HIGH SCHOOL HEROES

A CENTURY OF EDUCATION & FOOTBALL
AT ANNAPOLIS HIGH SCHOOL
1896 – 2003

Jane E. Good

To Lisa Leitholf –
The current principal and caretaker of the oldest school house in Anne Arundel County!
Best wishes –
Jane E Good
May 2004

HERITAGE BOOKS
2004

HERITAGE BOOKS
AN IMPRINT OF HERITAGE BOOKS, INC.

Books, CDs, and more – Worldwide

For our listing of thousands of titles see our website
at
www.HeritageBooks.com

Published 2004 by
HERITAGE BOOKS, INC.
Publishing Division
1540 Pointer Ridge Place
Bowie, Maryland 20716

COPYRIGHT © 2004 JANE E. GOOD

All rights reserved. No part of this book may be reproduced or transmitted in any form or by any means, electronic or mechanical, including photocopying, recording or by any information storage and retrieval system without written permission from the author, except for the inclusion of brief quotations in a review.

International Standard Book Number: **0-7884-2521-8**

*To my sons,
Alex and Nick,*

*and to all the
teachers, counselors
and coaches who helped them
succeed at Annapolis High School,
most especially:*

*Tony Anzalone
Mike Ballard
John Brady
Roy Brown
Dave Gehrdes
Phil Greenfield
Della Hanna
Sue Hersman
Rick King
Jim Kruse
Jennifer Manning
Donzella Parker-Bert
Pat Suriano
and
Daryl Watkins*

Table of Contents

Author's Preface	vii
Acknowledgements	ix
CHAPTER 1: *The Tigers on Green Street, 1896 – 1900*	1
CHAPTER 2: *Honoring Their Home Town, 1900 – 1910*	23
CHAPTER 3: *Annapolis High's Warriors, 1910 – 1919*	53
CHAPTER 4: *Red Jackets in the Roaring Twenties, 1919 –1929*	71
CHAPTER 5: *Depression and Wartime, 1929 – 1945*	105
CHAPTER 6: *Panther Pride Promotes School Spirit, 1945 - 1959*	131
CHAPTER 7: *Same Neighborhood, Different Worlds, 1959 – 1970*	155
CHAPTER 8: *Big Al and The Boys, 1970 – 1989*	181
CHAPTER 9: *Into the Twenty-First Century, 1989 – 2001*	213
EPILOGUE: *Changes and Challenges, 2001 – 2003*	247
APPENDICES:	255
A: *Annapolis High Football Season Results, Captains & All-County*	257
B: *Annapolis High Football Opponents, 1899-2003*	271
C: *Annapolis High Football Coaches*	274
D. *Annapolis High Football Honors and Records*	276
E: *Anne Arundel County Football Champions*	277
F. *Chronology: Principals and Buildings*	279
G. *Superintendents of Anne Arundel County Schools*	280
CITATIONS	281
BIBLIOGRAPHY	299
PHOTO CREDITS	304
INDEX	305

Author's Preface

Annapolis High is the oldest public secondary school in Anne Arundel County and the only one serving today's students in Maryland's state capital. When the school celebrated its centennial in 1998-1999, I was surprised to discover that only a collection of yearbooks and a pile of unsorted photographs had been preserved from its early years. Records, papers and trophies were lost or destroyed. Nobody remembered the names of the school's principals, copies of the school newspaper had vanished and results of its athletic competitions were unknown. Research for this book began as an attempt to recover the school's history so that today's students might better appreciate the heritage they are carrying into the 21st century.

Until the 1960's Annapolis High operated as part of Maryland's segregated school system. Secondary education for Anne Arundel County's African American students was not available until 1917 when the Stanton "Colored" School added a high school division [1]. In 1933, the new Wiley H. Bates High opened to provide secondary education to black students living anywhere in Anne Arundel County. After the federal government ordered county schools to desegregate fully in the mid-1960's, the vast majority of Bates students entered Annapolis High. Although this book focuses specifically on Annapolis High, each of the first six chapters includes a section on the parallel developments at Stanton and Bates in order to set the stage for discussion in chapters seven and eight about the integration process. The ninth chapter and the epilogue celebrate Annapolis High's racial and economic diversity that serves as the main source of the school's obvious strength and pride today.

Each chapter includes discussion of administrative and academic issues, including biographies of principals, analysis of the school's curriculum and discussion of student activities. The book's unique perspective is football, a sport Annapolis High boys began playing in 1899. For the next 103 years, football teams representing the school won two-thirds of the 645 games played. That so many of its teams have been highly successful makes the story of Annapolis

---

1. See citation 6 (page 281) for discussion of my use of terms *colored, Negro, black, Afro-American and African American* in this book.

High football compelling from a purely sports angle, while including sketches of players, coaches and games also serves to re-create a microcosm of the larger Annapolis community as it evolved in the 20th century.

Much of my initial research centered on filling in the holes in the school's history, but I soon found that I wanted to better understand the relationship of the school to the community it served. I first arrived in Annapolis a quarter of a century ago to teach history at the Naval Academy and raise my two sons. I got to know the city and its many neighborhoods by picking up their friends in Eastport Terrace and Annapolis Gardens, on Clay Street and Fairfax Road, off Riva and Bestgate Roads, under the Route 50 overpass and behind Annapolis Middle School, and ferrying them to their favorite spots – Truxton Park and Hillsmere Beach, Twilight Zone and AMAC karate, Apex/Crown Theaters and PAL Field, Chris' Charcoal Pit and Mamma Lucia's. This Annapolis struck me as not only wholly different but also infinitely more interesting than the colonial city celebrated in books as if it were little more than the home of the Naval Academy and the capital of Maryland.

This book is intended to honor ordinary Annapolitans of the 20th century, those who lived here and attended the city's public schools. The absence of education records forced me to find a way to uncover the names of students from bygone days so that through census records and genealogical references I could trace their social origins. Football proved an ideal vehicle because it has been the only activity routinely reported on in the local press over the entire history of the school. Indeed, the choice of football seemed particularly propitious when my research revealed the crucial role sports in general – and particularly football – played in facilitating the eventual integration of Annapolis High. I was also intrigued to find so many of the high school's heroes carried their courage from the gridiron to the battlefield as soldiers and sailors during America's wars of the 20th century – thereby suggesting the book's title.

Many histories of education are available, but this is perhaps the only one that explores the importance of a specific school within its community as seen through an athletic team. My hope is that many people in Annapolis will find the story touches their lives in ways they had not previously considered

Acknowledgements

Original research for this manuscript includes census records, military records, microfilmed newspapers, yearbooks, county school board records and the personal papers of Annapolis High students, teachers and coaches. Invariably the staff and administration at Annapolis High cheerfully assisted my frequent questions and searches for any shred of evidence about the school's past. My gratitude extends especially to former principal Joyce Smith and her administrative assistants Judy Trumbower and Cathy Wilson, head of the guidance department Anthony Anzalone, media center director Sallie Kravitz and her assistants Carol Baker and Mary Ellen McKurell, athletic directors Fred Stauffer (retired) and Dave Gehrdes, coaches Roy Brown and John Brady and newspaper advisor Diana Peckham.

The library staff at St. John's College always greeted me cordially and willingly gave me access to search their collection of old yearbooks and college bulletins. The sports department of the *Capital* – most notably Joe Gross, Craig Anderson and Bill Wagner – were equally generous in permitting me to mine what stories and photos are preserved in their high school athletic files. The Naval Academy's Academic Dean, William Miller, at the prompting of Academic Center director Eric Bowman and History Department chair Mary DeCredico, generously granted me a sabbatical from teaching so that I could complete the research and writing of this study even though it is far removed from my academic specialty, Russian history. I especially appreciate my colleague and friend Nancy Ellenberger's encouragement about pursuing the topic.

Local historian Jane Wilson McWilliams (AHS, '56) was always willing and able to supply needed bits of information about the region. Her many corrections and suggestions kept me – a girl born and bred in Ohio – from displaying total ignorance about Maryland. The guru of high school football in Maryland is Sheldon Shearer, an editor for the Frederick *News-Post* and the *Maryland/Virginia Varsity Football Annual Preview*. His quick, fulsome and insightful responses to my numerous e-mails helped me fill in much missing information about the development of high school football in the region.

Many Annapolis High alumni, teachers, administrators and coaches whose names are listed in the bibliography generously shared their recollections and whatever Annapolis High mementoes they or their relatives had saved. Sandy and Cathy Downs deserve special thanks for providing a treasure trove of photographs that Sandy's grandfather A.Z. Holley (AHS, 1910) had preserved from his days as a student and coach at Annapolis High as well as memorabilia from his years as a soldier in the Annapolis Machine Gun Company on the Mexican frontier in 1916 and in France 1918-19.

Many people helped sustain me through the years since I began this project. Naming them all is impossible, but a few whose interest and support have come at crucial moments must be mentioned. My sister, Bonnie Good Buzzell, joined me on a quest to visit Columbus, New Mexico, where a dozen Annapolis High boys bivouacked during the Pancho Villa expedition in 1916-1917. Her companionship and good humor on the endless drive across west Texas and through the maze of El Paso streets seeking the shortcut across the Rio Grande and into the New Mexico mountains kept me from giving up short of the goal. Bonnie and my longtime friend Joni Noel from Denver, Colorado, devoted valuable vacation days that were supposed to be spent on the beach at Bethany to reading and commenting astutely on several chapters of the manuscript.

I now count as good friends three fellow Annapolis High mothers who have stuck with me through the project's ups and downs. So I extend special thanks to: Susan Reimer for the encouragement that only a fellow author struggling with writer's block can offer; Rhonda Pindell Charles for helping me see Annapolis High through African American eyes; and Carol Mason for not only suggesting the book's title, but also for her thoughtful and meticulous editing of the many drafts I left at her front door. The mistakes that remain are, of course, my responsibility.

Finally, to my sons Alex and Nick, my gratitude knows no bounds. Without you I would never have walked through Annapolis High's front door, nor would I have met your many friends and teammates – people who over the years invited me into their world as I drove all of you to playgrounds and practices, karate tournaments and wrestling matches, movies and comic book conventions. So, thanks to all of you guys, especially to Camaro Henson, Jamal Jacobs, Albert and Alvin Johnson, Mike Melton and Trevon Williams. The journey you took me on made we want to write this book for you.

CHAPTER 1:
THE TIGERS ON GREEN STREET, 1896 – 1900

The first Annapolis High School football team, fall 1899

1. W. Brady, coach
2. W. Smith, mgr
3. H. McCardell, sub
4. R. League, sub
5. Frank White, lhb
6. J. Strohm, fb
7. J. Arth, lt
8. W. Jones, le
9. J. Pennell, lg
10. A. Ward, rg
11. A. Prosperi, sub
12. L. Cresap, qb
13. A. Williams, rhb
14. I. Machin, re
15. O. Bartlett, rt

> "This is the day of football. The hero of the gridiron succeeds the heroes of Manila in the public gaze."
>
> *The Evening Capital,*
> 5 October 1899

Origins of Public Secondary Education in Maryland

Secondary education in Maryland had long been the domain of private academies and college preparatory schools when at the close of the Civil War the state first initiated a program to support free public high schools. The Education Act of 1865 established a uniform system of public schools throughout Maryland under the overall direction of the state's superintendent of schools. Baltimore City, which had its own school administration, was exempt from the new provisions. Although the law focused on primary education, it stipulated, *"There shall be for each county at least one High School in which instruction shall be given to males and females in the higher branches of English and Science Education, and in the Latin and Greek languages, and math."*(1) Although the state created a general fund to help defray costs for establishing and running these new secondary schools, the law's intent was that every county should provide students a high school education supported by local taxes. As a model the counties could look to the third oldest public secondary school in the United States, Baltimore City College High (BCC) that had been in operation since 1839.

Eastern Shore counties took the lead in implementing the law. Easton High School in Talbot County opened in 1866, followed the next year by New Town High School in Worcester County. Wicomico High in Salisbury dates its founding to 1872. But most counties protested that a public high school would replicate their recent efforts to place deserving students in nearby private academies and college preparatory schools, with the tuition being paid through an annual state appropriation. Obviously a private school did not want to lose this state money, which by the 1870's constituted a significant part of its annual revenue. St. Mary's County, for example, could argue Charlotte Hall Academy had been doing such an excellent job of providing secondary education since its 1774 founding that no public high school was necessary.

Apparently Anne Arundel County took a similar position regarding a public high school. Not only was the county home to Patapsco Academy (Brooklyn), West River Institute (Owensville), and the Anne Arundel Academy (Millersville), but also to the preparatory school associated with St. John's College in Annapolis. This school offered teenage boys a three-to-four year curriculum that primed them for eventual matriculation in the college. The state gave

St. John's an annual appropriation to defray the cost of educating one boy from each election district in the county (2). Apparently a similar arrangement existed with Washington College in Kent County and may have existed at Carroll County's Western Maryland College.

Any pressure for the counties to open public high schools evaporated in 1867 when a new Maryland constitution rescinded the 1865 provision mandating secondary education. The state allowed each county to devise its own plan utilizing whatever educational facilities were already in place. Thus during the last third of the 19th century a three-tiered system of secondary education appropriations evolved that allocated Maryland state funds to public high schools, private academies and college preparatory schools.

In Annapolis prior to 1896 free public education for children, regardless of color, stopped at seventh grade. The city's schoolhouse for white students, which began operation in 1828, was located at various sites on Green, Main and Duke of Gloucester Streets prior to the Civil War. Beginning in1840 boys and girls were sent to separate buildings, but in 1881 the Stockett house on Green Street began serving as the schoolhouse for all children. William Harwood, the county Examiner of Schools, arranged to purchase this property for five annual payments of $1,300 and a final $4,000 payment made in November 1886 (3). Although the location was praised, the house itself drew complaints because it was "unadapted [sic] in every way for school purposes." On September 4, 1888, the city's local paper, the *Evening Capital,* bluntly addressed the need for an appropriate schoolhouse: "The time has come for the city to be aroused [to satisfy] a long felt need – the building of a school, not the purchase of a building." Nine years would pass before the idea was realized.

White families desiring education for their sons and daughters beyond the seventh grade had many options – as long as they were willing to pay. Small, private schools that most often were operated in or adjacent to the teacher's home were a popular choice for many. Daily front-page advertisements in the *Evening Capital* provide a sampling of such schools, including these from September 1895: Miss Kate P. Elliott's School for Boys and Girls (78 Conduit Street), Mrs. A.J. Watkins' Home School at 13 Francis Street, The Annapolis Institute to prepare "pupils of both sexes for admission to College" (59 Main Street) and the Arundel School that offered "instruction in French, German and Elocution" to "young ladies and children" from kindergarten through college preparatory levels.

Many girls attending such private schools were interested in becoming teachers, a goal that could be accomplished through two years of academic study at the secondary school, followed by a course of instruction at the state Normal School in Baltimore – today's Towson University (4). An option available only to boys was attendance at one of the numerous private schools in the city designed specifically to prepare them for the official Naval Academy written entrance examination. Werntz Naval Prep, Wilmer's Navy Prep, Bobbie's Prep and the Severn School (founded 1915) were among the best known of these programs. St. John's Preparatory School, housed on the campus in Humphrey Hall, continued to educate Annapolis lads seeking eventual admission to the college.

Maryland's public schools were segregated until the mid-1960's. Provisions were made in an 1869 Maryland school law for county boards of education to direct the "establishment of schools for colored children" and to maintain them through "the total amount of taxes paid for school purposes by colored people in the county." (5) This funding arrangement resulted in a separate and vastly inferior school system for these children. The tax base from their segment of the population was insufficient to support the costs of buildings, supplies and teachers' salaries equivalent to what was provided to the schools for white children. The idea of a high school for these students was not even considered. Fortunately a great deal of valuable historical work has been done about the establishment and operation of colored schools in Anne Arundel County. Especially well-documented is the story of the Stanton School in Annapolis, which originally opened in a hastily constructed wooden structure shortly after the end of the Civil War and moved into a new brick building on Washington Street in 1899. Not until 1917 was a high school division attached to the Stanton School that provided the county's Negro teen-agers the opportunity long overdue to pursue secondary education (6).

Annapolis High Opens, September 1896

In the fall of 1896, white teenagers in the city were offered a new opportunity to continue their educations for free when a high school department was attached to the Annapolis schoolhouse. Initially the high school consisted of only three grades: eighth (freshmen), ninth (sophomores) and tenth (juniors). An 11th grade (seniors) was to be added in 1897. Together these four grades would comprise the high school until 1917, when the state mandated a 12-year system that resulted in eighth grade being attached to the grammar department and ninth becoming the first high school year.

Why Anne Arundel County decided to open a public high school at this time is unknown. The state certainly was not pressuring the decision; Maryland continued its tripartite funding of secondary education until the early 1920's. The county's decision appears to have been wholly voluntary. Indeed, a general movement throughout the state to start public high schools occurred at the turn of the 20th century. Talbot County played a lead role by opening Denton High School in 1887. Other counties establishing high schools in the 1890's included Prince George's (Laurel), Montgomery (Rockville), Washington (Hagerstown), Frederick (Frederick and Middletown), Queen Anne's (Centreville) and Dorchester (Cambridge). Only three of Maryland's 23 counties (Calvert, Charles and St. Mary's) had no public high school by 1904.

Perhaps public secondary education spread rapidly at this time because Americans were beginning to appreciate that an educated citizenry was a vital component of a fully functioning democracy. Denying secondary education to children whose families could not afford to pay private school tuition did not square with the democratic spirit of the age. In many areas of America this attitude encompassed everyone in the community, including taxpaying immigrants and Negroes. In fact, the question no longer was whether there should be free public education for white and black children but whether such education should be mandatory, a proposition that Marylanders long resisted.

One key question the Anne Arundel County school board debated was how to staff the high school division. Especially important, they believed, was finding the right principal to lead the school. Because the genders were educated in separate classrooms, the grammar school had two heads, one male and one female, who had control respectively over the boys' and girls' divisions. The school board decided that a single male principal should be appointed to oversee the entire school complex, from first grade through high school seniors. They chose Professor William E. Smith, a taciturn New Englander, for the job. Smith wasted little time making his presence felt. On the first day of school in 1896 he announced several radical reforms. The first was to divide the younger children into separate primary (grades one through three) and grammar (grades four through seven) departments. Next he decreed the lengthening of the school day, moving dismissal from 2:30 to 3:00. He also insisted that classrooms above the fifth grade should be "integrated" with boys and girls mixed in the same classroom (7).

Professor Smith's regime also marked a definite change in the rigor and discipline of the public school. Evangeline Kaiser, future valedictorian of the Annapolis High School 1903 graduating class, remembered her first years in school – before Smith's arrival – fondly. She praised the principal of the girls' division, Mrs. Elizabeth Dorsey, and her staff for teaching the three R's with "loving kindness and cheerfulness." Mr. John "Peggie" Ray, whose nickname was a cruel reference to his peg leg, used "a chastising ruler" to instill discipline in the boys' division. But even Ray's methods were mild in comparison to the "cold, austere Professor Smith" whose *"authority over us, a group of warm-hearted, friendly Southerners [was] a fearful punishment. We were completely regimented in almost lockstep formation for dismissal or assembly of school, all done by clockwork and ringing of bells."* Kaiser claimed that Smith administered daily "whippings among the boys" and "completely terrorized the girls." Although she admits Smith improved the school during his four years at the helm, she concludes, *"The launching was such an ice-cold dousing [that] we never quite recovered from our resentment of his methods."* (8)

Professor Smith's first major task was to work with the board of examiners to oversee the building of a specially designed school on Green Street land that had been part of the Stockett house purchase. The state contributed $12,000 towards construction costs, and the city added another $6,000. Smith envisioned a campus with two buildings – the new one would temporarily house both the high school and grammar school until the Stockett house could be completely refurbished to accommodate the older students (9).

The new Annapolis Schoolhouse was a three-story brick building with large classrooms on the first two floors and a third floor assembly room. The indoor plumbing and heating facilities were a marked improvement over the pot-bellied stoves, water buckets and outhouses typical of the many one-room schoolhouses scattered across the county. To enter the school, however, it was necessary to walk on a wooden sidewalk laid across the Stockett property. A front entrance with steps cut through the Green Street wall would not be completed until 1904.

8 *A Century of Education and Football at Annapolis High School*

When the Annapolis Schoolhouse opened in the fall of 1897, there was no front entrance through the high wall on Green St. A model for its time, the school has remained in use continuously and today is home to Annapolis Elementary School

Annapolis High's first principal, William E. Smith (3rd row, with moustache), poses with the school's students. The below photo of the Class of 1900's seven graduates includes football star John Strohm (back row on right) and is often wrongly used to illustrate the first graduating class.

Stanton School for the county's "colored" students remained in use through the 1958 school year. Today the renovated building serves as a community center.

The still unfinished school was dedicated at a May 15, 1897, ceremony that featured the grammar school children entertaining local dignitaries with songs and recitations. Throughout the summer of 1897, citizens' committees under Professor Smith's direction selected textbooks and debated the feasibility of buying new furniture for the school. In July the *Evening Capital* supported the purchase, declaring the city would be "disgraced" if the new building were to open with the old, dilapidated furniture. Further, the paper pointed out that new furniture would "persuade the better classes of people to send their children to the public school," something that would "improve [the public school's] overall educational atmosphere." (10)

An order for $2,000 was duly placed with the Hudson School Furniture Company of Athens, Ohio, but unfortunately the shipment did not arrive in time for the desks to be installed before the first day of school on September 7, 1897. The 521 students aged six to 21 who showed up that hot Tuesday morning were forced to return to their former classrooms in the Stockett House. Four days later, on Friday, September 10, 1897, the doors to the new school were thrown open to students for the first time. Today this building – having withstood several fires and numerous remodelings – is Annapolis Elementary School, the oldest structure in continuous service as a school in Anne Arundel County (11).

The high school department was temporarily located in the assembly room on the new building's top floor while the Stockett House next door was remodeled to accommodate the needs of high school students. Funding for the project was so slow in materializing that three years would elapse before the high school moved back into the refurbished classrooms. In the meantime, enrollment at the Annapolis schoolhouse skyrocketed beyond what its original planners had anticipated. Classrooms for the early grades routinely had over 50 students, a situation that made teaching and learning nearly impossible. Many of the students came from outside the school district, especially from Eastport, Annapolis Neck and from across the Severn River, attracted by the superiority of the new facility and its high school department. On the first day of school in 1899, 700 children were enrolled and 70 had to be sent home for lack of space. On September 16, 1899, the *Evening Capital* noted, "A large contingent [of new students] came from the Naval Academy who heretofore have held aloof from the public schools of this city, and were sent to private schools. But these [schools] which flourished before the new school building and the present system have all been abolished, therefore causing the overcrowded condition of the public school today." The return of the high school students to the refurbished Stockett house in 1900 did little to relieve the congestion. Only five years later the situation would force the school board to seek funding to construct a new, larger building to accommodate the secondary school students.

The high school's curriculum in 1896 was strictly academic in content. Professor Smith oversaw instruction in Algebra, Geometry, Physics, and Physiology. His assistant, Miss Louise W. Linthicum – still shy of her 20th birthday – taught English (writing, grammar, and rhetoric), Latin, vocal music and drawing. German-born Walter Schaefer, an 1895 St. John's graduate, lectured in history (Maryland, United States, and General) and health (including the effects of narcotics and stimulants).

Few details survive about clubs and school activities during these first years. Christmas programs were held in December at which the students of all grades performed and presented gifts to their teachers. At the December 23, 1898, program the teachers presented a "Morris Chair" to Professor Smith and he, in turn, presented each of them with the rather odd gift of a nail file complete with "instructions on how to use it." The only indication of athletics in these first years is a report in the *Evening Capital* from April 1897 that a school baseball team had formed, but no announcements of games subsequently appeared.

The Class of 1899 – AHS's First Graduates

In June 1897 five 10th grade students were promoted for the coming year to 11th grade, which at that time was the final (senior) year of high school: The Linthicum siblings, Georgiana, Matilda and John, their cousin J. Francis Linthicum, and Frances "Fannie" Duvall. These five eventually would comprise Annapolis High's first graduating class. Two years were necessary for them to complete the 11th grade curriculum required to earn their high school diplomas, a delay attributed to the school's difficulties purchasing necessary course materials and books.

The first commencement, held in the school's assembly room on June 25, 1899, was a nervous time for the five graduates. Before the presentation of diplomas, each candidate had to deliver an oration to the room filled with dignitaries, school officials, teachers, classmates, family and friends. Their topics reveal much about the optimism of *fin-de-siecle* Annapolis. In "The Golden Mean" John Linthicum argued, "The station in life which brings to man the greatest happiness, contentment, and safety is the medium, being free from the wants that pinch the poor, and feeling not the plagues that haunt the rich." Frank Linthicum struck a similar chord in "Independence of Character," suggesting that to maintain a high purpose in life, his fellow graduates should set their own individual standards and not be dragged down by the "uselessness of national institutions." Matilda Linthicum spoke about the "Beauties of Nature," while in her salutatory address Georgiana Linthicum revealed that she had developed a "stout heart" in her quest to realize her dream of earning a high school diploma. Her determination must have been steadfast – Georgiana was already 23 years old by graduation day! And finally, class valedictorian Fannie Duvall spoke movingly about "The Pleasures of Memory" that would allow them in the future to recall these special years spent studying and learning together in their quest to become the first graduates of Annapolis High School (12).

The ceremony's main speaker was Professor James W. Cain, Vice President of St. John's, who urged everyone in the audience – relatives, teachers, and graduates – to take an interest in the future welfare of Annapolis High School to ensure that its prestige and influence would continue to grow among local citizens. He assured the graduates that their diplomas would allow them to take their place among the city's "honored men and women." The future lives of the female graduates would not disappoint the good professor – all became teachers or librarians – while the two boys went on to prosperous lives as a local businessman and a farmer.

At the turn of the 20th century, the city of Annapolis could boast of its own public high school and had celebrated the achievements of its first class of graduates. The school had yet to move into its own building and to separate its administration from that of the elementary school. These changes – and many others that took place during the coming century – will be discussed fully in the subsequent chapters, as will the stories of the men who coached and the boys who played football for Annapolis High School over the course of the next 103 years.

Football at the Turn of the 20th Century

Football frenzy swept the United States following its Spanish-American War victory. Citizens who cheered with patriotic fervor in 1898 as their team of soldiers and sailors easily whipped Spain transferred the object of their hero worship to college football players. Consensus held that the lads bracing for battle along the scrimmage line on fall afternoons exemplified the manly traits of courage and toughness that in the popular imagination were associated with triumphant warriors.

The rugged and dangerous nature of this distinctly American game as it was played at the turn of the century fed the combat analogy. Football evolved from two British schoolboy games to combine the brutality of a rugby scrum with soccer's emphasis on booting a ball. Eleven men per side lined up for the opening kick-off. A well-dressed team sported quilted canvas knee britches and sleeveless canvas jackets belted over a jersey in the team color. The same 11 played the entire game – offense and defense – unless serious injury to a player required him to leave the field for a substitute. The center began offensive play by snapping a large, egg-shaped ball to a stationary quarterback who then tossed the ball backwards to the fullback or laterally to the right or left halfback (forward passes were illegal). Meanwhile the seven linemen formed a wedge around the ball carrier to help push and pull him forward. The offense tried to advance the ball down the 110-yard field and across the defensive team's end line to score five points by "touching" it "down" on the ground. A successful "goal-kick" over a crossbar 10-feet high mounted on posts 18.5 feet apart added a point. The offense could also score a "goal from field" by dropkicking the ball over the crossbar (worth five points, equivalent to a touchdown).

The 11 players on defense had to punch through the mass blocking formation to tackle the ball carrier. Downing him behind his team's end line was ruled a safety, awarding two points to the defensive team. If they held the offense to less than five yards in three attempts, the ball was turned over to them. The offense generally punted on third down unless in scoring range. If the offense took possession deep in its own territory, the fullback often "quick-kicked" the ball away on second or even first down. A team with a superior punter had a decided advantage; games in which both teams had good kickers tended to be defensive, low-scoring, strategic struggles (13).

The 1894 Princeton team captain enthusiastically noted that "force was the thing then, and smashing, battering plays were depended on solely." Particularly dangerous was what the players called the "murder pile" – the heap formed as a mass formation play ended, as described in this 1903 account of a Michigan high school contest: *"The game was mostly played between a mass of players from one team struggling to advance the ball against a mass of players from the other team. Nearly everyone on the field was in the same place at the same time. The game's opponents complained that letting players interact in such close quarters made it convenient for them to inflict injuries without being seen. And they were right. Kicking, gouging, or disabling your opponent with heavy blows about the eyes, nose and jaw happened all the time. So did knees to the head and gut."* The account goes on to describe how play along the scrimmage line contributed to injury. No neutral zone existed then, so an offensive lineman actually took his stance with his forehead nearly touching the forehead of the opposing defensive lineman. At the snap of the ball, they banged their foreheads together causing faces to be "gashed and bruised and bathed in blood" by the game's end." (14)

No wonder fans equated football with military combat. And, as in any battle, casualties often ensued. Uniforms provided little padded protection, and the helmet had yet to be introduced. Head, neck, shoulder, arm, leg, and ankle injuries were common. Too frequently, players died. Reformers called for rule changes to make the game safer, but not until the 1905 season's 18 deaths and 159 serious injuries did the Rough-Riding hero of the Spanish-American War himself – President Teddy Roosevelt – mandate modest safety precautions (15).

Football-Crazy Annapolis

Maryland's capital city, Annapolis, with a population in 1900 of not quite 8,000 people, was home to two fine institutions of higher education: the United States Naval Academy and St. John's College. Well known is Navy's association with football, which began in 1879, just a decade after Rutgers and Princeton played what is considered the first football game. Less familiar is St. John's history as a military school whose students were required to wear uniforms and to drill, and who organized their own football team as early as 1885. By 1899 the neighboring colleges had played each other 11 times, and although Navy won eight of the games, the Johnnie cadets never thought of themselves as underdogs to the rival midshipmen. Annapolitans flocked to see their hometown heroes in action against many of the East's best teams, including Penn, Princeton, Georgetown, Rutgers, Lafayette, Lehigh, Bucknell, Swarthmore, and Virginia. Special trains were arranged to depart from Annapolis for traditional season-ending rivalry games in Baltimore (St. John's versus Johns Hopkins) and Philadelphia (Army versus Navy). Throughout the autumn of 1899, the *Evening Capital*'s front page brimmed with news about the local teams' games, practices, scrimmages, rosters and injuries as well as with other football features from across the nation.

Boys growing up in Annapolis naturally sought to share the limelight. In the late 1890's teams such as the "Down-Town Boys," the "Murray Hill Gang" and the "Slippery Hill 11" settled many neighborhood grudges on the gridiron. The *Evening Capital* is sprinkled with their line-up announcements and challenges to "all-comers" for games. Such teams, by necessity, included boys aged eight to 18 with a corresponding range in size and ability. The son of a local waterman remembered, *"We had groups, we had teams, but it was necessary for . . . you and your friends . . . to initiate the ideas, develop the programs, and in the case of sports, you had to subsidize your own interests."* (16)

By 1899 boys from these rival teams shared classrooms in the grammar and high school departments of the public school on Green Street. Of the 600 students attending the new Annapolis schoolhouse in the fall of 1897, very few were destined to earn high school diplomas; the first graduating class in June 1899 numbered just five. Not until 1907 did a graduating class reach double digits. The rigorous academic standards often resulted in an age spread of six years in the same classroom. Most male students left school early; the wealthier continued to rely on private prep programs before taking college entrance exams, while by age 15 most working-class boys were lured away to earn a paycheck. Although several ways to attract more boys were floated, one creative suggestion drew enthusiastic support – the formation of a football team that would draw the best white teenage players from the whole city away from their neighborhood teams to play under the banner of the high school that represented Annapolis.

The idea of a football team was attractive to the local boys wanting to test their skills against teams outside Annapolis. Many such schoolboy teams were beginning to form across the region, although it should be pointed out that at the turn of the century no requirement existed that boys playing on a high school team actually had to be enrolled as students. In fact, teams had no established age limit for players. Instead squads were classified according to the weight of the players. Thus a post-graduate or even a player who wasn't a student could legally join and play on a school squad until he exceeded weight limitations for the team's classification. Not until 1914 would basic eligibility criteria for high school players in Maryland be regularized to ensure that only full time students could participate (17). Despite the fact that football players for Annapolis High technically did not have to be students in the school, Professor Smith apparently thought that some boys attracted to the sport might also decide to investigate the classrooms. Once the formation of a high school football team was proposed, the idea took hold. Annapolis High football was born.

Seventeen boys formed the first Annapolis football team. Thirteen of them, decked out in football gear, posed for posterity on a grassy slope beside the school, their game faces forever fixed in a photograph for future generations to contemplate (the 1899 team picture is on the title page for this chapter). Their demeanor is serious – only substitute quarterback Gus Prosperi, son of the Naval Academy's pharmacist, dared to smile. Their casual, yet careful, arrangement, with faces scrubbed and hair parted, reveals an obvious pride in themselves and their team. Who were they, these boys who started Annapolis High School on its path to football excellence? Only one – left end W. Jones – remains a complete mystery. The others left a trail that can be traced through census records, blurred newspapers on cracked microfilm, crumbling college yearbooks, military service records, local history books, scattered memoirs and an excellent published genealogy of Annapolis families.

The team's star player is easy to spot. Holding the '99 ball at the picture's center is senior captain John Strohm, a powerful fullback and kicking specialist who led the team in scoring. Strohm's athletic prowess came naturally. His father Matthew, a German immigrant, was the boxing master and gym instructor at the Naval Academy for 42 years (1867-1909). At the high school's second commencement, held on May 25, 1900, John chose "Physical Training" as his topic for the required graduation speech. His justification of athletics embodied the Naval Academy's philosophy that the moral, mental and physical development of a person are all interrelated: *"Physical training prepares man for work and opens the way to better intellectual development. Athletes do not fall into the habits of the drunkard or the gambler. Man has a body that stands as much in need of strength as his mind, and examples show that the physically strong overtake the mentally strong but physically weak. What is beneficial to the body is beneficial to the mind."* (18)

Two of Strohm's teammates, quarterback Logan Cresap and tackle Owen Bartlett, must have shared his enthusiasm for physical fitness because they had dreams of entering the Naval Academy (both of their fathers were naval officers and graduates of the academy). Cresap and Bartlett left Annapolis High in 1900 to prep for Naval Academy entrance exams. Cresap returned to school a year later, graduating with the class of 1901. Both boys eventually earned Naval Academy appointments and graduated with the classes of 1905 and 1906. At Navy, Bartlett showed obvious spunk, playing a year on the "Hustlers" (the "scrub" football team for plebes) and rowing crew for the following three years. Cresap, who excelled playing quarterback in high school, apparently chose to be what today is labeled a "stealth midshipman." His classmates described him in the yearbook as *"a distinguished representative and worthy citizen of Annapolis, [who] does less with more effort than any man alive."* (19)

Others who contributed to this first football season reflect a measure of Annapolis' ethnic and economic diversity: German, Greek and Italian immigrants played beside third-generation Annapolitans. The sons of enlisted sailors and local politicians blocked for blue-collar and businessmen's boys. One-third of the city's population, however, was not represented at all. The segregation of Anne Arundel County schools meant that only white boys were on the Annapolis High team. An annual game between Howard University and the "pick of the colored gridiron talent" began sometime before 1905. The November 24, 1906, *Evening Capital* reports that the Annapolis team beat Howard for the first time ever "by a score of 10 to 6 notwithstanding the fact that the local team was greatly outweighed." The two teams played on the Naval Academy's Marine Corps barracks field in 1914. When the high school division of the Stanton School was added in 1917, the school's hastily organized football team continued the tradition of playing Howard. After 1933 the "Little Giants" of Wiley H. Bates High began fielding some excellent football teams that competed throughout Delaware, Virginia and Washington D.C. against other segregated high school teams (20).

The Annapolis High backfield included Frank White, son of the county clerk, at right halfback, and Albert Williams, son of an Eastport gardener, at left halfback. Center Richard Stone, the son of the *USS Santee*'s master-at-arms, was in charge of positioning the other linemen. The players on his left and right were called "guards" because their job was to protect the center following the snap. Guarding Stone to his left was a bricklayer's son, Joe Pennell, and on the right stood Arthur Ward, whose father served as first mate on the state police schooner *May Brown*. Isaac Machin, whose father was the St. Anne's cemetery superintendent, patrolled the right end of the line next to tackle George Parlett, whose city alderman father owned a prominent Main Street lumber and hardware store. Right tackle Joe Arth came to Annapolis from Washington, D.C., when his musician father was transferred from the Marine Corps to the Navy Band.

Substitute players included Harry Jewell, also a bricklayer's son, Richard McCardell, another Class of 1900 Annapolis High graduate, and the team's "hard luck" story, Richard League. League's mother had died when he was only three years old, and on February 15, 1898, less than two years before the team picture was taken, his father – Navy Chief Yeoman James League – was killed aboard the *USS Maine* when it exploded in Havana Harbor. Both of League's older brothers were already in the Navy; he would join them when he dropped out of school in 1900 to enlist as a machinist.

One other player on the team remains something of a mystery. In the season's last game in late November, a running back named Burtis appeared on the scene. Most news accounts of games in those days only included last names, and since this Burtis is not in the team photo, his identity can only be guessed. He was probably Solomon Burtis, the son of William H. Burtis, the former captain of a police cruiser in Maryland's "Oyster Navy." Captain Burtis' sloop *Synbad* had been "badly wrecked" in hurricane-force storms that hit the Chesapeake Bay on Halloween. Solomon may have been working for his father, but now had enough time on his hands while the boat was being repaired to take up playing football.

These were the boys who made up Annapolis High's first football team. They chose a tiger as their mascot and selected red as their jersey color. Their coach was Walter L. Brady, a newly minted St. John's graduate who starred for the Johnnies at halfback on the gridiron and shortstop on the baseball diamond. Although football rules at the turn of the century strictly prohibited coaching during games, teams were allowed to receive guidance during practices and between halves. A boy on the field – usually the quarterback – had to call every play without any input from the coach. The coach's job was to work on game strategy and conditioning during practice. Annapolis High had no playing fields because the land behind the school that backed on Compromise Street was swampy and rutted. Fortunately an arrangement was worked out with St. John's for the high school boys to practice on the college's athletic fields.

The Annapolis High team manager was none other than the school's taciturn principal, Professor Smith. Because athletics were funded completely outside the school, and no official state organization existed to arrange games, the manager had to seek out opponents, arrange a suitable date for the contest and negotiate who would get "home field" advantage. Sometimes an offer to pay for the opponent's travel expenses was necessary before a team would agree to play at an opponent's field. The length of the game also had to be agreed upon, something that was often left until just before kickoff. The longest a high school team could play was two 30-minute halves, but most often Annapolis played halves of 15 or 20 minutes. Given the game's brutality, even 15 minutes could seem a lifetime (21).

The Tigers In Action

Professor Smith's duty to schedule games was no easy task in 1899 when only a handful of public high schools in the state had teams. Baltimore's City College High School was home to a two-year junior college as well as to the full academic high school. BCC started playing football in the 1880's; by 1899 it fielded a varsity (mostly college boys) and a "scrub" team (mostly high school boys). BCC's varsity schedule was filled with other college freshmen teams, while its "scrubs" lined up against other scrub or high school teams. Baltimore Polytechnic Institute's team played only informal games because its administration thought athletics were antithetical to serious scholarship. Poly had begun playing BCC's scrubs in 1889, but the Poly players probably thought sneaking off to a game in Annapolis was too risky. Frederick High School was rumored to be forming a team, as was the high school in Laurel. The "Hustlers" from the Naval Academy played only other college scrub teams. A neighborhood team called "The Young Hustlers'" lineup of grammar school boys was considered beneath high school caliber (22).

Fortunately, the best prospective opponent for Annapolis High turned out to be willing, able and convenient. Annapolis was home to scores of teenage boys who were preparing for entrance exams at either the Naval Academy or St. John's College. In the past, most of these boys lived in boarding houses throughout the city. Apparently "preps" and "townies" were bitter rivals, especially for the affections of the local girls (23). Lack of proper supervision led St. John's to formalize its program into a Prep School that housed its students on campus. Meanwhile a Naval Academy professor named Wilmer decided that 26 candidates studying for Navy's entrance exam needed more supervision, so he leased a large building on Prince George Street "for school purposes and as a home for the [boys]" and hired a lieutenant to live on the premises to supervise them. Wilmer's Prep would not form a football team until 1905, but the preps at St. John's announced in the fall that their recently organized football team would soon be ready to "play its first game with the Annapolis High School." (24)

Thus it came to pass that on a crisp Saturday morning in late October 1899, the Annapolis High Tigers kicked off to St. John's Prep for what was the inaugural football game for both schools. The *Evening Capital* reported that the game was "well-contested," with the high school lads ending up on the short end of an 11-0 score. All three Annapolis High running backs – team captain John Strohm, big Joe Arth and fleet Frank White – were singled out for praise. The preps scored both of their touchdowns in the first half, so the scoreless second half was considered a moral victory for the high school. In fact, the Tigers gained so much confidence that at game's end they challenged the preps to a return contest, but apparently the victors refused because they did not want to risk losing bragging rights to the claim that they were the city's best schoolboy team (25).

Smith had to look outside Annapolis to find another game. The closest high school with a team was about 25 miles away in Laurel. The schools agreed to play on Tuesday afternoon, November 21, 1899, at a field on the grounds of the Laurel Outing Club. The Tigers and their fans rode the train from the Bladen Street *Shortline* depot in Annapolis to the *Baltimore and Ohio* Main Street station in Laurel. Certainly the trip was worth the effort. The *Evening Capital* the next day announced the first-ever football victory for the school: *"Annapolis High took the Laurel team into camp by a score of 11-0.*

The Laurel players outweighed the Tigers, but Annapolis went into the game to win, and win she did."

Shortly after the opening kick-off, right end Isaac Machin went down with an apparent dislocated shoulder. He was carried off the field and loaded on the next train to Annapolis. When play resumed, halfback Frank White was pulled over the goal line by Albert Williams to score the school's first-ever touchdown. (Such a play was then perfectly legal; indeed, some halfbacks wore a belt with a handle on it so teammates could pull him forward.) The goal kick failed, leaving Annapolis in front 5-0 at halftime. After intermission, captain John Strohm frequently carried the ball 20 yards or more from his fullback position. He scored a touchdown and kicked the extra point. Strohm's effort led the reporter to dub him Annapolis High's "Flying Dutchman" – a nickname borrowed from baseball star Honus Wagner, but hardly apt for the German Strohm.

Following the final gun, Annapolis immediately accepted Laurel's challenge to play again in College Park on Thanksgiving Day. Cocky with victory, they repeated in print their challenge to the St. John's Preps for a return game. Undoubtedly they celebrated their first victory aboard the train back to Annapolis. Their arrival late in the evening did not stop them from putting on a fine display of team spirit and camaraderie. The entire squad went from the depot "direct to Machin's house" where they "gave the plucky player three rousing cheers and a tiger." (26)

The Turkey Day contest against Laurel proved "something of a walkover" as Annapolis High won easily 29-0! The *Evening Capital* of December 1, 1899, called the game *"a leading feature of the holiday, witnessed by a large number of people, [who found it] interesting throughout."* The high school lads were credited with playing "finely." The boys on the line were praised for "good interference always being given the runner." When the Tigers were on defense, their "tackling was good and hard." Several players drew special mention for their "splendid play," including center Richard Stone, guard Joe Pennell, tackle Joe Arth, and halfback Albert Williams. Because no coaching could take place during the game, the quarterback was responsible for calling all offensive plays and setting defensive alignments. The Annapolis quarterback, little Logan Cresap, was lauded for showing "judgment and coolness in giving his signals." Strohm, still dubbed "The Flying Dutchman," played his usual "first-class game." But the newcomer Burtis stole the show, playing "a splendid game, making four rushes of from 40 to 60 yards" in scoring several of the Tiger's touchdowns.

Back in Annapolis, the team continued practicing until the middle of December in anticipation of a return game with St. John's. After several more weeks of waiting for the preps' reply to their challenge, the Annapolis players gathered on December 17, 1899, to disband for the season and make plans for the future. With spring around the corner, they elected Frank White and Joe Pennell serve as captain and manager of the baseball team. The "Flying Dutchman" Frank Strohm was suitably selected to form a track team. They then turned their attention to the fall 1900 football season, selecting their big right guard, Arthur Ward (Class of 1901) to captain the team and Donald Riley (Class of 1902) to replace Professor Smith as football team manager, a position Smith resigned in anticipation of his impending commission in the Marine Corps. Before his departure, Smith helped the boys establish an Annapolis High School Athletic Association, an organization that sought to raise money to support various sports activities in the school (27).

Thus Annapolis High's first football season consisted of just three games. The team could take pride in its 2–1 season record and the knowledge that for five straight halves they had held their opponents scoreless. During next fall's football season, Burtis and Pennell garnered favorable press mention for their efforts in several Annapolis High victories, but controversy surrounding the violence of the game may have contributed to the school playing very few games over the next several years.

Players on this first team went on to hold a variety of occupations. Several were employed by the Naval Academy, including brick and mason worker Harry Jewell and electrician Albert Williams. John Strohm served as longtime director of the county public works department, and reporter Frank White was a stringer for the Associated Press before settling in as the *Evening Capital*'s city editor. Three – Isaac Machin, George Parlett and Arthur Ward – pursued business careers in Baltimore, while Augustus Prosperi ventured off to Philadelphia. Naval Academy graduates Logan Cresap and Owen Bartlett commanded ships during World War I, both retiring from the Navy in the 1920's – Bartlett to a farm on the ocean in Rhode Island, Cresap to New York and a job as head of the Isthmian Steamship Company (28). Richard Stone went on to St. John's College, eventually securing an Army commission and a career as an infantry officer that carried him through both world wars and eventual retirement as a full colonel. Joe Arth was in the Annapolis High Class of 1903, studied a science curriculum at St. John's and graduated with a medical degree from George Washington University. He set up practice in Washington, D.C., where he died in February 1919 tending patients during the great flu epidemic (29)

* * * * * * * * * * * *

The first Annapolis High team in 1899 should be remembered for its pioneering efforts on the football field. Their on-field heroics set a high standard for schoolboy football in the region, one that the Annapolis High School teams would continue through the 20th and into the 21st century, playing under various nicknames but always wearing jerseys of reddish hue. They also demonstrated that high school football served as a social equalizer for boys from disparate economic and ethnic backgrounds who put differences aside when they lined up together to play.

CHAPTER 2:
HONORING THEIR HOME TOWN,
1900 - 1910

The 1909 undefeated Annapolis High School football team

"The plucky and scrappy little football team of the Annapolis
High School has brought great credit upon themselves
and great honor to their home town."
Annapolis City Council Resolution,
November 8, 1909

"Today all Annapolis does honor to our High School heroes.
Too much praise cannot be given the boys, who are a credit
not only to the High School, but to the town they represent."
The Evening Capital
May 16, 1910

Education was a prime concern to many Annapolitans at the turn of the 20th century. Monthly school board meetings and semi-annual Teachers' Institutes were covered in the local press. The city's white students were on very public display. The *Evening Capital* published front-page quarterly grade reports and monthly attendance records, along with detailed descriptions of grammar school promotion ceremonies and high school commencement exercises. The merits of curricular innovations were scrutinized, as were teachers' salaries and school calendars. Much less emphasis in the *Evening Capital*'s pages was given to the progress of the city's minority youngsters at the Stanton School that relocated to a new building on Washington Street in January 1899. Three issues related to Annapolis High School received a great deal of coverage during this decade: low salaries that produced a rapid turnover of principals, the need for a modern secondary school building and the dearth of male students.

Wanted: A Dedicated, Long-Term Principal

Annapolis High's most persistent problem in the 20th century's first decade was securing steady leadership. Salary disputes were at the heart of the trouble. These were difficult to resolve because oversight for schools was divided among several competing groups. All financial decisions were in the hands of the county's board of school commissioners, eight citizens appointed by the governor. From among its members this school board elected a president to serve as its spokesman and hired the county's superintendent of schools (earlier called the school examiner), a salaried administrator who usually had significant experience working in the local school system. The superintendent had responsibility for the day-to-day operation of all schools in the county and served as the school board's secretary. An 1896 state law mandated that the school board appoint a separate board of trustees for each school in its district. Each board of trustees consisted of three people whose job was to serve as advocates for their school. The trustees brought requests for such things as maintenance, staffing changes and salary adjustments to the superintendent, who presented them at the school board's monthly meeting. The trustees' most important responsibility, however, was to select a principal and recommend teachers for its school.

Naturally the appointed school board, its elected president, the superintendent (hired by the school board), the selected trustees and a specific school's principal (hired by the trustees) did not always see eye to eye on issues. Politics added to the problem because the governor had no restrictions on his appointments to school boards. All eight could be from one political party. The trustees, however, were supposed to represent both major political parties. This arrangement led the *Evening Capital* on June 17, 1910, to lament, "There is a sneaking suspicion that again the Anne Arundel county public schools are tied up in politics." Most often the politics showed up in the handling of the principal's salary. The choice was technically in the hands of the trustees, but the school board's power to determine the salary helped create a revolving door to the principal's office through which seven men in only ten years entered and exited.

The Annapolis trustees believed that a high school should have a male principal. Prior to the opening of the high school division, two principals – one female, one male – shared the responsibility for running the grammar and primary school, largely because girls and boys were taught separately. The trustees believed that consolidating the two former principals' positions into one job to head the entire school – that is, the primary, grammar and high school departments – would allow them to offer a more generous salary to the man they selected for the job. Thus, they advertised for a male principal who would be given administrative authority for the entire Annapolis public school (kindergarten through 11th grade - the last year of high school). The job was demanding and difficult, surely deserving of generous compensation. Yet the school board's control of the purse strings kept the salary below what was standard in other Maryland counties.

The first man to occupy the position of principal for the entire Annapolis Schoolhouse was New England-born and educated William E. Smith, who immediately elevated academic standards while imposing harsh disciplinary measures on the students. (Smith is discussed in more detail in the first chapter). The rapid turnover began when in the summer of 1900 Smith resigned after four years at the school's helm to accept a commission as a captain in the United States Marine Corps, a calling that students probably agreed seemed better suited to his martinet temperament.

The trustees scrambled to hire a replacement before classes started in September 1900. They settled on an 1893 St. John's College graduate named Charles E. Dryden. The new principal began with enthusiasm, initiating such popular activities as the publication of *The*

Annapolitan, a monthly school newspaper. He also directed several improvements to the grounds, the most important of which involved a public conscription campaign that raised $1,500 to purchase land behind the school that fronted on Compromise Street. The 125-by-200-foot lot was drained and transformed into a much-needed playground for the younger children (1).

At the commencement exercises for the six female members of the Class of 1901, Robert Moss, a former state Senator, a future judge and the then chairman of the St. John's Board of Governors, specifically praised Dryden for his "efficient management" and foresaw continued improvements under his guidance. Unfortunately, Moss's predictive powers proved poor. In the summer of 1903 Dryden resigned to become principal at the high school in Frostburg. Although his reasons for leaving were not fully disclosed, it appears that the salary offer at Frostburg was significantly higher than the $1,000 he earned as principal for the Annapolis school (2).

The next man to occupy the principal's office was Professor Irving L. Twilley, a native of Baltimore and a graduate of Washington College in Chestertown. Following his post-graduate work at Harvard, Twilley traveled abroad extensively, even penning a book entitled *Kodak in Foreign Travels.* He came to Annapolis from Susquehanna, Pennsylvania, where he had taught for a decade before serving as superintendent of schools. At the end of his first and last year in Annapolis, the *Evening Capital* enthused, *"Twilley is a man of good judgment [with] a keen sense of what is best for the school over which he presides, and an educator of experience, whose ability has been felt and recognized and who has improved the school in numerous ways."* (3)

One improvement to the school grounds was a towering flagpole erected in 1903 adjacent to the original 1898 school bell. The Order of United American Mechanics donated the pole and two United States flags, a large one for good weather and a smaller one for rainy weather, in the fall of 1900. The flags long ago disappeared, but the bell is on display in Annapolis Elementary School's main entrance and the flagpole still stands by the main entrance where a fifth grader has the honor of daily raising and lowering the colors (4).

Twilley's decision to resign – like Dryden's before him – was driven by financial concerns. He had signed the standard $1,000 principal's contract in the early summer of 1903, but before Labor Day the board of education decided that the school could remain open only seven of its usual nine months during the coming year because of a budget shortfall. They then informed Twilley that his salary would be cut to reflect the reduced amount of time on the job. The *Evening Capital* editorialized, "It cannot be expected that a man of education and ability will be bound to such a state of affairs as exist in the Annapolis school board regime." The paper's assessment proved correct. Twilley accepted a teaching position at Baltimore Polytechnic Institute, where he eventually became head of the science department. Annapolis was again left without a principal only weeks before the opening of school. The irate *Evening Capital* noted on August 8, 1903, "Good teachers cannot be retained at such meager salaries, and Annapolis must expect to lose those of her educators who value their services."

Critics were temporarily silenced when from among the 13 applicants for the vacancy the trustees selected Henry R. Wallis, who turned down an offer to be headmaster at Glenwood Collegiate Institute in Matawan, New Jersey, to accept the Annapolis position. Wallis had compiled an impressive resume for a man not yet 30 years old. Educated at Dickinson College and Princeton, he taught several years at Glenwood before resigning to become principal of the Anne Arundel Academy in Millersville. The Annapolis trustees were impressed with Wallis' stated desire to remain in Maryland and to make education his career. Certainly they hoped Wallis was a man who would remain in the principal's office more than one year

Like his predecessors, Wallis took over with enthusiastic plans to improve the school. During his first year enrollment at the Annapolis Schoolhouse ballooned from 750 to 900 students, about 100 of whom were in the high school division. Finding enough qualified staff to teach all these students was the most immediate problem he faced, in large measure because the salary ($200 for permanent substitutes, $400 for grammar school teachers and $500 for high school teachers) was lower than in other Maryland counties. The state regulation that required female teachers to be unmarried made staffing more difficult, especially when resignations from women about to marry could come mid-year. Wallis addressed this problem by keeping several substitutes on the payroll, including the two top women in each year's graduating class (5).

Of the 22 teachers at the school in 1904, only four were assigned to the high school division. Wallis taught the sciences, his vice-principal, Louise W. Linthicum, handled English and history, while two other female teachers – Miss Heller and Miss Bell – were respectively in charge of mathematics and foreign languages, Latin and German. Wallis instituted rigorous academic standards that contributed to the state board of education's decision to add Annapolis High to its list of accredited secondary schools (6). Months of wrangling between Wallis and city officials resulted in a major improvement to the school's grounds. An opening through the stone wall and high bank in front of the school was cut so that entrance could be gained directly from Green Street by walking up several steps, proceeding past the flagpole and the school bell to the main door, the same path used by Annapolis Elementary students today (7).

Wallis seemed settled in the principal's office for the foreseeable future when in November 1905 the popular county superintendent of schools, F. Eugene Wathen, suddenly died. The school board followed the tradition of offering the vacant position to the best-qualified person in the local educational system – Wallis (8). Although the school board spared itself a lengthy search for a new superintendent, it put the trustees in the uncomfortable position of hiring yet another principal. One noteworthy applicant was longtime teacher and current vice-principal Louise Linthicum, but her candidacy was not considered because the trustees were still unwilling to place a woman in what they insisted was a man's job. Instead they turned to the state's superintendent of public instruction, M. Bates Stephens, for advice about a possible replacement. Stephens suggested William S. Crouse, a recently retired administrator and teacher from the Eastern Shore, be hired on an interim basis while a search for a permanent principal was undertaken.

The trustees acted quickly on this recommendation – only 14 days following Wathen's death, Crouse accepted the offer. The new principal's credentials were impressive on paper: over thirty years' experience as an educator, including principal of three high schools (Denton, Easton and St. Michael's) and superintendent of Caroline County schools. Yet the Annapolis High students were not much impressed with their temporary principal, perhaps because they were accustomed to the much younger men who had held the position. Burton Starr, valedictorian for the Class of 1906, left this amusing description of Crouse in her senior memory book: *"When I entered the High School, Mr. Wallis was principal and held that office until my senior year when Mr. Wathen, the school examiner, died and Mr. Harry Wallis was selected to fill his place; then Mr. Crouse came and*

Annapolis High School's Early Principals

William E. Smith
(1896 – 1900)

Charles E. Dryden
(1900 – 1902)

Irving L. Twilley
(1902 – 1903)

Henry R. Wallis
(1903 – 1905)

Andrew J. English
(1906 – 1908)

George B. Pfeifer
(1908 – 1910)

This building next door to the grammar school on Green Street was constructed in 1907-1908 for Annapolis High School

was principal my senior year. And what a funny little man he was to be sure. He really was very well read but being a little man, I think, he must have gotten easily flustered . . . so that he never gave the impression of knowing anything." (9)

Crouse's reaction to the Annapolis students is unknown, but he wasted no time returning to the eastern shore when the school year ended. Certainly the salary wasn't high enough to keep him in Annapolis. In fact, just two days before the 1906 commencement exercises, the three Annapolis High teachers protested to the school board about the practice of withholding a portion of their $500 salary when the school year was shortened to less than 10 months. The board, unmoved, instructed superintendent Wallis to tell the teachers that "all salaries are based on a 10-month year, but will be cut off if the year is shortened for lack of funds." (10) Apparently the shortage was a result of the state legislature's decision to cut the tax rate for educational purposes from 16.75 cents to 16.0 cents. Although several other counties met their contractual obligations, the Anne Arundel County school board continued to expect teachers to sign contracts for a stated amount with no reciprocal obligation to pay the full salary.

The trustees had started to search for a new principal before Crouse's departure. This time their efforts netted Andrew J. English, a 29-year-old Dickinson College graduate who came "highly recommended as a teacher and disciplinarian" based on his three years' classroom experience at a Keating, Pennsylvania, school. The September 6, 1906, *Evening Capital* described him as "six feet tall and of athletic build [with] a pleasing countenance, a strong face and striking personality." Despite this positive first impression, English was not to remain in the job much longer than his predecessors. He began auspiciously, bringing considerable energy to bear on several projects that would leave his mark on the school long after he was gone. Most significantly he worked with the trustees to secure public support and funding for the construction of a new building for the high school (see next section). He also initiated several significant curricular changes. In 1908 Annapolis became one of the first high schools in the state to introduce a two-year commercial course open to students who had completed ninth grade. The curriculum offered stenography, typing, shorthand and related subjects to students interested in pursuing a business career. Annapolis High used half of a $1,000 allocation from the state to purchase typewriters and furniture necessary to equip the commercial classroom. The other

$500 paid the salary of a teacher assigned to the program. For students interested in becoming teachers, Professor English introduced a "normal course" with two recent graduates of the Normal School at Towson as instructors. Meanwhile, the regular four-year academic course was reserved specifically for those preparing to enter college (11).

Everyone hoped English's tenure would be a long one, yet at the close of his second year he resigned in what turned into a very public salary dispute. The first hint that trouble was brewing occurred with the July 10, 1908, *Evening Capital*'s report that "Andrew J. English will not return next year unless his salary is increased... [to] $1,200." Five days later the newspaper printed a study commissioned by the school board about the salaries paid to the teachers and principal at the Annapolis Schoolhouse. The report's authors, Superintendent Wallis and longstanding board member George T. Melvin, concluded that the current salaries ($1,000 for the principal, $500 for high school teachers and $400 for grammar school teachers) were "manifestly inadequate," especially "considering the great number of pupils (about 900), an average of over 40 to each teacher, and taking into account the high order of work done." The report urged the school board to raise English's salary to $1,200, noting "a man of sufficient ability to fill the position ought not to be expected to be satisfied with less than this." They urged the salary of the assistant principal, who had been earning the regular $500 teacher's salary, be increased to $800 and that other teachers receive a raise of $100.

Curiously the board adopted all the recommendations except the increase in the principal's salary, and even Melvin – who helped author the report – voted against the raise for English, who promptly finalized his resignation. Perhaps Melvin opposed a raise for the principal because $1,200 was the current superintendent's salary, so if English's salary had been raised, then Wallis might have expected a raise, too. Of course, when the principal's salary increase was denied, Wallis could see the handwriting on the wall. Thus, the announcement in the *Evening Capital* on August 20, 1908, that Wallis had accepted a "much more lucrative offer" to become principal of Miles City, Montana, High School was hardly surprising. That Wallis could earn more money as a school principal in a small western town than he could as school superintendent in the capital city of Maryland reveals how paltry the pay in Anne Arundel County was for educators (12).

The resignations of English and Wallis put the school board in the embarrassing position of trying to hire a new superintendent and a new principal for its flagship school only weeks before the start of the fall semester. The obvious candidate to fill the superintendent vacancy was English, who apparently was still in town. After all, English had been a respected principal, and the former principal – Wallis – had been promoted to the superintendent's job when it became vacant. Also the $1,200 superintendent's salary would meet English's stated request for a raise. The news that the school board instead hired Naval Academy language professor Samuel Garner can only be interpreted as a snub to English. Perhaps the public airing of his salary grievances made him *persona non-gratis* to the board.

Meanwhile, the Annapolis school trustees were able to bring a new principal to town just before the end of summer vacation. Virginia Military Institute graduate George B. Pfeifer had five years' experience teaching at South Carolina State Military College. During his interview Pfeifer revealed his intention to split time between his Annapolis school duties and the pursuit of a "professorial degree" at Johns Hopkins University, but the desperate school board could hardly object (13). Pfeifer won widespread public approval for the school and its programs during his tenure. The benefits of the commercial and normal courses were obvious to all who attended the 1910 commencement to witness a record 19 graduates receive their diplomas. The commencement celebrated the school's success while simultaneously bidding an appreciative farewell to Pfeifer, who upon completion of his Johns Hopkins degree had accepted the offer to become the Winston-Salem, North Carolina, superintendent of schools at a salary of $1,800 per year (14).

Thus, in 10 years the school's trustees had said hello and goodbye to seven principals – a merry-go-round ride that must have left them increasingly dizzy. The vacancy created when Pfeiffer resigned brought a surprising application from Lieutenant William E. Smith, U.S.M.C. – Annapolis High's first principal! The *Evening Capital* reported on June 7, 1910, that Smith had found his decade of service in the Marine Corps to be surprisingly uncongenial. He was now eager to return to Annapolis if a salary comparable to his $2,000 lieutenant's pay could be arranged. However, before the trustees could hire Smith they learned they no longer had the power to act in the matter. A new state law mandated the administrative separation of high schools from grammar schools and placed the authority to select principals in the hands of county school boards. Although the board was willing to raise the principal's salary to $1,200, Smith withdrew his application because he could not afford an $800 pay cut.

The school board, caught in yet another public salary dispute, decided the time had come to abandon the notion that only a man could do the job. After all, the seven male principals that had occupied the office to date had been strident in their salary demands and fickle about their devotion to the job. With no apology for passing her over in the past, the board announced on June 14, 1910, just one week after Smith's apparent hiring, that assistant principal Louise Linthicum had been asked to assume duties as principal of Annapolis High School. Another woman, Miss Josephine Riordan, a 23-year veteran of teaching first grade, was named principal of Annapolis Grammar School. Although women had served earlier as elementary school principals, Linthicum may have been the first female high school principal in the state (15). She certainly provided the constancy the school board was seeking, remaining in the job for 18 years until health concerns in 1928 led her to transfer to the less demanding principal's job at the much smaller Arundel High School. Indeed, Linthicum's tenure ushered in a span of 60 years in which Annapolis High would have only four principals!

Wanted: A High School Building

Despite the school's early leadership problems, enrollment in all departments (primary, grammar and high school) skyrocketed beyond what the early planners had envisioned. The three-story brick Annapolis Schoolhouse that opened in September 1897 was a magnet to parents living outside the city whose children were legally required to attend the inferior schools in their home district, many of which were one room and all of which ended by seventh grade. In its second year the 500 students enrolled in Annapolis included many from Eastport with others from Davidsonville, Germantown, Brooklyn and the eastern shore of the Severn River. On January 11, 1899, the *Evening Capital* published a school board resolution to ensure Annapolis children had first claim to seats in the school. The principal was instructed to "enforce the regulations of the trustees governing the attendance of children whose parents do not reside in the city" and to suspend any student who had been "absent five sessions, in any term, without satisfactory cause."

To ease the crowding the Stockett house, which had been used previously as the elementary school, was renovated thoroughly in 1900 for the high school department. Eighth and ninth graders were housed on its ground floor, with juniors and seniors occupying its second story. But this, too, proved only a stopgap solution. By 1905 the Stockett house was filled to capacity of 150, with over 50 students relegated to the waiting list for seats when they became vacant.

School board member George Melvin, president of the Annapolis Banking and Trust Company, lobbied the state legislature to support the county's proposal to replace the Stockett house with an entirely new high school building. The General Assembly authorized the school board "to expend $20,000 and to issue bonds for the same in order to erect a new high school building and a heating plant for the whole new group of buildings." The initial bids exceeded budget, but at the close of a second round the contract was awarded to Edward D. Skipper & Company (16). During construction in 1906-1907 the high school department squeezed into the third floor assembly room of the Annapolis Schoolhouse (17). The new high school building's two lower floors were ready for use in September 1907, but not until October 15, 1908, was the completed three-story Annapolis High School formally turned over from the contractors to the building commission.

Annapolis now boasted the most modern high school building in the state. After a special tour of the school, an *Evening Capital* reporter gushed, "*It is a magnificent specimen of art in all departments of work. All the ceilings are metal, painted in beautiful pastel shades. The rooms are large, bright, airy and perfectly ventilated. It is a credit to the town and certainly to the contractor [E. D. Skipper, who] gave many extras not included in the contract.*" The school was specially fireproofed, with "iron, granite and slate stairways between brick walls and the numerous exits and entrances which assure safety to pupils in case of fire." Another marvel was the "perfect system of electric lights" that allowed all the fixtures in the school to be controlled from central switchboards. The three-story school had nine "commodious class rooms," four on the top floor and five on the middle floor, which was also home to the library, the principal's office, a large lobby and several cloakrooms. The largest assembly room in the city – "2,180 square feet of floor space and a stage 21 x 17 feet" – took up much of the top floor. The reporter raved about the assembly room's "perfect acoustics." The stage was equipped with footlights and headlights, and adjacent to the performance area were several dressing rooms (18).

The reporter was also impressed with the basement, which housed classrooms to accommodate the school's latest curricular innovation, manual training. The *Evening Capital* of May 31, 1907, enthused, "There has probably never been a movement in American educational methods which has effected such great changes in so short of a time as this manual training school movement." The Annapolis High program was modeled on Baltimore's Polytechnic Institute, which had been founded a decade after Russian educators introduced the "Sloyd system of manual training" at the 1876 Philadelphia Centennial Exposition. The curriculum began in third grade with paper folding exercises to develop hand-eye coordination by forming models of various shapes (pentagonal pyramids and octagonal prisms were two standards). In sixth grade basic whittling and special constructions in cardboard were introduced. High school students developed advanced whittling, drawing, drafting and bench skills to produce picture frames, flowerpot stands and shelf brackets. Special Sloyd benches and general carpentry tools were required in the standard manual training classroom. The state education department allocated $500 to purchase "machines, tools and all sorts of implements used in a work shop" as well as "nine drawing desks and 10 drawing tables" for the mechanical drawing room. Annapolis High's new facilities for the study of drafting and basic engineering concepts were said to rival those of any college (19).

Also on the school's ground floor was a room given to the Annapolis High School Athletic Association (AHSAA) to be used as a dressing room where the boys could "keep their togs" provided that "they keep it clean and paint the metal ceilings of the three rooms on this floor." Because physical education was not a required part of the curriculum, the new building had no indoor gymnasium, but the AHSAA had spent the previous year grading and improving the condition of the playgrounds behind the school for voluntary outdoor sports activities after school.

The Stanton School

Public schools in Anne Arundel County were strictly segregated until forced to integrate in the decade following the Supreme Court's 1954 ruling in the *Brown v the Board of Education* case that declared the practice unconstitutional. For two-thirds of a century (1866 – 1932) the Stanton School was the sole public educational facility for the city's black children (20). Located on Washington Street in the heart of Ward Four's thriving African American neighborhood of shops and homes, the original school was constructed of lumber that had been used to build some barracks at St. John's College during the Civil War; Secretary of War Edwin Stanton's permission to use the lumber led to naming the school after him. A brick schoolhouse was constructed in 1898 to replace the dilapidated wooden structure after "the colored people demanded $10,000 for a new school building" equivalent to the one recently opened for white children on Green Street. The case that an interracial group of civic leaders presented to the Annapolis city council and the school board was hard to deny: *"The present school building for the colored pupils of the public schools of this city has been both condemned by the Grand Jury as in an unsanitary condition, and as totally inadequate for the numerical accommodations of the school's scholars."* (21)

The city responded with a $4,000 authorization to construct a new school and the county covered the remaining $6,000. The state also provided $1,500 to install workbenches and other equipment so that boys could take manual training and girls could study the domestic arts, cooking and sewing (22). Completed towards the end of 1898, the three-story school had 12 classrooms, an attic assembly room and, according to the November 28, 1898, *Evening Capital,* was equipped with "all the modern conveniences." The principal, J. W. Chase, and his eight teachers were optimistic about the school's future, especially when enrollment reached 300 students in six grades. Their enthusiasm, however, proved short lived. Lack of enough money to keep the school running pitted the city's black citizens against the school board, whose authority over Stanton included approving expenses for educational materials and building upkeep, hiring staff and setting the school calendar. The length of the school year was a constant source of conflict between the board and educators throughout the county schools, white and black. The teachers did not receive their full salaries when the school year was shortened, but they also objected for pedagogical reasons. Fewer days meant covering less of the curriculum.

The problem was most acute for the "colored" schools because of the peculiar manner of financing education. Segregation also extended to revenue sources. No taxes collected from white citizens were supposed to be used for the education of Negro children. Thus, the length of Stanton's school year was dependent on taxes collected from the third of the city's population that included most of the poorest residents (23). A 1905 textbook on the history of Anne Arundel County required for use in grammar schools makes the prevailing opinion of white county residents on the issue clear: "*The serious difficulty in the present school system of the county is the large number of colored children for whom Anne Arundel is expected to provide education. The parents of the children are not [taxpayers] in any degree commensurate with the expense of the school so that the burden is thrown upon the white taxpayers to support both the white and colored schools. The taxpayers do not feel able to support both classes of schools as the conditions require, and yet the county cannot afford to let the colored people grow up in ignorance.*" (24)

In the period 1900 to 1905 the potential student pool for Annapolis and Stanton Schools were comparable. Yet while white enrollment soared at the Annapolis schoolhouse to over 900 pupils, the Stanton students numbered less than 600, none of whom were promoted in 1905 because the school's lack of funds forced its closure after only one semester. To avoid a mid-November closing in 1906, the school board decided to take action to circumvent the taxpayer shortfall: each Stanton student was asked to pay 50 cents to keep the school running. A half dollar may not seem like much today, but the school tax at that time was 25 cents for every $100 of income. So a 50-cent payment was equivalent to the school tax levied on a person with a $200 per year income, the salary of a first-year teacher and clearly beyond the means of many of the Stanton School's families. To raise money for students who did not have 50 cents, the Maryland Inn waiters put on an entertainment that netted $86.55 and the Naval Academy Wives' Club held a tea to which each guest was asked to donate a piece of silver to be sold for the school. These and other similar efforts provided the payment for over 600 children who otherwise would not have been able to go to school and allowed the school to stay open approximately seven months (25).

Stanton School closed in 1958, replaced by the new Adams Park Elementary School, but in 2000 the building that housed the school was renovated and reopened as a community center. The project included refurbishing a classroom with authentic desks, chairs, and other relics from the school's past. The following year Philip L.

Brown, who was graduated from the school in 1922, published *The Stanton Elementary School Story* that includes mementoes and photographs of students and teachers.

Boys and Football

Only 12 of the 73 students in Annapolis High School's first 10 graduating classes (1899 to 1908) were males. Of the 15 graduates in the Class of 1908, 14 were female. The previous three classes had no male graduates. Although the primary and grammar departments were generally evenly divided between the genders, most boys dropped out of school by age 15. Some began earning money, often in the family trade or business. Others sought to complete their education at a private preparatory school before entering college. Uncle Sam recruited some for the armed forces. A June 16, 1908, *Evening Capital* editorial noted that school-age boys could be found around town "working in stores, telegraph offices, printing offices, selling soft crabs, etc." The editor lamented that these boys (and their parents) clearly undervalued the best public education opportunity in the state of Maryland. "*A thorough English, mathematical, scientific and classical course is offered, and a diploma is [granted] to those whose studiousness and efficiency attain it [but] year after year the boys drop out of school as they reach the higher grades.*"

The school board attacked the public perception of Annapolis High as a "girl's school" on several fronts. St. John's College agreed to advertise that male graduates of Annapolis High School could bypass freshman year and enter St. John's as a college sophomore. The decision to finance a manual training program was also an obvious attempt to attract more male students to the school. On June 11, 1908, the local newspaper printed a laudatory description of manual training and praised the teacher, Professor A. Garey Lambert, for setting high standards in performance and discipline. "*Not a student has ever been brought up or reported for a violation of discipline since Mr. Lambert has had charge of the department, and this commends him even more highly [than] the splendid work done by the scholars under his instruction.*" The story announced that the Isaac Benesch and Sons store on Main Street would turn over its large front windows for an exhibition of the students' work to include "*a number of useful and beautiful things . . . [such as] carved umbrella stands, tables, large and small, medicine cabinets, clock frames, candle-sticks with shades, two Morris chairs in mission style, beautifully made handkerchief boxes and almost every conceivable article in wood both useful and ornamental.*" The paper called on every citizen interested in the school to see the display, and predicted "those who do not know what work the school is doing along this line will be astonished." The June 16, 1908, editorial reminded its readers of the exhibition and urged parents who doubted the school's educational value to visit it with their sons.

The emphasis on manual training was not only a bow to blue-collar families whose sons would be entering a trade, but also to the white-collar parents who wanted their sons to acquire masculine skills. Manliness may also have been what prompted the re-examination of athletics and physical training as a means to entice more boys to stay in school. Thus, in the fall of 1908 the AHSAA launched a campaign to raise money for the construction of a school gymnasium. In a bow to the morality of the period, the association argued in the September 22, 1908, *Evening Capital* that a gymnasium would provide a wholesome after-school environment where boys could develop their minds and bodies "instead of running the streets and oftentimes associating with boys of bad character." The AHSAA argued that a gymnasium would "keep boys in the High School longer than usual." To guard against having boys in school ONLY to play sports, the association proposed rules that to be allowed to participate, a boy would have to be in good academic standing. This, they argued, would "excite more interest in the regular curriculum, and . . .will have effect on the best athletes who now are back in studies by making them work harder so as to have all athletic privileges."

The AHSAA proposed an elaborate scheme to charge boys 50 cents and girls 25 cents to go to school – similar to the fees put in place just to keep Stanton School open – with the proceeds going to a gymnasium fund. Apparently the idea never progressed beyond the planning stage, and the Annapolis High building on Green Street never did have a gymnasium. However, the lack of an indoor facility did not hamper the AHSAA's other major plan to attract boys to the school. In the fall of 1908, after a decade of on-again, off-again seasons, Annapolis High School decided to field a football team with a full eight-game schedule. The results would be successful beyond what anyone imagined.

Following Annapolis High's promising first football season in 1899, teams representing the school played only sporadically from 1900 through 1907. A careful reading of the *Evening Capital* turned up results for only a handful of games the AHSAA sponsored during this period. In the spring of 1901 the AHSAA had converted the land behind the school along Compromise Street into a playground – including space that could be used for football practice. However, to field a team on a regular basis more boys were needed. Even though matriculation was not a precondition for playing on a high school team, consensus was that if a boy were enrolled it was easier to keep tabs on him and thus more likely that he would be available for games. The growing controversy over football's casualty rate may have also led the school to back away from the sport.

To pick up the athletic slack at the public school, a city athletic association was organized in 1902 that was "open to all white men of this city, young and old, who are gentlemen, regardless of social caste. . . interested in promoting physical culture and pure athletics in the city." (26) This Annapolis Athletic Association [AAA] set about immediately procuring space in the Opera House to use as a gymnasium equipped with "*one parallel bar, one horizontal bar, one jumping board, one jumping stand, one jumping rope, four mats, three-dozen one-and one-half pound dumb bells, three dozen two-pound dumb bells, three dozen wands, one basketball, two basketball goals, six dozen hooks, one indoor baseball, two indoor baseball bats, one punching bag, and two sets of boxing gloves.*" (27)

Football equipment is conspicuously absent from the laundry list. Although the AAA clearly stated its intent to form a football team, the public outcry over the increasing violence of the game may have hampered its efforts. A steadily growing list of serious football injuries and deaths led many across America to call for the brutal sport to be banned. Even the *Evening Capital* joined the football bashing bandwagon on September 8, 1908: "*The football season will soon open and those who engage in the game will vie with reckless motor car drivers, canoeists and bathers in making up lists of killed and injured. Football, perhaps more than any other sport, is liable to bring serious after results.*" The paper's criticism certainly was valid. Forty-five football fatalities occurred nationwide between 1900 and 1905, along with countless broken necks and backs, concussions and spinal injuries. Many victims were "found unconscious, buried under a pile of players with indications they had been kicked in the head or stomach so as to cause internal injuries or concussions." Lockjaw, blood poisoning and meningitis were also associated with the game. The 18 deaths and 159 serious injuries in the six-week long 1905 season led Stanford, Northwestern, Columbia and the University of California to disband their collegiate teams (28).

President Teddy Roosevelt fretted over football's "unnecessarily rough mass blocking and wedge plays." Roosevelt had long admired football as "a manly game," and he endorsed the idea that preparatory schools require all boys to play it. In February 1907 he wrote, *"There is no justification for stopping [football] because it is sometimes abused, when the experience of every good preparatory school shows that the abuse is in no shape necessarily attendant upon the game."* Desperate to preserve a game that he valued for instilling qualities of cooperation and bravery, Roosevelt invited Yale, Harvard and Princeton to send representatives to the White House for a candid talk about how football could be saved. He proposed that football players guilty of "brutality and foul play" should be penalized quickly and decisively, in the same way "summary punishment is given to a man who cheats at cards." (29)

Following the White House meeting, Chancellor Henry M. McCracken of New York University decided to take action. He invited 13 other eastern colleges to a conference on December 9, 1904; before the end of the year representatives from 62 colleges attended a follow-up meeting that resulted in the creation of the Intercollegiate Athletic Association of the United States, which five years later would change its name to the National Collegiate Athletic Association (NCAA). A football rules committee co-chaired by Yale's Walter Camp and West Point's Captain Palmer E. Pierce was appointed to suggest modifications that would make the game safer for players and more interesting to fans. They recommended a major innovation aimed at neutralizing the game's emphasis on players' size and weight along the line of scrimmage: the legalization of the forward pass, which put a premium on players with speed and agility. Other adjustments that helped restore public confidence in football included adding a third official, creating a neutral zone between the offensive and defensive lines, increasing the yardage needed for a first down from five to 10 and prohibiting offensive linemen from forming a wedge around the ball carrier behind the line of scrimmage. The overall effect of these rules was to usher in a new era of football that eventually would transform it from the "heavy-handed, unimaginative mass attack of brute force and labored progress toward an open, quick-striking offense." At the same time, the game became much more attractive for the spectators and safer for the players (30).

The Murray Hill Gang, 1905 – 1907

The rule changes made football more palatable to Annapolis High's new principal, George Pfeifer, who allowed the school to field a football team that over the course of the 1908 and 1909 seasons would prove to be one of the best in the school's entire history. On the rosters of these teams were nine players from the renowned "Murray Hill Gang." Murray Hill was an area of the city named after James Murray (1786-1866) who in 1830 purchased the 383-acre Greenfield estate to the east of Annapolis. Murray deeded much of the land back, but he kept 100 acres surrounding the estate's original mansion, Acton Hall. This neighborhood came to be known as Murray Hill after 1890 when George Melvin bought and subdivided the land surrounding Acton Hall into plots that he marketed for less than $400 (31). Over the next 15 years frame and brick houses slowly cropped up along Southgate, Murray and Franklin Streets, but fields and woods stretched west of Southgate towards Spa Road and south of Franklin towards Spa Creek.

Boys who lived in Murray Hill or in adjacent neighborhoods along West Street, around Church Circle, and down Main Street towards Market Square claimed this open land as their playground. They dubbed themselves the "Murray Hill Gang" when they started their own football team before the turn of the century. By 1905 they had gained local renown for a long winning streak against other neighborhood teams. Six boys born between November 1890 and July 1893 formed the nucleus of the 1907 Murray Hill team: center John Kaiser hiked the ball to quarterback Andreas Zillinger (A.Z.) Holley who could hand it off to running back Philip Clayton or throw a pass to ends Frank Thompson, Howard Claude and Guy Parlett.

In the opening game of 1907 the Murray Hillers extended their three-year winning streak by beating their rivals, the Young Tigers, 5-0. The only score came when Claude fell on a punt by Clayton that a Young Tiger fumbled in the end zone. (A scoring change in 1904 made touchdowns worth five points, field goals four points, a safety netted two points and a goal kick following a touchdown one point.) Later in the season, the October 26, 1907, *Evening Capital* reported that the Murray Hillers' unbroken list of victories came to an end as "the Young Tigers took the Murray Hillers into camp yesterday on the College campus to the tune of 17 to 0." Another great defensive play, this time a pass interception returned for a touchdown, allowed

44   *A Century of Education and Football at Annapolis High School*

The all female class of 1901 poses with Annapolis High principal Charles E. Dryden on the grass slope beside the school. The lack of male students concerned education officials, who feared Annapolis High might become a girls' school. To counter this perception, football was again promoted at the school. Below is the undefeated 1908 team, many of whom played for the Murray Hill Gang.

1. Claude	2. L. Medford	3. L. Thompson	4. H. Thompson	5. J. Hyde
6. C. Jones	7. G. Parlett	8. C. Hill	9. R. H. Elliott	10. H. Claude
11. G. Tisdale	12. P. Clayton	13. A. Johnson	14. Coach McMackin	15. A. Holley
16. B. White	17. F. Stevens	18. J. Kaiser	19. W. Schulz	20. R. Ennis
21. L. Hill	22. Coach Lambert	23. A. Clark	24. Mascot (Hill)	25. A. Stone

Murray Hill to win the third game in their 1907 series, again by the score of 5 to 0. The next time these two groups of boys would meet on the gridiron the Murray Hillers' would be wearing the red jerseys of Annapolis High School.

1908: AHS's First Undefeated Football Team

By the fall of 1908 the attempt to attract more boys to Annapolis High was in high gear. The new high school building was nearing completion with its facilities for the manual training program in place. Professor Garey Lambert, the male teacher who a year previously had been selected for the program, earned high marks from parents for instilling discipline while teaching practical skills to his pupils. Another innovation designed to attract boys was the expansion of the commercial curriculum to include various business courses beyond typing and stenography. A basement room was converted into a locker room. The dividends from these improvements were seen on September 14, 1908, when 100 new pupils, about half of whom were boys, enrolled in the high school.

The boys wasted no time deciding they wanted a football team to represent the school. Only four days after opening day, a notice ran on the front page of the *Evening Capital* announcing that Annapolis High had "reorganized a football team." Challenges from other high schools or from private athletic club teams in the 125-130 pound weight class were to be sent to the team's manager, Arthur Stone, the younger brother of the 1899 team's center, Richard Stone. Playground and club teams of the time played according to weight categories. That high school players weighed so little compared to their counterparts today reveals much about nutrition and caloric intake prior to the First World War.

The boys' first chore was to raise money to improve the land behind the school that was in "very bad condition." In the center of the field "a large waste pipe had burst underground, and all sewerage water flowed to the surface and kept nearly one half the field in a marshy, unhealthy condition." A revitalized AHSAA held a bazaar that netted $500. The boys then enlisted Professor Lambert's help to repair the broken pipe and to grade the field. They also repaired the stone wall along the lower end of the field next to Compromise Street and enclosed much of the playing area with a wooden fence (32).

Now that they had a suitable practice field, the boys needed a coach. Lambert again stepped forward. The tall, athletic teacher had played many sports as a young man, and now he lent his time and expertise to coaching the high school team. The players practiced hard under his guidance while team manager Stone and team captain Howard "Frank" Thompson put together an ambitious eight-game schedule. The money left over from refurbishing the field was used to buy equipment including red jerseys trimmed in blue, matching high socks, padded canvas pants and canvas helmets with leather straps.

The season for the Red and Blue opened with a game on the refurbished field played Monday afternoon, October 5th, against the Chesapeakes, the successor team to the Young Tigers. Annapolis pulled out a hard-fought 5-0 victory against their old rivals. The only score came at the end of the first 15-minute half when Howard Claude fell on a Chesapeake player's fumble in the end zone for a touchdown. According to the local reporter, the stars of the game all played for Annapolis: quarterback A.Z. Holley got free for several long runs, team captain Thompson recorded the most tackles, and fullback Albert Clark picked up steady yardage with his line plunges (33).

The next game was scheduled the following Saturday morning against a club from Mt. Washington. The high school 11 was dressed and ready to play on the St. John's College field, but their opponents failed to show up. Coach Lambert attempted to get the St. John's preps to play, but the candidates refused. So the team and its fans were forced to head home "disappointed," through no fault of their own, and hoping "not to have a similar occurrence" in the future (34).

The following week the school's second team took on the juniors of the Chesapeakes. The fact that they both had what today would be termed "junior varsity" teams suggests how serious these boys were about football. The high school's first team again took the field on Tuesday October 20th, against Wilmer's Naval Preparatory School, another local school geared to preparing boys from across the United States for the Naval Academy's entrance exams. Professor Wilmer's school, located close to the Emergency Hospital on Cathedral Avenue, was in a handsome building that contained classrooms and a dormitory. Annapolis scored a touchdown on a pass from little quarterback Holley to Claude, his second touchdown in two games. Holley kicked the extra point to make the score 6–0, and then Annapolis extended its lead to 10–0 when Holley added a four-point field goal before the end of the first 15 minute half. After intermission the candidates narrowed the margin to five points on a 70-yard touchdown pass play, but their point after failed. The Annapolis defense toughened, allowing no more scores, thus securing for the high school boys the second victory of their young season.

The Red and Blue's next game produced one of its most impressive victories. Early on Saturday morning, October 24th, the team from Hagerstown High School arrived in Annapolis by train. The featured front-page story of the *Evening Capital* trumpeted the news of how the local boys thrashed the westerners, 36-0. Fullback Albert Clark had a huge game, scoring four touchdowns on line plunges. Other players drawing praise were quarterback Holley for his passing and running, as well as Clayton and Stone for their end runs. The city's growing pride in its schoolboy team is evident in the story's third paragraph, which pointed out the boys "represent Annapolis in even a closer sense than any of the other teams as the players all come from the city or vicinity." The paper attributed the fact that the local lads were "far ahead of other Maryland teams of their size and weight" to their long experience playing together as the Murray Hill Gang.

A week later the Annapolis High 11 totally "outclassed" the reserve team from Baltimore Polytechnic Institute, winning 21-2. Poly was the technical counterpart to Baltimore City College High (BCC), which offered a liberal arts curriculum that included a two-year college curriculum. Both of these schools enrolled several thousand boys, which allowed them to field football teams that routinely played college reserve teams, so the fact that the Annapolis boys lined up against the Poly reserves was appropriate. The news account of the game does not detail how Annapolis scored all of its touchdowns, but it does mention the highlight of the game occurred when Philip Clayton scored on a 75-yard touchdown run.

On the first Wednesday afternoon in November, Annapolis High faced its toughest test of the season, the candidates from Werntz Naval Preparatory School. The oldest of the local prep programs, Werntz had been fielding a football team for several years. The Candidates had a decided weight advantage of about 25 pounds per player, but the high school lads "fought like gladiators" to a scoreless tie. Running backs Clayton and Stone managed several long end runs, and as the game ended the locals were on the Candidates' ten-yard line. A serious accident took place during the second half when Holley threw a long pass to Claude at the lower end of the field towards the recently constructed wooden fence concealing a stone wall. The defenders "plunged through the fence and down on the other side of the wall." One of the Candidates was knocked out and was "in a very bad condition," but fortunately he regained consciousness a short time later (35).

The tie game with Werntz was the only blemish on the 1908 team's 7–0–1 record. The season ended with victories over BCC's reserves and Charlotte Hall Military Academy, but the game scores are unknown because the newspapers from mid-November 1908 through May 1909 have not been preserved. However, in November 1909 a story noted the high school defeated its opponents in 1908 by a combined score of 127 to 7, which means in their last two games they scored 44 points and gave up none (36). Fortunately the gap in the *Evening Capital* ends before the June 25th commencement for the Class of 1909. Two of the 10 graduates were boys – Frank Stevens and Walter Schultz, the starting guards on the football team the previous fall. The only other player to leave the team was a reserve end named Walton Childs, a serious scholar who was admitted as a special student to Baltimore Poly (37). That nine of the 11 starters, including all the star players, anticipated returning to the gridiron for the fall 1909 season boded well for the team's continued success, but nobody predicted the 1909 team might actually top the previous year's record.

Playing to Perfection – The 1909 Season

When the 1909 football team lined up for its preseason photo in front of the High School, the boys and their coaches may have wondered if they could replicate the previous season's record. Newcomers Charlie Jones and Roland Thomas were slated for the vacant guard spots. The September 30, 1909, *Evening Capital* noted, *"The Annapolis High School team is doing some hustling these days to get into shape for the opening contest of its schedule. The practice yesterday under Coach Lambert was fast and showed that the new men taken into the 11 are fitting in nicely in the team work."*

A surprise returnee to the team was graduate Frank Stevens. Coach Lambert learned that other high schools, including both BCC and Poly, routinely included players on the roster who were no longer matriculated students, a practice that was finally ended in 1914 when City and Poly signed an agreement that allowed only students in good academic standing and taking a "full work load in a regular course (a

Honoring Their Home Town, 1900–1910

minimum of 15 periods per week)" to participate in athletics. This agreement also limited boys to four years of eligibility, and set 22 as the top age a player could be at the start of a season (38).

Coach Lambert moved Stevens to the backfield, where he lined up with the "smart little quarterback, Holley, the swift Clayton at left half and the tough Albert Clark at fullback." Lambert knew his team was small in size, but he had no doubt they would be faster than most of their competitors. The four in the backfield, along with end Frank Thompson and center John Kaiser, were the key members of the Annapolis High track team. The previous May these boys missed winning the seventh annual Maryland Interscholastic Track and Field Championship at Tome Academy in Port Deposit by one point (39).

Any worries Coach Lambert may have had about his squad were quickly dispelled on Saturday, October 4th, when – as that day's *Evening Capital* so delicately put it – Annapolis High opened its season by "drubbing the aggregation from the Boys' Latin School by the score of 26 to 0." Playing on the St. John's College field, the local boys' speed and greater knowledge of the game sent the Baltimore school to "ignominious defeat." Clark, Clayton, Kaiser and Stevens scored touchdowns, Kaiser made three extra points and Holley added a field goal from the 35-yard line.

The easy victory over Boys' Latin gave the Annapolis 11 a sense of confidence as they approached the biggest game in the school's first decade. At 1:30 p.m. on Wednesday the 13th of October the "snappy fast little team of Annapolis High, along with a host of loyal rooters" boarded a train carrying them to a contest against the varsity squad of Baltimore City College. The previous year the Red and Blue defeated BCC's second team, but playing against their first team – often considered the top prep team in the state – would be a huge step up for the smaller Annapolis lads. BCC, with two starters nicknamed "Husky," was bigger and more experienced. The only other high school team City had played in 1909 was its Baltimore rival Poly; the rest of BCC's varsity games were against college second teams. "Plucky" little Annapolis High would have its hands full against the highly regarded BCC team.

The next day's *Evening Capital* splashed the joyous news about the game's outcome on its front page: AHS 11, BCC 5. Annapolis kept its opponent on the defensive the entire first half while building an 8 - 0 lead. Holley capped the team's first possession with a surprise field goal – now worth 3 points – from the 10-yard line.

Before the end of the half, guard Roland Thomas recovered a blocked BCC punt in the end zone for a touchdown. Holley capped the high school's scoring with another field goal in the second half. BCC's only score came on a late second half touchdown. The 1909 BCC yearbook, *Green Bag,* used an excuse common to many losers when discussing the game – they blamed the defeat on what they claimed was a weight differential in favor of their opponents: *"The next game on the program was Annapolis High School. . . . When one gets down to bottom facts, weight is the thing that counts in football. They had it and we did not. The score ended 11 to 5 in their favor."* (40).

The Annapolis lads followed their victory over BCC with a 35 to 5 defeat of Werntz's Naval Prep, the only team Annapolis High had failed to defeat the previous year. The *Evening Capital* noted that the high school boys "completely outclassed the future middies" by showing "their thorough knowledge of the game and executing a variety of plays that the heavier candidates could not solve." (41)

Word of the victories over BCC and Werntz's - two powerhouse teams – reached the western region of the state, causing Hagerstown to send a telegram announcing its decision to forfeit the game scheduled for the coming weekend rather than travel all the way to Annapolis for what likely would be a thrashing. Charlotte Hall also telegraphed its decision to forfeit, leaving Annapolis with only a game against St. John's Prep on its schedule. To Coach Lambert's surprise, St. John's sent their college reserve team instead of the preps (42). The switch in opponents had little effect on the Tiger team that dominated the entire contest with their "fast, open attack" and "speedy, aggressive defense." Fullback Albert Clark plunged into the end zone for the first touchdown. Roy Clark intercepted a St. John's pass and ran it back 30 yards for another score. Frank Stevens caught a Holley pass for the high school's third touchdown. John Kaiser kicked all three extra points, making the final score AHS 18, St. John's Reserves 0. Quarterback Holley was singled out for praise, as he had been all season, for his smart play and punting ability. The lads on the line were also applauded for their rugged blocking and tackling (43).

With no other teams willing to play Annapolis High, Coach Lambert had little choice but to declare the season ended. Officially the team's record was 6 victories and no defeats; in the four games actually played they outscored their opponents 90 to 10. Three days after their final victory of the season, the Annapolis City Council unanimously passed a petition praising the "plucky and scrappy little football team of the Annapolis High School" for the "credit they have done themselves" and the "honor they have brought to the town." (44)

Although football was over for the year, five of the star players – Philip Clayton, A.Z. Holley, Albert Clark, Frank Thompson and John Kaiser – returned to the Tome Institute in the spring of 1910 for the Eighth Annual Interscholastic Track and Field Championship. This time they left no doubt about which high school had the best athletes in the state. Twelve other scholastic teams from across Maryland competed in the five contested events: the broad jump and runs of 75, 220, 440 and 880 yards. Medals were awarded to the first three finishers in each event. The Tigers won eight of the 15 medals, scoring 26 of the possible 40 points to claim Annapolis High's first-ever state championship. Clayton set new state records in the 440 (54.4 seconds) and the broad jump (20 feet, more than a foot longer than the previous record). Clayton capped his day with a silver medal in the 75-yard dash. Other Annapolis medal winners were Clark (gold in the 220), Kaiser (silver in the 220 and bronze in the broad jump), Thompson (silver in the 880) and Holley (bronze in the 880).

In its lead story on Monday, May 16, 1910, the *Evening Capital* lavished praise on the "home lads" who "covered themselves with glory," declaring that "the athletic victory of the High School is appreciated by all the townspeople, who are immeasurably proud of the boys." In an editorial entitled "Our High School Heroes," the paper proclaimed that "too much praise cannot be given to these boys who are a credit not only to the High School, but to the town they represent." Predicting "this great achievement should go down in the history of the school," the paper reported that the handsome championship trophy – a bronze shield engraved with the school's name and mounted on an oak tablet – would be displayed in the front window of Green's Drug Store before being permanently installed in the school's main hall, the first championship trophy of the many that school teams would win in the course of the 20th century (45).

Alas, almost a century later, no trace of the bronze championship shield remains, and the glory these boys earned on the Annapolis High playing fields only recently has been commemorated in the school when a banner honoring all the championship teams in the school's history was hung in the gymnasium. Several went on to achieve great athletic success at St. John's College, especially Roy Clark (a four-year football starter), Phil Clayton (a three-sport star) and Frank Thompson. These three were to earn more lasting laurels, along with virtually all of their Annapolis High teammates, in service to their nation. Quarterback Holley, center Kaiser and reserves Richard Elliott, William Strohmeyer and Guy Parlett enlisted in the local National Guard's Company M, a machine gun unit that was sent to the Mexican frontier in 1916 to guard the border against Pancho Villa. They returned home in 1917 only to be federalized into the Army's 29th Division, 115th Regiment and shipped overseas in 1918 to front line trenches at Verdun. Altogether nine of the starting 11 found themselves fighting together in France, including two who remained career officers to retire as colonels – Clayton and Leslie Medford.

Following the war most returned to Annapolis. Businessmen Albert Clark and Frank Thompson won election as city aldermen. St. John's graduate William Strohmeyer retired as a major in the Army, then chaired the Annapolis housing authority and won election to the Maryland House of Delegates. Richard Elliott became a local fixture as a reporter, then editor-in-chief, of the *Evening Capital*. Frank Stevens worked as the city's postmaster, but spent much of his spare time for 54 years as volunteer head of the Annapolis Fire and Rescue Company. Holley became Annapolis High's football coach in the early 1920's, but then moved to New Jersey to begin a 45-year career teaching history and coaching at Rutgers Preparatory School. Robert Ennis took a position as a sales engineer with Bethlehem Steel in New York but returned to Annapolis to live out his retirement. Kaiser enjoyed a long, distinguished career in the Foreign Service. Only one of the boys on the 1908-1909 teams, Guy Parlett, died young. Shortly after being sent with the 115th Regiment to Alabama for training, Parlett passed away from pneumonia. Holley volunteered to escort the body of his teammate and comrade-at-arms home for burial.

* * * * * * * * * * *

The undefeated 1908 football team and the 1910 state championship track team bookend two pivotal years in the history of Annapolis High. From its tentative beginnings in the 1890's, this public secondary school had struggled to win an identity for itself in a city whose loyalty was attached to its two colleges – the Naval Academy and St. John's. With its new building completely finished, with innovative curricular changes and expanded course offerings in place, with a growing student body that included a better gender balance, and with local pride swelling as a result of athletic success, Annapolis High School exuded a well-deserved spirit of confidence as it entered the second decade of the 20th century.

CHAPTER 3:
ANNAPOLIS HIGH'S WARRIORS, 1910 – 1919

Football practice behind Annapolis High, circa 1910

We cannot afford to turn out . . .men who shrink from physical effort or from a little physical pain. In any republic courage is a prime necessity for the average citizen if he is to be a good citizen, and he needs physical courage no less than moral courage; the courage that dares as well as the courage that endures, the courage that will fight valiantly alike against the foes of the soul and the foes of the body. Athletics are good, especially in their rougher forms, because they tend to develop such courage. They are good also because they encourage a true democratic spirit, for in the athletic field the man must be judged, not with reference to outside and accidental attributes, but to that combination of bodily vigor and moral quality which go to make up prowess.
                    President Theodore Roosevelt, 1910

A Woman Takes Charge

Louise Linthicum assumed duties as principal of Annapolis High in the fall of 1910. Her $1,200 salary was equivalent to what her male predecessor earned, but the enthusiasm that greeted her appointment to a traditionally male job was far from universal. On June 17, 1910 – just three days after Linthicum's promotion from assistant principal to the top job at Annapolis High was announced – the *Evening Capital* editorialized: "*The Annapolis public school is now a manless school. There is no man in the entire teaching force that is now composed of women. It is claimed by those who have had experience that women cannot look out for boys' interests after school hours, as can male teachers. With the manual training teacher gone, as well as the male principal, the school will next year probably be taught entirely by women.*"

Linthicum may have privately bristled at the suggestion that female teachers were incapable of handling male students, but publicly she acted quickly to quiet her critics by hiring Ivan T. Morton to teach manual training. A native Marylander from Elkton, Morton graduated with a manual training degree from the state's normal school. Under Morton's direction, Annapolis High's program continued to attract boys to enroll in the high school because they, and more importantly their parents, recognized the value of the practical design and construction skills being taught to these future husbands and fathers. A companion domestic science curriculum with its own teacher was soon added so that girls would be well prepared to cook, to sew and to handle the everyday issues of household management when they became wives and mothers (1).

Indeed, whatever misgivings Annapolitans may have had initially about the new principal soon dissipated as the high school prospered under Linthicum's leadership. Anne Arundel was one of only a few counties that by 1910 still had no compulsory school attendance law. Determined to increase Annapolis High's enrollment, especially of boys, Linthicum worked to attract new students in a variety of ways. Initially public high schools were designed to provide preparatory work sufficient for students to be admitted to a college or normal school, but the majority of young Annapolitans had no such expectations. Instead, they sought skills that would allow them to advance in the business world. Addressing their needs, Linthicum improved the commercial curriculum, adding courses in banking, bookkeeping and clerical skills such as stenography. The purchases of new typewriters, duplicating machines and other office equipment kept the program current with the latest innovations. The commercial track allowed a student to graduate without taking such traditional college preparatory courses as Latin, Greek and higher mathematics. At the same time, Linthicum continued to emphasize the importance of the academic curriculum to those students aiming for higher education so they would be fully prepared for college and normal school. The entire curriculum was infused with a strong dose of moralistic patriotism, a reflection not only of the rampant nationalism of the era, but also of Linthicum's own personal view that high school graduates should assume civic leadership roles. The steady growth in the overall enrollment from less than 100 pupils in 1910 to nearly 200 in 1916 reflects Linthicum's success in selling the value of a high school education to the local community (2).

In 1916 the state superintendent received a report from a task force that had conducted a three-year study of public education. The Maryland legislature passed a revised school law based on the report's recommendations for improving the overall quality of education. The new law set the school year throughout the state to a uniform nine months, devised a plan that equalized financial support between wealthy and poorer districts, added 12th grade to high schools and made school attendance compulsory for younger children. The subsequent increase in the number of students attending Annapolis Grammar School brought about a 400 percent increase in Annapolis High's enrollment during the following decade. Those who had worried about the small percentage of boys enrolling in the high school applauded mandatory grammar school attendance because it naturally led to a dramatic increase in the number of male students promoted into the high school, and thus also to a higher percentage of male graduates.

The addition of popular extracurricular activities helped to maintain student interest in school. These included publication of a monthly school newspaper called *The Red and Blue* that began to appear in November 1910, a literary society and a drama club that several times a year put on elaborate productions ranging from *Alice in Wonderland* to Shakespeare's *As You Like It* and *Hamlet*. By the fall of 1917 the largest club in the school was the Junior Red Cross, perhaps because it allowed students to feel good about contributing now that the country was at war. Class organizations sponsored events such as luncheons and tag days to raise funds that were forwarded to the national Red Cross Office in Washington, D.C. (3).

Linthicum's personal attitude towards athletics is not recorded, but clearly she facilitated Annapolis High's burgeoning sports program. The school budget did not provide any funds for physical education or athletic teams – intramural or interscholastic. Money for teams had to be raised through the community. Generally high schools created their own athletic associations with student leadership, but often citizens interested in seeing the school compete in a specific sport would bankroll a team. The AHSAA raised funds to purchase uniforms and training equipment for football. It also sponsored a fundraiser with proceeds going to refurnishing the small basement space that served as a boys' locker room. The new manual arts teacher Ivan Morton helped AHSAA members revamp the fields behind the school and construct an outdoor basketball court (4).

Annapolis High's first organized physical education program began on a voluntary basis in 1911; the boys meeting after school with Morton on Monday, Wednesday and Friday and, under the guidance of domestic science teacher Mary Tate, the girls gained permission to have their own after school recreation period on Thursdays. When weather grew too cold to play outside, the students petitioned the school board for permission to take down the chandeliers in the Assembly Room so it could be used for indoor games during the winter (5). Although soccer and basketball were introduced during this period, the game the boys most wanted to play was the one that had first brought fame to their school – football.

Football – Too Violent for Schoolboys?

In the decade before the outbreak of World War One (1905-1914), 73 different boys wearing the red and blue jerseys of Annapolis High played football, most for two or more years (6). Following the undefeated 1908 and 1909 seasons, enthusiasm for the sport remained high among the schoolboys. Although teams were fielded for the next five years, game results are hard to uncover. Stories about Annapolis High football results virtually disappeared from the *Evening Capital,* perhaps because *The Red and Blue* editor, football player "Dillard" Tisdale, gave enthusiastic although somewhat sporadic coverage to the Tigers (7). Of the 19 documented games played from 1910 to 1915, Annapolis recorded eight victories,

Louise Linthicum became principal in 1910 after 15 years teaching and serving as the vice-principal. Not athletic herself, she supported football, including the 1910 team and coach Ivan Morton as a way to attract boys to the school. Eight boys in this photo served together on the Mexican frontier and then in France during World War One.

seven losses and four ties against opponents that included military preparatory schools for St. Johns and the Naval Academy (Bobbie's, Werntz's and Wilmer's), civilian prep schools in Baltimore (Boys' Latin, Friends, Gilman and Marsten) and only two other public high schools (Baltimore City College and Wicomico in Salisbury). Games are referred to in the *Evening Capital* against eastern shore high schools in Easton and Cambridge but no stories reporting results have been located.

    The game accounts that have been preserved identify several gridiron stars. The best player in the years leading up to the war was Samuel Edgar Clark, the youngest of the three Clark brothers who played running back for the Red and Blue. Most game stories from 1912 to 1914 mention Clark, who early in his high school career established himself as "the fastest man on the team." The *Evening Capital* reports on October 5, 1912, that in the first minute of his first game for Annapolis High (against the St. John's College freshmen team), Clark scored a touchdown on a 60-yard run. A year later, on October 31, 1913, Clark scored the only touchdown in the school's 19-6 loss to Gilman Country School in Roland Park when he "winged right end for twenty yards." His best effort came on October 28, 1914, when he quarterbacked Annapolis High to a 47-0 victory over Baltimore's Boys' Latin School. The next day's *Evening Capital* reported "Edgar Clark . . . was the star of the game. The diminutive youngster scored five touchdowns and worked the ball down field when the other two were scored. Clark made six sensational runs, one of which was good for 80 yards." In what was probably his last game for Annapolis High, Clark lined up at the fullback position and scored one of the team's touchdowns in the 14-0 victory over the Friends' School in Baltimore. Earlier in the season Friends had defeated all the other Baltimore prep schools, so Annapolis High's victory catapulted the team to the top tier of schoolboy 11's in the state.

Coaching the boys during these years was the manual arts teacher, Ivan Morton. Taking advantage of the loose eligibility rules, A.Z. Holley and Frank Stevens continued to play in 1910 and then assisted Morton with coaching Practices were held on the hard-packed dirt field behind the school, while home games were generally played at St. John's. The game remained very rough, certainly not for the faint-hearted. Although rule changes introduced in 1906 had opened the game to the forward pass, the ball was not allowed to be in the air more than 20 yards, and no pass could be thrown in the end zone for a touchdown. Teams without good passing quarterbacks still relied on plays that called for linemen to mass around the ball carrier, sometimes interlocking arms to form an interference line, at other times simply pushing or pulling him forward. Inside the 25-yard line one of the offensive lineman was allowed to position himself behind the backfield before the snap so that he could more quickly begin to push the ball carrier from behind as the other linemen pulled him forward – into a throng of defenders, some of whom surrounded the mass formation while others threw themselves on top of the heap.

Most of the serious injuries in football came from hitting, stomping on and kicking opponents inside the "murder pile." One Michigan high school player left a vivid description of play degenerating into brawling: "*A mass of players from one team struggled to advance the ball against a mass of players from the other team.. . . .The players tore at each other like wild dogs, pushing, kneeing and slugging at every opportunity. Soon they were smeared head to toe with sweat and mud, and as they gasped for air you could see their hot breath exploding into plumes of steam. Linemen on both sides were bleeding, mostly from bashed noses and split lips, and I saw several players spit loose or broken teeth onto the field. Even those who weren't injured had blood from other players splattered on them. Although football rules prohibited such brawling, players were* seldom penalized because field judges could not see what was happening inside the mass formations." (8)

From 1910 to 1912 additional rules were introduced that opened the game to more scoring while eliminating some of the most flagrant violence. The field was shortened from 110 to 100 yards. The value of a touchdown increased from five to six points, while a field goal was dropped first from five to four points, and then to three. To eliminate blockers from pushing the ball carrier from the rear, seven offensive players were required to be on the line of scrimmage when the ball was hiked. Limits were removed from the length a forward pass could travel and touchdown passes were legalized.

The new rules certainly did enhance the offensive side of football, thus generally heightening the fans' enthusiasm for the game. Especially popular were forward passes – the longer, the better! Annapolis High had a series of fine passing quarterbacks. Team captain Warren Feldmeyer was lauded in the November 1, 1911, *Evening Capital* for his "cleverly executed forward passing." The team's 5-0 victory over Werntz Naval Prep was attributed to "its superiority with the forward pass," which "kept their opponents guessing with their variety of trick plays."

In 1912 quarterback Henry Boettcher was labeled a "sensation" and his "work behind the line" was declared "the best that has been seen at the school for years." One of the favorite targets for both Feldmeyer and Boetcher was Harry Newton, whose name frequently appeared in the paper for both his runs and his catches. In 1914 Harry's younger brother Clarence took over as Annapolis High's signal caller and kept the school's reputation for good quarterbacks alive. Along with Edgar Clark, other noteworthy running backs were Fred Hyde and "Dillard" Tisdale. The local paper did not confine its compliments to offensive play. Among those singled out for their excellent tackling were Louis Hoff, Kenton Strange, Nicholas Woodward and 1913 classmates Fred Bielaski and captain of the 1912 team Willis Martin. In one game an AHS touchdown was nullified for "pushing from behind," an indication that the new rules eliminating the "murder pile" were being enforced (9).

Although the game remained extremely popular with the boys, the new rules did not completely silence football's critics. In 1913 Colonel C.P. Townsley, the Superintendent of the Military Academy, called for football's elimination because of the large number of cadets hurt while playing. He cited statistics that showed "75 percent of all the injured treated by the surgeons in the season at West Point are due to football casualties." He claimed 40 to 50 cadets per year were kept from normal military training while rehabilitating football injuries. He concluded that the only value of football at Army was "the interest, entertainment and excitement it affords to the other members of the corps and the thousands who attend its principal contests." The Surgeon General of the Navy, Dr. Charles Stokes, supported Townsley's evaluation with his own study in which he claimed that after commissioning as officers, former midshipmen athletes suffered more often from "vulvular disease of the heart, general poor health, obesity and tuberculosis" than those who had not been involved in "spectacular athletics." Dr. Stokes concluded "over training and over straining" caused the health problems (10).

Although Army and Navy continued to play football, the arguments against the game extended beyond service academy walls. One increasingly vocal opponent of football was the Public Athletic League (PAL) of Baltimore. Robert Garrett, the 1896 Olympic champion in the shot put and discus, founded PAL in 1900. The organization embodied Garrett's belief that boys and girls could benefit from supervised athletic activities. In 1911 physician William H. Burdick assumed the directorship of PAL. He tirelessly traveled throughout Maryland to promote the organization's credo: "healthful play and exercise build resistance, keep the body fit and provide for growth and development." Burdick's "healthful play" excluded all contact sports, especially football. Instead he championed soccer and baseball for boys. For girls he suggested volleyball and fieldball, a game played on a soccer field but instead of kicking the ball, players tossed it to each other as they ran up and down the field. Throwing a ball in the opponents' soccer goal scored a point. Burdick was also enthusiastic about the relatively new game of basketball, a sport that both boys and girls could play (11).

Burdick shared Garrett's passion for track and field. In the spring of 1915 he organized PAL's first "Olympiad" for Baltimore boys. PAL emissaries arrived in Annapolis the next summer. When school opened in the fall Annapolis High did not field a football team, a move that appears to have been a direct result of PAL's influence. In the spring of 1916, Anne Arundel County held its first Track and Field Day with students from Annapolis High, Annapolis Grammar, St. Mary's and Eastport participating. Running, jumping and throwing events for boys were organized in five weight classifications. A dodge ball game for girls was also included. Winners of each event earned the right to participate in the state Olympiad held in Baltimore every June (12). In the autumn of 1916 Annapolis High boys began playing soccer after PAL employee Daniel Miller came to the school several times to help lay out the field, explain the rules and teach techniques of the "previously unknown game." Inter-class basketball contests for both boys and girls also were organized (13). By 1918 these popular PAL-sponsored activities seemed to have buried any demand for football, perhaps partially because many young men were being called to action on fields far removed from the old gridiron behind Annapolis High.

Annapolis High Boys in the Great War, 1917 – 1918

By November 1918, 57 of the 73 boys who once wore the red and blue Annapolis football jerseys had been issued new uniforms designed for work, not play – the uniforms worn by the 4.25 million Americans who answered their nation's call to arms during World War One. Forty dressed in the Army's drab olive green. Twenty served together in the American Expeditionary Force's 29th Division, some in the 115th Infantry Regiment, the rest in the 112th Machine Gunners. Remarkably, ten of these young men showed enough leadership to be promoted to the officer ranks by the war's end (14). During the summer of 1918 the 29th Division, nicknamed the Blue & Gray because its soldiers came mainly from Maryland and Virginia, shipped overseas; by early fall they took up positions along the front line in eastern France. In October they fought during a three-week offensive in the Meuse-Argonne region north of Verdun, the last major battle on the Western Front.

Pvt. Edgar Clark, the star halfback of Annapolis High's pre-war teams, described the action – and his reaction to having survived it – in a letter to his mother that appeared on the *Evening Capital*'s January 19, 1919, front page: *"After being in one of the hardest battles ever fought by our doughboys, the same lasting for 21 days and nights, can you imagine me sitting in a French YMCA listening to an American melody which is being played by a French soldier? Mother, to be frank with you, I am congratulating myself on coming out of the conflict alive. . . . Believe me we surely had 21 days of hardship. . . . The worst thing that we had to endure was the continuous fire of the Boch artillery. They kept a barrage of artillery fire on the ground which we had taken day and night. It was almost impossible, too, for a human being to live through the same. I would write more about our four times over the top, but I am certain that the less I write would be best. I received quite a few letters while in the trenches, but I didn't know as to whether or not I would ever answer the same. We took seven miles from the Huns and most of it was work. Just imagine fighting in a forest. We also took several thousand prisoners. I am feeling quite well."*

Others from Annapolis High in the Army were scattered in a wide variety of units. John C. Martin, future chief of staff at the Annapolis Emergency Hospital, was a lieutenant in the Medical Corps. Frank M. Conor's training in the Engineering Corps enabled him to have a 33-year career as a Naval Academy electrician. Lt. Laurens Claude transferred from the 115th regiment to the Aviation Corps; his training as a pilot eventually led to a career with Pan American and then with American Airlines, but perhaps blaming himself for a 1949 crash at Love Field in Dallas that took 28 lives, he committed suicide in 1958. Seven of the youngest, including several who finished high school in May 1918, were still in Student Army Training Centers (SATC's) on college campuses when the war ended. Some in the Annapolis High contingent took to the military so well that they made careers of it; Philip Clayton, Fred Hyde and Raymond Stone (USMA 1923) all eventually retired as colonels after lifetime service that included World War Two.

The dozen Annapolis High boys who joined the Navy drew assignments to troop transports and destroyers in the North Atlantic, patrol boats along the American and British coasts and sub-chasers in the North Atlantic. Three were naval officers, including brothers George and Ryland "Dillard" Tisdale who were Naval Academy graduates in the classes of 1913 and 1915 respectively. Dillard was one of three from Annapolis High who returned after the war wearing decorations earned for specific acts of courage and bravery. On October 17, 1917, his ship SS ANTILLES was torpedoed and sank off Brest, France. According to a special commendation from the Secretary of Navy, Tisdale "showed coolness and courage in command of the forward guns," did not leave his post "until he was forced to dive from the bridge of the sinking vessel" and then "assisted other ANTILLES survivors onto life rafts." Tisdale's naval career took him to China, where the Yangtze River gunboat he commanded in the 1920's evacuated Americans and other foreigners

ANNAPOLIS HIGH WORLD WAR ONE VETERANS

Of the more than 70 boys from Annapolis High who served in the armed forces during World War One, only three died. Two pictured here are Private Benjamin Skinner Carr (left) who was killed in action at Verdun on 23 October 1918, just weeks before the armistice. Lt. Guy Parlett died of pneumonia at Camp McClellan in Alabama during basic training.

Football stars (from left to right) Lt. A. Z. Holley, Pvt. Edgar Clark and Capt. John Kaiser were members of the Annapolis Machine Gun Company, a Maryland National Guard unit that saw service on the Mexican border during the Pancho Villa scare in 1916. They returned briefly to Annapolis before American entry into World War One when the unit was augmented to the 29th Division and shipped to France, where all three took part in the fighting at Verdun. Kaiser won a citation for his bravery in action.

Lt. Laurens Claude (left) also served with the Machine Gunners in Mexico, but was selected for pilot training during World War One. Lt. Ryland "Dillard" Tisdale (right) was founding editor of "The Red and Blue" newspaper in 1910 and played football, but he left Annapolis High to enter the Naval Academy (Class of 1915) He was decorated for bravery for his actions when his ship, the SS Antilles, was torpedoed off Brest, France in October 1917. His long naval career ended with his death while resisting the Japanese in the Philippines during World War Two. The Navy later named a destroyer in his honor.

caught in the battles during the civil war between communist and nationalist forces. Although he retired in 1936, Tisdale was recalled to active duty in 1940, sent to help defend the Philippines prior to Pearl Harbor and was killed while resisting the enemy on May 23, 1942, shortly after the American surrender at Corregidor. The destroyer escort SS TISDALE (DE-278) was named in his honor (15).

Two other Annapolis High graduates were decorated for bravery while the 115th Regiment was in the trenches north of Verdun. Former quarterback Fred Bielaski ('13) captured an enemy machine gun while on night patrol in late August 1918. After graduating from Annapolis High, Bielaski was the honor graduate of St. John's class of 1916, but at the war's outset he had to enlist because he was too young to be commissioned an officer. His obvious leadership qualities did not escape his commanding officer's attention. Although Bielaski fought to remain a sergeant at the front, he was sent to officer's training camp and commissioned a lieutenant shortly before the armistice was signed (16).

John Kaiser ('11), who had played center on Annapolis High's championship teams in 1908–09, was with the 112th Machine Gunners during the Meuse-Argonne offensive. According to his citation, Kaiser displayed "courageous conduct in the fighting North of Verdun on the 11th of October 1918, when he captured 16 prisoners and an automatic rifle." By the war's end, Kaiser had been promoted to the rank of captain, which made him the senior officer present when Annapolis threw a victory celebration after the return of the 29th Division to Camp Meade in May 1919 (17). Interestingly, both Bielaski and Kaiser joined the diplomatic corps following the war and enjoyed careers that took them to many foreign posts.

Several from the Annapolis High contingent were injured or wounded, with only one suffering a serious disability. The youngest of the three Tisdale brothers, James William, was so impatient with his country's idleness that he disenrolled from Cornell University and crossed the border in March 1917 – a month before America declared war on Germany and its allies – to enlist in Company C of the 14th Canadian Battalion. Young Private Tisdale shipped overseas in late 1917 and immediately was thrown into action during the Somme campaign. At the battle of Amiens on August 18, 1918, the same shell that killed the soldier next to him "blew off the flesh from Tisdale's left leg below the knee, leaving nothing but the bone, which was sawn off in the hospital." Evacuated back to Canada, he underwent seven operations before being fit with an artificial leg and sent home to Annapolis to convalesce. He eventually took up a career selling insurance, married and had four sons (18).

Another former football star demonstrated striking determination to serve his country. A. Z. Holley, who had starred as the quarterback for Annapolis High from 1907 to 1910 and then volunteered to help Morton coach at the school, was a first lieutenant with the 115th when he was temporarily disabled during a training exercise and discharged. He reluctantly returned to Annapolis, rehabilitated his injury and then re-enlisted in time to ship to France with the 115th. In the process he lost his lieutenant's bars. Considering this a great injustice, the commanding officer of the 115th managed to get Holley promoted to the rank of second lieutenant at the war's conclusion. While in Paris awaiting orders home, Holley joined 51 others as a founding member of the American Legion (19).

Following the Armistice in mid-November 1918, the city of Annapolis turned its attention to planning a suitable welcome home for their boys who had fought overseas. Although the February 3, 1919, *Evening Capital*'s headline blared "Annapolis Soldiers To Come Home Soon," the 29th Division remained in France until mid-May. Their troop transport arrived in Newport News, Virginia, on May 24, 1919, and three days later they entrained for Camp Meade. Annapolis officials were frantic that they would not be able to squeeze in a suitable celebration for their war heroes before the start of the Naval Academy's commissioning week on the first of June. Fortunately a meeting between Camp Meade's commanding officer and a delegation from the city resulted in an agreement that granted a day's leave for the Annapolis soldiers (20).

The Red Cross, Salvation Army, Marine Corps, Odd Fellows, Order of Mechanics and the Knights of Columbus prepared floats for a grand parade. Bands from the fire department, the Naval Academy and the USS *Alabama* agreed to march. So did the local ukulele ensemble. The entire front page of the May 31, 1919, *Evening Capital* was devoted to the festive day, including the following lead story: *"On all sides this morning, satisfaction is expressed over the complete success of the parade which was held yesterday in honor of the youths of this community who fought the battles of America and humanity across the seas. . . . Led by the boys of the 115th, the Machine Gun Company, . . .a parade which is universally declared to be the finest which Annapolis has ever had, marched through the streets of*

Annapolis, causing the heart of everyone here to swell with emotion and to recall the day nearly two years ago when these boys marched through the streets preparatory to leaving for training camp. The community will never forget the sight of these noble young men who have done their trying work so well and have upheld the traditions of state and city so nobly. It was one of the big days in the history of Annapolis."

One float in the parade struck a more somber note. Decorated in green, it featured a large gravestone upon which were etched the names of those who were not returning home. Three former Annapolis High football players were on the list. Lt. Guy Parlett became the first from the city of Annapolis to die in service after war was declared, succumbing to pneumonia in late April 1918 at Fort McClellan (21). Cpl. John Frazier ('14) enlisted in the Army in August 1918, shortly after completing his education at St. John's. Six weeks later he died from influenza while undergoing training at Camp Meade. The third Annapolis High graduate to die was 20-year-old Corporal Benjamin Skinner Carr. "Skinner" had enlisted shortly after the outbreak of the war. His promotion to corporal earned him the distinction of being the youngest non-commissioned officer in the unit. Carr's father Maynard was the Chief Judge of the Orphans Court, and through his mother he was descended from such "fighting men" as Lafayette and D'Arcy de Rochambeau. His brothers James and Revell also served overseas; the latter was wounded and gassed at Chateau-Thierry in June 1918 (22). Although Skinner died on October 23, 1918, more than a month would pass before his family was notified. The November 26, 1918, *Evening Capital* headlined the sad news: "Skinner Carr is First Local Boy to Die in Action." All of Annapolis was said to mourn the loss of this "patriotic, clean, and high-principled boy" who died valiantly less than three weeks before the Armistice brought an end to the slaughter.

Why So Many Fought

Annapolis was justifiably proud of its sons who served the nation during the war. Anne Arundel boasted that it was the only county in the state to exceed its quota of men registering for the draft. More than 2,100 county residents joined the Army and Navy, including 700 African-Americans who served in segregated units. In fact, a higher percentage of eligible blacks than whites from the county served in the nation's armed forces. The *Evening Capital* gave scant coverage to these troops, but a front-page story on March 18, 1919, announced "Annapolis Colored Soldiers Back Home." In laudatory terms the service of 35 Annapolitans in Battery E, 351st Field Artillery is detailed, including a stretch of front-line combat during early November 1918. The unit was fortunate to have "lost no men in action" while "under the fire of the enemy's long range artillery and of aeroplanes continually." The paper concludes, "Not one of the Annapolis men failed to do his full duty or did anything to discredit himself as a soldier or man." On March 25, 1919, the black troops of Maryland were honored in a Baltimore parade and reception. Annapolis commemorated the "return of colored service men" in a parade in the city's Fourth Ward and an evening ceremony at Adam's Electrical Park (23).

Another identifiable group that stood out for its extraordinary rate of participation in the wartime military was former Annapolis High football players. A stunning 80 percent of these young men joined the Army or the Navy, while less than 20 percent of draft age males nationwide served in the armed forces (24). Why did such a high percentage of these football players seek wartime service? Perhaps they had heard of the Duke of Wellington's remark that the British victory over Napoleon at the 1815 Battle of Waterloo was "won on the playing fields of Eton." Or maybe they had heard the comments of America's own former president, Teddy Roosevelt, who claimed that participation in athletics – especially football – could transform an ordinary boy into a courageous soldier. Back in 1893 Roosevelt had praised the game for providing an arena in which schoolboy athletes could test their courage and physical toughness while forging a sense of loyalty to their teammates. As already discussed in this chapter, Roosevelt intervened while in the oval office to save the game from its harshest critics.

This idea that athletic competition hones warriors has persisted to the present at America's service academies, where midshipmen and cadets are required to play sports – intercollegiate or intramural – as an integral part of their officer training. While the athlete/warrior correlation is more theory than fact, the boys who played football at Annapolis High in the years leading up to American entry into the war certainly proved to be more than satisfactory soldiers when duty called. Indeed, football memories may have spurred their decision to enter the military. After leaving high school, many of these young men may have missed the camaraderie and glory of their gridiron days. One way to replicate such aspects of their adolescent experience was to join an organization that rewarded the same traits and fostered the same allegiance – the military.

That the Annapolis High athletes were drawn to the armed forces after their playing days were over was evident even before America's 1917 entry into the world war. By 1916, a dozen of the boys who played football between 1907 and 1915 had joined the Maryland National Guard's Company M – a machine gun unit – headquartered in Annapolis. Any notion that they were just playing soldier was dispelled in June 1916 when Company M was mustered into federal service and ordered to Columbus, New Mexico, to guard the border while General "Black Jack" Pershing and the Regular Army chased Pancho Villa across Mexico. Company M returned to Annapolis in January 1917, but only four months later was again mustered into federal service as the 115th regiment after the American declaration of war on Germany.

At least eight other teammates from the prewar Annapolis High gridiron squads volunteered to serve in the 115th while the unit was undergoing training at Fort McClellan in Alabama. Before being inducted, they had to pass a required physical exam. During the course of the war, slightly more than 30 percent of draftees flunked pre-induction physicals. Indeed in the first two months after America declared war, almost half of the 366,143 men who tried to enlist were found to be physically unfit for service. The American general staff even worried about the poor health of many recruits who passed medical examinations. According to the Army's Chief of Staff, General James G. Harbord, "The majority of our World War recruits were narrow chested, awkward and under weight in proportion to height." (25) Former football players like those from Annapolis were likely to be more robust than others presenting themselves for military service and therefore less likely to be rejected on medical grounds, thus contributing to their high rate of induction.

Another cause for a young man to be rejected for service was illiteracy. Nationwide roughly two percent of volunteers and recruits were unable to read. Again this difficulty did not apply to the Annapolis High lads. Their educational experience may have contributed in another way to spur their participation in the war. Principal Louise Linthicum consciously imbued the curriculum with a hefty dose of patriotism, driving home to the high school students that their free public education incurred the ethical obligation to serve their city, state and nation. She introduced the daily salute to the flag that included a promise by each student to " . . . give my head, my hands, my heart to my country: one country, one language, one flag." The pledge continued, *"Flag of our great Republic, inspirer in battle, guardian of our homes whose stars and stripes stand for bravery, purity, union, and truth – we salute thee. We, the children of many lands . . . do pledge our lives, our hearts, and our sacred honor to love and protect thee, our country, and the liberty of the American people forever."*(26) Can there by any doubt that young men from Annapolis High School had these words in mind when they lined up for military duty after their nation's call to arms?

* * * * * * * * * * *

Louise Linthicum and the faculty of Annapolis High must have been proud that the school had prepared its boys so well for their future military service – physically through its athletic program, mentally through its curriculum and morally by inculcating in them a sense of obligation to demonstrate their love of country.

CHAPTER 4:
RED JACKETS IN THE ROARING TWENTIES, 1919-1929

1926 Public School Champions and the first Annapolis High team to defeat Severn
J. Bernstein, J. Legum, C. Jones, B. Turner, C. Hoban, M. Wilson, G. Noble, J. Bossert; (back) unknown, E. Tomanio, G. Stevens, W. Dulin, W. Kimball, N. Boettcher, Coach White

The Old Team

Some time when the years seem weary and long
And life is old and our time is by,
Dim ghosts from the days when life was strong
Will come from the dreams that would not die.
We'll see again a trampled field
And a cheering grandstand that rocked and roared
And muddy men who would not yield
Fight on and on 'til the goal was scored.
Or maybe we'll vision a windswept field,
When the hearts and lungs and limbs were dead,
'Til forth the voice of a captain pealed
And men strove on 'til their own team led.
The games we played when our lives were new
Will bring forgotten triumphs back,
And crown the end of the things now through
With the youth that our burnt-out beings lack.

Maurice Wilson, 1927 *Crablines*

Secondary Education in Anne Arundel County in the 1920's

Annapolis High's Class of 1922 was the first to publish a yearbook. Its name, *Crablines,* honored the students' ties to "Crabtown – our quaint little town by the Bay." The editors hoped *Crablines* would be "a benefit and joy to all who read its pages: students who will find a record of their past history, alumni who will renew old and pleasant memories, and friends who will gain a little insight into school life and its activities."(1) *Crablines* was intended to show that Annapolis was, in their words, a "real high school." Their success is still evident eight decades later. Preserved in its pages is an Annapolis High that is surprisingly familiar today: faces of stern teachers and smiling students; clubs and athletic teams posed in the auditorium at the front entrance or on the lot behind the school; class wills and prophecies written with a glib humor perhaps only the authors themselves could appreciate and advertisements for local shops and companies, some remain in business today (2).

The student editors of the 1922 *Crablines* believed Annapolis High was as fine as any secondary school – public or private – in Maryland. Their parochialism can be forgiven; after all, their acquaintance with other high schools was limited. The only other public secondary education offered in Anne Arundel County was the high school department at Stanton School that had been added in 1917 to the original 1899 grammar school. The basic curriculum at both high schools was state mandated: mathematics, science, history, Latin, English, and domestic science for girls or manual training for boys. In 1920 two young women were awarded diplomas during Stanton High School's first commencement; by 1928 the number of graduates had risen to a dozen. Most Stanton High students lived in the Annapolis and Parole area, although some county residents with access to rail lines could commute to school. Stanton continued to house the high school division until 1933 when Wiley H. Bates High School opened its doors to black secondary students throughout Anne Arundel County (3). That Annapolis and Stanton High students had scant knowledge of each other is a safe bet.

By the early 1920's the options for private education in the Annapolis area had changed significantly. Annapolis High's archrival had been the St. John's Preparatory School located on the college's campus. The Prep School was disbanded in 1914 when the college began granting provisional admission to academically deficient applicants. Such students were classified "sub-freshman" until remedial work had corrected their scholastic weaknesses. While this arrangement may have worked well for those needing only modest tutoring before beginning classes for full college credit, the St. John's coaches stretched the rules to stock their athletic teams – especially football – with local boys who had little or no interest in becoming fully matriculated students. In 1922 the state board of education, which still provided an annual appropriation to the college, criticized St. John's practice of admitting inadequately prepared students. Given the choice of continuing state funding or changing its admissions policy, the college ended the "sub-freshman" program in 1923. From this date onwards, every St. John's applicant had to pass the entrance exams to be granted admission (4).

Also largely gone by 1920 was the network of small preparatory programs for the Naval Academy that professors had operated from their homes. Only Werntz Naval Prep limped along past 1920 by utilizing housing facilities in a local hotel. Army-Navy Prep in Baltimore attracted that city's candidates for service academy appointments. Anne Arundel county boys in search of a Naval Academy appointment increasingly turned to the new Severn School in Boone, just north of Annapolis. Founded several months after the start of World War One, Severn's mission was to "prepare young men to pass the entrance examination at the United States Naval Academy." Initially a one-year program, by 1921 Severn had grown to a boarding school with a three-year secondary curriculum that supported its post-graduate naval prep year (5). Severn's success probably drove many of the smaller preparatory programs out of business and certainly caused Werntz Naval Prep to shrink in size. By the mid-1920's Severn had taken the place of the defunct St. John's Prep as Annapolis High's archrival.

In the fall of 1922 two new Anne Arundel County public high schools – Glen Burnie and Tracy's Landing (re-christened Southern in 1933 when its new building opened in Lothian) – began holding classes. George Fox, the county superintendent of schools for a 30-year period (1916-1946), had backed the opening of the new high schools to quiet demands from north and south county citizens for secondary schools closer to home. Glen Burnie rivaled Maryland's capital city in size, yet its students seeking secondary education had to travel by train either north to Baltimore or south to Annapolis. Students from the southern part of the county had to choose between a long trip north to Annapolis and one west to Washington, D.C. Local residents in the north and south were equally pleased to have their own high schools, each of which would eventually become fierce competitors to Annapolis High (6).

Fox also pushed for the new secondary schools to help alleviate the crowded conditions at Annapolis High. Originally designed in 1907 to house a maximum of 270 students in its nine classrooms, the school was near capacity before the state passed a 1916 law making attendance compulsory for students through age 16. By 1922 when some 360 students were crammed in the school, learning and discipline declined as teachers coped with classes of 40 students. While Glen Burnie and Tracy's Landing siphoned some students from the Annapolis pipeline, the board recognized additional classroom space was needed for the high school. Although a few voices calling for a completely new building were heard, the board instead opted to construct a two-story wing off the back of the existing Green Street school (7).

The history of the county's fourth public high school is more complex. As early as 1908 professors at Maryland Agricultural College (now the University of Maryland) petitioned the state board of education to introduce agricultural courses in county high schools. The Anne Arundel Academy, a private school in Millersville founded in 1854, met this request by adding a series of agricultural courses to its curriculum. The academy's operational funds came from an annual state stipend of $4,000 supplemented by tuition of $10 a year from each of its 50 students. Facing bankruptcy after the state unexpectedly withheld its 1916 contribution, the academy's trustees voted in early 1917 to donate its buildings, ten acres of surrounding land and the $10,000 in its treasury to Anne Arundel County if the board of education would promise to operate a public agricultural high school at the site. Action on the offer was tabled, perhaps due to American entry into the First World War. Then a fire at the academy destroyed the classrooms; rebuilding meant tuition had to be raised beyond what area students could afford. In 1923 the Anne Arundel County's board of education agreed to take responsibility for tuition costs of students taking the academy's standard high school curriculum. Meanwhile the federal government passed the Smith-Hughes law to provide subsidies to public schools teaching an agricultural curriculum. The prospect of a significant federal allocation to help pay costs of running the academy as a public high school led to an agreement in 1924 for the buildings, adjacent land and the remaining $6,000 in the academy's coffers to be transferred to the Anne Arundel County board of education. That fall Arundel High School officially opened, offering students a choice of academic or agricultural curriculums (8).

Back at Annapolis High, enrollment continued to grow beyond the school's capacity. In September 1926 over 600 students crowded its classrooms, while the other four county high schools – Glen Burnie (110), Tracy's Landing (103), Stanton (93) and Arundel (63) – enrolled a combined 369 students. To gain an additional classroom in the Annapolis High building, the domestic science sewing classes were moved next door to a refurbished basement room in the Grammar School. A complicated, and controversial, block scheduling system was implemented with staggered opening, lunch and closing times. Every four weeks the schedule was rotated so students and teachers would have "a fair distribution of morning and afternoon work." Although the block scheduling system did allow all students to be accommodated in the building, it also forced unsupervised groups of students to hang around on the city streets during times they were prohibited from being in classrooms. Those living close by could go home, but most loitered downtown or congregated in shops catering to them (9).

According to James "Banny" Eppes ('30), a particularly popular spot for the boys was Joe Droll's store at the bottom of Green Street, where they could purchase candy, soft drinks, cigarettes, home made hot lunches, ice cream, school supplies and gadgets. An indication of Droll's importance in the life of the school is found in the 1927 *Crablines,* which lists under "Problems of the Seniors" the question, "What would boys do without Joe Droll's?" The schedule implemented to deal with the cramped conditions naturally led many in the community to demand a larger school. During an entire week in February 1927 teachers devoted homeroom period each day to discussion about the need for a new school, but Fox and the school board resisted replacing a building that was only 20 years old and had just added a new wing.

Controlling the Crowded Classrooms

The congestion in Annapolis High's hallways and classrooms posed challenges to principal Louise Linthicum, her faculty and the students. The 1927 *Crablines* notes the student council led a campaign to keep "the building neat and tidy so that the crowded conditions will be bearable." The safety of the students in case of fire was also a concern. The original builders had declared the school "fireproof" in 1907 based on its wide stairways and superior construction (10). They failed to envision the necessity of getting over 600 students safely down the stairs and outside, so no external fire escapes were attached. Required fire drills in the fall and spring had been held for years, but the congested exit paths prompted the student council to turn the drills into a contest aimed at decreasing the time necessary to empty the building. During September 1926 the fire bell rang daily for three weeks, with a record of 1 minute 40 seconds set. By 1928 the record had been lowered to 1 minute 15 seconds (11).

Large classes inevitably led to an increased number of disciplinary problems. Having heard rumors that the principal and teachers had no control over the students caused Anita Allio McIntire ('32) to fear starting high school in the fall of 1928. From her seat in the grammar school next door she had seen high school students hanging out the windows, calling to friends and throwing marbles, hard candies or other tiny projectiles at passers-by below. "Banny" Eppes recalls boys hiding peashooters in their pockets to use against unsuspecting targets when the teacher's back was turned. Once during an assembly he "got pinged" on his neck, but did nothing about it because he didn't want to stir up trouble.

Contributing to the perceived rowdiness in the school was a hazing system directed at the freshman "rats" who stood out wearing special beanies. Sue Gee Smith, author of the 1922 class history in *Crablines*, notes that as sophomores *"we had felt the responsibility of inducting [the freshmen] into the right paths and gently but firmly taught them a few things [like] sharing their pencils, tablets, and Droll's drollest confections with a truly generous spirit."* Lee Offut and Samuel Bloom recall that during freshman year the Class of 1925 was "the subject of many pranks of the upper classmen." Frances Owings notes that she and her 1926 classmates were "forever doing something wrong [as freshmen] to invoke the wrath of the higher powers, [but we] bore the hardships with dignity." At the 60th Class of 1932 reunion, Bernard Gessner described the "paddling ritual" in which freshmen boys were required to "walk through the older boys as they hit them with wooden paddles." (12)

Certainly the principal and faculty were aware of the hazing; in all likelihood they tried to keep it within acceptable limits. But students, being students, just as likely had devious ways to keep their elders in the dark. They clearly liked many of the teachers, and most were given nicknames. Banny Eppes chuckles when he remembers students calling principal Louise Linthicum "Baby Lou" (of course, never to her face). Like students today, Eppes and his friends just "tried to stay out of the principal's way." He still feels fortunate to have never been sent to her office. His wife, Elizabeth Fuller Eppes (Class of 1936) had an older brother who was not so lucky. Towards the end of his senior year a teacher accused John Fuller of cheating on an examination. Although John denied the charges, demonstrating that he could not have copied from another student's paper because he sat right in front of the teacher's desk, Linthicum expelled him. Mrs. Fuller sought the help of school board president Frank Munroe, but he advised her to "forget about it" because Linthicum "would always side with a teacher in a dispute with a student." So instead of graduating from Annapolis High, John eventually enlisted in the Marine Corps and shipped out to Central America during the Nicaraguan civil war in the late 1920's.

An episode in 1922 suggests Linthicum did, on occasion, side with students. Shortly before graduation a particularly egregious hazing incident involving all 18 senior boys was uncovered. Superintendent Fox decreed the culprits would not receive their diplomas. The boys were embarrassed and their parents were understandably angry – at their sons and at Fox. To show solidarity with their brethren the 40 girls in the class demanded the ceremony be cancelled and diplomas distributed to everyone – male and female – on the last day of school. Linthicum worked out a compromise - the boys were allowed to pick up their diplomas 10 days after commencement exercises and the girls would attend the ceremony to represent the entire class. The *Evening Capital* of June 15, 1922, reports, "*The principal, Miss Louise Linthicum, drew a round of applause from the audience by starting her brief address with the announcement [in reference to the missing boys] that all the members of the graduating class were good sports.*"

Fox, who shared the commencement platform with Linthicum that night, may have interpreted her remarks as a challenge to his authority and grounds for dismissal. Five years would pass, however, before opportunity presented itself. On September 23, 1927, an apparent heart attack forced Linthicum to take a medical leave of absence. Fox appointed Evelyn C. Wingate to serve as acting principal. Wingate had joined the faculty as an English teacher in 1923 after graduating from Blue Ridge College in West Virginia. Wingate's nickname "The Good Samaritan" reveals her popularity with students, but as principal she apparently had little control over their increasingly raucous pranks. The call for a "stern disciplinarian" better able to manage the boisterous boys grew from a whisper to a shout. Fox started to search for a permanent replacement for the ailing principal. He thought he had found his man in Howard A. Kinhart, principal of Pocomoke High School, considered "one of the best male principals in Maryland." Linthicum, however, threw a monkey wrench into Fox's plans when she returned fulltime to her duties on February 1, 1928. Fox continued to woo Kinhart, who had an offer to become principal at Towson High in his pocket, while negotiating retirement terms with Linthicum. Unwilling to step down completely, the two protagonists reached a compromise that allowed Linthicum to be appointed principal at the much smaller Arundel High School. Kinhart promptly tore up the Towson offer and accepted appointment as Annapolis High's ninth principal.

Fox's public announcement of the changes just prior to the commencement ceremony for the Class of 1928 put a decidedly positive, and exceedingly verbose, spin on Linthicum's reassignment. In the *Evening Capital* of June 14, 1928, the superintendent explained, "*Miss Linthicum's health has not been of the best during the last year due in large measure to the multifarious duties devolving upon her with the steady increase in numbers of students at Annapolis High.*" He explained that her transfer to Arundel was "in recognition of the long and faithful service she has given the county." He said he was pleased that Linthicum would "continue her splendid work with the children of Anne Arundel County" without having to endure the "heavy responsibilities the Annapolis High School principal must, owing to its congested condition, face for the next year or two."

Linthicum's reaction to her transfer is not recorded. Perhaps she left willingly, but more likely she was unhappy that after 34 years as a teacher and administrator in the Green Street schools she was sent packing to finish her career in Millersville. She could not have helped but notice the argument that was advanced in 1928 to oust her was the same her opponents had used 18 years earlier to keep her out of the principal's office – that a man is necessary to control boys, but

"Baby Lou" in 1928
before transfer to
Arundel High School

George Fox
Superintendent of Schools
1916-1946

Evelyn C. Wingate
Acting AHS Principal,
Sept. 1927- Feb. 1928

Elizabeth. Davis
English teacher

Lorene Marking
Foreign language teacher

Mary Louise Hicks
Social Studies teacher

like the good trooper she had been her entire career, she moved from her Spa Road home in Annapolis to a Millersville boarding house close to her new school. In the summer of 1929 she and Josephine Riordan, the longtime principal of Annapolis Grammar School, motored west with three other maiden teachers on a well-publicized eight-week tour of the national parks that included attending some courses in the University of California at Berkeley's summer school – an indication that Linthicum was not planning an imminent retirement. Arundel High's smaller size didn't result in the hoped for lessening of the stresses on its principal. On 28 May 1931, less than three years after her transfer, the *Evening Capital* reported the "terrible shock felt by Louise Linthicum's family and numerous friends" when they learned she had been found "dead in bed this morning of an apparent heart attack." She was only 53 years old.

The Quality of an Annapolis High Education

Louise Linthicum deserved to be proud of her many contributions to the high school she, quite literally, helped found. Her fingerprints are particularly evident on the curriculum. Immediately after assuming the school's helm in 1910, she began tinkering with the academic program. Her philosophy of education stemmed from direct classroom experience; as a 17-year-old with a diploma from the state normal school she was hired to teach at Annapolis Grammar School; four years later she was promoted to the faculty of the school's new high school department. Linthicum acquired additional theoretical foundation to support her classroom experience in her studies for the Bachelor of Science degree and Master of Arts degree she earned respectively from Johns Hopkins and Columbia Teacher's College in New York City (13).

Linthicum's policies suggest she shared the belief common among administrators that a public secondary school was obliged to provide an education tailored to the specific needs of its students and the community it served. The bedrock of her philosophy was an insistence that a high school should offer strong academic preparation for students with college aspirations. Yet at the same time Linthicum believed high school graduates should be prepared to assume adult responsibilities in the home and, for those not going to college, to find employment in the many shops and offices around Annapolis. The state mandated a core curriculum of English, history, science and mathematics courses for all students. Prior to becoming principal, Linthicum had played a role in introducing required manual training courses for future husbands and fathers and domestic science classes in cooking and sewing to prepare girls for their fated roles as homemaker. The remaining courses were selected from one of two tracks. The academic curriculum added requirements in Latin, French, upper-level math and science, while to earn a commercial diploma a student studied typing, shorthand and bookkeeping. About the time St. John's ended its pre-freshman program in 1923 Linthicum created a rigorous college preparatory diploma for those wanting to improve their chances of gaining acceptance to four-year colleges. Some students who already had earned a regular academic or commercial diploma could stay on to take a postgraduate year at Annapolis (14).

Several measures can be used to judge the quality of an Annapolis High education in the 1920's. One is to look at the qualifications of its faculty. During its first two decades, most Annapolis High teachers were young women with two-year diplomas from the State Normal School. Often they stayed only a couple of years until marriage forced them to resign (not until the late 1920's were married women permitted to teach). By 1928, all 28 teachers had four-year Bachelor of Arts or Science degrees. Thirteen had earned diplomas at in-state colleges: Western Maryland (eight), Goucher (two) and one each from St. John's, Hood and Johns Hopkins. Others were educated in the neighboring Pennsylvania (Lebanon Valley), West Virginia (Fairfield), Virginia (Shenandoah) and the District of Columbia (American University). The remainder came from across America, including three graduates of the University of Kentucky, and one each from Columbia Teacher's College, Muskingum (Ohio) and state universities of Minnesota and Colorado.

Although Marylanders represented the majority of the faculty, the presence of teachers from nine other states must have helped to broaden their students' outlook. That all had four-year college degrees at a time when a two-year normal school diploma was the only requirement to be hired suggests the Annapolis High faculty was hardly typical for the times. When asked about "the best teachers" she'd had, Anita Allio McIntire, who had a love of French acquired as a young girl while living in Europe with relatives, immediately mentioned foreign language teachers Mary Louise Hicks and Lorene Marking, along with drama club advisor Elizabeth Davis and history teacher Mary Frances Neighbors. She also had no trouble recalling her "least favorite" teacher, Helen Mary Sheller, the head of the Domestic Science Department. Apparently McIntire's aptitude for sewing didn't match her flair for languages. Miss Sheller told her that she was fortunate to be a "tomboy" because she would never be able to "properly stitch a dress."

Banny Eppes also praised Miss Hicks, but called math teacher B. Bryan Leitch "incompetent." Eppes had an older sister, Carolin, in the Class of 1928. Their father, a Naval Academy professor of mathematics, tangled with Leitch on several occasions over the grading of Carolin's tests. Several "discussions" convinced the professor that "Leitch understood only enough math to copy answers from the teacher's manual." Leitch was not the first, and certainly would not be the last, Annapolis High teacher to endure criticism from a Naval Academy or St. John's professor/parent.

Another way to measure the school's educational quality is to assess how prepared its graduates were for college or employment. Throughout the 1920's Annapolis High served as a steady feeder of students to Maryland's many institutions of higher education. Graduates in the five classes from 1922 to 1927 sent at least 15 boys to the Naval Academy, 33 boys to St. John's College, and 10 more to the University of Maryland. Several other young men gained admission to Loyola and Johns Hopkins. Very few, however, matriculated out of state. Two boys went off to Western Pennsylvania College, while one ventured all the way to the University of Cincinnati.

Girls continuing to post-secondary schools generally had ambitions to be teachers, nurses or secretaries. Some wanting to hone their secretarial skills returned for a post-graduate year at Annapolis High to take advanced shorthand and typing. Marjorie Evans Smith ('22) did just this; after earning an academic diploma, was looking for a job after taking the postgraduate commercial course. She happened to be seated next to principal Louise Linthicum on a train one day. According to Smith's daughter, Marjorie Layng Roxburgh ('55), when Linthicum learned Smith had secured an interview with the president of St. John's College, the principal said she would speak to her friend, the president; within days Smith was offered the job.

Twelve girls from these classes went to the State Normal School in Towson, while another 13 were in Nursing School (about equally split between Baltimore's Union Memorial Hospital and the Annapolis Emergency Hospital). Young women from Annapolis High also flocked to Western Maryland College (six), Goucher College (five), Strayer Business College (four), the Maryland Institute of Art (six) and Notre Dame of Maryland (three).

The 51 graduates in the Class of 1926 provide a more in-depth look at the postgraduate aspirations of Annapolis High students. Of the 18 (equally divided by sex) who earned the most prestigious college preparatory diploma, only one – a young woman who accompanied her family to the Philippines – failed to matriculate in college. Three boys gained appointments to the Naval Academy; three each also went to the University of Maryland and St. John's. Western Maryland College enrolled two female graduates, while three others entered the rigorous Union Memorial Hospital Nursing School. The remaining three who earned college preparatory diplomas went to the

State Normal College, Peabody Music Conservatory and Eaton & Burnett College.

The seven girls and four boys awarded academic diplomas also had college aspirations. Seven went directly to higher educational institutions (one each to Loyola College, University of Maryland, Notre Dame College of Maryland and Strayer Business College; two enrolled in the Annapolis Emergency Hospital Nursing School). Two young men returned for a postgraduate year at Annapolis High; one who spent two additional years eventually was appointed to the Naval Academy's Class of 1932.

Forty percent of the class (21 students) earned commercial diplomas, including 15 girls; four were married within a year after graduation and one entered nurse's training. The other young ladies found employment as stenographers for Montgomery Wards, as typists for Western Union, the Naval Experimental Station or local law firms and as clerks at local shops. The six young men with commercial diplomas were employed in sales and management positions with an insurance agency, a boat parts supplier, a dry goods store, a recreational club and two local repair shops (15).

Explosion of Extracurricular Activities

That Annapolis High graduates from the 1920's were successfully employed or enrolled in college suggests the school's teachers led by its principal had created a curriculum that met the community's educational needs. Many of the extracurricular activities contributed to the school's academic mission. Miss Wingate helped a group of students establish a school library in 1922. They solicited book donations from townspeople and teachers, constructed shelves, organized a card catalog and monitored circulation. They regularly supplied book reviews for publication in the *Evening Capital* (16). Other students improved their writing and editing skills while working on the yearbook *Crablines* and the newspaper, variously called *High School News* and *Hi-Signs,* was published bi-weekly in the *Evening Capital.* Latin and French clubs also were formed. Besides the clean-up and fire drill activities already mentioned, student council members gained experience raising money for school improvement projects, patrolling traffic in the school corridors and devising a policy for tardiness that required late students to stay for an hour after school in "detention hall." In 1922 English teacher Emily

The Annapolis High Jazz Band set the Roaring 20's tone at the school, while the "Crablines" staff (below) recorded the good times.

The guys liked to hang out at Joe Droll's shop located adjacent to the wall at the base of Green Street. Albert Droll (2nd from left) was class of 1926 president. Cy Kimball (right) was a three-sport star. His younger brother James ('28) signed AHSAA membership cards as president. The organization sponsored basketball games at the Armory and held Tag Days to raise funds. The school's version of flappers appearing in the 1928 Crablines were Lillian Talley, Lillian Noble and Helen Thomas.

Dryden suggested the student body be divided into two literary societies, the Philologians and the Euepians. Annually the societies sponsored a wide variety of intellectual and cultural events. In 1926, for instance, they booked the Circle Theater for a formal debate on "States Rights as an American Theory." The yearly talent show pitted Philologians and Euepians against each other in categories that included poetry recitation, dramatic reading, instrumental solos and persuasive argument. Originally each society put on an annual play, but eventually they joined forces to produce an original drama in the fall and a musical in the spring (17).

In fact, musical activities became increasingly popular during the 1920's. Annapolis High's first orchestra was formed in 1923. Under the direction of Dr. William Reichel, a local dentist, it featured an unusual combination of instruments: drums, a piano, a saxophone, a xylophone, violins and two banjos that were crucial to the success of the popular minstrel show held to raise money for the general activity fund. By 1928 the orchestra had grown into a larger 17-member symphony with eight violinists, three saxophonists, two pianists and one musician each on the coronet, clarinet, trombone and traps. No banjos. Along with the high school's choir, the symphony performed at parties, pageants, school board functions, assemblies, graduations and the state's convention for music teachers.

Several particularly ardent student musicians pestered the principal for permission to form a jazz band. This was, after all, the Roaring 20's – the decade in which Louis Armstrong and "Duke" Ellington's bands and Al Jolsen's hit movie *The Jazz Singer* brought the distinctive style of music out of New Orleans to an American public revved up and ready to party. The 1928 *Crablines* notes, "The Jazz Band had more obstacles to overcome than any other organization, but finally the principal approved." Featuring several saxophones and violins, drums, a piano, clarinet, trumpet and – yes – two banjos, the Jazz Band quickly gained a local following. Bandleader Arthur Krapf was lauded for "his interpretation of jazz melodies" as well as for his "snappy drumming." Pianist Lillian Noble and Saxophonists Basil Johnson and Charles Garner were reportedly "a trio that would do justice to any orchestra." *Crablines* gushes, "When the trumpet and trombone come in with their wailing and moaning, there are not enough words to describe the results." Everyone liked to dance to this band's music that was "different from any ever heard."(18) Their enthusiasm for jazz shows that although ignorant about their contemporaries at Stanton "Colored" High School, Annapolis High students wanted to be considered thoroughly modern and cosmopolitan kids *au courant* with the nation's latest fads. The photographs and essays in *Crablines* reveal how deeply Jazz Age styles and *mores* affected Annapolis High students. The media (radio, movies, magazines, newspapers) portrayed a wealthy nation enjoying itself. Of course the materialism of the times didn't extend to everyone, and the more traditional elements in society turned their backs on the easy pleasures that were daily on public display.

Annapolis High students appear to have embraced the frivolous behaviors popularly associated with the Roaring 20's. The girls strove to achieve a "flapper image" – bobbed hair, short skirts, boyish figures and seductive behavior that included a decidedly casual attitude towards sex. Every one of the 46 senior girls pictured in the 1928 *Crablines* looks like a Zelda Fitzgerald imitation with short hair and a "come-hither" expression. Lillian Talley, nicknamed "Giggles," is described as "gay and talkative," while Lillian Noble (mentioned earlier in connection with the jazz band) could be found "tripping the light fantastic" in the school's main hall or "tickling somebody's ivories," qualities said to make her the "foremost representative of the type gentlemen prefer." And then there was "tall, slim, dark-haired" Helen Thomas; under her yearbook photo is a quotation from poet Byron, "She walks in beauty, like the night." Can there be any doubt that these three made many a boy swoon?

Certainly the good times were flowing for these lucky students in 1920's crabtown. Dances, parties and picnics litter class histories and society notes in every edition of *Crablines*. Generally each class sponsored a picnic in the fall and two dances during the year. Parties were held to celebrate Halloween, Christmas and Valentine's Day. Banny Eppes remembers enjoying the dances held Friday nights after basketball doubleheaders at the Bladen Street Armory. The social news in the 1927 *Crablines* lists 12 parties and dances during January and February – a very full social calendar for these kids!

Many boys still had enough time on their hands to join the Blue Finkle, a fraternity whose future names included Centaurs and Hippogriffs. Membership criteria and meetings were carefully guarded secrets. Perhaps all they did was hang outside Joe Droll's at lunchtime. The most popular boys combined good looks (hair combed back or parted in the middle) with the right clothes (a loud tie or better yet a bow tie, worn with a vest or sweater under a tweed jacket). Having a "flivver" to drive was a definite plus. Being quick-witted was an asset, but the strong, silent type was also admired. Jamey Kimball was a three-sport star athlete, president of the Athletic Association, and a member of the Philologians and Hippogriffs. Under his 1928 *Crablines* photo is the quotation from Alexander Pope: "Men of few words are the best men."

In 1923 senior girls decided they wanted a secret sorority. Originally called Super-Sex, its name changes included Phi Chi and Devilettes. The 1928 *Crablines* reports the "Devilettes" planned to call their "novel dance" at the end of the school year the "Cabaret Hades." They would create a "mysterious atmosphere" with dim red lights and "the keenest Negro orchestra imaginable." Boys were lured with promises of an "intriguing" experience in the "underworld," especially at the intermissions. Such brazen language coming from the mouths of their daughters suggests why many parents may have backed Fox's efforts to replace Linthicum with a principal who would cleanse the school of the unsavory atmosphere that by 1928 seemed to be taking over the school.

Red Jackets at Play

Yearbooks, newspapers, orchestras, plays, debates and secret societies kept Annapolis High students busy, but many still found time after school for athletic practices and games. In the decade after World War I, the school fielded teams in nine sports, five for boys (baseball, basketball, soccer, football and swimming), two for girls (basketball and fieldball) and two co-ed (tennis and track). Uniforms continued to be a deep red color offset with blue trim; nicknames included Red Jackets, Red and Blue and the Red Cyclone.

State and county education funds had never been used to support high school sports. Even physical education was largely a voluntary after-school activity. Beginning with Annapolis High's first teams at the turn of the 20th century, the students who wanted to play had to raise enough money to cover all expenses. High school sports enthusiasts turned to the Naval Academy Athletic Association (NAAA) as its model for organizing and funding sports. This private organization made all decisions regarding Navy athletics and raised funds to cover team expenses and coaches' salaries. The athletic director headed an elected NAAA board of control; the superintendent's approval was necessary for any decision to be final. Similarly the Annapolis High School Athletic Association (AHSAA) had a board that was made up of officers with a teacher or coach as supervisor. The principal had the right to veto any decision. The AHSAA actively solicited donations and organized fundraisers throughout the year to generate the revenue necessary to cover all team expenses, including the cost of uniforms, gymnasium rental, athletic awards and travel to away contests.

This system served Annapolis High very well for several reasons. One was Linthicum's support. No athlete herself, she nevertheless believed sports were essential to the healthy development of children. Another was the interest the NAAA took in Annapolis High athletics. During the 1920's Navy athletic directors often spoke at AHSAA fundraisers and Navy coaches gave special clinics to the athletes. Finally, local townspeople supported the AHSAA's efforts to finance a competitive athletic program. Annapolis High was fortunate in this regard. Elsewhere in America independent booster clubs, many with ties to local gambling interests, often controlled high school teams. Football was the likely sport to have such a booster club, but basketball teams also were frequently funded in this way. The more unsavory of such booster clubs acted as owners of the team and its players. Since their main interest was betting on games, the potential for abuse was obvious. Especially objectionable were attempts to pressure players to throw games (19). Fortunately, the AHSAA kept such rackets' influence away from Annapolis High School.

Most of the AHSAA's proceeds came through its fall membership drive. Each student at the school was expected to buy a $1.00 membership that granted admission to all Annapolis High athletic contests for the coming year, and then each student was instructed to sell at least one membership to somebody else. During this two-week period in the fall, the *Evening Capital* ran daily full-page headlines urging people to "Join the High School Athletic Association." Tag days were held in conjunction with the drive. A nickel bought a special school logo tag to wear for the day. The Republic Theater and the Circle Playhouse annually donated proceeds from a day's matinee to the AHSAA. In 1921 their combined contribution came to $179.50, a handsome sum back then. Dances and card parties were other popular AHSAA fundraisers (20).

The 1927 baseball team, coached by Bill White, compiled an outstanding 14-4 record.

Three 1926 basketball stars (from left) John Bernstein, Cy Kimball and Ernie Tomanio were also standout baseball and football players.

In their modest middie blouses, culottes and kerchiefs the 1923 Annapolis girls' basketball team compiled a 2-2 record against outside teams.

The 1925 fieldball team was declared county champion after compiling a 6-0 record with two victories each over Arundel, Glen Burnie and Tracy's Landing.

The good economic times in the 1920's made soliciting donations comparatively easy, but the overall success of Annapolis High teams also helped. When the decade began, the Public Athletic League [PAL] still outlawed football. Soccer was the featured fall sport for boys; the soccer team won the County Championship with an 8-0 victory over Tracy's Landing in the fall of 1922. After Christmas, basketball took center stage. From 1922 to 1928 the boys had an overall 67-30 record, with the 1925 team gaining particular renown for its 14-2 season that included victories over all the Maryland teams they played (their losses came at the hands of Central High from Washington, D.C.). The featured boys' team in the spring, baseball, was undefeated against other high schools in 1924 (its only loss was to the St. John's College freshmen) and in 1927 had a 14-4 campaign that included two victories over Baltimore's Polytechnic Institute team, the city champions.

Not surprisingly, the Annapolis High girls clamored to get in on the action. Interclass girls' basketball games dated back to the pre-World War One era, but the lack of a gymnasium hampered efforts to put together an interscholastic schedule. The girls' efforts to find suitable practice space finally paid off in 1923 when the Bladen Street Armory became available. In their white middie blouses, blue scarves and red culottes, the AHS girls defeated Sparrows Point High and an alumnae team; they lost to Towson and Western High Schools in Baltimore. In 1928 tryouts for the team drew an astonishing 54 girls. Coach Elizabeth Carroll, a science teacher at the school, eventually cut 40 girls. The team won nine games while losing only two. Highlights included victories over St. Mary's Seminary and three public high school teams (Arundel, Ellicott City and Hyattsville).

Even more successful was the girls' fieldball team. Played in the fall on the soccer field, the game consisted of nine players passing and catching a soccer ball as they ran up and down the field trying to score by throwing the ball past the goalie into the soccer net. Coach Carroll led the undefeated 1925 team to its first county championship. The season consisted of two games each against the other county schools: Glen Burnie, Tracy's Landing and Arundel.

Annapolis High's co-ed tennis team lasted only two seasons because court space was difficult to arrange for practices and matches. Swimming fared better, lasting four years. The boys came away victorious in all four county swimming championships held at the Naval Academy pool. The meets were discontinued in the mid-1920's when a new superintendent decided to close Academy facilities to townspeople. Boys and girls continued to participate in the PAL Track Olympiads held each spring. The Annapolis High contingent won the county meet every year from 1918 to 1928, and went on to their best finish in the State Olympiad in 1927 when they finished third out of 20 teams (21).

All these sports had enthusiastic participants and fans, but the team that again became king at Annapolis High in the 1920's was football. Pressure from PAL (which in 1925 switched the first word in its name from Public to Playground) persuaded Linthicum to halt football in the years before World War One. The 1922 *Crablines* tells how Annapolis High boys, determined to revive the sport, took matters into their own hands: *"For the past few years the Public Athletic League has controlled athletics in Annapolis High School. In 1920 the boys organized a football team without PAL's consent as it thoroughly disapproves of football."*

A. Z. Holley volunteered to coach the team. Holley, the star quarterback of the 1908-1910 Annapolis High squads, had helped to coach several teams prior to being sent with Company M to New Mexico during the Pancho Villa scare and then to France during World War One. In 1920 he returned home to recuperate from war injuries and to explore career opportunities. Coaching football was a nice way to fill some spare time. Holley held practices behind the school on the hard-packed dirt playground embedded with glass and sharp rocks, certainly not ideal for tackle football! Banny Eppes, who played in the late 1920's, recalls twice being cut up so badly during football practice that the coach took him to the hospital. Fortunately, the 1920 team secured the use of St. John's field for its home games. Manager Bowie Duckett arranged four games: twice the Red Jackets crushed Werntz Naval Prep (42-0 and 36-0); they also soundly defeated Baltimore's Calvert Hall (21-0), but only managed a tie with Baltimore's Donaldson Academy (13-13).

Players from the 1920's were much smaller than is typical today. A "big man" on the high school's team stood less than six feet tall and weighed in at 150 pounds. The Annapolis players wore shoulder pads under red jerseys with some blue trim; not until 1937 would they be required to wear numbers on their backs. Most linemen wore some protection on elbows and forearms. Eppes' helmet was made of heavy flannel with leather straps. Canvas britches, high sox and heavy shoes completed the player's gear. AHSAA funds paid for all the equipment. Shoes were kept in a box for the boys to pick through before practices and games. According to Eppes, by 1929 all the equipment was "in pretty sorry condition."

In most respects the games played in 1921 would look familiar to a 21st century fan. Additional rule modifications after 1911 marked the beginning of modern football. These changes included:
- Outlawing all mass formations (prohibiting blockers from interlocking arms and from pushing or pulling the ball carrier)
- Modifying the point system to the same used today for touchdowns, field goals, etc.
- Standardizing the ball's size and shape to make passing easier (essentially the ball became less spherical, longer around its ends than at its middle)
- Making the size of the playing field uniform: 100 yards in length with 10 yard end zones at each end
- Dividing the game into four quarters (instead of two halves) with a longer break at halftime. Annapolis High played 10-minute first and third quarters, 12-minute second and fourth quarters

A major difference between the games played in the 1920's and today involved the single platoon system that was in use until 1941, which required the 11 players on the field at the beginning of the contest to be used on both offense and defense. Except to replace an injured player, substitutions could only be made at breaks between quarters. Rule and equipment changes had reduced the number of serious injuries, but football was still a brutal sport that left too many players with bumps, bruises and broken bones. Concussions were still common, and efforts to improve football helmets were high on the agenda of A.C. Spalding and Brothers, the nation's primary football equipment supply company (22).

Holley coached the first three teams of the 1920's to a combined record of eight wins, five losses and two ties, more than respectable considering no other public high schools were available to play. Instead Annapolis High lined up against teams with much older players (Company M and St. Mary's College scrubs) and preparatory schools (Mt. St. Joseph, Army-Navy Prep, Loyola, Donaldson, Leonard Hall and Rock Hall). One advantage for prep players was being able to practice on the well-tended grass fields that typically surrounded these exclusive schools, especially in the Baltimore area.

The 1921 Red Jackets team shows off their uniforms and their form.

Coach A.Z. Holley (2nd row, left) with his 1922 Annapolis High team that compiled a 3-2-1 season record.

Annapolis and Severn began their football rivalry in 1921, with Severn notching a 21-0 victory. Beating Severn soon became the team's top goal. In 1922 the Red Jackets almost pulled off a big upset. Tied with seven points each at halftime, neither team scored during the third quarter as "the ball see-sawed in midfield." With five minutes to play, the Red Jackets began a long drive to Severn's goal. An Annapolis High reporter picks up the action: "*The fans of Severn called for their team to hold as we neared the 15-yard line. . . .On [fourth] down we decided to try a pass, but instead of it bounding into one of our boy's hands, it was received by Hubbard [a Severn player] who, like a flash, was off toward our goal. Two of our men leaped for him but it was of no use, as he shook them off and then with two men as interference, he passed our quarterback, the only man in his way. He then scored – he had run eighty-five yards. The game ended with a score of 13-7. We had been outscored, but not outplayed.*" (23)

Holley took a teaching job in White Plains, New York, at the end of the 1922 season. His replacement as football coach was none other than math teacher Byron Leitch, whose one year at the helm resulted in a winless season. No doubt he was happy to turn over the coaching duties to Willis H. "Bill" White, a 1922 St. John's graduate from Easton, Maryland, with three years' playing experience on the college's football and baseball teams. Linthicum hired White to teach mechanical drawing, but soon she turned to him to coach baseball, basketball and football as well as to serve as the school's first physical education instructor. The handsome young man quickly became a favorite of principal and students alike.

Annapolis High teams prospered under White's guidance. During his five years at the school, the football team compiled a record of 14 victories, 14 losses and 5 ties. Finding public high schools to play continued to be problematic. Glen Burnie, Tracy's Landing and Arundel lacked enough boys to field football teams. Unfortunately Maryland's strict segregation laws kept Annapolis from playing an adversary less than a mile away. Stanton School formed its first football team in 1923. The players wore old blue and gold uniforms donated by the Naval Academy Athletic Association. Stanton could only schedule other Negro teams, including Cambridge High on Maryland's Eastern Shore, Douglass High in the nation's capital and Bowie Normal School (24).

White tried to restructure the Annapolis schedule by replacing squads consisting of college freshmen or soldiers with teams whose players were more similar in age and size to the Red Jackets. A group of Baltimore schools, including BCC, Poly and several preparatory academies joined together in 1919 to form the Maryland Scholastic Association (MSA). Annapolis High's basketball and baseball teams often scheduled MSA schools in the early 1920's. By 1925 White had shifted the Annapolis High schedule to include MSA schools Severn, Loyola, Mt. St. Joseph and Calvert Hall, along with Devitt Prep in Washington, D.C., and Charlotte Hall Military Academy in St. Mary's County, Maryland. He also scheduled the only public school within 50 miles of Annapolis with a football team, Alexandria in Virginia.

By 1925 White had assembled a core of solid players. Junior quarterback Norman Boettcher, a younger brother of Annapolis High's 1912 quarterback Henry, was especially impressive. Before the start of the season, White named Boettcher team captain, quite an honor for a junior. Boettcher certainly didn't disappoint his coach. Almost single-handedly he engineered what came within minutes of being the Red Jackets' first victory over Severn. On a cold, wet Saturday at the end of October 1925, Annapolis was trailing 6-0 at the end of the first half when Boettcher heaved a long pass that Cy Kimball (Jamey's older brother) caught inside Severn's 10-yard line. On his third successive line plunge, Boettcher managed to cross the goal line for a touchdown; he then drop-kicked the ball for the extra point to give Annapolis a 7-6 halftime lead. As rain turned to snow in the game's second half, neither team could advance the ball. It looked like Annapolis would hold on to its lead, but during the final minute an Annapolis player fumbled on the Red Jackets' 30-yard line. On the next play, the Severn quarterback Patten also fumbled – but the ball bounced forwards until a Severn halfback fell on it near the Annapolis goal line. On the next play Patten carried the ball into the end zone as time expired to give Severn a 12-7 victory. The *Evening Capital* concluded, "Annapolis outplayed Severn through most of the contest . . . [until] the prep school turned defeat into victory." (25)

The 1925 season ended on a high note. The two previous years the Red Jackets had met Alexandria High School on Thanksgiving; both contests had ended in ties. On Turkey Day 1925 the hometown boys carved up Alexandria, 34-0. That victory, indeed the entire 1925 season, left Coach White feeling very optimistic about the future of Annapolis High football. Although they had lost the first two games of the season badly to teams that eventually played for the MSA championship – Mt. St. Joe's (47-0) and Loyola (33-0) – Coach White saw his "scrappy warriors" improve their play on a weekly basis. He guardedly predicted that continued hard work at conditioning during the off-season would allow them to compete the next fall with the best teams in the state (26).

Indeed, his enthusiasm led White to hold several weeks of spring practice for any boy – veteran or newcomer – with a desire to play football. In these sessions Boettcher showed skills as a "triple-threat man with his running, punting and aerial tosses," and Kimball looked to be "one of the best pass receivers in the state." The team's "crack running back" Wilber Dulin and two top subs from 1925, Gerald Stevens and Eugene Tomanio, were elevated to the first team's backfield. Returning to anchor the offensive and defensive lines would be the team's best tackle, Harry Feldmeyer (first cousin of Warren, the 1911 Red Jacket quarterback and captain), and guard Clifford Jones, who scored two touchdowns after blocking punts during the 1925 season. Three players from 1925's second team were expected to fill in the rest of the line positions: Allison Trader, Leo Hantske and Will Vanous. Yes, 1926 certainly looked promising.

The 1926 "Scarlet Cyclone"

Back in the 1920's, high school football practice generally started about a week after Labor Day. After 3 weeks of drills, a team generally played a schedule of six to eight games from the season opener around October 1st until a final clash on Thanksgiving. For 1926 White put together a challenging six-game schedule that included past foes Mt. St. Joseph, Charlotte Hall, Loyola, and Severn. New on the schedule was Pikesville's McDonogh, originally opened in 1873 as a military school for poor boys. Alexandria High, after being drubbed 34-0 the previous year, no longer wanted to play Annapolis. White was pleased to receive an invitation from Hagerstown High School to play on Thanksgiving Day. The "Maroon and Gray" team from western Maryland played in the Cumberland Valley League against high schools in Virginia (Handley High in Winchester), West Virginia (Martinsburg High), Pennsylvania (Waynesboro High and Chambersburg High) and the only other public high school in Maryland outside Baltimore that fielded a football team, Cumberland. Hagerstown hadn't lost a game in two years. White was determined to show that Annapolis was a worthy opponent for Hagerstown by playing tough against the MSA teams on its schedule.

During the first week of fall practice White's hopes for the season suffered several blows. The first was the loss of Harry Feldmeyer, the team's biggest and best lineman, from injuries sustained falling off a mule. Three other boys elevated to starting positions on the line from 1925's second team failed to report for practice: Leo Hantske and Will Vanous had dropped out of school; Al Trader quit the team claiming "lack of time," which probably meant practice interfered with after school employment. Problems increased during the second week of practice when the team's top two running backs were hurt: Wilbur Dulin injured a knee and Eugene Tomanio sprained an ankle. With the October 2nd opener against reigning MSA champion St. Joe's only a week away, White scrambled to patch the line and the backfield with younger players without much game experience (27).

Despite the presence of so many newly elevated starters, the Red Jackets gave Mt. St. Joe's all it could handle in the season's opening game played at Gibbons Field in Irvington. Brother Vincent, the long-time St. Joe's coach, anticipated an easy game, but the Josephites barely squeaked out a 7-0 victory, the only score coming on a 50-yard punt return in the second quarter. After the gun sounded at the game's end, Brother Vincent said with relief, "We were fortunate to score at all." White, while happy with his team's defensive effort, knew he needed to have Dulin and Tomanio back in the lineup to jumpstart the offense (28).

Fortunately the team was at full strength at Monday's practice to begin a week of preparations for the contest against a Charlotte Hall team that was coming off a big victory over the usually tough Severn School. The two teams lined up at St. John's field on the following Saturday morning. The Annapolis defense continued its high level of play from the previous week, but not until midway through the second quarter did the offense find its rhythm when Boettcher scored the season's first touchdown at the end of "a steady march down the field." Only a few minutes later Cy Kimball "broke loose for a 50-yard run to a touchdown" that gave Annapolis a 14-0 lead at the half. Towards the end of the third quarter, Boettcher's second touchdown "on a pretty run" seemed to break Charlotte Hall's spirit, for in the last quarter "Stevens and Dulin used speed and clever dodging to run past several defenders" for the team's fourth and fifth touchdowns, Tomanio caught a Boettcher pass for another score and John Bernstein added to the drubbing when he converted a pass interception for the team's seventh touchdown of the afternoon. Final Score: Annapolis 47, Charlotte Hall 0 (29).

The Red Jackets had certainly discovered their offense. At a pep rally the following Friday, the day before they were to meet Loyola, the Naval Academy Athletic Director, Commander Bill Ingram, gave each of the previous week's starters a ticket to the upcoming Navy-Michigan game. Ingram also promised a ticket would be awarded the next day to the substitute who played the best. More than 1,000 fans lined St. John's field to watch the local lads battle the Baltimore power. Annapolis was ready to score in the first quarter, but a "fumble killed the chance." Several other times the Red Jackets "began victorious marches but lacked the final punch to get the ball across the goal line." Neither team had scored by halftime. As the game continued scoreless in the third quarter, Loyola's "huge end" Crowley – the brother of the team's coach – "slugged Dulin wickedly in the head while the Annapolis player was defenseless in a heap." As the fans booed, the referee removed Crowley from the game. In the waning minutes of the fourth quarter came the turning point. As they had against St. Joe's, the Red Jackets allowed a long punt return. This time they tackled the ball carrier on the Annapolis five-yard line. An *Evening Capital* sportswriter described the ensuing controversy: It required four downs to put the ball over and then referee Whitely Taylor of Navy football fame could have called it either way. Captain Kelly carried the ball through Annapolis left end while in the air and was driven back on the playing field. Taylor ruled, however, that the score had been made. Coach White plainly thought the runner had not crossed into the end zone, but the score and extra point stood: Loyola 7, Annapolis 0 (30).

After the game the Red Jackets were "fighting mad to wallop somebody." Their next opponent was McDonough, another tough challenge. Coach White devoted several practices to the fundamentals of defending against punt returns so that Annapolis wouldn't lose another game through sloppy coverage. The team traveled by bus to Baltimore for the game that turned into another defensive struggle. This time, however, Annapolis showed no weakness on its punt coverage. As the game clock ticked down in the fourth quarter a Boettcher pass to Dulin gave the Red Jackets the only points they'd need. Final score: Annapolis 6, McDonogh 0 (31).

Star players Boettcher, Dulin, Tomanio, Kimball and Stevens look forward with Coach Bill White to the 1926 season.

The Annapolis-Severn Game

There once was a school whose football team wore red jackets
And press-men called them the "Scarlet Cyclone."
Another school gave red shirts to its football men
And papers at once called them a "Maroon Tornado".
Late in the year these two teams played,
And the "Maroon Tornado" turned out to be a gentle zephyr
After a fighting "Scarlet Cyclone" had finished with it.
  by Henry E. Kobe
  1928 *Crablines*

The 1927 Annapolis and Severn teams clash on St. John's College Field. The Severn players have numbers on their uniform backs.

This victory was exactly what the Red Jackets needed to give them confidence going into the game they most wanted to win – against Severn School at their field in Boone. Both sides had loud, raucous cheering sections. Less than a minute into the game, the Red Jackets showed they had come to win. Cy Kimball scampered on a 50-yard touchdown run the first time Annapolis had the ball. Soon "howls of pleasure and groans of dismay swept over the field" as the Annapolis backs "ripped down the field for score after score." Kimball ended the day with three touchdowns and Tomanio tallied two. A sixth Annapolis score came on a pass from Boettcher to Dulin. While Annapolis was rolling up 41 points, all Severn could manage was a second quarter field goal. Each of the previous five contests between the schools had been a one or two touchdown affair. Never before had one of the teams so completely annihilated the other. A reporter coined the phrase "Red Cyclone" to describe the damage the Annapolis team had inflicted on the Boone field. Annapolis had always been the team in the past that had to console themselves with the words, "Wait until next year." Now, as the Red Cyclone jubilantly stormed off the field it was Severn's turn to hang their heads and vow they'd avenge the defeat the next time the teams met (32).

Coach White put the two-week break before the only game remaining on the schedule, the Thanksgiving Day clash in Hagerstown, to good use. Practices were light to allow several of the banged-up boys a better chance of healing their injuries. White drove one weekend to the western part of the state to scout the Hagerstown team. Impressed with the Maroon and Gray's running game, he used the week leading up to the game to develop defensive tactics to stop Hagerstown's patented end sweeps. Meanwhile, Hagerstown was headed for its third consecutive undefeated season. Since Hagerstown had beaten Cumberland, and Annapolis had only lost to private academies, the *Evening Capital* dubbed the game the "Public School Championship of Maryland." Many Annapolitans decided to drive to Hagerstown for the Thursday game, then to head on Friday to Philadelphia for the next day's Army and Navy game. The entire Red Jacket squad left Wednesday morning on "Miss Virginia," the team bus. Following a light practice the locals hosted the visiting team to sightseeing and dinner before the boys and their coach turned in for the night at a Hagerstown rooming house (33).

Kick-off the next day on the Willow Lane Park field was at 11 a.m. The local Hagerstown *Morning Herald* reported the crowd was "one of the largest ever to attend a game in this city." In the first quarter neither team was able to move the ball on offense. The surprised hometown fans watched as the visitor's defense stopped Hagerstown's running game cold. Towards the end of the second quarter, the Hagerstown quarterback Widmeyer caught the Red Jacket defense napping with an 80-yard touchdown pass (the extra point failed) to leave Annapolis on the short end of a 6-0 score at intermission. The second half, however, belonged to Annapolis. The Red Cyclone struck quickly in the third quarter. An Annapolis lineman tackled the Hagerstown punter on the 35-yard line before he could get off his kick. Boettcher then hit Dulin on a 34-yard pass play; the Annapolis end "could have easily scored a touchdown but became confused by the markings on the field and downed the ball within a yard of the goal line." Embarrassed by his mistake, Dulin "rammed the ball across for a touchdown" on the next play. With Boettcher's perfect extra point kick, Annapolis took a 7-6 lead. Boettcher opened the fourth quarter with long passes to Tomanio and Kimball that again got the ball to the one-yard line. This time "Cy" dove across the goal line for the touchdown. A failed extra point kept the result in question until the very end, but Hagerstown failed to score in the second half. Final score: Annapolis 13, Hagerstown 6 (34).

Back home in crabtown, the victory was hailed as the greatest in Annapolis High football history. The school pulled out all the stops to hail the boys and their coach. The Phi Chi girls hosted a special party for the team. At a school awards assembly Coach White praised all the players for their "hard work and cooperation that were responsible for their development as a team." He must have taken satisfaction from season statistics that showed the Red Jackets had scored 107 points while allowing just 23. Kimball's five touchdowns led all scorers with 30 points, while Dulin's four touchdowns and two extra points meant he contributed 26 points. Boettcher had a hand in 32 points – two on his own touchdown runs, two touchdown passes, and eight drop-kicks for extra points. Tomanio (two touchdowns and one PAT), Stevens (one touchdown) and Bernstein (one touchdown) also scored. White pointed out that without the blocking of linemen Cliff Jones, Joe Legum, Charles Hoban, Maurice Wilson and Barney Turner nobody would have scored. White also thanked the "second team that forced the regulars to a fast pace to hold their jobs." At the end of the assembly, the AHSAA presented commemorative gold footballs to 13 boys on the first team and silver to another 13 on the second team. The Student Council decided the school should have a trophy case in the main hall where the Severn and Hagerstown victory balls would be put on display (35).

As Coach White stood on the platform surveying the 26 boys who had played under his guidance in 1926, he must have had mixed feelings about the future. The top three offensive players – Boettcher, Cy Kimball and Dulin – would not be back. Altogether six starters and six reserves would be gone when practice started in September 1927. But big tackle Harry Feldmeyer, having finally recovered from his fall off the mule, would lead a strong Class of 1928 contingent, including Tomanio (Boettcher's replacement at quarterback) and three linemen – Turner, Hoban and Legum. Indeed, the 1927 team would record a fine 3–1–3 season, with an expected victory over Army-Navy Prep (47-6), an unexpected win over Mt. St. Joe's (7-6) and a season-ending repeat rout of Severn (20-0). Three ties against Baltimore-area powers McDonogh, Forest Park and BCC also were impressive. The lone loss was to Loyola, 30-20, but Annapolis could take some consolation from having scored more points against the Dons than any other opponent that season (36).

If White could have seen further into the future, he undoubtedly would have been proud of the men these 26 players would become. Ninety percent finished high school; a quarter went on to college, including three who would play football for St. John's. One admitted to the Naval Academy joined four of White's former players who were already midshipmen. All five became career naval officers, while nine would serve Uncle Sam in the Navy or Army during World War Two. Everyone eventually became a family man. Several worked for the government, and one – "crack running back" Wilbur Dulin – earned a law degree at the University of Maryland, represented Anne Arundel County in the State Senate from 1943 to 1949 and then served as president of the county bar association. Others had careers as policemen, insurance agents, government clerks and plumbers, including star running back Cy Kimball. Two of the half dozen civilian employees at the Naval Academy were quarterback Norman Boettcher and Cy's younger brother James Kimball, who was the assistant registrar for over a quarter of a century.

Another Naval Academy employee, Charles Mason "Daffy" Russell, became perhaps the most renowned of White's former players. Only a freshman scrub in 1926, by his senior year Daffy was still playing football and had started Annapolis High's first lacrosse team. He enlisted in the Navy during World War II, earning nine battle stars and a Purple Heart. After the war he returned to the Naval Academy, but he devoted much of his life to coaching football and lacrosse at Annapolis and then St. Mary's High School. Before his death in 2001 at age 91 he was inducted in the National Lacrosse Hall of Fame for being the father of lacrosse in Maryland (37).

* * * * * * * * * * *

Dulin with victory balls from Severn and Hagerstown games

Yes, White surely must have been happy with how his boys turned out. But he certainly could not have been pleased with what lay beyond 1927 for him and Annapolis High football. The 1926 football trophies for defeating Severn and claiming the Maryland Public School championship would be put on prominent display in the main hallway, but by 1929 both he and the principal who had hired and supported him throughout his tenure at Annapolis High would no longer be around to admire them.

CHAPTER 5:

DEPRESSION AND WARTIME,

1929 -1945

Football stopped with this 1929 team until resumed in 1947

1st row: Brown, Boettcher, Johnson, Kaler, Eppes, Kotzin, Paige, Leitch; **2nd row**: Banas, Skordas, Fisher, Emory, Greenfield, Shawn, Owens, Rosteberg, Wenzell; **3rd row**: Coach McCauley, LeTourneau, Fuller, Gray, Martin, Moreland, Woods, Russell, Winchester, Johnson, Frazier, Schenker.

Annapolis High School has made wonderful strides athletically, but the future in the great moleskin games does not appear so rosy as the past. Now the high school's aim is to aid in the development of students physically without hampering him or her scholastically. All in all the high school athletic department is doing its best to aid the whole student body rather than a select few.

E. M. Jackson, Sports Editor
Evening Capital,
12 February 1930

Depression and Wartime, 1929 – 1945 107

Between 1929 and 1945 the United States suffered through the Great Depression and dispatched millions of troops to fight in the Second World War. The era's economic and wartime hardships affected most citizens of Annapolis. Money was scarce, jobs vanished and lives were lost. The local high school was certainly not immune to these problems, especially after a costly fire destroyed part of the school's roof and third floor assembly room in February 1930. Principal Howard A. Kinhart reassessed priorities so that the school's educational mission could be met despite cuts to the education budget. Students could no longer afford to contribute enough money to sustain all of the school's most popular activities. Yet in the midst of the economic crisis, the state legislature passed a million dollar Anne Arundel County school bond issue, $400,000 of which was earmarked for construction of a new Annapolis High School building. In June 1932, when the Green Street school's doors closed on students and teachers departing for summer vacation, traditions over 30 years in the making came to an end, locked away as memories in the minds of everyone who had worked and studied there. Yet when the doors to the new building swung open the following September, routines began that soon would grow into the cherished customs of Annapolis High's next generation of students.

A New Administration at Annapolis High

So many changes greeted Annapolis High students returning after summer vacation of 1928 they may have thought they were in an entirely different school. Although the faces of their friends and many of the teachers were the same, one new to them belonged to the man who would, over the course of the next several years, alter much that had been familiar about the school: Howard A. Kinhart, the school's ninth principal. Kinhart would remain in this position for 21 years, making him the longest serving principal in Annapolis High history. A native of rural Jarrettsville, Maryland, Kinhart came to Annapolis in the fall of 1916 as a freshman at St. John's, where he enrolled in the Latin-Scientific curriculum, served as manager to the football team and mainly distinguished himself as a marksman in the mandatory military training. The *Rat-Tat* yearbook of 1920 teased "Kinny" about the daily "pink envelopes" he received in the mail from the eastern shore, apparently written by the "petite blonde" he was spotted dancing with at "nearly every Cotillion hop." Perhaps this young woman convinced Kinhart to accept a teaching job at Pocomoke High after his graduation from St. John's, but the relationship must not have endured. Photos of Kinhart's wife, Mildred, a longtime foreign language teacher at Annapolis High, show a dark-haired woman.

Once settled on the eastern shore, Kinhart followed a route similar to other Maryland educators serious about their profession, using his spare time on weekends and during the summer to drive north to Columbia Teacher's College in New York City to earn a master's degree. Later he completed a doctorate degree that conferred on him the title that would precede his name the rest of his professional career. Dr. Kinhart's reputation as "one of the best male principals in Maryland" convinced county superintendent of schools, George Fox, that he was the right man to enforce a stricter code of student behavior. (1).

Kinhart quickly let it be known that a new day had dawned at Annapolis High. He began by taking aim at extracurricular activities he considered either frivolous or counterproductive to the school's academic mission. To the dismay of the students, the yearbook *Crablines* and the newspaper *Hi-Signs* were discontinued. Secret fraternities and sororities were abolished. The literary societies were restricted to organizing such intellectual activities as formal debates. Although Kinhart valued culture, he imposed strict limitations on the number of drama productions put on each year at the school. Thespians were restricted to one senior class play in the spring. The school's orchestra and chorus continued, but the ax fell on the jazz band and minstrel shows. Doris Jarosik Purdy ('31) thought Kinhart's motivation was to "cut down on expenses." Blanche Taylor ('38) took a dimmer view; in her opinion, "Kinhart was mean and stingy – he just didn't want us to have any fun."

Although fiscal concerns may have contributed to Kinhart's stance on student activities, his motivation was grounded in an educational philosophy that mirrored that of the county school board and its superintendent. During his first summer on the job, Kinhart reorganized and expanded the curriculum. Projecting an enrollment of 700 students in a building designed to hold no more than 400, Kinhart managed to get basement space in the grammar school converted into three classrooms. He persuaded the school board to fund six more faculty billets, raising the total number of teachers to 29 (2).

Kinhart wrote an *Evening Capital* article to clarify his educational views. After stating his belief that a high school has the moral obligation to produce graduates united in their support of democracy, Kinhart explains, "The secondary school is the one agency [that can] unify the nation's people through the development of common knowledge, common ideals and common interests." To ensure this result, his new curriculum required all students to take a common series of social studies and history courses imbued with American democratic ideals and moral values. He strongly endorsed participation in student government so young men and women could experience the satisfaction of putting into practice the democratic theories learned in the classroom Equally vital to preparing model citizens was the required English curriculum that would "ensure all students achieve mastery of the mother tongue and its literature." (3)

Kinhart also built options into the curriculum to provide necessary specialization for students preparing for their life's work. Kinhart compressed Linthicum's four curricular tracks into two, each with a variety of choices. The first was a college preparatory curriculum for those with "distinctly academic interests and needs." Within this track students chose between Latin (humanities) and Scientific specialties. The other track was vocational, with specializations in "agriculture, business, clerical, industrial, fine arts and household arts." To determine the appropriate education and future vocation for students, Kinhart introduced a guidance program with fulltime counselors tasked to gain "intimate knowledge" of each student's abilities. Kinhart's goal was to graduate "products of the school [who are] able to live completely and happily in their social environment and contribute to the perpetuation and improvement of the democratic state."

Annapolis High Drops Football

Kinhart's emphasis on installing a common core curriculum extended to the physical development of students. Specifically, he wanted to introduce required physical education classes for entering high school freshmen. Initially this was impossible because the school had no indoor gymnasium. Instead he set his sights on revamping the interscholastic sports program to broaden participation. During his first year at the school he voiced dissatisfaction with the small number of students benefiting from the AHSAA funds that supported three interscholastic sports for boys (football, basketball and baseball) and one – basketball – for girls (fieldball was only played as an intramural sport in the fall of 1928). He criticized the idea of "sports for a few" at the expense of "training for all." (4)

Kinhart's attitude about athletics made him a natural ally of Dr. William Burdick, director of the Playground (formerly Public) Athletic League, the organization that since 1915 had supervised Maryland interscholastic sports outside Baltimore. In an address to the Annapolis Parent-Teacher Association, Burdick asserted, "The highest purpose of athletics is to prepare children for the responsibilities they will face as adult citizens." PAL sponsored the most inclusive athletic event in the state – the spring Olympiad for school children that since its initial competition in 1915 had spread to all Maryland counties. Individual running, jumping and throwing events in weight categories were held for boys, along with team competitions for girls in volleyball, dodge ball and softball. The only boys' team sport was baseball. Each event winner on the county level advanced to the statewide Olympiad held annually during early June in Baltimore. Anne Arundel County called its annual PAL Olympiad a Field Day. In 1928 it drew 4,505 student participants, many of whom were there to attempt the PAL physical fitness test (long jump, high jump, chin ups and 220 yard run for boys; balance exercise, leg raises and dodge ball throw for girls). Gold, silver and bronze badges were awarded to each student who met a predetermined mark in all three events. Elizabeth Fuller Eppes ('36) remembers everyone enjoying the day's activities that were held on the grounds of what was then the Navy Postgraduate School. She recalls winning a bronze medal, now long lost.

Burdick believed contact sports, especially football, were unhealthy for children. His opposition played a crucial role when Annapolis High dropped football prior to World War One. The team sports PAL promoted were soccer, basketball and baseball for boys, fieldball, volleyball and basketball for girls. Annapolis High boys were enthusiastic about hoops, and baseball had long been popular in the city. But soccer failed to generate enough enthusiasm to bury football completely. In 1920 some Annapolis High boys took the initiative to revive the gridiron sport behind Burdick's back (as previously mentioned in chapter four, page 92).

As the 1920's progressed, football again became the centerpiece of the school's athletic program, especially after Bill

White assumed coaching duties in 1924. In 1926 and 1927, White's teams were competitive against every team they played, including several in the elite Maryland Scholastic Association comprised of Baltimore city private and a few public high schools. At the end of the 1927 season the MSA invited Annapolis High to become a full-fledged member. White carefully weighed the pros and cons of accepting the offer. Scheduling a suitable slate of opponents had become increasingly difficult. The only other white public high schools in Maryland that played football were in Hagerstown and on Greenway Avenue in Cumberland (later named Fort Hill). They belonged to the Cumberland Valley League that included high schools in Waynesboro and Chambersburg (PA), Handley High (Winchester, VA) and Martinsburg (WV) High. Although Annapolis and Hagerstown played on Thanksgiving several times, a full slate of games against CVL teams would have involved long trips that the AHSAA budget could not fund. Thus, White reasoned, Annapolis High's most feasible option for a full slate of games was to accept the MSA's invitation (5).

White realized his team would be overmatched when lining up against most of the MSA squads. His players were younger and consequently smaller than the boys on the other side of the scrimmage line. In the mid-1920's limited classroom space had again forced Anne Arundel County's school board to revert to an 11-year system, eliminating eighth grade. Banny Eppes ('30) remembers taking a test when he finished seventh grade at Germantown Grammar School. Those who passed went directly on to high school; those who didn't were sent to Annapolis Grammar School for remedial work. With only 11 grades, Annapolis High's oldest students were often only 16 or 17 years old, while the private preparatory schools had many boys 18 or older on their teams.

The results of the 1928 football season increased White's worry about the ability of his team to survive in the MSA. The Red Jackets were competitive in every game but ended up on the short end of the score in close games against the MSA's Mt. St. Joseph's (6-0), BCC (13-12), Loyola (12-0) and Severn (6-0). The Red Jackets also lost on Thanksgiving to Hagerstown (27-21). Their only victory came against Forest Park, a Baltimore public high school whose players were equivalent in age and size to the Annapolis boys. Nobody was happy with such a losing season. White believed the best tactic to use against teams with such bigger and older players was speed. To help

Coach Bill White's 1927 team had a respectable 3-3-1 season, but he realized the stiff MSA competition would make it increasingly hard for the Red Jackets to win.

St. John's graduate James McCauley (left) came to Annapolis High in 1929 to teach history, but White's resignation made him the most logical choice to take over as the head football coach. Within a year he helped principal Howard Kinhart (right) disband the football team, arguing instead for a broader physical education program that was eventually realized as seen below as boys play on a field alongside the new Annapolis High building in the 1940's.

develop his players' quickness, he suggested replacing baseball with lacrosse as a spring sport. White's plan brought an enthusiastic response from several boys who had been clamoring to play this game that was rapidly growing in popularity throughout the greater Baltimore area. White worked with Daffy Russell, one of the most ardent lacrosse advocates among the school's football players, to form an Annapolis High club. Its first recorded victory came against the Severn junior varsity on May 22, 1929 (6).

Louise Linthicum had always given White a free hand to run the athletic program, but Kinhart left no doubt throughout the 1928-1929 school year that he intended to control all aspects of the school, including sports. One apparent dispute between principal and head coach was over the academic eligibility standards for athletes. Students failing more than half their courses had their names placed on what became known as the "black list" and were prohibited from playing on any school team until their grades improved (7). Declaring the policy far too lax, Kinhart instituted a "black list" that included names of students failing any class, including electives carrying less than a full credit. The result was that more than half the boys in the school were ineligible during the spring of 1929 – the major reason why the lacrosse team operated as a club rather than as an interscholastic team. The "black list" also dealt a deathblow to the baseball team that spring. Instead of playing for Annapolis High, the schoolboys were forced to organize a team under the sponsorship of the local Rotary Club (8).

In a June 1929 interview with *Evening Capital* sports editor E.M. Jackson, White discussed his plans for the coming fall's football season He gave no indication that he was thinking about leaving Annapolis. But on September 18, 1929, the newspaper ran a banner headline on the sports page announcing a major change in the athletic staff at the local high school. White was reported to have "resigned"; no explanation was offered, nor were his future plans discussed. Perhaps he found a better coaching job elsewhere. Maybe he left because he didn't agree with Kinhart's athletic philosophy. A rumor circulated that he became a racecar driver. Twenty years later, he was Dr. Willis White, an assistant superintendent of Maryland schools, so maybe he resigned to pursue graduate education (9).

Whatever his reasons, White's resignation at the start of the school year sent Kinhart scrambling to find a replacement coach. The only candidate was James W. McCauley, a 1929 St. John's graduate from Maryland's eastern shore who had just been appointed to the school's faculty as a history teacher. McCauley had played three years of football for the Johnnies, quite an accomplishment considering he had never seen a game before enrolling in college. McCauley also successfully took up lacrosse at St. John's. Although his ambition had been to go to law school, he now found himself appointed Annapolis High's new gridiron coach.

McCauley initially seemed to relish the challenge of coaching the Red Jackets. He honored the rigorous football schedule already in place – six games against MSA teams and a season finale on Thanksgiving against Hagerstown. He attempted to implement a "new grid system" that changed the defensive line to give more latitude to the tackles (perhaps because he had played the tackle position in college). On offense he introduced the huddle, a recent innovation to the game that he brought from St. John's. But clearly the coach's expectations for the season were modest. On October 4, 1929, he told the *Evening Capital* that his "classy boys" would hopefully be able to give "a creditable showing" against their opponents.

By season's end, McCauley's early assessment proved to be all too true. Again the Red Jackets were competitive against the bigger and older teams, but finished with only two victories in eight games. The record, however, shouldn't lead to the conclusion that the season was a waste. Banny Eppes remembers how much the boys enjoyed the season-ending trip to Hagerstown, especially the opportunity to stay overnight with his friends in a Hagerstown boarding house – an unusual luxury coming just a month after the Black Thursday collapse of the American stock market and the beginning of the Depression. Ed Gray ('30) preserved his team photo for over 60 years before donating it to the school in 1993. His most vivid memory of his senior year as a scrub on the team was that "our record was not very good," something Eppes also vividly recalls. Their coach shared the two players' assessment. Within a month of the season's close, McCauley told Jackson in an interview that he thought football was an unrealistic sport for public high school boys to play. Jackson disagreed, stating bluntly that if the school wanted to stay on the *Evening Capital*'s sports page, the boys would have to continue playing "major sports" like football.

Kinhart may have influenced McCauley's views about what the proper role of high school sports should be. On February 12, 1930, the banner headline on the *Evening Capital*'s sports page announced,

"Annapolis High Abandons Football." Jackson reported fully on McCauley's well-organized and persuasive explanation of the factors that had led to the decision. Topping the list was a financial analysis showing football had grown too expensive for the school to support. According to McCauley, $540.35 was expended on football for the 1929 season, which worked out to $19.29 per each of the 28 players. Team bills were paid with funds from the AHSAA ($350), Severn School (paid $50 to play at St. John's field) and a surplus from the Hagerstown trip ($25), which meant the school treasury had to cover the remaining $115.35. McCauley pointed out that to spend so much money on so few students wasn't fair to others, a view that mirrored Kinhart's stance on athletics.

McCauley then laid out the projected expenses if football were to continue. The team desperately needed new uniforms that would cost $550. Such a purchase would double the revenue necessary to field a team in 1930. Even raising $500 to cover field rental costs, bus transportation, officials and other incidental expenditures would be problematic, especially given the financial uncertainty facing many Annapolitans during the first months after the stock market collapse. Even the student's two-dollar contribution to the AHSAA could no longer be taken for granted.

McCauley's second major argument for dropping football was that Annapolis High simply could not be competitive against most MSA teams. He cited figures that showed the average Annapolis High player weighed 145 pounds while the opposition teams ranged in average weight from 155 pounds to BCC's 170 pounds. He also noted that both City and Poly had enrollments of several thousand boys, whereas Annapolis High had, at best, 250 male students (over half of whom were ineligible due to the black list). McCauley was also frustrated that MSA coaches raided his team, enticing away his best players who naturally were attracted to the private schools' better athletic facilities. He concluded that continuing football only would demoralize everyone involved, especially the players.

In the place of football, McCauley recommended Annapolis boys compete in soccer, basketball and baseball. The funds freed from football would also allow girls to have fieldball, basketball and volleyball teams. McCauley estimated that less money would be necessary to field these six teams than football, alone, had cost. His suggestion reveals PAL's influence in the decision to drop football. These sports were the six in which PAL sponsored annual state championship tournaments for public schools (outside Baltimore), hardly a coincidence.

McCauley's detailed argument even convinced Jackson, who previously had opposed the idea of dropping football. Although Jackson was far from happy that the "major sport" of football was to give way to soccer, he understood that the combination of finances and enrollment factors made the continuation of the "pigskin game" unrealistic at Annapolis High. Several weeks later, Jackson reported that "little protest" greeted the decision, Even star player "Stiff" Moreland said that he was "tired of losing" and he understood there wasn't enough money to field a team. Jackson reported Kinhart was "particularly gratified that the city and the boys had accepted the decision in a "fair-minded manner." (10)

Seventeen years would pass before another Annapolis High football team would take the field. During the early 1930's some of the most athletic Annapolis High boys tried to fill the football void by joining a group of alumni to form a local semi-pro team called the "Coca Colas." Some smaller high school lads fielded a 118-pound team decked out in the discarded red Annapolis High jerseys. They defeated Severn's lightweight squad in 1931 and 1932, but either interest or funding waned. By the late 1930's, organized football was only a distant memory at Annapolis High (11).

Meanwhile Kinhart appointed McCauley to serve as the school's athletic director and hired several physical education teachers tasked with implementing his vision for Annapolis High sports. In the winter of 1931 the girls' basketball team put together a 9-1 season that included double wins over Hyattsville High, Brewbaker College and an alumnae team, along with single victories over Catonsville High, Strayer's Business School and a coed faculty team. Sportswriter Jackson became a big fan of this "classy little group," especially the "perky little miss, Margaret Smith" who could teach some "masculine players" how to get their shot off faster (12). The boys' basketball team was right behind, with a 7-2 record, including victories over several MSA teams. Baseball had a .500 season against a "strictly PAL" schedule that included county teams from Glen Burnie and Tracy's Landing. The next fall the fieldball team won the county championship with a perfect 6–0 record, twice defeating each of the other county high schools. And in its first year returning to soccer, the Red Jackets also won the county crown.

Depression and Wartime, 1929 – 1945   117

As the decade of the 1930's progressed, Annapolis established dominance in two sports – girls' fieldball and boys' basketball, with both teams routinely winning county championships and faring well in the PAL state playoffs. In 1932 and 1935 the girls played for the state fieldball championship. The boys' basketball team made it through four rounds of tournament games in 1934 and 1936; in 1938 they reached the "western shore" championship contest played at Ritchie Coliseum in College Park (13). Thus, despite the disappearance of football, Annapolis High athletes continued to make a name for the school in the state.

FIRE!!

Coach McCauley's announcement that Annapolis High was abandoning football was supposed to be made on February 12, 1930, at the school. Instead the press conference was hastily moved to the assembly room in City Hall because on the previous day fire had destroyed much of the school's third floor. The blaze was spotted about noon when student Orville Hatfield returned from lunch and noticed flames at the bottom of the stage curtain in the assembly room. Hatfield shouted "fire," someone quickly sounded the alarm and all the practice fire drills over the years paid off as the 650 students and 27 teachers safely evacuated the building. Two girls who fainted were carried out by fellow students. Five firemen were injured: two from smoke inhalation, one smashed his hand, one twisted an ankle and one dislocated his shoulder. Some schoolboys reacted heroically as they helped the firefighters lug heavy ladders up the stairwells. They saved every typewriter before Kinhart ordered all but firemen out of the building (14).

By the time the fire was under control about 2:00 p.m., over $25,000 damage had been done. The roof on the grammar school side had a gaping hole, the floor in the assembly room was badly charred and the lower floors were waterlogged. Banny Eppes recalls seeing several boys throwing papers out the main office windows. His interpretation was they were destroying school records. The newspaper's more positive spin was the boys were trying to save valuable school papers. Whatever the motivation, almost all of the official papers ended up soaked inside the building or scattered in the muddy water on the ground outside the windows – one of the reasons why virtually no records from the school's first three decades exist.

The next day controversy erupted when insurance inspector Joe Daugherty from Baltimore quickly pronounced the fire to be the work of an arsonist, concluding that a box of rags under the stage had been set on fire purposefully. In support of his case, Daugherty cited another suspicious fire that had caused $12,000 in damages to the grammar school just three weeks earlier. The city's fire chief, Jesse Fisher, came to quite a different conclusion. From having seen the fire firsthand, he concluded a faulty flue in the chimney was its cause. His explanation made sense, particularly because several people had smelled smoke earlier in the day but hadn't been able to discover its source (15). The mystery about how the fire started still sparks heated discussion 75 years later among former students. Banny Eppes, who earned an electrical engineering degree at Johns Hopkins, believes the fire was accidental, caused by faulty wiring around the stage that sparked the flames. Other alumni smile slyly and quip that they're sure some student who wanted to have his records destroyed started it. No names are ever mentioned. The truth, it seems, will never be known.

Although Kinhart wanted to know what had caused the fire, his more immediate concern was how soon classes could be resumed. Originally the estimate for the repairs necessary before students would be allowed to return stretched to months because building inspectors said the entire roof would have to be torn off and replaced. Kinhart and superintendent George Fox developed a plan for space in the state capitol building to be converted to classrooms, but this idea was dropped when legislators protested about the damage the students could do to the desks in the senate and house of delegates chambers. Then came an elaborate proposal for shared space in the grammar school, with the younger students attending classes from 8:30 to 12:30 and the secondary school scholars from 12:30 to 4:30. The main obstacle would be trying to move all the equipment for commercial and manual training classes to the grammar school.

Then to everyone's surprise, the *Evening Capital* announced on Saturday, February 22nd that the high school building had been put in satisfactory condition for classes to begin the following Tuesday on a split-session schedule. Apparently building inspectors certified that temporary patching done to cover the hole in the roof had allowed the lower floors to dry out. Access to the top floor was boarded off, heat could be provided and a special covered entrance to keep debris from falling on anyone coming in or out of the structure had been erected.

The main hardship would be lack of electricity. Replacing wiring was deemed too disruptive to classes, so the necessary electrical work would be delayed until summer.

One benefit of the fire was an invitation from the Naval Academy Superintendent to hold commencement for the Class of 1930 in Dahlgren Hall. Every one of its 130 members was forever proud that they were in the first Annapolis High class to hold its graduation inside the Naval Academy walls. Over 3,500 people attended the ceremony, by far the largest audience in the school's history. Kinhart used the podium to congratulate the students, faculty and parents for successfully reducing the school's overall failure rate from 12.5 percent in 1928 (former principal Louise Linthicum's last year in the school) to 8.4 percent in 1930, an obvious effort to pat himself on the back for the rigor and seriousness he had introduced to the school. Kinhart also drew attention to the "overcrowding in the high school" that had become "desperate " since the fire. Although repairs had been budgeted, Kinhart said it was obvious that a "bigger school and better laboratories" were needed immediately (16).

The Third Annapolis High School

A year prior to the fire Kinhart, with the full support of the county school board, began a campaign to win local support for a million dollar school bond issue to cover the costs of building a new Annapolis High School. On February 16, 1929, Kinhart told PTA representatives at a county-wide meeting that Annapolis needed a new high school building, one that would "stand for 50 years" without becoming outdated (17). Superintendent George Fox gave a lengthy interview to the *Evening Capital* in which he sought to counter criticism about the increasing cost of public education. He methodically laid out some numbers that showed a rise in countywide enrollment of high school students from 133 in 1916 to 1,000 in 1929. Such an increase obviously demanded more buildings, more teachers, more books and more supplies. The per-pupil cost, which in 1916 was $64, had increased to $75 largely as a result of the costs to bus students to distant schools. He asked rhetorically if Annapolis wanted to revert to a system like Sleepy Hollow where Ichabod Crane had taught in a one-room school (18).

The Maryland legislature passed a one million dollar bond issue in the fall of 1929 for Anne Arundel County, $400,000 of which was for a new Annapolis High School. The remaining $600,000 was earmarked for high school buildings in Glen Burnie, Lothian (the future Southern High School), and the future Wiley H. Bates High School for "colored" students (19). The legislative action, however, served to launch major discord in the county about the location of the new schools, especially in Annapolis and the southern part of the county. At least a dozen sites were mentioned for the new Annapolis High. Downtown merchants, for obvious reasons of self-interest, wanted the new school to be built on its current site – a virtual impossibility given the desire for a large school surrounded by playing fields. St. John's College owned a parcel of land in Cedar Park that was offered to the school board, but its location on the "other side" of the railroad tracks led many to wonder if students would be courting danger walking to and from school. Others criticized the location because it was outside the city limits. Two locations along West Street – one adjacent to the ballpark (approximately where a Goodwill store sits today) and the other at Stehle's Circus – were popular with many teachers who rented rooms in houses out that way. After visiting 12 possible sites a committee of the PTA recommended the McGuckian house and its surrounding 25-acre parcel of land located at the head of Spa Creek at the western edge of Murray Hill (20).

The school's building commission seemed to focus attention on the West Street locations, so the announcement in the March 24, 1931, *Evening Capital* that the commission had bought the McGuckian property for $35,000 came as a surprise to virtually everyone. Yet in retrospect the Spa Creek site seems an obvious choice. The large parcel of land would easily accommodate the much bigger school building that was desired, along with several parking areas, playing fields and space for any necessary future expansion. The PTA group had especially liked the "commanding knoll" on the property that would make the school building visible for miles in each direction. The many streets feeding into the area would allow easy access from all directions. In fact, the only drawback the commission cited was the proximity to a "colored settlement," but they decided this was "not a sufficient impediment to make the land undesirable." The commission was referring to the Smithville Road area, which not only was "home to several Negro families" but also would become the site of Bates High School (21).

Depression and Wartime, 1929 – 1945 121

Spirits were high when school opened on September 11, 1931; the 675 students and their teachers realized this would be the last year they would have to tolerate the cramped conditions in their Green Street building. Everyone was looking forward to a year hence, when students and teachers would be filing into a new building designed to hold 1,000 students. Anticipation was heightened further on November 4th when the Baltimore architectural firm, Buckler and Fenhagen, released its winning design and formal bids on the project were opened. The brick school was to have 18 standard academic classrooms, four fully equipped scientific labs, two oversized commercial classrooms, large rooms for manual training, home economics and music, a library, two gymnasiums with adjacent locker rooms, an auditorium, an assembly room measuring 1,000 square feet, a cafeteria and a principal's office with outer waiting room and secretarial space (22). Although excavation began on December 8th, the groundbreaking ceremony wasn't held until January 20, 1932. Annapolis High students walked *en masse* to the new school site. One thousand people struggled to hear the speeches of Frank Munroe, president of the school board, and Kinhart over the noise of two steam shovels and 75 workmen. The ceremony concluded with the laying of a marble cornerstone with a copper box concealed inside that held the *Evening Capital,* the *Maryland Gazette* and a scroll signed by the school's students and faculty (23).

Originally plans called for the new building to be completed in time for the commencement ceremony in June 1932, but bad weather delayed the construction timetable, so diplomas were given to the 106 graduates at the Circle Theater. Over the summer plans were made to convert the now vacant main floor of the Green Street building into offices for the superintendent and board of education. The second story was prepared for possible use by the grammar school next door.

The day before all county schools were slated to open for the fall semester, the *Evening Capital* of September 7, 1932, announced that classes at the new high schools in Annapolis and Glen Burnie would be delayed a full week so that the grounds at both locations could be properly graded. Superintendent Fox also announced that both new high schools would be open three days for public inspection, with faculty on duty to serve as guides (24). Over 2,000 people had taken the tour of the new Annapolis High by the afternoon of the third day, but the line was so long that all 26 of the school's teachers volunteered to keep the building open that night until nine

The new Annapolis High School could seat 1,000-people in its auditorium.

New math classrooms and science labs were considered among best in the state.

AHS graduate William Strohmeyer and school board president Frank Munroe help lay cornerstone.

The school cafeteria served popular nickel sandwiches and deserts, but most students opted to bring sack lunches to save money.

o'clock. Altogether approximately 4,500 Annapolitans toured the building (25).

Early on the morning of September 15, 1932, students began to arrive at their new school. Many walked, but others traveled by "automobile, bus, train and bicycle." When the doors swung open at 8 a.m., about 850 students filed into the auditorium to receive Dr. Kinhart's rules about the proper "use and care of the school building." They then were directed to their homerooms to pick up books and class schedules. As the day progressed they found some school furnishings were still missing; desks for all classrooms and pieces of equipment for the manual training shop room had not yet been delivered. The cafeteria was staffed and well stocked to serve the school's first meal. Offered for a nickel were a selection of sandwiches, pies and cakes. The cost of a "cold plate" was 15 cents. Most students, however, brought sack lunches from home. By day's end, all agreed that the new era for Annapolis High had begun exceedingly well, better than could have been expected (26).

The new high school for the northern part of the county also opened on September 15, 1932. Its $200,000 price tag made it half as expensive as Annapolis High. Located on Route 2 just south of Glen Burnie, this 1932 structure still serves as the central part of the high school. The replacement building for Tracy's High School was delayed as various towns in southern Maryland fought over its precise location. The fourth new building opened on January 1, 1933, to serve the "Negro high school students of Anne Arundel County" that was named after Ward Four's prominent citizen Wiley H. Bates, who donated $500 towards the cost of land on Smithville Road less than a half mile from the Constitution Avenue location of the new Annapolis High building. Bates consisted of seven classrooms and a gymnasium built at a cost of $58,596, a much more modest price tag than its fancy white neighbor.

Certainly a new high school building for "colored students" was long overdue. The Stanton School had grown so overcrowded that rooms in neighboring buildings had to be used, often without benefit of any school furnishings or supplies. Transportation to Bates High School from many areas of the county was initially a major problem, but by 1937 a free bus system was implemented that helped make a secondary education accessible to all people of color in the county (27). Demand for seats soon exceeded availability, thus forcing the county to repeatedly expand the facility in the 1940's and 1950's.

The Class of 1938 posed for a group photo on the stage in the school's auditorium — note the presence of the previously banned short socks on the front row girls.

Well-dressed boys in the class sported slacks and sweater.

Students of the March 1932 musical "Riding Down the Sky" pose for a cast photo.

School Days During the Depression

During his first years as Annapolis High's principal, Dr. Kinhart put most of his efforts into improving the school's academic environment. Many students chafed under what they perceived to be overly strict rules. In his second year at the helm he faced a major rebellion when on the first day of school many girls appeared "in diminutive sports socks or entirely stockingless." Some of their male classmates showed up with "no garters" so that "their socks flapped over their shoes in the most approved collegiate style." The students' "nonchalance" earned a "stern rebuke" from Kinhart, who declared war on such fads. By the third day of school he decreed that henceforth all girls must wear proper stockings and all boys must wear garters. A rumored school boycott was avoided when parents and teachers persuaded the students to bow to the principal's edict (28).

As the years passed, however, Kinhart seemed to grow more tolerant towards the students. He modified many of his initial restrictions, while others were discarded completely. Nothing better illustrates his softening than a Class of 1938 photograph that shows 10 girls seated demurely in the front row sporting the previously banned anklet socks. Gradually a few clubs crept back into the school. One popular activity was the Traffic Squad, a group of two-dozen students who regulated the flow of students inside – not outside – the school, especially in the cafeteria and hallways. Chosen at the end of junior year based on their qualities of citizenship, leadership and responsibility, squad membership was widely perceived as both a privilege and an honor. *Tally Ho*, the student newspaper, reappeared in mimeographed form in 1937. Members of the Student Library Council volunteered free time to help the school librarian, although according to Elizabeth Fuller Eppes ('36), the library was "never open" for students to browse in at their leisure. The Student Council held mock presidential elections, while its social committee organized two dances, the most popular of which was the Christmas formal. Music again filled the school, with the girls' chorus, mixed glee club and orchestra (without banjos!) combining efforts to produce a musical each spring.

Kinhart's willingness to loosen strictures about extracurricular activities was part of his effort to help students find some refuge from the economic hardships of the depression. Another impact of the hard economic times can be seen in the school's enrollment that continued to rise, especially among boys. With jobs scarce, parents were more willing to let their sons go to school. They may also have been influenced by statistics that showed the average salary of high school graduates was 33 percent above workers with only an elementary school diploma (29). In 1937 one-third of all young people in the county between the ages of 16 and 25 were in high school or college, one-third were employed and one-third were unemployed. This led Superintendent Fox to urge the county high schools to establish early-intervention programs that would help every student, especially the boys, identify a feasible career choice so their employment options following graduation could improve. Kinhart responded by improving the industrial arts offerings. Statistics for the school show a remarkable increase in the number of male graduates. Between 1930 and 1935, Annapolis High averaged 52 boys per graduating class. From 1936 to 1940 the average rose to 76. The 207 students in the Class of 1941 included 104 boys, making it the first to have more male than female graduates (30).

Despite Dr. Kinhart's best efforts, the academic reputation of Annapolis High School apparently declined during the 1930's. In the fall of 1936 Elizabeth Fuller Eppes arrived at an interview with a University of Maryland dean without her Annapolis High transcript. The dean told her that it hardly mattered since "Annapolis High isn't accredited," a reference to the process begun in 1920 when the Commission on Secondary Schools of the Middle States Association was founded. The CSS/MSA's mission was to "promote the improvement of secondary education and to secure better coordination and understanding between secondary schools and institutions of higher education." They offered accreditation to high schools whose graduates (in academic, commercial or vocational tracks) met standards set by respected educators. By the mid-1930's many mid-Atlantic regional colleges began to insist that entering students come from schools accredited by CSS/MSA (31).

Kinhart's apparent hesitation to apply for accreditation is mystifying – certainly Annapolis High had well-qualified teachers (all with college degrees) and a curriculum geared to meet the needs of its students and the community. Perhaps he worried about the fact that the Anne Arundel County school system continued to operate an 11-grade system instead of the preferred 12 so that students had to begin high school with a year's less preparation than those in most other Maryland counties. The CSS/MSA might also have been critical of the county's pay scale for teachers that still lagged behind the rest of the region. Indeed, the bad economic times actually forced a reduction in pay for the 1932-1933 school year so that a teacher with 10 year's experience was slated to earn only $1,200, what a beginning teacher had earned a decade earlier (32). Then in June 1933 the teachers' paychecks were delayed for several weeks because the state had defaulted on its required $7,000 deposit to the county's education account at Annapolis Banking and Trust. Fortunately the state finally deposited the missing funds so paychecks were issued by the end of the month (33). Despite these problems, the Annapolis High faculty remained loyal to the school throughout the Depression years. Perhaps the stability of employment helped them overlook the smaller than deserved paychecks.

By the fall of 1939, 16 public high schools in Maryland had been accredited, including five in Baltimore (BCC, Poly, Forest Park, Southern and Western) and five in Montgomery County (Bethesda-Chevy Chase, Gaithersburg, Montgomery Blair, Richard Montgomery and Sherwood). Perhaps Glen Burnie's successful evaluation in 1936 finally spurred Kinhart to begin the application process, which resulted in full accreditation being granted to Annapolis High in 1940. Every 10 years a school must seek re-accreditation, which Annapolis High has now done successfully six times – the last during the 1999-2000 school year (34).

The Second World War

No event in its first half-century had a greater impact on Annapolis High than American entry into World War Two following the Japanese attack on Pearl Harbor. Dr. Kinhart's many lectures on the meaning of democracy and the obligations of citizenship suddenly seemed prescient. The nation was at peril, and everyone in the school focused on what they could do to help the war effort. All after-school activities, including athletics, were halted. The possibility of invasion seemed very real to people living along the Atlantic coast and Chesapeake Bay. Remains of the lookout towers built on the Delaware shoreline still stand today. Annapolis High students formed rescue and firefighting squads. In the place of assemblies, first aid classes were held. Air raid drills were practiced regularly, and the school developed its own blackout plan. Students raised a remarkable $20,000 in a war bond drive; they purchased pieces of equipment – including two jeeps, a flying glider and a 35-foot rearming boat – that

World War Two Deaths of Annapolis High Graduates
(42 former Annapolis High students were killed in the war; the names listed on this page are graduates whose deaths the author has been able to confirm)

1911 TISDALE, Ryland Dillard, Cdr. Navy (USNA '15) killed May 23, 1942, during the American defense of the Philippines.
1929 SCHNEIDER, Earle C., Cdr. Navy
SHILER, Earle M. Capt. Army (USMA '38) died of pneumonia at Fukoka Japanese POW camp (Silver Star)
1934 GILMORE, Morris D., Lt. Navy (USNA '39) was killed in action 3/1/1942, when the USS *Edsall* was sunk near Java
1935 HUGG, George E., 2nd Lt. Army (St. John's '40) was killed in action 4/4/1943, at the Battle of El Guattar during the Tunisian campaign
MEADE, Rowland H. 2nd Lt. Army Air Corps, died 4/17/1945 in collision of two planes during flight training, AFB Big Springs TX
SMITH, Arthur L., CMoMM Navy
1936 BAGBY, William W., AvC Army Air Corps, died 8/28/1942, during flight training in Alabama
JONES, Morris E. 2nd Lt, Army
MARKLI, Robert G., Sgt, Army
McNALLY, Charles H. , 2nd Lt. Army Air Corps (pilot), was killed in action on 7/16/1945, on his 40th mission (awarded DFC)
1938 KING, John M., T/5 Army
1939 WINDSOR, Robert D., 2nd Lt. Army Air Corps, was killed in action 8/1/1944, while on a flight over England
1940 HALL, Donald W. , Ens. Navy (USNA '44) was killed in action 5/15/1945, aboard USS *Morrison* off Okinawa
JACKSON, Hugh M., Sgt. Army
LEMKEY, James C. H., Pvt., Army, died in France 11/28/1944
PAPPAS, Anthony G., Ens. Navy Air (pilot), died in plane crash 5/30/1945
ROBBINS, Hugh W., 1st Lt., Army Air Corps (bombardier), died 1/2/1945, engine failed over France returning from mission
1941 DAWSON, Joseph F., S/Sgt. Army Air Corps (waist gunner) was killed in action on 3/16/1945, over England
KAVANAUGH, William P., S/Sgt. Army Air Corps (gunner) was killed in action 2/9/1945, when plane shot down over Yugoslavia
KING, James V., S/Sgt. Army
SHEFF, Bernard H., Pvt. Army
1942 CUMMINGS, Bernard, Pfc., Army
LEWNES, Thomas J., 1st Lt. Army Air Corps (65 combat missions), died 1/27/1945, when his B-26 crashed in Tyndell Bay, FL.
RIDOUT, Francis E., Pfc. Army, died 1/7/1945, in Belgium
1943 TUCKER, John C., F 1/C Navy, died 5/11/1945 during kamikaze attack on USS *Evans* off Okinawa
1944 FINKLE, William Walter, S/Sgt. Army
1945 DOYLE, William H., Capt. Marine Corps
MILLHAUSEN, Francis J., Pfc. Marine Corps

were presented to representatives from the Army and Navy at a special assembly. An obstacle course was constructed to prepare the boys for future military service. A Victory Corps was formed with five branches. The boys chose among Army, Navy, Marine Corps and Aviation – with each unit conducting pre-induction courses to "train the kind of fighters the United States needs to bring them ultimate victory." Most of the girls joined the Community Service branch, which included Red Cross work as well as volunteering at the new USO building on Compromise Street. A group of Annapolis High musicians formed a band that played *gratis* at many USO dances (35).

Although Dr. Kinhart believed the academic work of the school should take top priority, he seemed to realize that allowing students to have a few clubs and social activities would help lift morale. Thus, to the general amazement of the entire student body, the Class of 1942 was permitted to publish a yearbook. They decided to let the *Crablines* name rest in peace; instead they chose another nautical moniker: "As a ship leaves its tail, may these pages recall our *Wake*," and *Wake* has stayed its name for over 60 years (36). Leafing through the first four editions of *Wake* makes clear how profoundly the war touched Annapolis High students. Most of the boys in the classes of 1942 through 1945 mention service in the armed forces as their immediate post-graduation plan. Approximately 200 male graduates from the classes of 1940 through 1944 served in the military during the war. Many waited to be drafted, but a surprising number eagerly enrolled at their first opportunity. The 1945 *Wake* includes the photographs of six seniors who had left school a semester early to enlist – perhaps fearing that if they waited until graduation the war might be over before they could see action (37).

With so many graduates in uniform, Annapolis High braced whenever death lists were released. On March 30, 1945, the Student Council held an Easter Assembly dedicated to the memory of its own war dead. A year later, on Memorial Day 1946, the school again honored the 42 former students who had died while serving their nation in the armed forces from 1941 to 1945, one-sixth of all war deaths in the county. One was Thomas J. Lewnes, the popular president of the Class of 1942, who after 65 combat missions died in a B-26 crash in January 1945. Eight other AHS alumni died in the air, including Army Air Corps pilot Charles H. McNally ('36) shot down in July 1945 while flying a mission and bombardier Hugh W. Robbins

('40) who died when his plane's engine failed after a bombing run in January 1945.

One of the first from Annapolis High to die was Army Capt. Earle M. Shiley ('29), who reportedly succumbed to pneumonia in a Japanese POW camp after the fall of the Philippines. An early battlefield death was 2nd Lt. George Hugg ('35) who was killed in action during April 1943 after the American forces landed in North Africa to fight Rommel. Others died late in the war, including Bernard Sheff and Francis Ridout who were classmates in 1942. Both were privates in the Army; both died during the Battle of the Bulge in the winter of 1944-1945. Three graduates died at sea: Lt. Morris Gilmore ('34) went down with his ship, the USS *Edsall*, in March 1942 off Java. John C. Tucker ('43), a fireman 1/C in the Navy, was killed at Okinawa during a kamikaze attack on the USS *Evans* on May 11, 1945. Four days later Ens. Donald Hall (AHS '40; USNA '44), aboard the USS *Morison*, was also killed at Okinawa. Francis J. Millhausen, voted the "most athletic" boy in the Class of 1945, rushed out to join the Marine Corps, just in time to die before V-J day (38).

* * * * * * * * * * * *

When school began in September 1945, Annapolis High celebrated victory while mourning the loss of so many precious lives. Faculty and students were proud that their sacrifices had helped the nation overcome the dual perils of the Depression and the war. Yet victory would also bring profound changes to Anne Arundel County, beginning with a population boom that would continue for more than a decade. New people brought new ideas – especially about the role of women and the injustice of segregation – that soon would force dramatic changes across Maryland, changes that would directly impact the high school in its capital city.

CHAPTER 6:

PANTHER PRIDE PROMOTES SCHOOL SPIRIT

1945 – 1958

1950 Panthers Football team fostered school spirit during their 7-2 season.

1st row: T. Shores, R. Brown, A. Jones. **2nd row**: E. Hendricks, W. Brown, R. Purdy (co-capt), D. Olson (co-capt), N. Smith, A. Calabrese **3rd row**: P. Chaney, K. Barber, P. Clark, W. Mumford, J. Beans **4th row**: J. Belch, W. Kerchner, W. Kennerly, K. Belch, P. Parkinson, W. Donald **5th row**: Coach Rentschler, T. Coble, J. Jennings, D. Como, G. Springfield, W. Hughes, Coach Wetherhold **6th row**: C. Hortopan, D. Jones, H. Sullivan, R. Moyer, J. Simmons, M. Hyatt, J. Alvanos **7th row**: D. Nichols, W. Martin, R. Lee, J. Potee.

Alla-Beeba, Alla-Biba, Alla-Beeba, Alla-Brum
Go back! Go back! Go back where you're from!
You haven't got the rhythm, you haven't got the jazz.
You haven't got the spirit, that Annapolis High has!

Annapolis High School Cheer, 1950

"Football is a rugged, virile, knock 'em down and drag 'em out sport that . . . teaches you to play clean and to the letter of the rules. It is good for you physically, mentally and morally. I can never be sold on a school 100 percent unless it goes in for football. If they don't, they make some good, first class, drug store cowboys. This is a tough old world and to learn to meet it you need something you don't get out of a book. You've got to learn how to hand it out and how to take it. Football is the best sport to teach this type of courage."

Navy Assistant Coach Rip Miller to AHS Assembly, October 1947

Post-War Population Boom

Between 1940 and 1950 the population of Anne Arundel County increased from 63,375 to 117,392 – an astonishing 170 percent rate of growth (1). According to local historian Jane Wilson McWilliams, the expansion should be attributed to the impact of the Second World War on the region. The northern part of the county was home to several major war industries that attracted thousands of workers, including many women. Glen Burnie and Brooklyn Park were two of the communities that provided affordable housing for these industrial workers. Living away from home for the first time, they dated, married and began families. So they stayed.

Further south, Annapolis served as the official homeport for thousands of Navy officers and sailors. Many struggled to find some kind of housing for their families before shipping out. Summer bungalows in waterfront communities like Bay Ridge, Arundel on the Bay, Round Bay, Severna Park, Epping Forest, Herald Harbor and Sherwood Forest were quickly – and in many cases, barely – winterized to accommodate Navy wives and children while the man of the family was off fighting the war. When the veterans returned they found these small homes along the county's scenic waterways to be both affordable and pleasant places to live. So they stayed.

The county's population boom continued unabated in the 1950's as additional people were drawn to the suburban areas that began to crop up to the east of Washington, D.C., and to the south of Baltimore. Ritchie Highway running north from the banks of the Severn to Baltimore and Defense Highway headed west to Bladensburg outside the nation's capital made commuting from Anne Arundel county easy, especially after wartime gasoline rationing was ended. Planned communities with small, affordable houses were rapidly constructed to accommodate those seeking the "good life" away from the crowded cities. So they stayed (2).

Meanwhile, the Annapolis population of 10,000 remained virtually unchanged in the 1940's. Census figures that report the capital city's growth to over 23,000 citizens by 1960 are deceptive. Almost the entire increase can be attributed to the city's January 1, 1951, annexation of neighboring communities and land in the Back Bay and College Creek watershed – including Eastport and Parole – for inclusion in the Annapolis sewer system.

The county's population boom naturally resulted in scores of new faces around the corridors of Annapolis High. Although the school had always been a part of the county education system, Annapolis residents clearly took a proprietary interest in it. Their complaints grew at the end of the Second World War when more than half the students in the increasingly crowded school lived outside the city limits. Many came from the rapidly expanding area east of the city, especially Severna Park, Arnold and Cape St. Claire, but others arrived from the south and west (Edgewater, Cape St. John, Riva, Mayo and Davidsonville) and from communities north along the Severn and Generals Highway towards Crownsville.

Contributing to the corridor congestion were eighth graders who were added to the high school in 1946 when the Maryland department of education reinstated a 12-grade classification for the state's public educational system. The $7,000,000 Anne Arundel County school bond issue that passed in 1947 was earmarked for the construction of additional classrooms to house the eighth graders and to meet projected enrollment increases at all levels. Over $330,000 was diverted to repair and modernize Annapolis Grammar following yet another fire in the school. The building's distinctive Mansard roof and the entire top floor had to be removed. The school gained a cafeteria and a new assembly room that could be used as a gymnasium. Replacing the outdoor fire escapes were new – supposedly fireproof – stairwells (3).

Crowding at the city's grammar and high schools remained a problem. Both buildings had been near capacity without the eighth grade, and new enrollment projections suggested the high school would soon be cramped with its full complement of freshmen, sophomores, juniors and seniors. This caused the board of education to take a hard look at the best way to organize students into 12 grades. The solution agreed upon was to move towards reconfiguring buildings from the traditional two types of schools (grammar and high) into three: elementary (kindergarten through sixth grades); junior high (seventh through ninth grades) and high school (10th through 12th grades). More money was needed to implement the plan so another $5,500,000 school bond issue was floated in 1949 that funded several projects, among them the construction of what would be Annapolis Junior High adjacent to Annapolis High (4).

During construction, the seventh and eighth graders from the county's central sector were gathered together in what was dubbed

Annapolis Junior High located in the old Annapolis High building on Green Street. Marjorie Layng Roxburgh ('55) was among the first students to return to the Green Street school. Her mother Marjorie Smith Layng ('22) was very excited when she learned her daughter was going to be attending class in the old high school. Mrs. Layng took Marjorie on a special tour of inspection prior to the first day of classes. Jane Wilson McWilliams, who entered seventh grade the next year, recalls some space in the building was retained for the board of education offices, so additional classrooms were carved out of the ground floor in the former USO building (today's Annapolis Recreation Center) located behind the school on Compromise Street. McWilliams and her classmates entered Annapolis High in the fall of 1952, the last group of ninth graders to be a part of the school until junior highs were phased out in favor of middle schools for sixth through eighth graders in 1989. Annapolis Junior High opened in its new home on Chase Avenue in the fall of 1953 with a full complement of seventh, eighth and ninth graders, reducing its next door neighbor, Annapolis High, to just three school years – sophomores, juniors and seniors (5).

Shuffling Principals and Teachers

In the midst of the turmoil involved in these building projects came major changes in the school system's administration. In 1946 Superintendent George Fox retired after 30 years in office. Replacing him was David S. Jenkins, who in his 22-year term would oversee the addition of four more high schools to the county system (Brooklyn Park, which began as a junior/senior high school in 1953; Severna Park, 1958; Andover, 1961; and Northeast, 1965) and the slow integration of the entire system. Howard A. Kinhart's tenure as Annapolis High's principal ended in 1949 when he accepted appointment as the county's assistant superintendent for secondary education. Students, parents and faculty lamented the departure of the man whose name had been synonymous with Annapolis High for 21 years. During his tenure, Kinhart had shaped the school to meet his high academic standards. Clearly he left his mark on a generation of students, who continue to this day to remember their principal fondly Carolyn Banks ('49) recalls him as a "true educator," while Blanche Taylor ('38) says he had such a remarkable memory that he could greet his former students by name until his death in January 1946. The

Albert W. Fowble (left) became Annapolis High's 10th principal in 1949, but a year later began a leave of absence when his reserve Army unit was activated during the Korean conflict. The school's assistant principal, Ernest H. Herklotz (center), served as acting principal until Fowble returned in September 1952. Norwood S. "Woody" Wetherhold (right, was named acting assistant principal while continuing to coach football during Fowble's absence.

Veteran teachers (from left to right) Mary Louise Hicks (history), Lorene Marking (foreign languages) and Elizabeth Davis (English) were still teaching 30 years after they had joined the Annapolis High faculty in the 1920's. (Compare these photos to their 1928 Crablines photos on page 80.)

Among the other teachers who had been at the school for two decades or more were (from left to right) Mildred Kinhart (foreign languages) and English teachers Katharine Cox and Katharine Kibler.

students' affection for Kinhart is reflected in a large bronze plaque the Class of 1936 purchased to honor him that still hangs inside the main entrance of the Maryland Hall building.

Promoted to take Kinhart's place was vice principal Albert W. Fowble, a native of Fowblesburg, Maryland, a post stop along the Western Maryland Railroad in the northwestern corner of Baltimore County. Fowble earned a bachelor's degree from Johns Hopkins in electrical engineering and a master's degree from Cornell University. He taught at Sparks High School before joining the Annapolis High faculty in 1937 as a science teacher. During the Second World War Fowble attended officer's candidate school and then served in an Army research and development unit at the Pentagon. He remained in the Army Reserves when he resumed teaching at Annapolis High after the war. Soon he was promoted to assistant principal, which made him the logical choice to become the school's 10th principal when Kinhart resigned (6).

Fowble had just finished his first year at the school's helm when his reserve unit was called to active duty in September 1950 and shipped to Korea. For the next two years, Capt. Fowble was assigned to the Military Advisory Group in Pusan where he supervised Korean military schools. The job gave him the opportunity to travel throughout South Korea inspecting educational facilities, meeting with faculty and writing reports on how to improve teaching and learning (7). Because federal law protected the jobs of activated reservists, Fowble did not have to resign as principal while in Korea. Appointed acting principal in his absence was assistant principal Ernest H. Herklotz, an industrial arts teacher who had joined the school's faculty in 1943 after completing a Bachelor of Science degree at California State Teacher's College in Pennsylvania.

The sudden shuffle of principals naturally caused some turmoil, but a handful of experienced teachers long familiar with the school's daily routine helped minimize the disruption. Three women who had been teaching at Annapolis High since Louise Linthicum's regime had the most seniority: Lorene Marking (foreign languages), Elizabeth Davis (English) and Mary Louise Hicks (history). Hicks was valedictorian of the Annapolis High Class of 1917. She and her classmate Davis attended Goucher College (Hicks graduating in 1921, Davis in 1923), were colleagues for the next four decades at their *alma mater* and eventually retired together in 1965. Fred Stauffer remembers when he first reported to Annapolis High in the fall of

1963 to teach math that both women were popular, friendly and respected teachers. The 1965 *Wake* was dedicated to this pair whose lives had been entwined with Annapolis High School since 1913 (8).

Six other teachers at the time of the Kinhart to Fowble to Herklotz transition had been at the school more than two decades. Heading this list was Kinhart's wife, Mildred, the near unanimous nominee of mid-20th century alumni when asked who had been the most difficult teacher during their Annapolis High years. The mention of her name can still cause her former French students to quake and cower. To be fair, Mrs. Kinhart also had two *Wake* yearbooks dedicated to her during her long tenure at the school, an indication that among the hardworking journalism students her expertise and high standards were appreciated. Two other women whose arrival at Annapolis High dated to when the school opened at the Spa View site in 1933 were English teachers Katharine Cox, a graduate of Columbia University, and Washington College alumna Katharine Kibler, both of whom wrote short histories of Annapolis High and Anne Arundel County education found in the bibliography.

That all of the most senior faculty members were female is hardly surprising given that prior to the Depression very few men held career aspirations to be teachers. The difficult economic times in the 1930's made education more attractive to anyone, regardless of gender, seeking a secure profession. By 1941 the number of male teachers at Annapolis High had grown from two or three in the 1920's to 11 – one-third of the school's faculty of 33 – but that percentage quickly shrank during World War II when so many men were called to military service. Other male teachers left to take more lucrative jobs in industry. By 1944 only five of the 40 teachers on the payroll were men – four industrial arts teachers and an elderly math instructor, George Norris. Only three of the men on the 1941 faculty who went into the armed forces returned after the war to their teaching posts: Fowble, math teacher and soccer coach Calvin Rogers and Morris Rannels, who taught science classes (9).

The difficulty Kinhart faced hiring faculty – even female teachers – continued into the immediate post-war years. Throughout this period the Annapolis High faculty averaged 38 billets (the exception was between 1946 and 1948 when the addition of eighth graders swelled the faculty size above 45). Kinhart actually hired 77 teachers in the six-year period (1942-1948) – an average of 11 new faculty members a year. Over half (40 of 77) remained at Annapolis only one year and another 16 left within two years. Only six of the teachers hired during these years were still on the faculty in 1950. Kinhart believed the main difficulty keeping faculty more than a year or two was lack of affordable housing. He told the Baltimore *Sun* that the population boom had created a critical shortage of suitable housing in the Annapolis area for anyone trying to live on a beginning teacher's salary. Given the conditions, he claimed it was virtually impossible to attract and retain good, young teachers (10).

During the 1950's the yearly teacher turnover slowed, helped in part by the decrease in the number of faculty members at the high school from 45 to 31 when ninth graders started attending the junior high in 1953. As the baby boomers began arriving at Annapolis High during the early 1960's, Fowble could gradually grow the faculty by adding new teachers while holding on to more of the veterans. Sixty percent of the 1953 faculty was still teaching at Annapolis High in 1961. Housing, however, continued to be a major problem, in part because of an Anne Arundel County law that prohibited construction of apartment complexes. When Fred Stauffer and his wife Colleen, a newly hired teacher at Corkran Junior High, tried to find a place to live in 1963, they were forced to take space in a "tourist home" on Ritchie Highway until they located a small house in Linthicum to rent.

An Era of Academic Excellence

The two principals in charge of Annapolis High for nearly four decades, Louise Linthicum and Howard Kinhart, had devoted much of their attention to the school's curriculum. Fowble and Herklotz continued the stress on improving academic programs, in part by streamlining the various courses into two major tracks – academic and general – while shrinking the commercial program to just one major in stenography. The 233 graduates in the Class of 1958 included 98 who earned academic diplomas, 121 who were awarded general diplomas and 14 who completed the stenography program.

This breakdown reveals much about the aspirations of students in the "silent 50's." Most who completed the academic program enrolled in college. The Class of 1950 had 146 graduates. Of these, 37 percent went to college, most of which were within the state. The most popular choices were the University of Maryland, Frostburg and Towson Teachers' Colleges, Washington College and Western Maryland. Every year three or four boys sought entry to the Naval

Academy. Over the years the number selecting St. John's College declined steadily, perhaps because parents brought up during the Depression did not consider its rigorous Great Books curriculum to be preparing their children for a wage-earning vocation.

As the decade progressed, the percentage of seniors choosing to continue their education at the higher level increased, with many more applying to and selecting colleges outside Maryland. By 1961, 53 percent of the seniors had college plans, including 33 headed to destinations across the nation, from the Universities of Alabama, North Carolina, West Virginia, Iowa and Florida to Cal State, Ohio State and Rhode Island School of Design; from Amherst, Dickinson and New England College to MIT, NYU and BYU; from Mary Washington, George Washington, Emory and Drake to Cal Tech, Case Tech and Virginia Tech; from Florida Southern and Eastern Carolina to Portland and Pittsburgh.

Some credit for expanding the horizons of the Annapolis High students goes to the increased emphasis put on staffing the guidance department with professionals who had earned graduate degrees in counseling. Much credit for the students' increased interest in the world outside Maryland belonged to their teachers. Of the 48 men and women on the faculty and staff in 1961, two-thirds – 32 – held undergraduate degrees from colleges and universities outside Maryland. Two-thirds of the 33 in the core academic subjects also had graduate degrees from universities scattered throughout the nation. That Annapolis High teachers came from diverse backgrounds reflects well on the principals who hired them. Their presence in the classrooms surely served as a daily example to students of how wide the world outside their front doors truly was. Alumni from this era universally speak with respect and fondness of these teachers. Dick Purdy ('58) summed up what seems to be the consensus: "Our teachers were no-nonsense professionals who expected us to behave and encouraged us to learn. We liked and respected them and, for the most part, we behaved pretty well for them."

Several indicators point to the high caliber of an Annapolis High education in this period. Twice – in 1950 and 1960 – the school was reaccredited through the Council of Secondary Schools of the Middle States Association. Sandwiched between the CSS visitations was perhaps the most prestigious honor in the school's history. In October 1953 Annapolis High received the 12th annual Francis Bellamy Award. Named for the author of the Pledge of Allegiance, this national prize was bestowed annually on one high school in the country that had demonstrated exemplary patriotism and adherence to democratic ideals. Annapolis High's curriculum had been infused with such values since World War One, and its graduates' record of service and sacrifice in the armed forces during every war of the 20th century was widely known. The school's location in the city that was home to the Naval Academy was another factor contributing to its selection. Schools recognized in previous years were in Virginia, Indiana, Ohio, Pennsylvania, Florida, Nebraska, New York, Louisiana, California, Washington, Maine and Washington, D.C..

    Two ceremonies were held at the school to commemorate the honor. The first took place on Columbus Day 1953 to confer the award formally. The many dignitaries on hand listened to Bellamy's son read a citation praising the school's "excellent philosophy of secondary education and the success of its alumni in government, arts, sciences engineering, business, the professions and civic leadership." Offering personal congratulations were Gov. Theodore McKeldin, several legislators from the district, the State Supervisor of Schools (none other than the man who had coached Annapolis High football in the 1920's, Willis H. White) and alumni from the first graduating classes (including former football great John C. Strohm, who at the Class of 1900's commencement had spoken so eloquently about the need for physical fitness). Congratulatory letters arrived from President Dwight D. Eisenhower, 11 governors, 20 U.S. Senators, 50 high school principals, the Air Force Chief of Staff and even Walt Disney – who wrote that he had followed the Bellamy Award with interest since his *alma mater,* McKinley High in Chicago, had won it in 1946. Everyone then left the auditorium to encircle the pole outside the school's main entrance as the new American flag that was a gift to the school was raised. In its October 12, 1953, editorial, the *Evening Capital* summed up the feelings of local pride that day: "*It is a tribute to the Annapolis High School that . . . busy officials representing states stretching from the Pacific to the Atlantic and from the Canadian border to the Gulf of Mexico should join in complimenting the school for its achievement. We are certain the people of Annapolis and of all Anne Arundel County join with these dignitaries in commending the school for winning such wide-spread recognition by carrying out its mission so splendidly.*"

    Another less elaborate ceremony was held a year later, again on Columbus Day. The Daughters of the American Republic donated

Girls had many activities to choose from in the years after World War Two. Fieldball (right) was the most successful girls' sport. The 1947 team (above) won county and district championships. Some female athletes proudly pose (below) in their letter sweaters adorned with the school emblem and their class badges. Other girls enjoyed being majorettes with the band and leading cheers at sporting events.

small American flags to hang in each of the school's classrooms. A large bronze plaque in recognition of the Bellamy Award was mounted inside the school's main entrance. Today the plaque is on the wall in the foyer of the "new" building on Riva Road, a reminder that a half-century ago Annapolis High earned recognition as one of the best public high schools in the entire nation (11).

Two other indications of the regard in which Annapolis High was held nationally deserve mention. A *Reader's Digest* program named a monthly "honor school," a designation granted to Annapolis High in April 1957. For this issue of the magazine a panel of Panther students reviewed a group of articles submitted for publication. Also in 1957 the U.S. Department of State selected Annapolis High and Parsi High in Karachi, Pakistan, to take part in an experimental program designed to foster better international understanding. Annapolis sent copies of *Talley Ho* to Pakistan and in 1958 the Parsi principal personally visited Annapolis High (12).

Football Returns to Annapolis High

During the fall of 1945 a slow but steady return to normalcy occurred as student activities that had been curtailed during the war were reestablished. Soon clubs and student activities were meeting after school. The Student Council organized a legislature that had one elected representative from each home room. A Student Court was formed to deliberate the cases brought to them from the Traffic Squad, which continued to roam the hallways and cafeteria to enforce school rules against skipping steps, shouting, cutting in the food line and smoking in the lavatories. The school orchestra and glee club planned recitals. A three-year campaign raised enough funds to outfit the band and majorettes in handsome uniforms. Student journalists devoted an incredible effort to publishing *Tally Ho* and *Wake*. Soon the school was awarded a chapter of Quill and Scroll, the national journalism honor society. The Social Committee again swung into action, planning dances and other school parties. Members of the National Honor Society, founded in June 1944 to promote scholarship, were required to be actively involved in community service projects. A student-produced radio program on local station WANN aired once a week for 30 minutes.

Tally-Ho on November 7, 1947, announced a bi-weekly activity period had been inserted in the school day to give students a selection of 32 hobbies, including knitting, mechanical drawing, needle craft, photography, boys' cooking, book club, boys' gymnastics, archery, typing, Spanish, radio club and sewing. The Boys' Hi-Y and the YWCA's Girl Reserves brought Christian-based character building activities to the school. An Allied Youth Club that adhered to a nation-wide call for students to abstain from alcohol was formed. Future Homemakers, Future Teachers and Future Nurses were clubs that reflect the most popular post-graduation aspirations of many Annapolis High girls, while the mostly male Pre-Med and Pre-Law Clubs mirror the era's attitude that encouraged boys to seek careers as doctors and lawyers.

Reminders of the recent war and hard economic times could still be seen around the school. Some veterans returned to complete requirements for diplomas, helped by a county school board decision in May 1946 to allow them to proceed at their own pace, taking just one or two courses at a time if their jobs interfered with classes. Expenses were covered through the G.I. Bill that according to the May 11, 1946, *Evening Capital* would provide $15.28 monthly towards every veteran's costs of education. Meanwhile another federal program drew the attention of the entire school. *Tally-Ho* of October 17, 1946, lauded the National School Lunch Act that ensured low-cost, wholesome meals would be available to everyone. The two cents contributed by the government reduced the cost of milk to seven cents; and the price of a hot meal dropped from 34 to 25 cents. The meals also improved when a full-time nutritionist was added to the staff in 1947.

As the calendar turned from 1949 to 1950, events taking place on the international stage again penetrated Annapolis High's walls. The Korean conflict took away not only the school's principal, but also scores of students. Because boys could be drafted when they turned 18 even if they were still in school, Annapolis High began an accelerated program in the fall of 1950 so six boys could "step up" from their junior to senior year in order to graduate before becoming draft eligible. Soon the local chapter of the Civil Defense was holding assemblies at the school to show students how to survive an atomic bomb. Their motto was, "Don't be Afraid, be Prepared." Although not yet in high school, both Jane McWilliams and Dick Purdy remember air raid drills at Germantown Elementary School during the fighting in Korea. The communist threat continued even after the hostilities ceased. Joe McCarthy whipped the nation into frenzy over his accusations of "Reds" in the State Department, and America began sending advisors to help save Vietnam from communist insurgents.

Although Annapolis High students could not avoid hearing about these threats to the American way of life, most felt safe within the school's cocoon where they could focus energies on their daily routine. Many boys wanted nothing more than a cool car to impress their friends or to get a special girl's attention. According to Dick Purdy, some guys liked to spend the brief lunch period at Chris' Pool Room at the corner of West Street and Amos Garrett, where they could shoot a game while eating "the best hot dogs in town." Girls were more likely to stay at school, although some ventured out to the lunch counter at West and Monticello (where Reuben's is located today). Huntley Cross recalls that when he arrived at the school in the mid-1960's, faculty favored Jim's Corner for breakfast or lunch. After-school clubs and sports were popular with many students, but Purdy recalls that the "country" kids – those who lived outside Annapolis – were hard pressed to participate unless they had a transportation alternative to the school buses that left 15 minutes after the final bell. Some kids popped by Mrs. Brown's candy shop on Spa Road before heading home.

Athletic teams also began to practice for the resumption of interscholastic competition for boys in soccer, basketball and baseball, and for girls in fieldball, basketball and volleyball. To mark the return of interscholastic competition, the Student Council decided the school should have an official mascot. The student body picked an animal known for its quickness, ferocity and agility – the panther. They also voted to select official school colors. In recognition of the long association of Annapolis High with various shades of red and blue, the students officially selected maroon and royal blue with white trimming as the colors for uniforms. A cheerleading squad was formed that urged the Panthers on to victory. Accomplished athletes earned coveted school letters and emblems that they proudly wore on school sweaters to meetings of the Varsity Club.

One sport was still conspicuously missing from the Panthers' athletic lineup – football. Several tentative efforts to revive the game began during World War Two. A group of boys organized an intramural touch football league that, according to the 1944 *Wake,* was "the major factor of the school's sports program." Andrew Hewlett, hired to teach physical education after the war's end, volunteered to supervise boys who wanted to practice football drills in the afternoons. Soon Hewlett had them organized in weight categories to scrimmage. These indicators of interest in football served as justification to launch a well-organized campaign to reinstate the game. Leading the effort was the Annapolis Athletic Association (AAA), an organization founded by World War Two veterans in the spring of 1946. Originally an adult lacrosse club, the AAA expanded to support the expansion of all recreational athletics in the city. Soon an AAA adult football team was playing a full slate of games against other clubs throughout the mid-Atlantic region. The AAA also sponsored a series of clinics for boys ages 10 to 15 interested in learning to play football. The next logical step was for the AAA to push for the rebirth of football at Annapolis High (13).

As the fall of 1946 progressed, the AAA joined forces with the Recreation Committee of the school's PTA to host a series of evening meetings at which speakers respected in both academic and athletic circles promoted the game's value. One of the most influential was the University of Maryland President, Dr. H. C. Byrd. On November 12, 1946, he expressed his opinion that the absence of football reflected poorly on everyone in the audience. *"When a school the size of Annapolis High is without football, you're virtually admitting you have less school spirit than other smaller schools."* Nationally syndicated sports broadcaster Bailey Gross hit on the same theme when he spoke to the students, faculty and administrators two months later. *"You at Annapolis High have 1,000 students but don't have a football team. There are schools with less than 400 students who have teams traveling all over the country. Well, I say it's about time you get a team, too."* (14)

Such criticism must have made Kinhart bristle. One of his justifications for dropping the sport after the 1929 season was that only two other Maryland public high schools outside Baltimore had teams. Obviously now, with a dozen or more Maryland public high schools playing football, he could no longer claim a lack of competition as an excuse for not having a team. He was also better able to hear the voices of football's advocates because he no longer had the Public Athletic League whispering in his ear. PAL had folded shortly before the end of the war. Its opposition to contact sports in general, and football in particular, played an active role in Annapolis High's abandonment of football twice (in 1915 and 1929). The new organization overseeing interscholastic sports for public high schools (outside of Baltimore) was the Maryland Public Secondary School

Athletic Association (MPSSAA). That the renaissance of high school football coincided with the 1946 founding of MPSSAA was no accident. Although MPSSAA was not an active supporter of the pigskin game, its officials certainly did not speak against it as PAL once had (15).

Another attraction to football was the belief it would foster Annapolis High spirit. Kinhart had long believed that developing students' loyalty to school was an important stepping-stone to building good citizens. Blustery Cold War rhetoric lauding the democratic values of the game was reminiscent of Teddy Roosevelt at the turn of the century. The Naval Academy's assistant football coach Rip Miller launched into a locker-room style pep talk at a school assembly. *"Football is a rugged, virile, knock 'em down and drag 'em out sport that . . . teaches you to play clean and to the letter of the rules. It is good for you physically, mentally and morally. I can never be sold on a school 100 percent unless it goes in for football. If they don't, they make some good, first class, drug store cowboys. This is a tough old world and to learn to meet it you need something you don't get out of a book. You've got to learn how to hand it out and how to take it. Football is the best sport to teach this type of courage."* (16)

While such fighting words may have persuaded Kinhart that his refusal to resume football would make his beloved school look timid, what really caught his attention was another argument Rip Miller made that day. Football, Kinhart learned, could generate enough revenue through ticket sales to fund the school's entire athletic program. Superintendent David Jenkins and the county school board also were won over to the resumption of the game when Kinhart explained, "Football is the only sport that will pay for the others."

Thus Kinhart, the man responsible for ending football 17 years earlier, stood before a special assembly on Monday morning, October 27, 1947, to tell the cheering student body, "Annapolis High School is embarking on an enlarged sports program, including football." Equipment was scheduled to arrive within the week. If all went according to plans, an exhibition game would be played against an alumni team after Thanksgiving, and in the fall of 1948 football would become a varsity interscholastic team again. The assembly closed with the cheerleaders leading the students in several rousing chants and the singing of the alma mater. Kinhart could not have asked for a more solid display of school spirit.

Until a full coaching staff could be put in place, the AAA's Leo Hantske, who as a boy had played on the last Annapolis High football team in 1929, directed the practices. Physical education teacher Bruce Rentschler, a recent graduate of Penn State who had been hired to replace the departed Hewlett, was soon named permanent head coach. The school formed its own AAA chapter, with fees ranging from a dollar for one year to $25 for a lifetime membership. At a pep rally in front of the city's public library, where a thermometer had been erected to chart the AAA's fundraising efforts, Coach Rentschler announced that the 30 boys who had been working hard all fall to master the intricacies of blocking and tackling had earned the right to play a game against a group of alumni on December 6, 1947. In front of several hundred shivering fans, the high schoolers held their own in a 12-6 loss to the older, more experienced alums, many of whom played for the AAA semi-pro team. All on hand that day agreed the team's performance boded well for the future success of Annapolis High football (17).

Plans for the first full season were in the hands of Ernest Herklotz, the school's assistant principal and athletic director, who was responsible for arranging team schedules. In those days, the home team kept all of the gate receipts, so generally another school would agree to a game at Annapolis High only if the Panthers promised to return the favor the following year. Herklotz contracted games with four high schools for 1948 and 1949 – Cambridge, Havre de Grace, Westminster and Elkton. A four-year series was set with the Dover (Delaware) High School Senators. Rentschler continued as the 1948 team's head coach, with yet another new physical education teacher – Norwood "Woody" Wetherhold – as his top assistant. Wetherhold was an Allentown, Pennsylvania, native who had graduated from East Stroudsburg Teacher's College in 1937. He served with the Navy in the South Pacific during World War Two as part of boxer Gene Tunney's physical fitness program and returned to Pennsylvania before joining the Annapolis faculty in 1948.

The two coaches had their work cut out for them. Only 11 of the 27 players on the roster had practiced with the team the previous year. The Panthers' first true football game since 1929 was played in Cambridge, Maryland, the first Saturday in October, 1948. With no Chesapeake Bay Bridge in those days, the team had to take a ferry to the eastern shore. On the very first play of the game, Wetherhold was standing on the Annapolis sideline when he heard an "awful sound come all the way across the field." An Annapolis player had broken his leg. The game was halted as the boy was tended to and then "hustled back to Annapolis on the ferry." Despite this inauspicious start to the game, the Panthers managed to salvage a 6 to 6 tie. The following week Annapolis hosted Dover in its first home game of the year, which ended in a narrow 7-0 loss. Rentschler's boys finished with a 2–1–2 season record, defeating Havre de Grace and Elkton (18).

In those days, high school physical education teachers coached without any stipend. Although most probably relished the opportunity to coach, those with families had difficulty managing the demands of more than one team. Rentschler decided to take the vacant baseball coaching position in the spring of 1949, so he turned the football team over to Wetherhold, who promptly expanded the schedule from five to nine games with the addition of contests against Wicomico, Frederick, Sherwood and Bethesda. The home opener of the 1949 season was supposed to be a night game. Wetherhold arranged to rent equipment from a man in Chester, Pennsylvania. The steady rain during the day caused a delay in getting the lights set up and working. They finally came on for about 10 minutes, during which time the visiting Frederick High team scored a touchdown. When the lights again failed, the game was called and the fans were refunded their money. Wetherhold still feels embarrassed about the evening's debacle: "We lost the game and lots of money on that fiasco," he admits.

Although the 1949 Panthers were defeated in six of their nine games, the local press put a positive spin on the team's progress. The most significant game was actually a season ending loss to undefeated Wicomico High, favored to thrash the Panthers by 50 points. The score was close the entire game. Trailing 12-6 in the final seconds, Wetherhold put in a tackle eligible to catch a pass. The trick play unfolded perfectly with George "Breakaway" Springfield sprinting down the field past the surprised Wi-Hi defenders, but quarterback Paul Clark threw the ball just inches beyond the outstretched hands of the wide-open receiver. The Panthers declared the game a "moral victory" and left the field feeling optimistic about their future prospects. Even the 1950 *Wake* predicted next fall's team would be well worth the price of admission.

The high expectations for the 1950 team centered on a core of four-year veterans who had been teammates since freshman year. Co-captains Bob Purdy and Dan Olson led the senior class that included

Stars of Wetherhold's '51 team included "Mule" Jennings (10), "Big Bill" Kennerly (24), "Big Jawn" Simmons (18), "Pip" Moyer (28) and "Dimples" Kerchner (34).

One of its two losses was by one point to the Dover (DE) team (below) with Gene Zartman (#25) George Manlove (#43), Fred Frear (#39) and Jack Richter (#47). Dover also was the opponent at the Panthers' 1st home game (10/9/1948). Fans in the center section donated money the previous year to buy equipment and help prepare the field for varsity games.

guard Herb Sullivan, 200-pound tackle Melvin "Mose" Hyatt, leading scorer Charlie Hortopan and end "Breakaway" Springfield. The team also had a bevy of talented juniors: quarterback Jack "Mule" Jennings, fullback "Big Jawn" Simmons, center Roger "Pip" Moyer, and a matched pair of linemen, "Big Bill" Kennerly and Bill "Dimples" Kerchner. The Panthers crafted a superb 7–2 record, outscoring their opponents 173 to 59. The victory Wetherhold relishes most came in the 1950 season finale against Wicomico. Apparently Charlie Berry, the Wi-Hi coach, "didn't like losing," so defeating the Indians in a hard-fought 6-0 game was especially sweet revenge for Wetherhold and the Panthers after the previous season's narrow loss.

Annapolis High played its home games on the unlighted grass field next to the school on Saturday afternoons. Generally the visiting school was close enough to travel roundtrip by bus on game day. Overnight trips were rare, but Dover High Coach Evan Koons decided to bring his team from Delaware on the Friday before the game to avoid the long Saturday morning lines at the Chesapeake Bay ferry. Gene Zartman played in three games for Dover against the Panthers in these early years. With some help from teammates Jack Richter, George Manlove and Fred Frear, Zartman penned a revealing recollection of the Senators' overnight road trip to Annapolis:

"The 1950 Annapolis game was the one and only overnight trip for Dover High School during the three years I played. We arrived in Annapolis during the early afternoon of the day before the game. We stayed at the Annapolis Country Club. After checking in, we held a practice at one of the Naval Academy fields. We had dinner the night before the game and breakfast early on the morning of the game at the country club. We were assigned bunks on a lower level of the building. There was a large shower room next to the sleeping area, and when we woke up on game day morning someone decided it would be a good idea to take a hot shower. Soon, everyone else decided to jump in. When Coach Koons got word of what was going on, he charged down and made us turn off the water, telling us that hot showers would sap our strength. As it turned out, not even a cold shower would have helped us. The Annapolis team was physically much bigger than Dover. We were not as strong or quick as we needed to be on that day. Annapolis easily won, 31-7." (19)

The 1951 Panther team also produced a 7-2 record, scoring 205 points and giving up only 99. They opened with a 21-6 victory over Frederick, but the following Saturday they tasted defeat at Dover

High's new lighted stadium that featured a cinder track around a well-kept grass field and stands from the town's former minor league baseball park. Gene Zartman reports the Senators were "*out for revenge, still smarting from their only setback of the previous year. Once again the Annapolis team was physically bigger than Dover, but we were able to handle it better this time. Dover won 20-19 in what surely was an exciting game to watch.*" Annapolis had taken a six-point lead on a touchdown to start the fourth quarter, but "Mule" Jennings missed the extra point. Trailing 19-13, Dover drove the ball the length of the field to score a touchdown, then ran the ball across the goal line for the extra point to give Dover a one point lead. Annapolis tried several long passes that fell incomplete during the waning seconds of the game (20). The bus and ferry ride home must have been a long one for the Annapolis players.

The team then rolled off victories over Suitland, Bethesda, Elkton, Northwestern and Cambridge before suffering its second loss, also by the margin of a missed extra point. Before the start of the season, Wetherhold had reluctantly agreed to schedule Woodward Preparatory School. Public schools in the state used the National Football Federation rules, but the Maryland Scholastic Association schools, including Woodward Prep, played according to the college rulebook. The week before the game the Woodward coach called to ask Wetherhold to "take it easy" on his team. Graciously Wetherhold agreed to use the college rules, not realizing the switch would allow Woodward Prep to insert a 21-year-old quarterback into the lineup who would have been ineligible under federation rules. After a narrow 21-20 loss, the furious Wetherhold vowed "never to play a private school again."

The final game of the 1951 season was a Thanksgiving Day clash with Southern High School. The game marked the first time two Anne Arundel County public high schools played each other. The Bulldogs had already lost all three of its games in their inaugural season, and the Panthers easily defeated them 39-0. But Southern would improve quickly, losing just 6-0 in 1952 and defeating the Panthers 6-2 in 1953. Although Annapolis would come to dominate the series by the end of the 1950's, the two schools continue as fierce rivals regardless of the sport being played. St. Mary's, another local school that would assume rival status in several sports, was added to the schedule in 1953, and although the Panthers would also gain decided gridiron superiority over the Saints, their season-ending game was a Thanksgiving Day treat for local sports fans from 1958 to 1962.

Another landmark in the rebirth of Annapolis High football occurred during Wetherhold's tenure as head coach and came courtesy of the Annapolis Athletic Association. In 1949 the AAA began negotiations with the city to lease the old garbage dump behind the new incinerator site on Spa Road so they could convert it into an athletic field. After securing the lease, association members devoted four years to transforming the pit into a football field, a task that proved far from easy. Wetherhold recalls seeing "the custodian back there in the old junk yard shooting rats." After the land had been reclaimed from the vermin, it needed to be graded, seeded and tended. Tireless fund raising netted enough money to purchase lights, erect bleachers and build a clubhouse on Spa Road with locker rooms and showers. The first games were played on what was known as the "Athletic Association Field" in 1953. Besides Sunday afternoon AAA games, Annapolis High and St. Mary's games were played at the field. This allowed Annapolis High to mark off separate practice fields and an oval dirt track on the land adjacent to the school, giving all the school's teams more space for practices. Friday night high school football games now became a fixture in Annapolis.

On October 14, 1954, the AAA field was christened the Weems-Whelan Memorial Field to honor two AAA members who had died in service to the country. George F. Weems, brigade commander and Eastern Intercollegiate wrestling champion in the Naval Academy's Class of 1941, died while testing a Navy seaplane off the Delaware coast in 1951. Joseph F. Whelan, a 1942 Annapolis High graduate, served in the Marine Corps during World War Two and then joined the Air Force in October 1947; less than a year later he died when his transport plane was lost in the Pacific. Annapolis would play its football games at Weems-Whelan Memorial Field until the mid-1960's when land immediately behind the school was converted into Panther Stadium. St. Mary's continues to play many of their home games at Weems-Whelan today (21).

Wetherhold relinquished his coaching duties when he was named permanent assistant principal and athletic director in 1957. His football record was an honorable 34-36-5. Although three of his teams (1952, 1953 and 1955) had miserable seasons, winning a combined total of only four games, 1954 (6-3-1) and 1956 (6-3) provided Panthers' fans with many reasons to cheer. When asked which team was his best, Wetherhold replied that both the 1950 and 1951 teams were so terrific that to chose one over the other would be impossible. He was less reticent when talking about his best players. He considers "Mule" Jennings to have been the best all-around athlete at the school, starring in football, basketball and baseball. Jennings went to Washington College where he took up a new sport, lacrosse, and became an all-American player. Wetherhold cannot recall any of his players being on college teams, in part because the University of Maryland focused recruiting in Pennsylvania and had little interest in Annapolis players. Two – all-state tackle Bill Kennerly ('51) and fullback Ronald Jordan ('53) – were awarded scholarships to College Park, but neither played on the varsity.

* * * * * * * * * * * * *

The resumption of football after World War Two certainly helped boost Annapolis High School spirit. Much of the credit for the successful rebirth of the sport should go to Coach Woody Wetherhold and the boys who put in the hard work necessary to field a creditable team. Wetherhold was a no-nonsense coach, cut in the mold of the era. Dick Purdy, who admits to pulling some pranks during his years at Annapolis High, says everyone respected Wetherhold for being fair and impartial in handing out punishment, traits he would have to rely on during his years as vice principal during Annapolis High's transition to a multi-ethnic, diverse high school in the 1960's.

CHAPTER 7:
SAME NEIGHBORHOOD, DIFFERENT WORLDS, 1959 - 1970

The 1962 Annapolis High Panthers had a perfect 10 – 0 season

1st row: T. Nylund, J. Robertshaw, J. Hanna, J.B. Taylor, J. Russell, D. Macey, B. Gardner, W. Nemith, A. Frieman; **2nd row**: T. McWilliams, H. Langluttig, T. Parlett, D. Dickson, A. Smith, M. Rankin, K. Hunzeker, B. King, A. Pastrana; **3rd row**: A. Brewer, B. Nicewarner, S. McDonald, R. Baskett, H.R. Grau, W. Williams, D. Hendrick, B. Moeller, T. Rayhart. Coaches M. Ballas and N. Leonard are in back.

"We conclude that in the field of public education the doctrine of 'separate but equal' has no place. Separate educational facilities are inherently unequal. Therefore, we hold that the plaintiffs and others similarly situated for whom the actions have been brought are, by reason of the segregation complained of, deprived of the equal protection of the laws guaranteed by the Fourteenth Amendment. . . . We have now announced that such segregation is a denial of the equal protection of the laws."

Earl Warren, Chief Justice
U.S. Supreme Court
Brown et. al. v the Board of Education of Topeka, Kansas
May 17, 1954

The Other School in the Neighborhood

Dick Purdy ('58) and Jane Wilson McWilliams ('56) agree that every student at Annapolis High tried to make the Friday night football games in the fall and basketball games in the winter. Neither could recall a hangout where everyone congregated afterwards, although the Dutch Mill up on route 50 was a popular drive-in restaurant. They also agree that one place Annapolis High students knew little about, and with one exception seem never to have ventured even though it was less than a half-mile away, was Wiley H. Bates High School.

The original 1932 Bates building of only eight rooms had been enlarged several times to accommodate the ever-increasing number of "colored" students coming to the county's only high school that welcomed them. The board of education's decision in the late 1930's to provide free busing to Bates served as the principal catalyst to the school's expansion. In 1939 the old Germantown School on West Street was moved to the Bates site to help accommodate its one thousand students (1). The enrollment continued to grow so that after World War Two, over 1,500 students were crammed in the Bates classrooms. The school board had to decide whether to build another "colored" high school or to expand Bates. They settled on the latter course, ostensibly because the Negro population was so scattered throughout the county that no clear site for a second school could be determined. The decision resulted in extremely long bus rides for Bates students living in the far reaches of the county. Bates graduate Larry Brogden ('61) recalls being on the bus from his Dorsey neighborhood in the northwestern corner of the county to Bates for more than an hour each morning, an easy commute compared to the hitching and walking he had to do after football or baseball practice to get back home, sometimes not arriving until 11 p.m.

The decision to put all the county's money for colored secondary education into just one school resulted in Bates being transformed into the largest, most modern high school in the county: 45 classrooms; a 700-seat cafeteria; a 399-seat theater (the only such facility in the school system); a fully-equipped gymnasium; a home economics department outfitted for cooking, sewing, cosmetology and other homemaking skills; a 30-station language laboratory; a modern library; and a large vocational education wing with specific shop areas for auto mechanics, sheet metal work, building construction, mechanical drawing and other assorted industrial arts. At the new building's dedication ceremony on October 11, 1950, Morgan State College President Dr. Martin D. Jenkins praised Bates for having been the source of so many "first class citizens" over the years (2).

Accompanying the building expansion was a revamping of the Bates' curriculum to invigorate the academic courses and to expand the commercial department. One highlight was a new "capstone" program that arranged an internship for every interested senior with a local business. The school also took pride in its industrial arts program, one of the best in the state. The idea that anything might actually be "better" in the "colored" school was the cause of some hard feelings. Jane McWilliams recalls listening at the dinner table as her father, a BG&E employee, talked about visiting Bates to do some electrical work. He was angry that the shop classes were "so much better" than the comparable offerings at Annapolis High.

Meanwhile, activities at Bates were a mirror image of what the white students were doing at Annapolis High. The students were especially proud of their newspaper (*Chronicle*) and yearbook (originally called *Retrospect* and later *The Beacon*). The school band and a variety of singing groups attracted crowds whenever they performed. An active theater arts club put on several productions each year. Bates athletic teams were known as the Little Giants, a nickname the school adopted when Anne Arundel County had only 11 grades so the Bates players were often younger and smaller than their foes from 12-year school systems. The football and basketball teams (boys and girls) played from the 1930's through the early 1960's against other segregated schools throughout the Delmarva Peninsula, West Virginia and Washington, DC. The best of its early football teams was the 1939 squad that under Coach James Early won the South Atlantic championship with a 7-1 record. The *Retrospect* of 1940 pictures the players, including team captain Bill Baden and future Annapolis police chief Charles "Skinny" Randall.

The post-graduate plans of Bates students also were similar to those at the neighboring school. Annually one-third of Bates graduates went on to college – about the same percentage as Annapolis High – although they headed in very different directions because Maryland's state colleges were as strictly segregated as its public schools. Most Bates students matriculated at historically black colleges: Morgan State, Bowie State Teachers' College, Maryland State at Princess Anne, Coppin State Teachers' College, Hampton

Institute, Howard and Lincoln Universities. Also of note is Bates, like Annapolis High, was accredited through the Middle States Association in 1949 and earned re-accreditation in 1959 (3).

In short, every indicator suggests that Bates was an excellent high school providing its students with a rich and varied educational experience. Its main deficiency was identical to what was lacking at Annapolis High – knowledge of and familiarity with all the people living in Anne Arundel County. Until 1952 no evidence exists that Annapolis and Bates High had any interaction. Although both fielded boys' football, basketball and baseball teams, they never played a game against each other. Neither did the girls' basketball teams. Annapolis competed in the all-white Anne Arundel County leagues and against other all-white schools in eastern Maryland and Delaware. Segregated schools throughout the region continued to be the opponents of the Little Giants (4).

Then in February 1952, an event took place unprecedented in the history of the two neighbors. Some now forgotten group sponsored a National Brotherhood Week that led some unknown person or people to arrange for the Bates and Annapolis High bands to exchange visits at each other's school. What is known took place on Wednesday morning, February 20th, when Bates High's principal Douglas King, student council president Leo Simms, seven student dancers, several student singers, a handful of teachers and the 51-member school band led by its majorettes marched down Smithville Street, across Spa Road, up Greenfield Street and through the front door of Annapolis High to the auditorium where they put on a performance for the host school's entire student body and faculty. Included in the program were short speeches by the principals, two dance routines, several vocal numbers, a baton-twirling exhibition and a band medley of famous marches with John Philip Sousa's rousing "Stars and Stripes Forever" as the grand finale. Two days later the Annapolis High band and chorus paid a return visit to Bates High.

The 1952 *Wake* includes two photos of Bates students entertaining on the Annapolis High stage. Marjorie Layng Roxburgh ('55) remembers how talented the Bates performers were, including Betty (Brown) Fuller ('53) who recalls being frightened about how she and her friends would be received. Her fear, however, soon turned to pleasure as the Annapolis High students applauded the musical numbers and "acted respectful when Mr. King, our principal, spoke." King told the sea of white faces staring up at him from the seats in the

During Brotherhood Week in February 1952, Bates High School musicians put on a show for their neighbors at Annapolis High School. Shown at left is a photo from the 1952 Wake that shows a Bates student singing "May the Good Lord Bless and Keep You." Later in the week the Annapolis band paid a return visit to Bates, with the reception being just as positive. This exchange seems to have been the only such event in the decade prior to desegregation.

James Webb (left) and Neville Leonard (right) coached undefeated teams at Bates and Annapolis Highs in 1962. Among the many fine players on Webb's 1961 undefeated team (below) were the all-around athletic star #12 Charles Kirby and #40 quarterback and defensive back and Larry Brogden.

packed auditorium, "Your enthusiastic and courteous reception [shows] the caliber of our young American citizens." He closed his remarks with words that bear repeating 50 years later: *"Prejudice is a two-edged sword which cuts both ways because it affects the person who is being prejudicial as well as the individual or group against whom such a feeling is directed. We can never appreciate the worth and value of an individual or a race until we get to know them."* (5)

This one-time exchange between the neighboring schools stands in marked contrast to the 1950's landscape of daily life in segregated Annapolis. When asked today what they felt back then about rigid separation of the races, alumni from both schools shrug and admit – seemingly apologetic – that they just didn't think about whether things could, or even should, be different. The possibility of integration seems never to have occurred to them. Bates and Annapolis High certainly were neighbors, but their students lived in totally separate worlds, caught up in their respective school activities and private lives, unaware that they were living on the brink of massive change. On May 17, 1954, the United States Supreme Court ruled in the *Brown v Board of Education of Topeka, Kansas* case that the "separate but equal" justification for segregation of public schools was unconstitutional. The next day Superintendent David Jenkins implied that the Anne Arundel system would comply with the ruling only after the Supreme Court answered questions about redistricting and provided a timetable for implementation (6). In May 1955 the Supreme Court issued instructions that called for desegregation to proceed "in good faith [and] with all deliberate speed." Yet 11 more years would pass before Anne Arundel County's high schools would be integrated fully (7). In the interim, students at Annapolis and Bates High Schools continued to live their separate lives.

Two Perfect Seasons: AHS and BHS Football, Fall 1962

During the fall of 1962 two of the finest high school football teams in Anne Arundel County history played their home games on the same field. Although both ended their respective seasons undefeated, neither could claim full bragging rights as the "best" in the county because they didn't play each other. The teams were the Annapolis High Panthers and the Bates High Little Giants.

Annapolis entered the 1962 campaign after what head coach Neville Leonard termed a rebuilding season during which his young

Panthers had won only two of nine games. Leonard was still fairly new to the head coaching business, having taken over the Annapolis High football team in 1959 when Bill Best opted to limit his coaching to basketball. Leonard became cautiously optimistic about his team's prospects for 1962 when the Panther defense held St. Mary's scoreless in the final game of the 1961 season. Returning would be many of the players most responsible for that victory. Alan Pastrana, who was rapidly establishing his reputation as one of the best athletes in the history of the school, would start at quarterback. Halfbacks Rick Baskett and Hal Grau had plenty of speed, while little used Arnie Frieman was showing promise at the fullback position. The linemen were the team's real strength, especially three 200-pounders who were exceptionally mobile for their size: Buck Gardner, Doug Macey and Bert Taylor. Gardner was also an able kicker (8).

The 1962 season opener against Oxon Hill served notice to other teams on the Annapolis High schedule that the Panthers were no longer the patsies of the past. Leonard's charges tuned a 19-6 loss in 1961 into a 20-0 victory, a win even more impressive because an ankle injury had kept Pastrana on the bench (9). The next week the Panthers showed their opening victory was no fluke by steamrolling Howard High, 33-0. Pastrana, back in the line-up, broke a school record with his 60-yard pass to Buck Gardner that set up the Panthers' first score. Halfbacks Grau and Baskett each rushed for two touchdowns. By the end of the third quarter, Leonard had emptied his bench to give all the players a taste of game action (10).

Annapolis High continued to roll in its next three victories over the other white county public schools then playing football: Brooklyn Park (27-7), Southern (29-0) and Severna Park (13-0). At the season's halfway point the Annapolis defense had allowed only one touchdown, a long-pass on the second play of the Brooklyn Park game that had caught the Panthers' secondary by surprise. Meanwhile the offense was clicking on all cylinders, with Grau and Baskett responsible for most of the scoring. Pastrana was finding his passing groove after his early-season injury (11).

Leonard knew that the real test of his team's ability was its next game against Harford County's Bel Air High, a perennial powerhouse that Annapolis had never beaten in seven previous tries. Playing before a boisterous crowd at Weems-Whelan Memorial Field, the Panthers erased the bad memories of past losses by blanking the Bobcats, 13-0. After the game, Leonard proclaimed the outcome a

Same Neighborhood, Different Worlds, 1959 - 1970   163

"real team victory." The offensive line provided enough protection for Pastrana to get the ball to his running backs and receivers. And the defense continued to sparkle. Indeed, Bel Air never moved the ball inside the Panthers' 30-yard line (12).

The Bel Air victory made the idea of an undefeated season seem a realistic possibility. Victories against Eastern Shore opponents Wicomico and Cambridge would be necessary if this dream were to come true. Ever since Woody Wetherhold's unpleasant experience with Wicomico High in the early 1950's, little love had been lost between the two schools whose shared football history went back to 1912 when Annapolis twice beat Wi-Hi. Although the Panthers had won only two of the eight games played in the modern era, every encounter was fiercely contested. The 1962 meeting in Salisbury was no exception. Annapolis trailed 7-6 until the game's last minute when Buck Gardner recovered an Indians' fumble with time running out. Pastrana drove the team 44 yards down the field to the Wicomico 10. Rick Baskett carried the ball over the goal line for the winning touchdown as time expired (13).

Seven victories down, three to go for a perfect season. The eighth game against Cambridge proved the most serious challenge to the streak. Originally scheduled for Friday night, the game was postponed until late the following afternoon while a late fall torrential rainfall swept across the eastern shore. When the game finally got underway, Annapolis quickly tallied touchdowns on its first two possessions on passes from Pastrana to Grau and Baskett. Fortunately Buck Gardner made one of the two extra points because that early flurry ended the Panthers' scoring on the muddy field. Even more fortunate was Bert Taylor's heroic effort to block the Raiders' point-after-touchdown kick as time expired to preserve Annapolis High's 13-12 victory (14).

Two games remained on the schedule. The season would end on Thanksgiving at Navy-Marine Corps Memorial Stadium against St. Mary's. Suffering through a 2-6 season, the Saints weren't expected to provide stiff opposition. But before turkey day, the Panthers would play host to Forest Park of Baltimore, a team that had a much easier time beating Wicomico than Annapolis had. Before another boisterous crowd at Weems-Whelan Memorial Field, Buck Gardner and Rick Baskett scored touchdowns in the 14-0 win. The ninth victory was secured by stellar defensive plays, including fumble recoveries by Doug Macey and Dick Hendrick, a blocked punt by Tom Nyland and John Russell and the overall play of Tom Parlett (15).

The season finale against archrival St. Mary's was a 48-0 rout. All the players who had contributed to the perfect season had big games against the Saints – quarterback Alan Pastrana; running backs Arnie Frieman, Rick Baskett and Hal Grau; and linemen Buck Gardner, Tom Nyland, John Russell, Doug Macey, John Hanna, Burt Taylor, Tom Parlett and Mark Rankin. Indeed, the thrashing was so sound that the football series between the Saints and the Panthers was discontinued (16). Beginning in 1963, Severna Park took St. Mary's place as Annapolis High's turkey day adversary.

Looking back on the Panthers' perfect season, Coach Leonard gave equal credit to the offense and defense. The statistics tell the story. Annapolis gained 3,457 yards while racking up 127 first downs and scoring 222 points. By contrast, the defense held opponents to 26 points, 71 first downs and 1074 total yards – all team records. Pastrana set school records for completed passes (41) and longest pass from scrimmage. Halfback Rick Bassett scored 13 touchdowns and earned all-state honors. Buck Gardner's 22 extra points also was an Annapolis High record. A state poll at season's end placed the Panthers third, and a national poll ranked them among the top 50 high school teams in the country (17).

As exceptional as the Annapolis High 1962 season was, the Panthers may not have been the best team in their own hometown. That honor could easily be bestowed on the Wiley H. Bates Little Giants, a team that entered 1962 riding an 11-game winning streak dating back to the fourth game of the 1960 season. Head coach James Webb had been directing the football fortunes at Bates since 1950, gradually turning a losing program around. The school's first perfect season was 1961, and the 1962 Little Giants would be missing just one key contributor to the winning streak - quarterback and defensive back Larry Brogden. Yet Webb had 19 other returning players, including 13 lettermen, to welcome back. The most important was the young man Webb considered the best athlete in Bates High's history, Charles Kirby. Only a week before fall practice began, the Bates coaching staff thought the star quarterback, who would turn 19 in October, was too old to play his senior year. A recent MPSSAA rule, however, stated a player must be 18 or younger at the start of a specific sport season, so Kirby was eligible for football in the fall but would have to pass up his senior year in basketball and baseball (18).

Beginning with the season opener at Weems-Whelan Memorial field on Friday night, September 21st, the Little Giants stormed through its first seven opponents: Mace's Landing (Cambridge, MD), Good Counsel (Wheaton, MD), Fairmont Heights, Severna Park, Brooklyn Park, Pomonkey (Indian Head, MD) and William Jason (Georgetown, DE). The Little Giants' split-T offense amassed 216 points behind Kirby's arm and the legs of fullback Arthur Colbert, who led the team with 11 touchdowns. Meanwhile the Bates' defense had surrendered a total of only seven points – and even those were something of a fluke, the result of a fumbled pass reception that all the coaches and players on the Little Giants' sideline thought the referee should have ruled an incompletion [19].

The only game standing between Bates and a second straight perfect season was played on Saturday afternoon, November 17th, in Linthicum Heights against Andover High. The Little Giants pulled out the victory, 19-12, in a game that apparently was not as close as the final score indicated. Afterwards Coach Webb fumed that the "referees penalized us for as much yardage as we gained." A number of the calls came on blocks or tackles that the referees deemed "too rough." Nobody, however, could take away what Webb's team had achieved: an 8-0 season that extended their winning streak they'd carry over to the 1963 season to 18 games [20].

Thus it was that in the fall of 1962, the capital city of Maryland was home to two undefeated high school teams. The Annapolis High Panthers and the Bates Little Giants had much in common, beginning with loyal and loud fans who packed Weems-Whelan for home games and followed their teams on the radio – WNAV (Panthers) and WANN-AM or WXTC-FM (Little Giants) – when they weren't on the road to cheer in person. Both carried nice winning streaks into the next season and would, unfortunately, see them end on the same Saturday in late September 1963 when Bates lost to City 27-0 in Baltimore and Howard upset Annapolis 7-6.

The players for the two schools – except for their skin color – were virtually identical. Both teams had a slew of mobile linemen weighing over 200 pounds, fleet-footed halfbacks, pounding fullbacks, sure-handed receivers, steady kickers and hard-hitting linebackers. At the crucial quarterback position each had a three-sport star that coaches and classmates considered the best athlete in their respective school's history. Alan Pastrana had a magical senior year in which he captained the undefeated Panthers' football and lacrosse teams and was named most valuable wrestler for the metro area after an undefeated and unscored upon season at 165 pounds. Pastrana went on to set several passing records for the University of Maryland (1965-68), was drafted and spent two years on the Denver Broncos' roster and eventually returned home to coach football and lacrosse at Anne Arundel Community College (21).

Pastrana's counterpart, Charles Kirby, had an equally illustrious athletic career at Bates. As a freshman he made the Bates varsity basketball team and was named all county, an honor he picked up sophomore and junior years, too. His best sport may have been baseball. Several major league teams scouted him throughout high school, and he tried out with the New York Giants before his senior year in high school. The scout told Kirby to come back in a year after he "got more seasoning." The smaller rosters and fewer number of teams made it more difficult to land a major league contract back then than it is today. So Kirby returned to Bates and played a spectacular season of football that earned him the Annapolis Touchdown Club's prestigious Rhodes trophy emblematic of being the best high school player in the county, but because of his age he was barred from the "seasoning" on the Bates High baseball team the scout wanted. Today Kirby is retired from the county school system, but is still a terror on the Anne Arundel County "senior" softball circuit (22).

Trying to determine whether Bates or Annapolis would have won if they had played is difficult. On consecutive weekends in mid-October they faced their only common opponent, Severna Park. Their respective performances against the Falcons suggest Bates may have had the upper hand against Annapolis. Although both shut out the Falcons, the Little Giants rolled up 34 points on offense to the Panthers' 13. Yet when asked which of his opponents was the better team, Severna Park's coach said, "Flip a coin," although he went on to suggest Bates might be "a little more explosive." (23) That Annapolis and Bates High Schools played only one common team in 1962, indeed that they did not play against each other, could be interpreted as an indication of overt racism, but this argument loses force when analyzed more closely. In fact, as Larry Brogden suggests today, the main reason may have been scheduling difficulties. For decades segregation laws had forced the Little Giants to play other "colored" schools, some located hundreds of miles away. Brogden remembers leaving at 9 a.m. to arrive in time for a 7 p.m. kickoff at Page-Jackson High in West Virginia, then boarding the bus as soon as the game was over to ride all night back home. Bates was always eager to play opponents closer to Annapolis, but prior to 1960 the two county schools with football teams (Annapolis and Southern) were strictly off limits because of segregation strictures. Then in the early 1960's three county high schools began football programs – Brooklyn Park and two new high schools, Severna Park and Andover. All three faced difficulties trying to build a schedule because established programs were already locked into contractual obligations. Yet because desegregation of the county schools was in process, it was suddenly not only possible, but also desirable, for Brooklyn Park, Andover and Severna Park to schedule Bates, and the Little Giants were more than happy to get games closer to home. Thus, in 1961 Brooklyn Park became the first county opponent to play Bates, and the next year Severna Park and Andover were added. Meanwhile, according to Brogden, "As a long-established program, Annapolis High already had scheduled games for the early 1960's before anyone had thought of playing Bates." The neighbors finally did line up against each other in 1964, during Neville Leonard's last season, with the Little Giants winning 19-0. The next year, the last Bates High School team lost to Al Laramore's first Annapolis High team 26-0 (24).

To suggest that bigotry played no role in Anne Arundel County football at this time would be naive. Coach Webb's career after Bates High School closed in 1966 suggests that African Americans faced difficulties finding coaching jobs in the first decades of integration. Webb's resume showed at least 15 years as a very successful coach of the Little Giants football, basketball and baseball teams. As an educator he encouraged his players to make something positive out of their lives. One was named a Rhodes scholar, scores went on to college and hundreds became contributing members of the Annapolis community. Yet in the fall of 1966, Webb could be found watching football games from the bleachers rather than directing them from the sidelines. He remained at Bates Junior High as a physical education teacher, later moved to several elementary schools and finished his career as a drivers' education teacher at Annapolis High. He retired in 1980, a decade before his wife Laura Webb became the Annapolis High principal.

Despite his obvious qualifications, James Webb never again coached high school football after 1966. Perhaps at the time Bates High closed, he couldn't generate enough enthusiasm to start over somewhere else. Brogden believes Webb did not even apply for the

Homecoming was a tradition that began in 1950 and grew to the most visible celebration of Panther spirit. The weekend began with a parade on the night before the game from City Dock, up Main and West Streets to the school.

Cars carried the football captains and homecoming queen, the court and the cheerleaders, while each class contributed a float. Alumni marched, organized by class. At the school a huge bonfire was lit to start a pep rally. The queen and her court were formally introduced at the game's halftime and on Saturday came the crowning of the queen at the dance. In the 1950's many dances were held at the Annapolis Country Club.

head coaching positions at any of the four new high that opened from 1965 to 1980 (Northeast, Old Mill, Chesapeake and Meade), and perhaps as a former head coach he wasn't interested in becoming an assistant in somebody else's program. It is difficult to discern if Webb tried to coach again and was rebuffed, or if he just voluntarily packed away his clipboards and whistles with the purple and gold Little Giants uniforms when Bates High School closed in 1966.

Webb died thirty years after he last coached a Bates High School team. Yet the passage of three decades had not diminished the gratitude of the former players who packed his funeral on March 23, 1996. Many came to testify to the difference Coach Webb had made in their lives. They speculated about where Webb's career might have gone in another era, claiming that he should have made it to the pros. One insisted that Webb was very frustrated during his later years: "Coach Webb didn't die from pancreatic cancer; he died from desegregation." Let us hope that even if that statement were true, Webb was able to feel a large measure of pride in his former Bates players as they helped Al Laramore's Annapolis High teams take their first steps towards becoming the dominant football program in Anne Arundel County. In a larger sense, he must also have been aware that black and white students playing together on athletic teams served as the main vehicle to help ease integration at Annapolis High when it finally occurred in the mid-1960's (25).

Anne Arundel County Schools Desegregate

Until the mid-1950's Maryland was one of 17 states that segregated its public schools under the "separate but equal" concept legalized in the U.S. Supreme Court's 1896 *Plessy v Ferguson* ruling. Nearly six decades later, in the 1954 *Brown v the Board of Education* case, the court unanimously reversed the *Plessy* decision, declaring "separate educational facilities are inherently unequal and hence deprive the segregated person of equal protection of the laws, which is guaranteed by the 14th amendment to the Constitution." In May 1955 the Supreme Court declared its expectation that the states "make a prompt start" and "act in good faith" to end segregation of their public schools (26).

Following these orders, Dr. Thomas Pullen, superintendent of Maryland's schools, instructed county boards of education to undertake without "chicanery or devious methods" to "end racial discrimination in public education." Responsibility for devising and implementing procedures was left to the individual counties. This freedom allowed some local school superintendents, among them Anne Arundel's David S. Jenkins, to interpret the court's ruling in the narrowest manner possible. Publicly Jenkins announced the "spirit and intent" of federal law would be followed, but the school board's actions in the next decade suggest they interpreted this to mean that they were only required to dismantle discriminatory barriers without necessarily integrating the schools (27).

Indeed, the county's plan was quite simple. First the designation "colored" or "white" was to be removed from each school. Then every student was to be allowed a choice: stay in your current school or go to another if it is closer to your home. The implementation of the plan was to be gradual. Initially offered only to first, second and third graders in 1956, it was to be extended each subsequent year to the next grade until 12th graders would finally be given the choice in the fall of 1965. Twice the process was accelerated, in 1958 when fifth and sixth graders were permitted to choose and again in 1963 for juniors and seniors. With the completion of this "free choice within set geographic boundaries" process, Jenkins declared in May 1964 that the county's public schools were in compliance with the Supreme Court's *Brown v the Board of Education* order. The school board's pamphlet "Desegregation of Public Schools in Anne Arundel County; 10 Years of Progress" stated that about half of the county's 83 schools were "desegregated" according to geographic attendance areas. The remaining 42, including 12 elementary schools and Bates Junior-Senior High that had 100 percent black teaching staffs and student bodies, were labeled "desegregated" through "freedom of choice" (28).

Jenkins and the county board of education left moot the question of how many schools in Anne Arundel County were actually integrated as a result of their desegregation efforts. Civil rights groups refused to ignore the issue. After carefully canvassing the 300,000 people living in the county (11 percent of whom were African American), they found that black and white students were together in only about one-third of the county's schools. What really bothered them was that in Annapolis no school reflected the city's racial balance (about thirty percent of the city's 24,000 citizens were African American). The city's schools remained almost completey segregated. Not a single white teacher was transferred permanently to integrate the staff of a colored school. Not a single white student had opted to enroll in a neighborhood school with black students and teachers. Although these all-black and all-white schools technically met desegregation criteria (i.e., nobody was prohibited from going to them because of race), the NAACP insisted they should be integrated (29).

That so many schools remained *de-facto* segregated was hardly accidental. Following a pattern more associated with Deep South states, the Anne Arundel school board had consolidated several dozen small colored schools into seven schools (six new and one with a new addition) during the five years following the *Brown* ruling when they were supposed to be proceeding "without chicanery" and "with deliberate speed" to desegregate. These seven schools were then staffed with black teachers and administrators. When presented with the choice of attending one of these new schools (including the 20-room Adams Park Elementary School that was constructed for nearly one million dollars in 1958 to replace the dilapidated, inadequate Stanton School) or their present schools, white children stayed put. When asked if they wanted to attend an existing white school "closer" to where they lived or the new school that was replacing the building where they had been going, 75 percent of black students opted for the latter. Thus the county could claim they had desegregated the schools because the same "free choice" rules were applied to everyone when, in reality, three-quarters of African American students were in all-black schools (30).

Several additional school board policies were implemented to ensure students made the right choice. The segregation of faculties made clear which schools were intended for whites and which were for blacks. A particularly transparent ploy was to designate the student's bus pickup point as the school closest to his or her home. A 1966 Health, Education and Welfare Department investigation discovered that "*many Negro youngsters [are being] transported past white schools in their own neighborhoods to Negro schools as far as 15 or 20 miles from their homes [while] white children are transported past Negro schools to a predominately white school in an adjacent neighborhood.*" Jenkins' declaration that the school board had met the "intent and spirit" of the Supreme Court's ruling when such cynical methods were used to keep 75 percent of "Negro" children in all-black schools was nothing short of disingenuous.

The county's overall approach to desegregation also served to perpetuate the existence of Bates as an all-black school. Negro students ready for high school in the early 1960's could chose between Bates and another county high school closer to where they lived. If they were already attending Bates for junior high, they most likely stayed there, although some who would have to endure long bus rides from the northern half of the county did select Andover, Arundel, Brooklyn Park, Glen Burnie, Severna Park or Northeast (after its 1965 opening). Roy Brown, the future Annapolis High football coach, recalls there being "quite a few" blacks playing sports with him at Arundel High in the mid-1960's when he was a student there, and Larry Brogden also mentions Arundel as being "the most integrated" of the north county high schools (31).

Meanwhile Negroes in the south county theoretically had the choice between Bates and either Annapolis or Southern, but the latter, in whose geographic boundaries lived a significant black population, effectively argued that it could not accommodate such an influx of new students. Thus, when time came for African Americans in the Southern High area to have a choice of high schools, they were told that until a new school could be built, they would continue to be bused to Annapolis – to attend either Bates or Annapolis High.

It is tempting to point an accusatory finger at the board of education for placating south county whites resisting integration (32). To be fair, however, the board did face such serious overcrowding problems in the late 1950's in the more rapidly urbanizing northern half of the county that they overlooked the largely rural southern sector. On a yearly basis the board struggled to find additional building funds for a variety of projects including the new Adams Park and Eastport Elementary Schools, additions to Parole and Annapolis Elementary Schools and the new Severna Park High School, which was supposed to help ease crowding at Annapolis High. The system barely kept its head above water in the flood of new students (33). In the spring of 1962 Tony Anzalone, eager to venture out from his native Fitchburg, Massachusetts, accepted what he thought was a social studies position at Annapolis Junior High. Instead he found himself teaching all subjects to a class of seventh graders housed back in the old Green Street high school building. By the following fall, he moved to the new 1,800-student Annapolis Junior High at the intersection of Forest Drive and Spa Road. This new junior high allowed the high school to expand into three buildings: the original 1932 "Maryland Hall," the 1955-56 "Chesapeake Hall" annex to its rear (originally built for shop and music classes, but enlarged in 1959 to include science labs) and the 1953 "Severn Hall," the old junior high building. A new and enlarged Southern High was penciled in for sometime in the late 1960's (34).

Notice that Bates received no attention from the school board in this discussion. One conclusion seems obvious: Jenkins and the board expected that African Americans, when given a choice, would continue attending Bates rather than select a "white" high school. They were right. When juniors and seniors were offered the choice in the fall of 1963 between Bates and Annapolis High, only a handful of African Americans opted to integrate Annapolis. Indeed, about 95 percent of the seniors and 90 percent of the juniors pictured in the 1965 *Wake* are white. No African Americans appear as class officers or Student Council representatives. The only club with black students pictured is the Future Homemakers of America, but a dozen male black athletes are seen with the football, boys' basketball and track teams, and nearly a quarter of the girls posing with the basketball, volleyball, softball and on the county championship field hockey team are African Americans. Only one of the 86 teachers pictured is black, a female typing instructor. No changes in the Annapolis High management team had been made for over a decade, with the top administrators seemingly firmly entrenched: Principal Albert Fowble had been at the school since 1937, Assistant Principal Woody Wetherhold since 1948, and Supervisor of Instruction Roland Olson since 1950. The conclusion is inescapable: black students could enroll in Annapolis High, but only through sports were some being assimilated in the school's student body.

A school board doing its best to protect the status quo must have been gratified with these results. Civil rights groups clearly were not. In the summer of 1964, representatives from the local chapters of the NAACP and CORE (Congress for Racial Equality) began appearing at every Anne Arundel County school board meeting to point out that the *Brown* ruling was no longer the litmus test for determining if a school system was in compliance with federal integration laws (35). Title VI of the 1964 Civil Rights Act called for "the elimination of the dual structure of separate schools for students of different races as expeditiously as possible." Frustrated with the perception that Jenkins and the board were not intending to act quickly to implement Title VI in the county, they filed a formal complaint with the federal government. A HEW investigating team issued a damning report that first conceded, "There was little if any

Mrs. Gwendolyn Pindell (above, left) was a math teacher at Bates High School who was transferred in the summer of 1966 to help integrate the faculty of Southern High. Her daughter Rhonda graduated in the top 100 of over 600 students in Annapolis High's Class of 1972. She went on to Morgan State ('76) and earned a law degree from the University of Maryland ('79); today she is an assistant state's attorney. Math teacher and future Athletic Director Fred Stauffer came to Annapolis High in 1963, started the school's track program and also coached cross-country. In 1969 Butch Middleton (center, left) captained that team.

overt intimidation to keep Negroes from choosing previously white schools." Instead HEW concluded, *"Anne Arundel County's freedom of choice plans [failed to produce] substantial steps toward the expeditious elimination of a dual school structure due to the sense of inferiority imposed on Negroes by the social and economic traditions of society, the fear of what might happen to Negro parents and students if they sought a desegregated education and the designation of certain schools as intended for Negroes by staffing them with all-Negro faculties . . . combined to prevent integration."* (36) On the heels of this report, in March 1966, the U.S. Office of Education directly ordered Anne Arundel County schools – students and faculties – to be completely desegregated by September 1966. Bowing to the federal government's higher authority, the school board told Jenkins to devise a plan that would result in all grades in every school being integrated before the start of the next school year. Specifically targeted were the

13 Negro schools, including Bates, all of which were to become desegregated through the inclusion of white students and teachers in September 1966 (37).

Thus after years of resistance, sudden change was at hand. The Bates Class of 1966 learned it would be the last in the school's history. Beginning the next fall, it would house the entire city's ninth and about half of its 10th graders as one of five buildings comprising the greater Annapolis Junior and Senior High School complex. The remainder of the sophomores along with all of the city's juniors and seniors would utilize the three buildings on the Annapolis High campus. From this point forward, all public secondary school students in the city would be awarded diplomas from Annapolis High School upon graduation. Meanwhile, sixth grader Rhonda Pindell (Charles), who had been looking forward to trying out for the Bates precision marching group, the Rangerettes, instead found herself and her Parole Elementary classmates among the 2,099 seventh and eighth grade students at Annapolis Junior High on Forest Drive.

An incident during the summer of 1966 reveals how raw the emotions were among some white parents whose children were assigned to attend school in the Bates building. To appease their sensitivities the school board had already replaced teacher desks, refinished all student desks and thoroughly cleaned the inside and outside of the building, but when invited to inspect the school and meet with the principal some white parents expressed such bitter opposition to their children being assigned to Bates that Jenkins bowed to their demand to change the school's name. In an August letter he informed Principal Herbert Hilliard that henceforth his school would be officially called Annapolis Middle High School, presumably to reflect its status as a way station between junior and senior high school. No consideration was given whatsoever to the sensitivities of Wiley H. Bates' family, to the school's thousands of alumni or to the Annapolis African American community (38).

Despite the school board's clumsy and callous handling of the matter, the vice principal of the newly-christened Annapolis Middle High School, Philip Brown, reports that the only major problem students encountered during the first weeks of classes in the fall of 1966 was an increased level of confusion that he attributes to the "larger than usual number of children who had never been in the building before." He calls the board of education's fears of what would happen if "children and young people of both races [were] suddenly thrown together on a large scale" to have been "needless and unwarranted." He concludes, "*As the days passed and the students, through their association in the classes, began to know each other better, some of them began to sit together during lunch in the cafeteria and pass to and from classes together and in other ways began to appear to think of themselves as students rather than white students and colored students.*" (39)

    Rhonda Pindell Charles is one of many people to corroborate the conclusion that "the kids didn't really have any problem with integration." Larry Brogden points out that black and white guys in Annapolis already were acquainted from playing in recreation leagues and interscholastic games against each other, so being in the same classroom "wasn't that big of a deal." For instance, Butch Middleton ('70) was invited to play on an otherwise all-white age group team for under-12-year-olds that was coached by future county school superintendent C. Berry Carter, whose son Chris and Butch were to stay friendly and eventually start together their senior year on the Panthers' basketball team. Teacher Fred Stauffer recalls many of his students welcomed the change as part of their overall interest in the civil rights demonstrations, campus protests against the Vietnam War and the emerging hippie culture of free love and drugs.

    Charles and Middleton agree that "adults – parents and teachers – caused most of the problems back then, not the students." Indeed, according to Vice Principal Brown, a handful of teachers brought about the only major crisis at Bates in the fall of 1966. Because the county had to desegregate the faculties as well as the student bodies of its schools, 54 of the 72 Bates teachers were transferred to formerly all-white schools. One was Gwendolyn Pindell, a longtime math teacher at Bates, who was notified in the summer of 1966 that she had been transferred to Southern High where, according to her daughter Rhonda, she was the only African American teacher on her morning split-shift session at the school. The good news is that despite the ferocity with which various parents' organizations in the area had fought desegregation, Mrs. Pindell found Southern's principal, Mr. Wingate, to be "wholly supportive, backing her up when any parent complained or tried to force her to change grades." The bad news is that eight of the white teachers transferred to the former Bates High failed to report for their new assignments, forcing the school to scramble for qualified substitutes until permanent replacements could be hired. Undoubtedly those missing had been members of Teachers Association of Anne Arundel County that for several years after the *Brown* decision refused to accept the county's Negro teachers' union request to merge (40).

Based on testimony from African American students who helped integrate Annapolis High, some prejudiced instructors remained on the faculty. Butch Middleton saw teachers use very different discipline standards with black and white students. Rhonda Pindell Charles had one teacher who allowed black and white students to sit separately and then proceeded to turn his back on the African Americans while teaching. After several weeks, one student asked him why he was behaving in such a prejudiced fashion. He answered, "Because I'm a racist," and then assured everyone that he was kidding, but the behavior didn't stop. Complaints to the administration from black students and parents about such unfair treatment seemed to fall on deaf ears.

Black Student Outrage Explodes, Spring 1970

Annapolis High began the 1966-67 school year with about 1,200 white and 500 black students. The overall enrollment dropped from 1,933 the previous year to 1,727. Most of this decline apparently resulted from half the sophomore class being assigned to Annapolis Middle High School, but undoubtedly some white parents withdrew their children to "protect" them from the integrated school. Other than a printed brochure depicting the realignment of grades in the Annapolis Junior-Middle-Senior High complex, little effort to inform the community about the impending changes was made over the summer of 1966. The school's administration assumed a "business as usual" attitude that left students, parents and teachers to cope as best they could with the integration process. Fred Stauffer remembers no special advice having been offered to faculty about how to welcome the new students or to ensure that each received fair treatment. Communication between the school and parents was almost nonexistent, especially after the PTA – for obscure reasons – disbanded (41). Black students, who comprised less than 30 percent of the enrollment, were left to fit in wherever they could. Evidence that the administration ignored warning signs of student unrest can be found in its 1969 accreditation report that in 95 pages makes only this reference to integration: "The students attending Bates Junior-Senior

High School became members of the student bodies of the various hitherto all-white secondary schools in Anne Arundel County." (42)

Before classes began on February 12, 1970, several dozen black students rampaged through the school, breaking windows, tearing down posters, scattering school records, slightly roughing up a vice principal and throwing eggs at some police when they arrived on the scene. Fortunately nobody was seriously hurt. During the height of the melee, Principal Albert Fowble seemed unable to decide on a course of action. Huntley Cross, a geography teacher and assistant basketball coach, recalls the sense of chaos was heightened because the public address system microphone was inadvertently left on so that the angry shouting match between students and adults in the main office was broadcast throughout the school. Local radio stations announced students were being sent home before anyone had actually made that decision. Rhonda Pindell Charles and her friends left the school almost immediately. Butch Middleton hung around for a while to watch the action, but cut out when he realized he wouldn't be punished for skipping class. Fred Stauffer's track athletes – black and white – congregated in his room, hoping to be able to stay so they could practice for an important upcoming meet. At 11 a.m., everyone was sent home. Tony Anzalone was attending a family funeral in Massachusetts where he watched with shock as Walter Cronkite led the evening's national news with filmed coverage of the "race riot at Annapolis High School." Anzalone was unsettled to hear that four students had been arrested and charged with assault, destruction of property and instigating a riot and that 41 others were suspended, as was a white English teacher accused of helping the students organize the protest.

For several weeks after the protest, students were required to show identification before entering the school and armed police patrolled its corridors. Eventually 15 of the suspended were expelled from school, while the juvenile court found the four arrested to be "delinquent." Carl Snowden, one of the student leaders, transferred to a private school (43). Throughout the spring of 1970, mystified citizens – white and black – wondered what had gone wrong with their high school. Many blamed the events on outside agitators, accusing them of having spread the general air of unrest about civil rights and the Vietnam War from college campuses to high school students. Local black activists and civil rights advocates disagreed, arguing that the angry students' actions stemmed from systemic problems in the school. The black students who figured prominently in the day's violence wanted Fowble to respond to their two-week old demands about how to improve conditions for Afro-Americans in the school: more black faculty members, an infusion of black studies in the curriculum, leadership training and a guarantee that black students be included on the Student Council and cheerleading squad

The origin of these demands went back to 1966-67 when Bates juniors and seniors were required to attend Annapolis High. Nothing was done to prepare the students – those already at Annapolis as well as those coming from Bates – for the new school they would be building together. Blacks sensed an attitude from the administration and among some faculty and students that they were expected to be grateful for the opportunity to attend Annapolis High. As we shall see in the next chapter, those engaged in athletics did quickly acclimate to their new surroundings, but those former Bates students who had aspirations of assuming leadership roles in school government organizations and clubs were frustrated that their minority status in the school meant they had no realistic chance of being elected to the Student Council, to win a class office, to become a club president or even to make the cheerleading squad.

Ideally, African Americans wanted an opportunity to excel, to lead in ways they would have if they had their own school. At a minimum, according to Rhonda Pindell Charles, the black students wanted adults at Annapolis High to care about them, to encourage them in ways their teachers had at the schools they had previously attended. Mrs. Charles points to Wilber Mills, longtime principal of Parole Elementary, and his faculty as models for the type of effective and caring educators the black students and parents expected to find in the desegregated secondary schools. Instead they found a much more depersonalized – and at times hostile – atmosphere, one in which they rarely saw the school's principal and in which some teachers were clearly reluctant even to teach them.

The immediate consequence of the riot and the discussions it engendered was the announcement on April 4, 1970, that Principal Albert Fowble had resigned after 33 years at Annapolis High, 25 as its principal (44). Never a particularly strong leader, Fowble had grown accustomed to a school that, according to Fred Stauffer, "pretty much ran itself." For decades Fowble had relied on the Traffic Squad to control student behavior, but as the school expanded into three buildings to accommodate the influx of the new, diverse student body, the obsolete Traffic Squad was disbanded in 1968. Administrators and teachers were needed to fill the void, but Fowble seldom was seen outside his office. Anzalone, then a guidance counselor at Annapolis Junior High, was paired with Fowble in a special evening seminar the school board had hastily organized to help teachers grapple with issues related to student unrest. After several sessions, Fowble confided in Anzalone that in the mid-1960's he had requested to be relieved as principal but the school board told him to stay because he was "doing such a good job." Anzalone empathized with Fowble, who had devoted his life to the school and now was so perplexed about the students of the late 1960's that he wanted out. "He was a man," in Stauffer's words, "who had outlived his times."

Could the February 1970 riot and the subsequent hard feelings have been avoided? Yes, but perhaps only if Jenkins and the county school board had taken a very different approach to integration when first given the opportunity in the mid -1950's. By dragging their feet, obfuscating and expressing fear about the dire consequences of desegregation, Jenkins and the board gave sustenance to bigots who thought "the coloreds" should be grateful for the great favor the government had done for them Naturally blacks quickly came to resent the implication that their former schools were inferior. The "what-ifs" make a long list, but simply put – if Jenkins and the school board had embraced a vision of black and white children learning together harmoniously, taught by an integrated faculty of talented teachers, the results might have been quite different. Instead their actions helped perpetuate prejudices and to delay the assimilation of blacks in the desegregated schools.

* * * * * * * * * * * * * *

Severna Park Junior High principal Joseph Mirenzi was named to replace the ousted Fowble. Mirenzi knew he had to act decisively to meld Annapolis High's black and white population into a unified student body. A former physical education teacher, he sensed athletics could serve as a major avenue to achieve racial harmony. For help, he looked to the man whose name was becoming synonymous with Panther athletic success, the larger-than-life football, basketball and lacrosse coach, Al Laramore.

CHAPTER 8:
"BIG AL AND THE BOYS," 1970 – 1988

The 1978 State Championship Panthers Football Team (12-0)

1st row: C. Evans, T. Trescott, D. Hart, K. Thompson, D. Brown, D. Parker, D. Loman, D. Blanchard, Dave Laramore; **2nd row**: Dan Laramore, J. Dobyins, C. Chamber, A. Chew, C. Bowie, L Riek, T. Parker, R. Pittman, G. Dukes, E. Dementer, J. Bonner, B. Evert, Coach Phebus; **3rd row**: Coach Laramore, T. Simms, M. Colbert, T. Smith, R. Bradford, M. Jabin, A. Tongue, W. Downs, R. Mallow, S. Chambers, R. Wilson, K. McKinney, B. Wimple, Coach Villwock; **4th row**: J. Andreczyk, L. Spencer, J. Smith, P. Pearman, H. Bullen, C. Straaten, J. Jacobsen, J. Rodkey, M. Yu, B.. Nickerson, S. Quigg, J. Quarles, K. Kapchnick.

"The football field was the one place where it didn't make any difference what color your skin was. Pretty soon, the guys on the football team were just people, and eventually there was a progression. You got to know each other, and then you'd try and convince your friends not to do something because the other guy was all right. Sports bonded us together. I had a great coach who didn't see color. All he saw was performance. If you did it his way, you were OK. If you didn't, you were in trouble."
Bill Belichick, AHS '70
Head Coach, New England Patriots

On this field Al had some of his greatest moments. He was bigger than wins and losses His true legacy lies in the example he set. As the years pass the legacy will remain. Names may change but the thought on the field will forever by the same. IF YOU HEAR ANY NOISE, IT'S JUST "BIG AL" AND THE BOYS.
Commemorative plaque placed at Ensor Stadium
at dedication of Al Laramore Field Fall, 1989

"You Have a Good School"

Severna Park Junior High principal Joseph A. Mirenzi was transferred to Annapolis High following Albert Fowble's request to be reassigned in mid-April 1970. A graduate of Penn State University, Mirenzi was a veteran educator whose career included stints as a physical education teacher at Glen Burnie Junior High and vice principal at Annapolis Junior High. His move to Annapolis High placed him squarely in the public eye. The school gained statewide notoriety two months earlier when several Afro-American students instigated a protest that turned destructive – broken windows and furniture, scattered papers, ripped posters and some minor injuries. They achieved their goal of focusing outside attention on the administration's failure to act on a list of complaints about conditions for black students at Annapolis High. The reticent Fowble, overwhelmed and indecisive in the face of student unrest, was granted his wish to resign. Mirenzi, under orders from the school board to make Annapolis High more inclusive, immediately established himself as a hands-on, accessible and visible leader who walked the halls, ate in the cafeteria, listened to complaints and appointed committees to suggest changes. Yet at the same time the school's 11th principal let students know he would enforce all disciplinary rules and expected them to behave responsibly.

Mirenzi's efforts brought immediate results. Butch Middleton ('70) recalls how quickly the school atmosphere improved as blacks and whites worked together on several new committees and clubs. Comparing the 1970 *Wake* with those from the previous several years confirms his impression that things were, indeed, changing. Clubs and student government organizations in the 1965 to 1969 era have few blacks pictured; in 1970 new and clearly integrated groups are present, including the Student Advisory Board, the Assembly Committee and an Afro-American Culture Club. By the end of the year about as many blacks as whites were selected in the class poll for everything from Most Likely to Succeed to Class Clown. Middleton, for instance, was elected "friendliest," while a black male – Bruce Belt – was named the school's scholar-athlete. Mirenzi's crackdown on behavior also resulted in improvements in the school's learning environment. Leslie Finkle ('75) entered Annapolis High as a sophomore in the fall of 1972. She respected Mirenzi as a "strict but fair principal who set and enforced clear standards for everyone." As a result, her overall memories of high school are extremely positive.

Medical problems in 1973 apparently caused Mirenzi to accept promotion to a less strenuous administrative position supervising middle schools. Taking his place was assistant principal Richard G. Ensor. Only in his mid-30's at the time of his appointment, Ensor was offered the position after the opening failed to attract more experienced candidates. Math teacher, track coach and athletic director Fred Stauffer speculates that Annapolis High's "unfair reputation as a tough ghetto school" kept would-be candidates from applying. Stauffer's wife Colleen was often asked by her Corkran Junior High colleagues about why her husband continued to teach at Annapolis when positions at "safer schools" were available. The answer was simple – Stauffer liked his colleagues, felt supported by the school's administrators and appreciated the opportunity to work with students from diverse socio-economic backgrounds. Over the years he felt fortunate to have so many bright math students to teach and gifted athletes to coach.

Ensor shared Stauffer's view that Annapolis High offered an excellent opportunity to make a difference in the lives of students. Born and raised in Towson, Ensor earned a bachelor's degree at Mt. St. Mary's College in English and journalism, subjects he taught in Baltimore County for over a decade before joining the Anne Arundel County school system in 1970 as an administrative intern at Glen Burnie High. Although he lived in Severna Park and was father to seven children, Annapolis High's 12th principal was devoted to the school, seldom missing a home game, drama production or musical event. His enthusiasm for the job was contagious. Students and faculty felt energized, again unafraid to express pride in Annapolis High. One particularly popular tradition Ensor initiated was inviting students to decorate his door with spirit signs and messages.

As the 1970's progressed, Ensor continued to work for improved race relations in the school. He encouraged blacks and whites to share leadership responsibilities. Faculty sensitivity training and stepped up recruiting of minority teachers also contributed to the school's growing sense of community. Students seemed to pull together, with few divisive issues surfacing. Somewhat surprising is the lack of evidence that Annapolis students actively participated in the anti-war movement that was engulfing college campuses at the time. Perhaps because civil rights issues were of such immediate concern to many Annapolis High students, few had the inclination to protest the Vietnam War. Leslie Finkle recalls leaving school once with a group of other students to march about a mile in an anti-war protest to the state capital building, but she is vague about the details. Other students of the time recall the school's "hippies" formed a folk music group and an environmental awareness committee. Certainly young men from Annapolis High were drafted or enlisted, and several dozen served in Vietnam. Deaths were fewer than in other 20th century wars, with 1,014 Marylanders killed, including 17 who listed Annapolis as their home and three from Edgewater. At least four former Annapolis High students died in Vietnam – Marine Corps PFC Emidio Pasqualucci ('67), Marine Corps LCPL William Eugene Tucker ('64), Air Force Sgt. Teddy Waxman ('64) and Army SP4 Dallas A. West ('66) [1].

Ensor was concerned with the academic atmosphere at the school, too. He found time in his busy administrative schedule to continue teaching, and his classroom efforts were rewarded in 1977 when he was named Maryland's Journalism Teacher of the Year. Like many of his predecessors in the principal's office, Ensor tinkered with the curriculum to ensure the students' many and varied needs were met. The state department of education had for many decades offered three curricular tracks that led to different diplomas – academic, general and business. Annapolis High piloted several innovative curricular changes that allowed more diversity in course offerings and encouraged students to take more academic electives. One major modification, according to guidance counselor Anthony Anzalone, was arranging schedules on a semester rather than on a yearly basis so that departments like English could offer a wider range of topics in its literature classes. Such changes eventually contributed to the state's decision to grant a common diploma to all high school graduates.

The Middle States accreditation process in 1980 validated Annapolis High's success in meeting the educational needs of all its students. The visiting committee of educators immediately sensed the "special tone of the school," and they discovered nothing during their three days at Annapolis High to dispel the initial impression of the "favorable relationships . . . between faculty and administration, faculty and students, and students and administration." They reported that the students were "working happily" and "were being well prepared for their future." They applauded the breadth of the curriculum that included 175 separate academic, business, vocational

186 *A Century of Education and Football at Annapolis High School*

Annapolis High School had four principals between 1970 and 1989. They were (top row, left to right) Joseph Mirenzi (1970-73), Richard Ensor (1973-84), Kenneth Catlin (1984-86) and (left) Ken Nichols (1986-90). The biggest change in this period was the 1979 move to Annapolis High's fourth building. Outside the city limits on Riva Road, the new school was isolated from residential areas, in a location with enough land for the large, modern school to be surrounded by ample parking and athletic fields. Following his death as a result of a traffic accident, the football stadium was named to honor Ensor.

and enrichment courses each semester that were "multileveled in an attempt to serve each student at his level of instruction." In short, the committee praised Annapolis High's program for challenging students who ranged in ability from those with special remedial needs to those able to excel in the large array of Advanced Placement courses. Individual evaluations of the 13 departments offered some specific suggestions for improvements, but congratulated the faculty for its enthusiasm and dedication. The report concludes with words that must have made everyone at Annapolis High feel proud: "You have a good school!" (2)

Goodbye to the old Neighborhood

The one feature of Annapolis High that most impressed the Middle States accreditation team was the school's new building. In fact, the visiting educators marveled that Ensor and his faculty had been able to complete the "task of moving into a new educational plant in mid year" while at the same time "completing the required self-study documents." The *Report of the Visiting Committee* notes in its introductory paragraph, "Each is a major achievement on its own and worthy of note; both then become doubly significant. That they were brought to fruition with so few mishaps is indeed commendable." Ensor certainly deserved the praise Middle States offered "for the guidance and direction that he exerted in all phases of the development of this exceptional facility" that took something of a miracle to be built and still stands today as his lasting achievement.

Until the mid-1960's Annapolis High's immediate neighbors in Spa View Heights and Murray Hill were fairly tolerant of the occasional inconveniences that came from living adjacent to the school and its playing fields. Twice a day they had to close their ears to traffic noise from school buses and cars. Rowdy crowds after Friday night football and basketball games could be annoying. Integration, however, seemed to bring a measure of suspicion and even fear to some of the school's neighbors. Matters weren't helped when crowds at football games soared to several thousand after the larger Panther Stadium opened in 1965. Although alcohol was prohibited on the premises, some bold students and adults were able to sneak in beer or flasks with various heady concoctions that produced scores of loud, often surly, inebriated fans. Fights sometimes erupted in parking lots after games with rival schools like Southern. Then as the game against Rockville's Good Counsel High was winding down on October 27, 1968, several thugs attacked a boy in a dark area near the stadium. The victim, a Good Counsel student, remained in grave condition at Johns Hopkins for several days with multiple internal injuries and a skull fracture. An 18-year-old former Annapolis High student was eventually charged with assault and attempt to maim. That same night the 35 city policemen patrolling an area between the school grounds and Church Circle made six other arrests: four Good Counsel students who were "drunk and disorderly," a drunk 14-year old Annapolis boy and a 37-year-old Annapolis man charged with "carrying a concealed weapon, assault and discharging a firearm." (3)

In the wake of this latest and worst in a string of rowdy incidents, county superintendent Edward J. Anderson and the school board outlawed future night football games at Annapolis High. Mayor Roger "Pip" Moyer, a Panther athletic star of the early 1950's who later coached at St. Mary's, argued against the decision. He pointed out that there had been no incidents the previous two night games or during the school's homecoming bonfire. He feared that moving football to Saturday afternoons would only cause the "hoods" to find other venues to disrupt. He vowed, I'll double the police force, call in the National Guard or any other extreme you can think of before I'll sit around and watch young hoodlums ruin the city of Annapolis." (4)

The mayor also tried to quiet accusations among some in the white community that the civil rights movement was responsible for sending gangs of unruly Afro-Americans into their neighborhoods. He pointed out, "In the recent arrest of a Negro youth charged with disorder, it was responsible Negro citizens who helped police locate the youth charged with the offense." The protest of February 1970 at the school heightened neighborhood tensions. Not until 1975 was night football reintroduced at the school, and then only after the school's lacrosse team played several evening games without incident the previous spring.

Although no specific complaints of major property damage occurred in the 1970's, many residents in areas close to the school believed that its campus of three buildings was a blueprint for trouble. The only solution they could suggest was to move the high school to a new facility outside city limits where students could be contained in one building with access to it better monitored. Principal Dick Ensor tended to agree with the neighbors about the difficulty of monitoring students both inside and outside the school's buildings. The layout not only served as an open invitation to cut class by slipping away unnoticed between periods, but also made it practically impossible to keep outsiders from entering the school. Fire regulations prohibited locking doors, and although teachers formed what they jokingly called the "mod squad" to patrol the halls during their free periods, they couldn't cover every corridor at once. Fred Stauffer's math classroom was in the corner of Maryland Hall's basement where a group of students began congregating during the hour-long lunch period. After several days of their loud conversation disrupting his class, Stauffer asked them to move. Most willingly agreed, but one young man decked out in a fancy hat, gold watch on a chain and a cane, refused. Stauffer asked him where he was supposed to be. He replied, "I am wherever I am." Stauffer then suggested they go upstairs to sort out the situation in the office, whereupon the young man struck him on the head and neck with the cane and ran away. Fortunately Stauffer wasn't hurt, but unfortunately the culprit was never apprehended.

Maryland Hall's obsolete facilities also caused concern. Ensor wanted his students to have access to state-of-the-art technology, something hard to envision in the dilapidated Maryland Hall. Although not yet 50 years old, some walls and windows were cracked, graffiti covered lockers, floors were badly worn, bathroom fixtures were leaking and some classroom furnishings were broken. The gymnasium in Severn Hall (the former junior high school) had a capacity of only 600, totally inadequate for the huge crowds that wanted to see Annapolis High basketball games. While Coach John Brady and his Running Panthers were putting on a show to packed houses, some students found a way to sneak in through basement windows in the locker rooms under the gymnasium. Finally the school resorted to selling tickets in advance. Spectators had to show one to get in and could be evicted during the game if they couldn't produce it when asked. Obviously a bigger facility was needed.

To get a new school built at this time was no easy task. The state legislature had to approve all school construction, which was then funded through the Maryland State Interagency. Although privately Ensor's main concern was about school safety, his lobbying efforts stressed the need for a school facility on the cutting edge of technology. County Superintendent Anderson, an Annapolis High parent, backed the project, as did local Anne Arundel County delegate Robert Neall. Everyone associated with the school celebrated when legislative approval was finally secured and construction of the new Annapolis High began in 1976 on a 10-acre site five miles west of the city limits on Riva Road. The Board of Education's new offices were adjacent to the large parcel of land where the school was to be built. Anderson envisioned eventually adding a middle school at the site (where the county swim center sits today) so Annapolis would have an educational cluster similar to those built at South River, Old Mill and Chesapeake High Schools.

Not everyone was equally happy about the location of the new Annapolis High. Ensor and the faculty liked the open setting far removed from residential areas that presumably would facilitate improved monitoring of traffic to exclude unauthorized outsiders and to make cutting class more difficult. Families living in Annapolis, especially those whose teenagers were used to walking to school, voiced concern that the distance to Riva Road from their homes would greatly increase the amount of time to get to and from school. Those without cars would now be dependent on bus transportation, and some worried they'd be unable to participate in sports because they lacked transportation home after practices. Criticism was somewhat muted with promises of activity buses that would allow all students to participate fully in after-school activities.

The original plans for the $10.9 million facility also met with mixed reactions. The school board insisted on a design incorporating the latest educational trend towards open classrooms and flexible space. Ensor and most of his teachers argued that classrooms without walls were impractical for high school students. Guidance counselor Tony Anzalone still marvels that Ensor was able to secure a few modifications to the blueprints so that science, foreign language and some English classrooms were enclosed. Other academic departments consisted of a central office and teacher preparation room with a large space in which up to four faculty members might be teaching at the same time. These academic departments were situated on the top floor of the two-story central section of the building surrounding the large, open space media center. The business, art, home economics and computer classrooms were located on the main floor, as were a large open-space administrative center and the guidance department offices. The one-story south wing included a 650-seat auditorium, the cafeteria and a music complex with soundproof practice booths, numerous larger class areas, ample storage for instruments and even a repair facility. The physical education wing featured a gymnasium with two full-size basketball courts, two large general locker rooms, numerous smaller team rooms and separate areas for gymnastics, wrestling and weight training. A stadium complex with a natural grass field for football, soccer, field hockey and lacrosse games, a quarter-mile track, a concession stand and press box was slated to be built off the south end of the building. Behind the school was ample land for softball and baseball diamonds, several practice fields, a cross-country course through the neighboring woods and six tennis courts.

With all new furniture in the school, the faculty only had to worry about packing up their personal belongings, books and papers during moving week in late January 1979. The sole teacher who seemed to regret leaving was Coach Brady, who twenty years later was still telling stories to his varsity basketball players about the electric atmosphere during big games in the gym at the "old high school." Everyone else looked straight ahead with a sense of hope to the future, without a glance in their rear view mirrors to see the neighbors happily waving farewell.

Adjusting to their new surroundings took several years, but by 1984 the school was running smoothly. To maintain accreditation, Middle States requires an interim report be submitted at the five-year midpoint between visitations. Ensor oversaw the work on this report, but tragedy struck before it could be submitted. Shortly after midnight on April 28, 1984, Ensor and his wife Veronica were returning home when a car driven by a teen-ager crossed the center line on Old Annapolis Road and hit them head on. All were taken to the shock trauma unit at University Hospital in Baltimore. Mrs. Ensor and the 18-year-old driver of the other car had been released when on the morning of May 13, 1984, Annapolis High's beloved principal died. He was only 48 years old. Students, faculty and the entire community mourned the loss of this energetic educator. Annapolis High closed on the day of his funeral. *The Capital* eulogized Ensor as "a doer," and his wife remembered him as "an ideal father, a wonderful husband and a great asset to the community." (5) Fred Stauffer, who in his 38-year career worked as teacher and coach for seven Annapolis High principals, unhesitatingly calls Ensor the best of them all, a man who directed the school with a "firm but loving hand." At Stauffer's urging, the Booster Club voted to rename the school's stadium to honor the principal without whom it probably never would have been built. The plaque that was hung on the stadium's interior wall sums up Ensor's achievements and why his colleagues and students mourned his loss: *Richard G. Ensor dedicated his professional life to Annapolis Senior High School. He advocated, planned and gained approval for Annapolis High. His efforts have provided all of us with an excellent program and an outstanding facility to enjoy for many years to come. Dick was a visible spectator and cheerleader for his kids. He realized the need for a modern gym and stadium complex because he believed night activities would maximize student and community involvement. The spirit of Annapolis High lives in the hearts and minds of those touched so much by Richard G. Ensor.*

Kenneth W. Catlin, an assistant principal in the school, took over on an interim basis while a search was conducted for Ensor's permanent replacement. The Salisbury University graduate had been in the local school system since 1964. His familiarity with Annapolis High made the transition easier than it would have been with an outsider, and thus nobody complained when Catlin's appointment was made permanent. Catlin used a School Climate Survey to identify problems in the school. The results prompted the formation of the Annapolis Pride Committee composed of faculty, students and parents. Annapolis Pride organized poster contests, 10 kilometer races, honors assemblies, student-faculty athletic contests and *Pantherama* skits – the goal of all being to stress self respect, respect for others and respect for the school. A smaller steering committee identified two specific problems to focus on – homework and discipline. A follow-on climate survey in 1986 indicated great improvement in the targeted areas. Overall the Annapolis Pride program seems to have brought improved student motivation to succeed, illustrating the point that high expectations can result in improvement in overall performance (6).

After only two years in the job, however, as part of new county school Superintendent Robert Rice's policy of rotating administrators, Catlin and Arundel High Principal Kenneth Nichols exchanged offices. Nichols, a Frostburg graduate, had actually been an administrative intern at Annapolis High in 1973-74, the year before Catlin held the post. An affable and energetic educator, Nichols was tapped for numerous duties that required him to travel away from the school. He assembled a talented group of assistant principals who ably ran the school during his many absences, including two future Annapolis High principals – Laura P. Webb and Joyce P. Smith. (The accomplishments of Nichols, Webb and Smith are discussed in Chapter 9.)

A Quarter Century with "Big Al"

Five men served as Annapolis High's principal in the quarter century following the school's desegregation, but in the same period only one man held the position as head football coach. Although each principal made positive contributions to the school, all realized the coach played a pivotal role in successfully integrating Annapolis High. In particular, Mirenzi, a former physical education teacher, and sports enthusiast Ensor recognized that athletics could help ease the inevitable tensions that accompanied the end of segregation. Ethnicity didn't matter on playing fields and in the gymnasium as long as the coach cared more about putting together a competitive team than about skin color. Fortunately, this is exactly the kind of coach the Panthers had in Joseph Alvin "Al" Laramore, Jr.

A Dover, Delaware, native, Laramore was an all-around athlete who excelled at football. He attended Wesley College and West Virginia Wesleyan, where he earned a degree in physical education. Assistant Principal and Athletic Director Woody Wetherhold hired Laramore in 1962 to teach physical education, coach baseball and fill in as an assistant coach in football and basketball. Only six games into the 1962-63 boys' basketball season, the team was languishing with a 2-4 record under Ron Covington. With no explanation offered in the press, Laramore was promoted from directing the junior varsity to head coach of the varsity. Under the tutelage of this big, blustery, demanding and competitive man the team caught fire, winning 12 of its last 15 games and capturing the county championship. This initial success served notice to everyone associated with Annapolis High that, like one of America's rockets during this first decade of the space age, Laramore was about to boost Annapolis High athletics into orbit.

Laramore arrived at Annapolis High with the school's first Afro-American students, a happenstance that proved fortunate for everyone involved. He exhibited few of the prejudices that might have been expected of a man educated in segregated schools of Delaware. He welcomed the players from Bates in the very same gruff manner he used with everyone. He was an equal opportunity yeller when angry at an athlete's lack of effort. Nobody got a pass from his long, tough practices, nobody escaped his basic rule: be at practice on time, ready to work hard. The transfers quickly sized up the situation and

Coach Al Laramore should be remembered not only for his win-loss record, but also for successfully integrating the Panthers athletic teams, as seen in two of his squads, the county champion 1968 football squad that included Bates transfers Jack Reed (20) and three-year all-county Archie Pearman (83). A reserve who would start the following season was junior Bill Belichick (50, 3rd row), whose NFL coaching career would make him the most famous of Laramore's former players.

The 1970 basketball team compiled a 16-4 record behind the all-county play of Butch Middleton (14), Les Stanton (23), Phil Johnson (11) and Chris Carter (13), son of future county superintendent C. Berry Carter.

realized that Laramore would give them a chance to play if they put in the effort at practice

The task Laramore faced should not be minimized. Two rival high schools in the same neighborhood had their own treasured athletic traditions. One of them closed abruptly, with its athletes forced to attend the other school, try out for the other school's teams, wear the other school's uniforms and play their hearts out for the other school's glory. Meanwhile the athletes at the "other school" had to worry about dozens of new players – many of them really good – taking away their spots on the team and spoiling their chances of becoming stars. That the schools had been segregated, the defunct one black and the one still open white, further complicated the situation.

Jack Reed ('69) was a varsity football player for the Bates Little Giants as a freshman in 1965-66. He didn't start that year, but he did get to play "a considerable amount" in games. Then his school closed and his team was disbanded. As a sophomore he and his teammates had to try out for the Annapolis High squad along with all the returning Panthers' players. Laramore selected 10 former Bates players for the 1966 varsity, about one-third of the total roster. A disappointed Reed was sent to the junior varsity. To this day he believes he was as good as some of the guys Laramore kept on the varsity. Perhaps he was, but in Laramore's defense, he probably felt more confident keeping players with a year's tutelage in his Delaware Wing-T offense. The 1966 squad went on to win Laramore's first Anne Arundel County championship by fashioning a stellar 8-0-1 season record (the only blemish was a season-ending tie with Severna Park). Reed's classmate from Bates, sophomore Archie Pearman, was named all-county, an honor he garnered again as a junior and a senior. Thirteen other Panthers also earned post-season honors, a school record that still stands, and perhaps also an indication that Reed's placement on the junior varsity may have been a result of simple arithmetic – there were just too many talented upper-class players ahead of him. Reed went on to enjoy an all-county season his junior year, but a leg injury kept him from playing in all the games his senior year. An all-around athlete, Reed also was a track standout and while a student at Morgan State he played on the college's first-ever lacrosse team. Today he coaches basketball at St. Mary's High.

The number of Afro-Americans on the Panthers' varsity football team increased in 1970 to 16 (38 percent) and by 1975 reached 23 (52 percent), a ratio of black and white players that has continued ever since. An even swifter integration occurred in basketball. In 1966, 3 blacks (25 percent) made the varsity, but in 1970 the team was 90 percent Afro-American. Looking over his entire career it appears that in the mid-1960's Laramore may have given some preference to juniors and seniors already on the varsity, but once they had graduated he picked players based on their ability. Basketball and football player Barry Booth ('79) puts it bluntly, "Coach Laramore played the best guys, period. Race had nothing to do with who started." *The Capital* editorialized on January 12, 1989, just two days after his sudden death, "[Al Laramore] coached many of the tough kids from the city's public housing projects and made better men of many of them. White or black, rich or poor, Laramore showed no favorites. The rules were the same for all."

Laramore obviously relished having talented athletes to coach, but he also treasured those with fewer natural gifts who grabbed his attention through hard work. Bill Belichick ('70), the future head coach of the 2002 Super Bowl champion New England Patriots, was such a player. Belichick moved to Annapolis as a young boy when his father Steve was hired in 1956 as an assistant football coach at the Naval Academy. His sheltered life inside the academy's walls and as a student at Germantown ended abruptly in 1966 when he entered ninth grade at the old Bates High building. Years later Belichick told the story of his high school experience to Ron Borges, a *Boston Globe* reporter: *"Back when I was growing up in Annapolis, there was a black high school, Bates, and a white high school, Annapolis High. When I was a freshman, integration began, and I got sent to Bates for two years. The schools were only a few blocks apart. . . .[but] the neighborhoods were so different. I was in over my head.. . . There would be three fire alarms a day, cherry bombs going off in the toilets. I still can remember the day I heard Martin Luther King was assassinated* [4 April 1968]. *You can't imagine how tense that was."*

Belichick understands what helped him change from the nervous boy lost in his new school into a confident young man comfortable in the diverse environment. Although his classmate Butch Middleton remembers him as a "small, kind of pudgy kid," Belichick was determined to play football. He took one of Laramore's favorite maxims to heart. "Football can be explained in four words – HIT OR BE HIT." Belichick's knowledge from studying Navy game films with his dad, coupled with his refusal to let anyone out hit him in practice, eventually earned him the starting center position his senior year. According to Belichick, the football field was *"the one place where it didn't make any difference what color your skin was. Pretty soon, the guys on the football team were just people, and eventually there was a progression. You got to know each other, and then you'd try and convince your friends not to do something because the other guy was all right. Sports bonded us together."* Belichick is just as candid praising the person responsible for making it all work. *"I had a great coach who didn't see color. All he saw was performance. If you did it his way, you were OK. If you didn't, you were in trouble."* The coach Belichick was referring to, of course, was Al Laramore (7).

Title IX – The Girls Take to the Courts and Fields

While Al Laramore was leading Annapolis High boys' football and basketball to state prominence, athletic programs for girls went through a roller coaster ride. By the mid-1960's, Annapolis High girls had been playing some form of organized competition for nearly six decades. The first record of a girls' game is in the October 16, 1908, *Evening Capital* story that lists the line-ups for the senior and junior girls' inter-class basketball competitions. The tone of the story suggests that similar class games had taken place in earlier years. Detailed coverage of girls' basketball can be found in the 1910 and 1911 school paper, *The Red and Blue*. The Public Athletic League (PAL) endorsed basketball as excellent exercise for girls in 1915; the following year all girls in the fourth through 11th grades were assessed a fee of 10 cents a month to help defray the costs of constructing two outdoor basketball courts and a playing field behind the grammar and high school buildings on Green Street (8). When winter curtailed outdoor play, the boys' basketball team moved its interscholastic games to the Bladen Street armory. Meanwhile, the girls eventually succeeded it getting the superintendent's permission to transform the third floor assembly room in the high school temporarily into a basketball court so they could continue their intramural games (9).

After World War I, the girls asked to be allowed to form interscholastic teams in several sports. By the 1920's they were playing a full slate of basketball games at the armory, often as part of a double-header with the boys. Soon PAL was sponsoring state championships in several girls' sports, including basketball, fieldball and softball. Although Annapolis High girls never won a state title, they fielded many excellent teams in both basketball and field ball

AHS Girls' Basketball

The "girls' gym (on the second floor of Maryland Hall) was site of fierce interclass games (right), but by 1948 the girls' team played interscholastic games in the "lower gym" before making it to the state finals the "lower" gym, where the boys also played.

The 1964-65 county champs (below) crafted their 10-1 record playing games in the gymnasium at the new Annapolis Jr. High

The 1976-77 Lady Panthers were the 4th AHS team in a row to make it to the AA state final 4. They lost to DuVal 55-52 in the finals to finish 2nd in the state with a 20-3 season record.

until World War II brought a halt to all interscholastic competition in the county. After the war they wasted no time reorganizing teams. The 1948 girls' basketball team lost the state championship to Towson by only one point, and in the 1950's, the Lady Panthers won several county basketball championships (10).

The decade of the 1960's was not a good one for girls' sports. The basketball team was disbanded twice, first from 1960-62 and again after 1967. During the first hiatus, the girls continued playing field hockey, volleyball and softball. During basketball's brief reprise in the mid-1960's, the Lady Panthers put several superb teams on the court, including the 1964-65 county champions that compiled a 10-1 record. Then, without warning, the county dropped all girls' interscholastic varsity sports except basketball in the fall of 1966. No field hockey, no volleyball and no softball. Basketball survived the axe for just one more year. The girls expressed their dismay at the turn of events in the 1967 *Wake*. The Girls' Varsity "A" organization that had been composed of female athletes who earned varsity letters had to change its rules so intramural participants could be considered for membership. By 1970, Rhonda Pindell Charles' only opportunity to play interscholastic basketball and softball came when one of the local high schools hosted a field day of round robin competition.

Why female varsity sports were cut at this time is puzzling. Certainly the girls didn't request their teams be disbanded. Several possible explanations can be suggested. Perhaps the continued growth of enrollment in the county schools to over 66,000 students – an increase of 2,843 from the previous year – created budget concerns that led administrators to cut the expense of running a girls' athletic program (11). Although it is certainly curious that this decision coincided with the full desegregation of the county's schools, it is hard to imagine that racism played a role in canceling girls' sports. Another possibility is that there was a shortage of enough fields and gymnasiums to accommodate the competing demands of both boys and girls for practice and game venues.

At Annapolis High, for instance, by the fall of 1965 the land behind the school that had been used by the girls' field hockey and boys' soccer teams was appropriated for a new 5,500-seat Panther Stadium the school was slated to share with a short-lived professional football team called the Annapolis Sailors (12). Laramore, in his first year as the Annapolis High athletic director and head football coach, was so worried about the new sod on the field that he prohibited any other teams from playing on it. According to coach Paul Verrillo, his soccer team had to play at Germantown Elementary School, while field hockey players ended up staking out a small field in front of Severn Hall to play their few games. The Sailors folded after a year, leaving Annapolis High with a debt of over $30,000 and a half-finished concession stand and press box. With such money worries, Laramore likely would have used what influence he had to cut the expense of running a girls' sports program (13).

In June 1972, however, the prospects for female athletes changed dramatically with the passing of Title IX of the federal education act that stated, "*No person in the United States shall, on the basis of sex, be excluded from participation in, be denied the benefits of, or be subject to discrimination under any educational programs or activity receiving federal financial assistance.*" These words started a revolution in interscholastic and intercollegiate athletics. At the time Title IX was enacted, fewer than 300,000 girls in the United States were participating in high school sports. Twenty-five years later, the number had grown to 2.4 million. Basketball serves as a good example of the rise in participation: In 1972, 132,299 high school girls were playing basketball; in 2000 that number has risen over 300 percent to almost half a million (14).

Anne Arundel County's reaction to Title IX regulations was swift. Girls' volleyball, basketball and softball teams were fielded during the 1972-73 school year. Opportunities for girls to play other sports, however, took longer. Leslie Finkle remembers there "was no big deal" about the girls playing interscholastic basketball again, but some females were frustrated that sports they wanted to play weren't available. Finkle was on the basketball team, but her dream was to play tennis. Her problem was resolved when coach Robert Pauli allowed Finkle and another girl to join the boys' tennis team in the spring of 1974. The county gradually added girls' teams in field hockey and cross-country (fall 1977), indoor and outdoor track (winter 1978), soccer (fall 1979) and lacrosse (1981). Although Annapolis High has produced outstanding female athletes over the years in every sport, basketball was the school's premier sport in the first decade of the Title IX era. Starting in 1973-74 the Lady Panthers won four straight county and district titles, compiling a 70-15 record. They improved their fourth place finish in the 1975 state tournament to third in 1976 and second in 1977, when under head coach Judy Svec they lost 55-52 in the finals to DuVal. Fred Stauffer recalls the frustration among Annapolis High fans during this game when the referees failed to notice that the same DuVal girl went to the charity stripe regardless of who had been fouled. Hard to win when the opponent's best free throw shooter is allowed to take all the foul shots! Although the girls' team fell off somewhat in the late 1970's, Coach Calvin Vain directed them to a 20-7 season in 1982 that included another appearance in the state finals. The team that would eventually replace basketball as the school's most successful sport for girls was lacrosse, which in the 1990's under Coach Dave Gehrdes won one national title and several state championships.

1978 State Football Championship

As the girls' sports program recovered after the passage of Title IX, Al Laramore struggled with his health. In 1972 and 1977 he was forced to take extended leaves-of-absence as he grappled with emotional problems that today can be routinely managed through medications. He came back from both sabbaticals rip-roaring for action. His 1973 team responded by improving from the previous year's 5-5 record (under stand-in coach Lou Thomas) to a county championship, 9-2 season. The team's recovery in 1978 was to be even better. Prospects for the season were uncertain when players reported for its first practice in late summer 1978. The previous year defensive coordinator Bruce Villwock had taken over the young, inexperienced team while Laramore was hospitalized. The 4-6 record in 1977 marked the Panthers' first losing season since 1964, and one of only four in the nearly forty years since then (1965-2003). Laramore was quick to point out that the previous year's experience would prove invaluable now that the players were older and stronger. Villwock recalled that on the first day of practice, Laramore told the players he expected "dedication, positive thinking, teamwork, togetherness and no shenanigans." (15) With one exception,. the team followed the coach's orders.

The Panthers opened the season with a 45-0 thrashing of Baltimore's Kenwood High. According to the *Evening Capital,* "Laramore attributed the Panther's inaugural success to total school involvement and positive senior leadership," a theme he would return to many times as the season progressed. Under the daily drilling of offensive coordinator Bill Phebus, the offensive line was emerging as one of the finest in Annapolis history. Center Lenny Riek, guards

John Dobyns and Gary Dukes, tackles Mike Colbert and Jeff Jacobson and ends Bruce Wemple and Dan Loman could open holes that allowed backs Randy Pittman, John Rodkey and Kevin Thompson to break into the open after taking a pitch or handoff from quarterback Darryl Brown. The potent attack would produce 375 points in 12 games, a record that would last until 1999, while linebacker Tom Parker keyed the stingy, hard-hitting defense that would surrender just 82 points.

In their second game the Panthers managed a narrow 19-12 victory over Westminster, but the next weekend they easily defeated South Carroll, 22-7. Next up was longtime nemesis, Bel Air, a school that since 1955 had defeated Annapolis in 17 of their 23 annual meetings. Several days before the game, Tommy Parker left a classroom to go to the bathroom without the teacher's permission – a violation of school regulations that led to a one-day suspension. Laramore's policy was to bench any player who had been suspended from school, so the Panthers went into the contest without their defensive captain and leading tackler. Phebus points out that "*most coaches would have looked the other way rather than bench their star player before the biggest game of the year, but not Al Laramore. Parker broke a school rule, so he sat out the game. No discussion.*" In what would be the closest game of the season, the defense held Bel Air to just 7 points while the offense managed to score 12. They then ran off five convincing victories over Chesapeake (27-0), Old Mill (40-0), Meade (48-13), Andover (47-0) and Glen Burnie (34-6). Laramore said of the nine-game winning streak, "*The 1978 Panthers are a team with the most sincere dedication to teamwork – and each other – I have ever coached.*" (16)

The last game on the regular season schedule was against the Falcons of Severna Park coached by Laramore's rival coach and close friend Andy Borland. These two teams had met annually since 1960, with the last 15 games played as the regular season finale. By 1978 Annapolis held a narrow edge in the series, having won nine times to Severna Park's six (three games ended in ties). Borland had his team sky high for the game, challenging them to spoil Annapolis High's chance for a perfect regular season. The Panthers, already assured of making the state AA playoffs, were lackluster in the first half, but they stepped up their intensity enough to secure a 19-13 victory that wrapped up just the third perfect regular season in Annapolis High history (the others were 1909 and 1962). Unlike past seasons, however, the equipment wasn't ready to be packed away. For the first time, Annapolis High had earned the right to play a post-season game the next weekend.

The Maryland Public Secondary Schools Athletic Association (MPSSAA) state playoffs in football were first staged in 1974. Schools were arranged in four classifications based on size, with the four teams in each class that had accrued the most playoff points vying for the champion's crown. Annapolis High's 10-0 regular season put them at the top of the AA classification for the biggest schools in the state. The playoff games were held at high schools with suitable stadiums. Ironically, the school hosting the Panther's semi-final game against Crossland from Prince George's County was Severna Park. Although Annapolis had a better record, predictions were for a close game, in part because other counties regarded Anne Arundel County football lightly. The Panthers' convincing 34-10 victory "gave Anne Arundel County football a shot in the arm." Laramore credited the offensive line for "opening gaping holes in Crossland's defense" that allowed the Panthers to rush for nearly 300 yards. Meanwhile linebacker Tommy Parker and the Annapolis defense held the Cavaliers to just 54 yards on the ground. After the game, Laramore said the decisive win should "quiet those critics who think Anne Arundel football doesn't stack up with the rest of the state." (17)

The victory propelled the Panthers into the finals where on the Saturday after Thanksgiving they took on Montgomery County's Walt Whitman High for the state championship. For the third weekend in a row the Panthers played on Severna Park's Roberts Field. Annapolis fell behind 7-0 in the first quarter when the Vikings converted a fumble recovery into the game's first score, but then took the lead on a surprise two-point conversion (their first all season) after Kevin Thompson scampered 80 yards for a touchdown on a simple trap play. They cushioned their lead on a 14-yard swing pass from quarterback Darryl Brown to wing John Rodkey on the last play of the first half. Brown passed for two more touchdowns in the second half, one each to Thompson and Rodkey, while the Vikings mustered only one more touchdown late in the fourth quarter. Final score: Annapolis 28, Whitman 14. Laramore and the Panthers had their first football state championship (18).

In the joyous locker room after the game, Laramore was generous doling out praise to everyone on the team, again singling out

204 *A Century of Education and Football at Annapolis High School*

Celebrating the state championship for 1978 are Tommy Parker and Darryl Brown (holding the trophy) surrounded by John Rodkey, Dan Loman, Kevin Thompson, Ed DeMeter, Alex Chew, Daryl Parker, James Quarles, Philip Pearman and Bruce Wemple.

The 1984 football team was unblemished in the regular season and easily won its semi-final playoff game against Churchill, but Randallstown upset them in the state finals, 14-6. Laramore's sons, Dan (12) and Dave (83), were starters, along with captain Rico Stewart and Marcus Hayes (44), selected to be in the Big 33 all-star game.

The 1973-74 boys' team won AHS's first state basketball championship. Players were (top row, l to r): Bunk Stansbury, Jeff Brooks, Larry Beavers, Albert Mills, Gilbert Allen, Tyronne Jones, Larry Snyder, Sherman Douglass (bottom row): Brewer Gray, Steve Anderson, Kim Jones, Otis Evans, Henry Downs, Larry Johnson and Kevin Slade.

the offensive linemen for coming off the snap so well that they controlled the scrimmage line all afternoon. On defense, the press hailed linebacker Tommy Parker as "the best of the best." *Evening Capital* reporter Ted Simendinger piled on the metaphors, calling Parker, *"The demon of the Annapolis defense, the hardest hitter this side of inflation, and a fellow so tough a clock won't tick until he passes by. He hits with the force of a truck every time, every down. He doesn't tackle people. He rearranges them so that even their hairdresser does not know for sure. On occasion he alone has been worth the price of admission."* Laramore put it more succinctly: "Parker is by far the best at his position I've seen in 16 years of coaching in Maryland." (19)

Over the years Laramore had the opportunity to coach many other outstanding players who wore the maroon and white uniforms of the Fighting Panthers. High on the list was Donald "Turkey" Brown ('81), who during his Annapolis career set rushing and scoring records that stood for 18 years. He accepted a full scholarship to play at Oklahoma, but left after a year saying he liked the football, but not the western lifestyle. A problem transferring credits led to a wasted year, but he eventually played two seasons for Maryland and was selected by the San Diego Chargers the in the fifth round of the 1986 NFL draft. He also played for Miami and New York before a compound shin fracture ended his professional career in 1989 (20).

In 1984 Laramore again led an 11-0 team into the state championship game, but this time Randallstown defeated the favored Panthers, 12-7. The next year the MPSSAA playoffs expanded to eight teams. Annapolis played in the quarterfinals four seasons in a row, but lost each time – to Meade (35-20 in 1986), to Severna Park (12-7 in 1987) and twice to Winston Churchill (3-0 in 1985, 31-14 in 1988). Instead of being in his customary spot on the sideline during this last game, Laramore was restricted to a hospital bed while he recuperated from pacemaker surgery. Assistant Bill Phebus visited Laramore several hours before game time and told his mentor that the truck was waiting downstairs to take him in his bed to Potomac for the game. Laramore, going along with the joke, asked for his shoes. Then in a more serious mood, he asked Phebus to "tell the team I'm doing fine and I'll be back." (21). If the two men could have seen into the future perhaps they would have pulled off the stunt so that "Big Al" could have seen "his boys" play one last time. Although Laramore did get back to the school after Christmas, he never again was to walk

AL LARAMORE MEMORIAL SCHOLARSHIP WINNERS

These student athletes were selected for this honor because they best exemplified the enthusiasm, spirit and ideals of Coach Laramore. Football, basketball and lacrosse head coaches nominate a senior who best exemplifies these qualities; Coach Laramore's wife, Dorothy Laramore Coyle, interviews the finalists to help select the winner. Certainly Coach Laramore's legacy lives on in these graduates of Annapolis High School.

1989 Patrick Pope
AHS football & lacrosse
Air Force Academy ('94)
Lacrosse recruit; varsity starter

1990 Nathaniel Cook
AHS football
Dartmouth College ('94)
Football recruit, varsity captain

1991 Erin Cannelli
AHS field hockey & lacrosse
James Madison University ('95)

1992 Robert Wooster
AHS basketball
St. Francis College ('96)
Basketball recruit, varsity starter

1993 Matthew Criscimagna
AHS football & baseball
Salisbury State University ('97)
Football & baseball varsity starter

1994 Matthew Smear
AHS football and wrestling
Duke University ('98)
Ph.D. in neurobiology, California

1994 David Winegrad
AHS soccer & lacrosse
University of Virginia ('98)
Lacrosse recruit, varsity starter

1995 Teshawn Cooper
AHS football & basketball
Chesapeake Community College ('97)
Basketball recruit

1996 Brian McNew
AHS soccer & lacrosse
Washington College ('00)
Lacrosse recruit, honor student

1997 Donald Snowden
AHS football & basketball
Newport News Apprentice ('05)
Football recruit, varsity starter

1998 Michael Donlin
AHS football & lacrosse
Loyola College ('02)
Lacrosse recruit, varsity starter

1999 Keith R. Buckingham
AHS football & basketball
U. S. Naval Academy ('03)
Ensign, U.S. Navy

2000 Will Phillips
AHS soccer, basketball & lacrosse
University of Pennsylvania ('04)
Lacrosse recruit, varsity player

2001 Nick Good-Malloy
AHS football, basketball & tennis
Salisbury University ('05)
Football recruit, varsity starter

2002 Chester Feldmann
AHS soccer & basketball
University of Maryland ('06)
Presidential scholar

2003 Demario Harris
AHS football & track
Wesley College ('07)
Football recruit

the sidelines during a Panthers football game. On January 10, 1989 he stayed after school to have coffee with John Brady and Roy Brown. He told them that since a magnet was inserted in the pacemaker he really had been feeling much better. Later that afternoon he was at home carrying firewood with his son David when he felt weak, sat down and then slumped over. Rushed to Anne Arundel Medical Center, he was pronounced dead of cardiac arrest. He was only 53 years old (22).

Memorializing Al Laramore

During his 26-year tenure at Annapolis High, Al Laramore held two major administrative positions: athletic director (1965-72) and physical education department chair (1971-89). He also served as head coach of four sports: baseball (1962-65), football (1965-88), boys' basketball (1962-77) and boys' lacrosse (1982-88). Although he only had one winning season in baseball, nobody in the history of Anne Arundel County has surpassed Laramore's lifetime winning percentage in the other sports – football (156-66-2, .697), basketball (243-81, .750) and lacrosse (71-27, .717) – for a combined 470-174-2 (.730). His led teams to 24 county championships (three in lacrosse, 10 in football and 11 in basketball) and 15 district/regional championships (3 in lacrosse, 5 in football and 7 in basketball). We can only guess at how many more victories Laramore might have added to these records if he had lived a normal life span. Despite his early death, he is the only person in Maryland public high school history to coach state championship teams in three sports, basketball (1974), football (1978) and lacrosse (1983, 1984 and 1987).

Tributes to Laramore poured in following his death. He was posthumously inducted in the Maryland State Football Coaches Hall of Fame in 1990 and enshrined in the Anne Arundel County Athletic Hall of Fame in 1992. His name was attached to the Touchdown Club's outstanding lineman award and a major high school lacrosse tournament. His family requested that donations go to a scholarship fund that would annually honor a graduating Annapolis High student-athlete who best embodied Laramore's enthusiasm, spirit and ideals. That his widow and sons wholeheartedly supported the plan for a memorial scholarship reflects one of Laramore's most admirable characteristics, his devotion to his family. Laramore married Dorothy Boltz shortly after beginning his Annapolis teaching career, and soon were the proud parents of twin sons, David and Daniel. His former

208 *A Century of Education and Football at Annapolis High School*

Dan and Dave Laramore played football for their dad, graduated from Annapolis in 1985 and then played college football. Bill Belichick, AHS Class of 1970, became a successful NFL coach. He has been loyal to Annapolis high school and his coach, Al Laramore.

The Annapolis High Booster Club backed the construction of Panther Stadium in 1965 in partnership with the short-lived pro team, the Sailors. At left, the 1966 team storms the field to open practice for the season.

Donald "Turkey" Brown (left) set school rushing and scoring records in 1981 that stood for almost two decades. A University of Maryland graduate, Brown's promising professional career was cut short by leg injuries in 1989.

One lasting tradition born during the Laramore era was the Panther Drill, a routine the entire team performed as to psych-up before each half and after victories. Here the 1980 team executes the drill.

player Bob Mosier, a sportswriter for *The Capital*, remembered, *"Laramore loved his wife, Dorothy, and twin sons David and Dan, more than anything in the world. Often I thought that everything he did, he did with his family in mind."* (23)

Severna Park's football coach Andy Borland also pointed to Laramore's family loyalty as the bedrock of his longtime rival and friend's character. *"When Al sent his men in motion you would hear the quarterback calling the names of his wife and children. He named his signals after them because they were important to him and he always wanted them out on the field with him."* (24) As soon as the boys could walk, Laramore took them to practice; by the time they were 10, their role as managers merited inclusion in team yearbook photos. Both started on the 1984 state finalist team, graduated with the Class of 1985 and then played college football, Dave as a tight end at Shepherd and Dan as the quarterback for Hampden-Sydney (25).

Roy Brown, Bill Phebus and Bruce Villwock (who had left Annapolis High to help establish the football program at the new Broadneck High) headed a group that wanted to ensure Laramore's name would be remembered at the school where he been a fixture for a quarter of a century. After prolonged negotiations with other school organizations, agreement was reached that the field at Richard G. Ensor stadium be named after Laramore. At the dedication ceremony on September 5, 1991, a letter was read from the head coach of the Cleveland Browns, Bill Belichick. Unstinting in his praise for his former coach, Belichick said he had learned from Laramore how to keep plays simple but to insist on perfect execution. He claimed to have used the same philosophy with great success as the Giants' defensive coordinator. "Al really meant a lot to me and I think what is happening is great for his family and the school." (26)

Belichick later demonstrated the depth of his sentiments about his high school coach when he donated the $1,000 speaker's fee from the 1993 Anne Arundel County Touchdown Club banquet to the Al Laramore Memorial Scholarship fund. He also returned to Annapolis High School at the invitation of Anne Arundel County schools Superintendent C. Berry Carter, the father of Belichick's friend and teammate Chris Carter. Belichick urged his audience to follow the "never quit" philosophy of life he had learned from Al Laramore. *"You have to take some risks. Whatever direction you choose there will be some rough spots. I've been fired, lost games, won games. You* have to be resilient enough to work hard. *When you get knocked down, you have to get up and keep on going.*" To repay his coach and the school for these "valuable lessons," Belichick and his wife Debby, also a 1970 graduate, established their own annual scholarship to honor a senior scholar-athlete (27).

The most lasting memorial to Laramore is what perhaps would have mattered most to him. The men who inherited the Annapolis High football program in 1989 consciously retained Laramore's coaching philosophy, techniques and playbook. Head coach Roy Brown and assistants Larry Brogden and Bill Phebus never wavered from Laramore's Wing-T as the team's signature offense. They have taught contemporary players to revere Laramore as the man who began most of the traditions still associated with Annapolis High football, including the pre and post-game Panther Drill, listening to a scratchy recording of college fight songs in a darkened room before taking the field for warm-up drills, putting the starting offensive linemen front and center during pre-game and halftime talks, holding practice the night before the last regular season game on the lighted field of Ensor Stadium and ending that practice with the seniors running a lap together around the field while the rest of the team stands and applauds them.

According to a trio from the 2000 state finalist team – Nick Good-Malloy, Camaro Henson and Mike Melton – Coach Brown wanted to pass on to them Big Al's lessons about qualities like perseverance and loyalty that nominally were about football but also could help them better live their lives. For example, when Brown saw some players were upset after being chewed out during August tryouts, he called the team together to explain that his yelling wasn't meant to be personal, that he didn't "hate them, just what they were doing." He then described the method Laramore used to decide which players he wanted on the team. "*He would pick people out, yell them to death to try and make them quit. Those who looked him in the eye and wanted to kill him but said nothing, stayed on the team. If you didn't quit on him, he wouldn't quit on you.*" Brown, angry after a lackluster practice, challenged the team to play every down according to one of Laramore's favorite sayings: "If I stumble, push me forward. If I fall, pick me up. If I surrender, shoot me." (28)

Laramore's former colleagues and players enjoy telling tales that add color to the picture of the man who figured so prominently in their lives. Math teacher and track coach Fred Stauffer, who replaced

Laramore as Athletic Director in 1972, admits that his predecessor did not take "no" for an answer easily. To avoid acrimony and shouting matches, Stauffer learned to tell Laramore that he needed some time to think over any request he knew he'd have to deny. Usually that proved to be the end of the issue, probably because Laramore lost interest as his active mind filled with other ideas and schemes. Stauffer chuckles as he imitates Laramore's habit of seizing the microphone during morning announcements to exhort the students, "Don't forget, don't be late. Tonight the Panthers are coming out of the gate." Barry Booth ('79) relates a story when Laramore actually became a cheerleader. While playing a close basketball game in DuVal High's packed gym, everyone was surprised when Laramore suddenly got off the bench and walked around the sidelines of the entire court waving his arms, a move that quieted DuVal's fans and fired up the few Panthers' supporters who had managed to get seats. The Panthers went on to win the game. Keith Mathews ('75), a football player on several of Laramore's teams, remembers the physical education class when "Big Al" reappeared after being absent for several weeks pedaling a tiny tricycle through the door and circling the gym floor while the startled students cheered him on.

Clearly, however, Laramore wanted to control reactions to his antics. Jack Reed ('69) recalls the afternoon he laughed as the hefty Laramore came to practice in a sweatshirt too small to cover his belly. Laramore's tirade ensured Reed never again made the mistake of laughing at a teacher or coach. Laramore also expected a measure of respect from game officials. His most infamous dispute with referees occurred in the first quarter of the game to decide the 1970 boys' basketball county championship at Arundel High School. Laramore sent his team to the locker room and refused to let them return to the court following a technical foul he considered unjustified. Arundel was awarded the victory, 2-0. Butch Middleton ('70) still bristles when he recalls Laramore's actions that night. The team, he insists, wanted to play but was powerless to override the coach's decision. Jerry Mears, the Arundel coach, blasted his Annapolis counterpart in the February 21, 1970, *Evening Capital* for poor sportsmanship. Laramore may have had misgivings himself. The following Monday he called each of the seniors to his office to discuss his decision. Although Middleton doesn't know what the others said, he reports telling his coach that the decision had been wrong because Laramore himself had taught his players "never to surrender." This was the only time Laramore allowed his actions to cause his team to forfeit a game. Perhaps he realized that instead of protecting his players from an unfair referee's call, he had actually penalized them and the school by denying them a chance to let their playing do their talking for them.

Although Laramore was as fiercely competitive as any coach around, he was not just about wins and losses. According to longtime assistant Bill Phebus, "*Al was not the kind of man young kids easily forgot. Good or bad, he left an impression. He was a man who had strong convictions about how young athletes should carry themselves both on and off the field. If you broke his rules, you paid the price and it didn't matter who you were. He wanted his athletes to be upstanding citizens, first and foremost.*" (29) Roy Brown agrees that dedication to principles set Laramore apart from most other coaches. "*Al used to say a handshake is one of the most important things in the world. He had principles that he lived by and believed in and never strayed from them. I think that is probably how he'd like to be remembered.*"(30) Brown and his entire coaching staff have done their part to ensure Laramore's legend lived on in the next generation of Annapolis High Panthers.

* * * * * * * * * *

The decade of the 1980's at Annapolis High was marred by the deaths of two men who were in many ways the school's heart and soul: Principal Dick Ensor in May 1984 and Coach Al Laramore in January 1989. The challenge for Annapolis High as it approached the centennial of its founding was to find quality people who could step into their empty shoes. Two women would eventually step forward, and although their feet were small, their actions more than filled the principal's office with creative and steady leadership that would carry the school into the 21st century.

CHAPTER 9:

INTO THE TWENTY-FIRST CENTURY, 1989 – 2001

2000 Panther Squad (11-2) played for State Title in Byrd Stadium

1st row: Kevan Simms, Charlie Dammeyer, Camaro Henson, Nick Good-Malloy, Neanders Nixon, Kion Mackell, Brandon Gulley, Bobby Baker; **2nd row**: Kareem Reed, Karl Butler, Che Carr, Eric Venerable, Andre Toney, Mike Melton, James Forrester, Trico Morgan, B.J. Zadera, Mike Brown; **3rd row**: Maurice Taylor, Ken Brashears, Delano Watkins, Darren Johnson, Demario Green, Davon Watkins, Brandon Johnson, Kevin Jones, Demario Harris Marcus Whitehead, Daniel Esposito, Tavon Hines; **4th row**: Derek Curran, Sung Yang, Tyrell Forrester, Phil Boyd, Brian Powell, Karl Acker, Ben Youngs, Erron Silva, Delray Johnson, Mark Neptune, Pat Cerone

> *"I'm happy for the tight-knit bunch of 20 seniors on this team. They have been with us for the last three years when we went home in the first round of the state playoffs. They are a great bunch of guys and just weren't going to quit. They don't all play, but they pull hard for each other. The only way we could have won tonight was with a total team effort and that is what we got from everyone."*
>
> Head Coach Roy Brown
Following victory over Douglass
in state semi-final game
November 25, 2000

Return of the Freshmen

On opening day of the 1989 school year, half of the 1,740 students at Annapolis High had never before been in the school – 400 sophomores who had completed their freshman year in junior highs, and another 400 ninth graders who entered Annapolis High as part of a county-wide reconfiguration of students that ended elementary school with fifth grade and created middle schools for sixth, seventh and eighth graders. Accompanying Annapolis High's new freshman class were an additional assistant principal and 22 teachers. Former Annapolis High Principal Joseph Mirenzi was an early advocate of four-year high schools, arguing that ninth graders needed access to a broader range of courses than was available in the typical junior high curriculum. Mirenzi rightly pointed out that too many ninth graders in junior highs failed to realize they were actually freshmen whose coursework counted towards high school graduation requirements. He reasoned that moving ninth graders into high school buildings to mingle with older students in the hallways and even sit beside some in classes might encourage them to put more effort in their studies (1).

Among the most enthusiastic early supporters of the change were coaches who salivated at the prospect of having freshmen athletes eligible to play varsity sports (2). Also adding strength to the pro-middle school argument were demographic studies that indicated siphoning sixth graders from elementary schools and ninth graders from junior highs would permit better allocation of existing facilities. Certainly Annapolis High had ample space to house freshman. Originally designed for 2,100 students, enrollment reached 2,300 in 1980, but as the tail end of the baby boom generation born before 1965 completed high school, the number of students dropped steadily so that in the late 1980's between 1,500 and 1,600 names appeared on Annapolis High's roster.

Opponents of the change worried that neither sixth nor ninth graders were mature enough to flourish as the youngest students in middle and high schools respectively. Psychologists suggested that placing them with older students might increase social stresses to the detriment of their academic performance. Concrete evidence to support such a fear was lacking. Almost 35 years had passed since Annapolis High's last freshman class had entered the school in 1952. Discipline, which had improved as the result of the Annapolis Pride program, again became an issue in the fall of 1989, as freshmen lacking maturity soon became behavior problems in the freer high school environment. According to guidance counselor Tony Anzalone, their academic achievement also began to decline markedly relative to their predecessors who had been educated in junior high schools. Despite these problems, however, the county continued its transition to middle schools and four-year high schools.

Unfortunately Ken Nichols, in the fourth year of his tenure as Annapolis High principal, was often called away from the school during this important transition period. The talented educator was sought on the state level to head accreditation teams, serve on various boards and chair education association meetings. A group of teachers, including basketball coach John Brady, liked to rib their affable principal. They designed a "missing person" ad that featured Nichols' picture on a grocery bag with the question, "Have you seen this man?" They rigged up a life-size dummy they propped in the often-empty chair behind his desk. A flip sign for his office door read "Out of the Office" on one side and "Still Out of the Office" on the other.

Obviously November 1989, less than three months after the arrival of Annapolis High's first freshmen, was not the optimal time for the Middle States team to evaluate the school. The 10-year interval for re-accreditation was, however, a requirement set in stone. The previous visit in 1979 had also come at an inconvenient time, immediately after the school had moved into its new Riva Road location. Nichols, who had experience chairing Middle States teams assigned to study other high schools in the region, did not anticipate problems. Indeed, he encouraged Annapolis High's self-study team to be candid about problems, especially those stemming from the open-space classrooms in the school's academic areas on the second floor.

The 47-member visiting team spent three days at Annapolis High and then took almost six months preparing its report. They applauded "the stable core" of veteran faculty and staff, commending them for creating such a "caring atmosphere" for the diverse student body. They also praised Nichols for articulating a philosophy of education based on equity rather than on equality so that everyone at Annapolis High was given a fair opportunity to succeed. The "extensive curriculum" crafted to challenge the academic ability of students in classes ranging from special education to advanced placement exemplified the philosophy in action. So, too, did the Maryland's Tomorrow program that provided special services to students targeted as being at-risk of dropping out of school.

Despite such praise, however, Middle States informed Nichols that full accreditation would be delayed while the school took appropriate action on several of its recommendations. The local press pounced on the report when it was released. The school's positive aspects were all but ignored in a Baltimore *Sun* story printed under a headline that called the evaluation "highly critical" and focused on the visiting committee's censure of the school's leaders for allowing discipline to decline dramatically (3). In candid language the evaluators alleged that the teaching and learning environment had been eroded by the failure to "unilaterally and consistently enforce rules and regulations." They specifically objected to "hats in class, vulgar pictures and images on shirts, lateness to class without teacher recognition and the absence of remediation laboratories." To improve the school's climate, they recommended the implementation of "more consistent controls on the students' freedom" and challenged teachers to "hold individual students accountable for consequences of their actions." Finally, the report suggested administrators, especially the principal, needed to "focus more of their attention and time on their roles as instructional leaders of the school," a not-so-subtle rebuke of Nichols' frequent absences (4).

Nichols naturally took umbrage at the report's tone. He was particularly irritated by its failure to link the open classrooms and the recent arrival of ninth graders to the school's shortcomings. Although he agreed to take "all the recommendations back to the individual committees . . . to develop appropriate responses," he objected strongly to the criticism directed at how his students dressed, how his teachers taught and how he led the school. He wondered how "somebody could think their standards should be our standards. We do not feel we need to monitor whether hats are worn. We already have school standards." And in defense of his own leadership, he commented: "The question when you are a principal is: Are you a manager or an innovator?" Which he considered preferable wasn't clear (5).

The Two Female Principals of the 1990's

Despite Nichols' vigorous defense, everyone at Annapolis High realized the need to make changes. Nichols was able to convince the school board that most discipline problems in the school stemmed from the open classrooms. Funding was approved to enclose the open spaces on the second floor and to partition the main office into several

In 1990 Laura P. Webb (left) became the first African American and only the second female principal of Annapolis High. Four years later Webb's friend and former assistant, Joyce P. Smith, replaced her when she retired.

Senior staff members during AHS centennial were (clock-wise from right): guidance counselor Helen Turner, Mike Svec (music), Phillip Greenfield (history), Thomas Neiles (German), Richard King (history), Donzella Parker-Bert (PE) & Tony Anzalone (guidance).

Svec began leading the band to its many local, regional and national honors in 1969. Neiles started coaching cross-country in 1970. King gave his time to girls' soccer starting in 1979 and later added tennis. Parker-Bert helped with several teams in the 1980's.

smaller rooms surrounding a central reception area. Anzalone also credits Nichols for taking the first steps to secure a Navy Junior ROTC program that offers the opportunity to excel for students looking for a special niche in the school.

The major rethinking of issues about student deportment and discipline would be left to a new principal. In the spring of 1990 Nichols was promoted to an assistant director position with the board of education. County Superintendent of Schools Larry L. Lorton, an Ohio native two years on the job, invited Annapolis High's 13 department chairs and the faculty council to convene with an assistant superintendent to brainstorm about the type of person they'd like to see replace Nichols. Consensus emerged that they preferred a compassionate yet firm leader familiar with the diverse Annapolis High community. Anzalone relates that towards the end of the meeting, they were asked to recommend people who met such criteria. Their response was surprising because, according to Anzalone, "those present seldom agreed on anything." Now they spoke with one voice. Everyone wanted the current assistant principal Laura P. Webb to get the job. Impressed with such a strong recommendation, Lorton complied by promoting Webb to be Annapolis High's second female and first African American principal in the school's 94-year history. Webb brought solid credentials to the task of leading Annapolis High in the last decade of the 20th century. Born in North Carolina, she majored in physical education at Greensboro's Bennett College, then moved to Maryland in 1961 when her former teacher Robert Jeffries offered her a physical education position at Calvert County's Mount Harmony Elementary School where he was principal. Eventually she came to Anne Arundel County, married former Bates High football coach James Webb and in 1984 joined the Annapolis High staff as an assistant principal (6).

Webb wasted no time addressing the problems identified in the Middle States report. The easiest recommendation to fulfill was improving the visibility and involvement of the principal in the school. According to her longtime friend and colleague, Assistant Principal Joyce P. Smith, "The students wanted and needed a steady presence and visibility from their principal. Webb was accessible to everyone [and was] present at every event." Smith was just one in the strong group of veteran administrators and teachers who advised the new principal. Webb and Smith made an especially formidable team. Smith admired Webb's ability to "get people to work together to accomplish a common goal." (7) Anzalone, who chaired the guidance department while both women were principals, credits Webb for her knack of being able to articulate an overall vision and Smith with the ability to figure out innovative ways to translate theory into practical programs.

Concerns about discipline and demeanor were turned over to an advisory group of student advocates. Webb adopted several of their suggestions at the beginning of the 1990 school year. A stricter dress code prohibited hats from being worn inside the building, an after-school detention program for those tardy to school or to class was organized and students were required to remain on Annapolis High grounds during school hours (8). Several months later some members of *The Capital*'s editorial staff held a "rap session with about 20 students from Annapolis High" during which the surprised adults discovered "[they] actually embraced the stricter disciplinary measures Mrs. Webb installed at the high school in her first year as principal." The newsmen left the session impressed by how much "Mrs. Webb is loved and respected by her students." (9)

Having satisfied the concerns of Middle States, Webb was free to tackle her own agenda. Raising expectations and performance of the minority students topped her list. She facilitated the formation of two new clubs in the school – Concerned Black Men and Committed Black Females – both of which enlisted the support of community leaders. Focused tutoring and special encouragement for marginal performers led to a significant increase in the number of minority students taking SATs and a whopping 50-point improvement in the school's overall test results (10). Webb also strengthened the Maryland's Tomorrow program to improve its success keeping at risk students in school. To help all ninth graders make a more successful transition to high school, Webb got permission from the board of education to limit the first day of school each fall to freshmen (11). Alex Malloy ('97) was in the first class to benefit from having a day in the building without being bothered by older students as he learned his way to his classrooms, found his locker, met his teachers and ate lunch in the cafeteria. "Freshman Only Day" proved so successful that other high schools in the county soon copied it. Webb also did some borrowing, including South River's "prom breakfast" held in the school cafeteria to provide seniors with a fun and safe event to enjoy after the dance (12).

The only blemish on Webb's record came in the spring of 1993 when students brought a feud simmering between two rival communities into the school. Police were summoned several times to break up fights. The first was on March 10, 1993, when two students started punching each other in a second-floor hallway; 40 to 50 others joined in. Nine teachers acted quickly to quell the disturbance. Of the seven students suspended, two were eventually expelled (13). Webb joined with community leaders to mediate with the feuding teenagers, but three weeks later another fight erupted, this time inside the school's main entrance. Thirteen students were arrested and eventually expelled. Webb, who was slightly injured when she inserted herself between brawling students, was clearly exasperated. She told *The Capital,* "I'm just very disappointed and frustrated the instructional day has to be hindered by the disrespect of a couple of students. It's just a disregard for law and order." Over the next several weeks the police worked closely with the school to reestablish confidence among parents and students that Annapolis High was safe. Police sergeant Ray Pearson believed the arrests and expulsions served "notice to these kids that their fighting in the school will not be tolerated."(14) The message was apparently received, and with the help of continuing mediation sessions, the feud was resolved. No such disruptions have taken place at the school in the decade since 1993.

Much of the credit for keeping the hallways safe goes to Joyce Smith, who took over the principal's office in June 1994 when Webb decided to retire so she could "leave while I still love it." Smith called Webb a "wonderful role model for anyone who wants to be an effective, compassionate and effective principal." Webb returned the praise, saying her departure was made easier because she knew she was leaving the school in good hands. Smith, an Oklahoma native and University of Arkansas graduate, brought her degree in history and English east in 1967 to begin her teaching career in Baltimore County's Woodlawn High School. She moved on to Fairlawn, New Jersey and then to Fairfax County, Virginia, picking up a master's degree in psychology and special education at the University of Virginia along the way. She eventually settled in Anne Arundel County and after filling several teaching and administrative positions with the county and state, she arrived in 1984 at Annapolis High as an administrative intern and then assistant principal. Smith briefly served as South River High's acting principal before being named to replace Webb at Annapolis High.

Although Smith considers her most important contribution to Annapolis High was convincing students to keep community disputes outside of school, her list of additional achievements is lengthy. Many were a natural outgrowth of her firm belief that students could only excel in their studies when they were comfortable in the school and free of outside worries. She set out to involve students in making decisions and establishing rules to give them a sense of ownership in the school. The centerpiece of her plans took shape in 1995 when the first T.E.A.M. (Together Everyone Achieves More) Days were held. In late August a group of students representing a cross-section of the school were trained to be T.E.A.M. leaders during an overnight retreat at Arlington Echo, the county's outdoor education facility. Then on several Fridays in the fall, larger groups of about 250-300 students accompanied the leaders to Sandy Point Park for a day of team building activities. Reaction by day's end was always extremely positive, with many participants stressing how they had made new friends after spending the day with students they hadn't known from different neighborhoods, classes or clubs (15).

"Celebrate Annapolis!" was another program Smith began to increase student pride in their school. On a designated day each spring, Annapolis High served as the stage on which current, past and future students were selected to perform everything from musical numbers and poetry readings to karate demonstrations and step dance exhibitions. The day ended with the induction of distinguished alumni from both Annapolis and Bates High onto the Wall of Honor, a ceremony that not only highlighted the accomplishments of the inductees but also allowed students to think about what they might be able to achieve in their own lives. Smith laughs as she relates how often a graduating senior told her to make sure to "save a place on the Wall of Honor for me." (16)

Smith's innovative programs soon attracted favorable notice. Honors for Annapolis High and its principal began to pile up. In 1999 the *Washington Post* chose Smith as the Outstanding Educational Leader in Anne Arundel County. The following year the Maryland Association of Student Councils picked her as its Principal of the Year. Annapolis High was selected as an honorable mention Blue Ribbon School in 2000, and then was named a national Green School in 2001 to recognize the many student-initiated environmental projects. Not surprisingly, the 1999 Middle States team of educators conducting its 10-year re-accreditation visit discovered much to praise and little to fault – a significant turnaround from the previous report. Everyone in the school shared credit, but everyone also recognized that the leadership of their two female principals – Laura Webb and Joyce Smith – had been crucial to the process of restoring Annapolis High's good name (17).

Annapolis High – 100 Years and Beyond

During the 1997-1998 school year Smith learned that Annapolis High was approaching the 100th anniversary of its first graduating class of 1899. Uncertain exactly when the school had actually been founded, 1998-1999 was designated as the appropriate time to celebrate Annapolis High's centennial. Always ready to seize any opportunity that would focus public attention on favorable aspects of the school, Smith asked students, teachers and parents to consider ways to commemorate Annapolis High's 100th birthday. To ensure everyone knew about the landmark year, two-dozen large, attractive blue and white vinyl standards with the slogan, "Annapolis High – 100 Years and Beyond" and the name of the sponsoring organization were displayed on the overhanging arms of parking lot lampposts.

Centennial activities were organized to coincide with Homecoming weekend in the fall of 1998. On Thursday October 29, 1998, the Wall of Fame induction featured the oldest known graduate of Annapolis High, 99-year-old Emily Rawlings Johns ('16), who attended in person and even sang an original song that she'd written while a student. Former Mayor Al Hopkins ('43) said he was delighted to have a chance to connect with today's Annapolis High students to let them know how much the school had meant to him and his Depression and World War Two-era friends. With the support of mayor Dean Johnson, the traditional parade through downtown Annapolis, which had been discontinued soon after the school moved to Riva Road, was re-instituted. About 750 graduates from both Annapolis and Bates joined current Annapolis High students to march from St. John's College, around Church circle and down Main Street to City Dock. An alumni band and alumni cheerleaders participated in the parade and then entertained the packed Ensor stadium during the Panthers' 35-7 victory over Old Mill. The Booster Club printed a special centennial football program that was distributed free to all fans. *The Capital* provided prominent coverage of the weekend's events, including an editorial that aptly summed up the good feelings the centennial homecoming generated. "*Individuals come and go, but certain institutions bind the community together decade in and decade out. Annapolis High School is one of those institutions, and, as the school completes its first century, we wish the best to all those who love it."* (18)

Among those who have loved Annapolis High through the course of its first 100 years are many of its more than 500 teachers. Huntley Cross, who began his 40-year career with the Anne Arundel County board of education as a teacher at Annapolis High, states that he looks back on his years at the school as "the best time of my life." Joyce Smith believes the smooth running of the school during her tenure as principal was largely due to the dedicated faculty of 98 teachers who at the time of the centennial celebration were a blend of enthusiastic newcomers, including some Annapolis High graduates, and a score of veterans whose tenure extended over 20 years to before the school moved into the Riva Road building. Among those with seniority were Anthony Anzalone (guidance); Mary Ford, Lydia Smithers and Ron Stafford (English); Lynn Kolarik and Tom Neiles (foreign languages); Larry Brogden, Catherine Cundriff, Chris Deterding, Fred Stauffer and Bob Walleck (math); Laura Hack, Sherry Hockenberry, Dan Pogonowski, John Rentch, Joe Ruddle and March Warner (science); Robert Carter, John Harrison, Rich King and Jean Nouri (social studies); John Brady (business); Marietta Smallwood (home economics); Michael Svec (music) and Donzella Parker-Bert (physical education).

In the mid-1980's these veterans were joined by another dozen teachers who would become stalwarts at Annapolis High, including: Helen Turner (guidance); Sam Salamy (administration); Leslie Gershon and Linda Harshbarger (English); Della Hanna and Barbara Rogers (math); Phil Greenfield and George Rossiter (social studies); Roy Brown and Dan Hart (physical education); Norma Clarke and Pat Suriano (special education). That over one-third of the teachers who comprised the Annapolis High faculty in 1998 had been there for more than 15 years speaks volumes about their commitment and dedication – to their jobs, to their students and to the school. Indeed, their tenure would doubtless have been shorter if they believed half of what they read in local papers about their safety. Many of math teacher Della Hanna's colleagues echo her sentiments about being assigned to Annapolis High: "The stories about violence in the school are completely overblown. "There were a couple of fights then years ago and that was it." Anzalone adds, "Some people mistake noise for misbehavior. Annapolis High students have always been loud, but that doesn't make them violent."

Taking the space to list all of these teachers is meant as a tribute to them and to their unnamed colleagues for having devoted their lives to educating the diverse, demanding and talented Annapolis High students. When asked to name teachers who have made a difference in their lives, former students seldom have to think longer than a minute to come up with several names, and the teachers are just as likely to smile and fondly remember the students who mentioned them. One explanation for the obvious bond between teachers and students is that so many of the faculty volunteer time to sponsor clubs and extracurricular activities. Those who devoted enormous amounts of time to school clubs in the 1990's include history teacher Marlene Ramey (SGS), English teachers Diana Peckham (It's Academic and *Talley Ho*), Ron Stafford (Forensics) and Sue Hersman (Drama and Music activities), math teacher Chris Deterding (National Honor Society) and language teachers Patricia Smith (Latin Cub) and Tom Neiles (German Club). Administrator Mike Flanagan has volunteered so many hours as the public address announcer at stadium events that if he ever retires, the press box should be named for him.

The Annapolis High band serves as an excellent example of the type of activity that would not have succeeded without the dedicated involvement of a teacher, specifically longtime music director Michael Svec. He, in turn, points to the support of an active Band Boosters group of parents who over the years have always been ready to respond to the needs of the young musicians as they marched in parades, competed in state and national contests, performed at concerts and accompanied school musicals. Every year Panther musicians are named to various all-state bands and orchestras. Their contributions to Friday night football games include playing the National Anthem, forming a phalanx for the players to run through onto the field, providing halftime entertainment with their innovative marching routines and rocking the stands with the school fight song at every opportunity.

Another group of teachers who give enormously of their time and talent after school are coaches of athletic teams. Among those in academic subjects who coached in the 1990's were German teacher Tom Neiles (cross country), science teacher Neill Russell (gymnastics), math teacher Mike Ballard (track), history teacher Rick King (soccer and tennis), math teachers Larry Brogden (baseball) and

The 1999-2000 Running Panthers won 25 straight games before losing in the state semi-finals. Coach Brady was proud that 13 went to college after graduation, and 12 played sports on the collegiate level: five basketball – Marcus Johnson (23) Thomas Hawkins (30), Marcus Neal (13), Scott Robinson (44) and Rodrick Simms (5); six football – Kyle Acker (12), Marvin Charles (20), Aaron Copeland (15), Nick Good-Malloy (43), Camaro Henson (33) and Rayvon Johnson (23); and lacrosse player Will Phillips (32). Joe Feldmann (10) won a prestigious academic scholarship to attend the University of Maryland.

Two of the most successful AHS coaches are business teacher John Brady (boys' basketball) and Dave Gehrdes, who coached wrestling, boys' soccer and girls' lacrosse until he had to drop the first two when he became athletic director in 2000.

Joy Eskuchen (softball) and the most successful boys' basketball coach in Anne Arundel County history, business teacher John Brady.

Coach Brady succeeded Al Laramore at the outset of the 1977-1978 season. Over the next 25 years his teams won 21 county championships and earned 15 trips to the state final four as district or regional champs. His 1990 squad won the 4A state title with a 23-3 overall record. A decade later his 2000 team brought their perfect record and 25-game winning streak to Cole Field House only to be upset in a semi-final heartbreaker by eventual state champ Paint Branch. After retiring from teaching in 2001, Brady continued as the boys' coach and also took over coaching the varsity girls' basketball team – a feat unheard of previously in Maryland history. Brady's overall record in boys' basketball reached 557 victories with only 95 losses by the end of 2003, an amazing .854 winning percentage.

The fiery, competitive coach is just as proud of what his players achieve after graduation as he is of their on-court exploits. Over 80 percent of Brady's players – male and female – have gone to college. Many have taken their hoops ability to the next level, with more than a dozen playing at NCAA Division I universities and many others at junior colleges and Division II or III schools. He's also coached scores of players who have earned scholarships in other sports or for their academic achievement. Six Running Panthers are Naval Academy graduates (Keith Buckingham, Hank Gibson, Dan Smalley, Frank Snyder, Mark Wiggins and Kevin Young). The 2000 state semi-finalist boys' team typifies the post-high school aspirations of his players. Of the 15 students on the roster, 13 went to college: five to play basketball, seven recruited for football or lacrosse and one who won a prestigious academic scholarship [19].

Dave Gehrdes is an example of a physical education teacher who thrives on coaching. He was teaching elementary school in 1981 when offered the opportunity to coach the Panthers' wrestling team. He added boys' soccer in 1986. Three years later he was hired to fill Al Laramore's vacant physical education billet. Gehrdes added a third sport, girls' lacrosse, in 1993, but when he replaced the retiring Fred Stauffer as athletic director in 1999 he had to give up two teams. Not surprisingly he opted to keep girls' lacrosse, a team he'd directed to state championships in 1996, 1998 and 1999. Meanwhile physical education teacher Dan Hart took the Whammin' Panthers boys' lacrosse team to state titles in 1994 and 1998 [20].

Transitions in High School Football

Despite the successes of the boys' basketball and both lacrosse programs, the Annapolis High team with the most fans in the 1990's was the same as it had been a century earlier. Football's popularity was partially due to its winning tradition, but the team's wide following also reflected the economic and racial diversity of the players. John Brady confesses to being surprised at how well integrated the Annapolis High football team was when he arrived at the school in 1977, a favorable situation he credits entirely to Al Laramore's influence. Sons of wealthy professionals, naval officers, business executives and artists played beside poor boys from working class families. According to guidance counselor Tony Anzalone, over 40 percent of the students in the school at the turn of the 21st century came from families with incomes below $10,000. That for a quarter of a century Al Laramore had given all comers an equal opportunity to play helped develop a wide fan base for the Fighting Panthers. Many in the stands felt a direct connection to the boys on the field who came from their neighborhood, church or civic club. Second and even third generation Panthers were carefully watched by fathers, uncles, brothers, cousins and even grandfathers who had worn the same maroon and white Annapolis High uniforms in years past.

Laramore's death in January 1989 meant a new head coach would be entrusted to protect the Fighting Panthers' traditions. Athletic director Fred Stauffer didn't have to look far to find the right man for the job. Assistant Roy Brown, who had been on the Panthers' staff for a decade, directed the team when Laramore was hospitalized the previous fall. Naming him to be the 13th head coach of the Fighting Panthers was a natural progression, one that would best ensure continuity in the program. Brown's coaching credentials were impeccable. A 1966 Arundel High graduate, he was a tight end on the school's first county champion football team, then played so well at Western Maryland College that the Chicago Bears invited him to their training camp in the early 1970's. When a professional career didn't materialize, Brown returned home to Anne Arundel County to teach middle school physical education. He caught on as an assistant football coach working for Jerry Mears at his *alma mater* and then moved on with Mears to Meade. His teaching transfer to Annapolis High in 1979 allowed him to join Laramore's football staff and eventually assist John Brady in basketball (21).

Brown considered himself fortunate to have had as mentors the two most successful coaches in Anne Arundel County history, Mears and Laramore. But neither was now around to help their pupil prepare for his first head-coaching job. Mears, who for 20 years had directed Arundel and Meade to 129 victories, died of cancer in November 1988, just two months before Laramore's death from a heart attack. Also missing from the county scene was Joe Papetti, who retired in the spring of 1989, bringing his 24-year run at Glen Burnie and South River to a close after 157 victories. Thus within the span of a year, three coaches who had dominated Anne Arundel County football with a combined total of 441 victories were gone. Their rival, friend and colleague Andy Borland, head coach at Severna Park, believed everything good about football in the county could be traced to Laramore, Mears and Papetti, "who for all practical purposes established the high standards the rest of us have to live by." (22).

Well before the county's "Big Three" were gone, high school football in the state was in flux. The Maryland Public Secondary School Athletic Association had been tinkering with the state tournament structure for many years. In the early 1970's the MPSSAA sponsored several district-level title games as trial balloons before crowning its first state champions in 1974 (23). For 14 years (1974-1987) the state tournament consisted of only 16 teams: the champions of the four regions (designated by Roman numerals I, II, III, and IV) in each of the four classifications (AA, A, B and C). Schools qualified for post-season play through a weighted system that awarded points according to the classification of a defeated opponent. Thus, defeating a B team earned more points than a victory over a C team.

During the early 1970's Anne Arundel County had eight public high schools. Annapolis, Glen Burnie and Severna Park were classified AA and assigned to Region IV (24). The other five (Andover, Arundel, Brooklyn Park, Northeast and Southern) were scattered in the lower classifications. By 1977 the county league had grown to include two new high schools, Old Mill (AA) and Meade (A). At the same time, recognizing how the MPSSAA weighting system hurt the playoff chances of teams with too many opponents from lower classifications, the county's single league was broken into two divisions. The larger schools played each other and filled in the rest of their schedule with out-of-county AA teams. The county's smaller schools then formed what came to be called the "ABC League." In 1981 the AA League grew to seven teams with the addition of Arundel, Chesapeake and Meade; Carroll County's Westminster High (the other AA team in Region IV) joined with them to form a conference known informally as the "Big Eight," which lasted until 1987 when Westminster was replaced by Broadneck, whose rapid growth since opening in the early 1980's elevated it to the AA classification (25).

In 1989 the MPSSAA expanded the playoffs to include 32 teams: four regional champs and four at-large teams in each of the four classifications, now renamed 4A, 3A, 2A and 1A. Annapolis, which went from AA to 4A status, joined with the county's seven other large high schools to form the Anne Arundel 4A League. The conference for the five smaller high schools was short lived. In 1990 Andover and Brooklyn Park were closed; all their students were then subsumed in the new North County High School that brought the number of teams in the Anne Arundel 4A League to nine, leaving only three in the 3A/2A conference. Broadneck would briefly drop to 3A following the 1992 season until renovations were completed to house freshmen from Severn River Junior High School (26).

Roy Brown's First Decade at the Helm

Roy Brown was faced with more pressing worries than how the county league was configured. The timing of his promotion to head coach was not much to his liking. At the start of the 1989 season he confided to Bob Mosier, high school sports editor of *The Capital*, that it had been tough trying to follow Al Laramore. "*I was pretty close to him. I thought he had some years left and I didn't feel like anybody should take over for him because of the things he had established here. I feel bad about that.*" (27) Fortunately Brown didn't have to worry about putting together a staff; veterans Bill Phebus (offensive line) and Larry Brogden (offensive and defensive backfield) remained with the program. Brown admitted, "*If I would have had to bring in new coaches and teach them our system, that would have been an extra burden. Billy and Larry [are] very knowledgeable and I can count on them.*" (28) Ken Dunn, a veteran physical education teacher and coach at South River, joined Brown's staff in 1990 to coordinate the defense.

Brown was under considerable pressure, some of which was self-imposed, to prove that Annapolis High football could be successful without Big Al calling the plays. The Panthers had struggled both years Laramore had been on leaves of absence (1972 and 1977). The surest path to success was to keep the "Laramore system," which on offense meant continuing the Delaware Wing-T, which relies on precision blocking, power running and as little passing as possible, along with Laramore's "tough, tenacious and hard hitting" defense. Brown knew his biggest mistake would be changing too much. "I'm not Al Laramore, but we're going to try to do the same things he did and continue the tradition he established." (29)

Narrow losses to out-of-county football powers Friendly (26-20) and Randallstown (14-13) to begin the season were frustrating, but then the Panthers ran off five victories before Glen Burnie upended them. Senior captains Nathaniel Cook (6'2", 215), a returning all-Metro center, and Jamie Cook (6'1", 190), a returning first team all-county defensive end, used their leadership skills to get the team back on the winning track to end the regular season 7-3, earning the county championship and the 4A East Regional title. Yet like Laramore's previous four teams, the 1989 Panthers ended their season in the 4A quarterfinal game, this time by a 20-6 score to eventual state runner-up Gaithersburg High from Montgomery County.

Although the 1989 season established Brown's coaching *bona fides*, two mediocre seasons in 1990 (5-5) and 1991 (6-4) caused concern about the direction the program was headed. The 1992 team quieted the incipient criticism by following an opening loss with nine straight victories to bring the county and regional trophies back to Annapolis High. Finally breaking the playoff jinx, the Panthers stunned Friendly 21-6 in the state quarterfinals. Standing between Annapolis and a trip to Byrd Stadium for the Maryland 4A title game was an old nemesis, Gaithersburg. The Panthers were overmatched from the start of the semifinal game, losing 35-6 to the eventual state champs.

Over the course of the next four years the Panthers struggled through a slump in which their overall 21-19 record left the school without a title for the longest stretch since the county began crowning football champions 30 years earlier. Meanwhile North County coach Chuck Markiewicz implemented an aggressive "run and gun" passing attack that not only brought the Knights 4A county titles in 1993 and 1994, but also took them into the state playoffs five of the school's first six years, including a trip to the state finals in 1992 and a state championship in 1994 (30). Arundel, with a 10-0 regular season in 1995, and Meade, winners of county-best 17 out of 23 games in 1995-

1996, joined North County in pushing Annapolis High out of the limelight. By 1997 many of the Annapolis High faithful were openly disgruntled with the string of mediocre seasons. Self-styled "coaches" in the stands wanted Annapolis to abandon the Wing-T offense for either a passing attack like North County's run-and-shoot or a run/pass balance similar to what they saw at Arundel and Meade.

Fortunately Brown and his staff stuck to their guns, partially because they wanted to protect the Laramore tradition but also because they believed they had the athletes to run the Wing-T to perfection in 1997. The senior-laden squad included nine players who by season's end would be named to one or more all-county teams: center Mike Donlin (6'1", 175), two-way linemen Derek Johnson (5'10", 230), Joe Plattner (6'2", 230) and John Paul Williams (5'10", 280), quarterback Pete Ludlum (5'10", 165), end S.J. Womak (6'2", 180), flanker Donnell Foote (6'3", 210) and backs Albert Creek (5'10", 175) and Curtis Jones (5'9", 170). The Panthers opened with victories against two tough Prince George's County schools, Largo and Paint Branch, giving the coaches "positive vibes" that a good season was at hand. They were right – Annapolis kept winning week after week, running their record to 9-0, including easy decisions over Arundel (28-8) and North County (49-6) and a thrilling 25-21 victory over undefeated Meade on a rainy Friday night late in October. Assured of a trip to the playoffs, the Panthers missed an undefeated regular season when they lost 21-14 on a sloppy, muddy field to Severna Park in a game delayed a day because of torrential rain. The following week they hosted a 4A quarterfinal game against High Point of Prince George's County, but came out flat and never seemed to get in sync during a 33-14 loss (31).

To end the once-promising season with such a resounding thud was particularly disappointing because prospects weren't great for 1998. Returning would be only four players with much game experience. Missing from Brown's preseason analysis was any mention of a junior who had showed up in August to try out for the first time, a young man who over the next two years would rewrite both the Annapolis High and the county record books – Rayvon Johnson. Although a virtual unknown to the coaches, Johnson had achieved near legend status on the county's recreational league playing fields where for the past two years he had been leaving other 140-pound boys in the dust. Now that Johnson had grown to 5 feet 10

Into the Twenty-First Century, 1989 – 2001

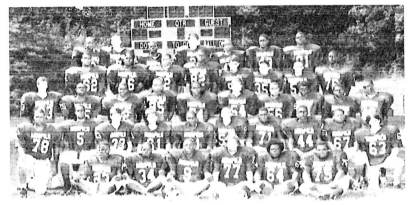

The 1997 Panthers brought back the county and regional titles to AHS after a 4-year drought. Severna Park spoiled their perfect record in the season finale. All-county players were (1st row from left) Curtis Jones, Albert Creek, Donnell Foote, Joe Plattner, John Paul Williams, Derek Johnson; 2nd row S.J. Womak (5), Pete Ludlum (33) and Mike Donlin (52).

Two years later, the undefeated 1999 team lost by a point to Broadneck in the season finale and in OT to Damascus in the playoffs. Rayvon Johnson (23) was one of many senior leaders including Kyle Acker (81), Aaron Fenwick (45), Aaron Copeland (25), Mike Phaneuf (5), Trevon Williams (66) & Marvin Charles (84).

inches, 170 pounds, friends talked him into playing for his school team. By the end of the preseason, Johnson had impressed the coaches enough to earn a starting position in the Wing-T backfield. His talent became more obvious in the season's first two games, close losses to tough Prince George's County teams from Largo and Paint Branch. In the third game, a 60-0 victory over Frederick, Johnson rushed for 205 yards before the third quarter ended. From that point in the season on, there was no stopping him or the Panthers as they steamrolled through the rest of the schedule to finish 8-2, a record good enough to win the county and regional championships for a second straight year.

The Panthers' 17-7 loss to Montgomery County's Sherwood High in the quarterfinals of the 1998 state playoffs was frustrating. With a few breaks, the Panthers could have won the tight, competitive game. Instead they had to swallow yet another maddening playoff loss. Eight all-county players were seniors: Dewayne Hunt (DB/RB), Kyron Belt (DB/QB), Jack Brooks (DL/OL), Henry Downs (OL/LB), Eric Toney (OL/LB), Charles Carter (OL/DL), David Hall (C) and Rashad Wills (OL/DL). Despite losing these terrific players, Brown couldn't help but look forward to the next season when he could welcome back 1998 Anne Arundel player-of-the-year Johnson, whose 2,060 yards had shattered the county season rushing record. Returning with him would be three other all-county players: receiver Marvin Charles (6'0", 175), defensive end Trevon Williams (6'1", 185) and linebacker Aaron Copeland (6'0", 180). Brown's main concern was putting together an entirely new set of linemen. He turned the problem over to Bill Phebus and his quarter-century of experience teaching the intricacies of blocking assignments in the Wing-T offense. By the season opener against Old Mill, Phebus had transformed three seniors (guard Williams and ends Charles and Kyle Acker, 6'4", 210) and four juniors (center Kion Mackell, 5'10", 210; guard Brandon Gulley, 6'3", 185; and tackles Nick Good-Malloy, 6'4", 210 and Bobby Baker, 6'1", 225) into a cohesive unit that opened enough holes in the Patriots' defense for Johnson to rush for 195 yards. As one lopsided victory followed another, it was clear that the best defender against Johnson was his own coach, Roy Brown, who routinely benched his star during the fourth quarter of blowouts.

Entering the season's 10th week the undefeated Panthers, averaging over 40 points a game on offense, had clinched both the county and regional championships for the third year in a row. Only Broadneck stood between them and a perfect regular season and the top seed in the 3A playoffs. The two schools were playing after a six-year hiatus during which Broadneck used its 3A classification as the reason for refusing Brown's repeated requests to schedule a game. Ironically when Broadneck was reclassified 4A for the 1999 season, Annapolis was dropped to 3A, but Brown embraced the challenge of continuing to play the county's largest schools. Indeed, athletic director Fred Stauffer played a key role in persuading his colleagues to re-establish a single league regardless of school size so that one champion could be crowned for the county's 12 public schools at season's end (32).

While preparing for their last regular season game, the 1999 Panthers made a classic mistake. They compared their 9-0 record to Broadneck's 6-3 and came to the conclusion that victory was assured. For much of the first half at the field in Cape St. Claire, the game looked like it would turn into a typical Annapolis rout. Leading 21-7 midway through the second period, quarterback Mike Phaneuf lofted an apparent 65-yard touchdown pass into the sure hands of Marvin Charles, but as one referee was signaling a touchdown, another back by the scrimmage line was throwing a yellow flag: holding. This late penalty both nullified the touchdown and changed the flow of the game. The Bruins then managed to score right before halftime, so the Panthers headed to the locker room leading only by eight instead of 21 points. After intermission, Annapolis put together several long drives as Johnson and Copeland churned up 307 yards, but mistakes and penalties on several crucial third down plays thwarted them each time they drew near the end zone. Meanwhile Broadneck put together a methodical scoring drive that ate up much of the third period by using a combination of short runs and passes, but their attempted two-point conversion failed. Annapolis clung to a 21-19 lead through most of the fourth quarter, but a Bruins field goal with six minutes left put Broadneck ahead, 22-21. That lead withstood two more Annapolis possessions in which the desperate Panthers again failed to score.

The disconsolate players on the Annapolis side of the field could not quite believe they had lost a perfect season for a second time in three years. Brown challenged his team to show its mettle the following Friday night when Montgomery County powerhouse Damascus High School traveled to Ensor Stadium for the state quarterfinal game. After a scoreless first quarter, the Panthers got the ball in good field position when defensive end Trevon Williams blocked a punt and nose guard James Forester fell on the loose ball at the Hornets' 44-yard line. With everyone expecting Annapolis to try to grind out a touchdown on the ground, Phaneuf took the snap from Mackell, faked a handoff to Johnson and hit a wide-open Marvin Charles for a touchdown. The extra point was good, and for the first time since 1992, Annapolis High had a second quarter lead in a playoff game. Damascus tied the score just before the half, then seemingly put the game out of reach with two more touchdowns in the third quarter. But Annapolis was not prepared to go down without a fight. After being held to just 10 yards rushing in the first half, Johnson began ripping off huge gains towards the end of the third quarter as he juked his way through the holes the offensive line started opening in an increasingly befuddled Hornets' defense. Taking possession with only 42 seconds left in the game and trailing by eight points, Annapolis was 57 yards from the end zone. Damascus now was looking for the Panthers to pass. Instead Phaneuf handed the ball to Johnson three plays in a row. He responded with breathtaking runs that got the ball to the 13, where with every Hornets' defender keyed on stopping him, Phaneuf lofted the ball to Kevan Simms who out-leapt two Damascus defenders to catch it in the end zone. Johnson scurried around right end untouched for the two-point conversion that tied the game and sent the Panthers' fans into a frenzy. Maybe the fates were, at long last, ready to smile on Annapolis High.

    To break a tie in high school football, each team is given a chance to score from the 10-yard line. Annapolis lost the coin toss so had to go first. On third and ten, Johnson somehow managed to race around left end into the end zone, but a poorly executed extra point kick was blocked. Damascus also scored in three running plays, and – to the dismay of the Panthers faithful – their extra point sailed straight through the uprights to give the Hornets a 28-27 victory. Instead of being kind, the fates had delivered a most heartbreaking blow.

    Afterwards there wasn't a dry eye in the Panthers' locker room. Brown told his players he thought they should hold their heads up high, that their refusal to quit made the game the best ever played on Al Laramore field. He pointed to the records they had set during the season. Their 420 points in 11 games set a county scoring mark. He complimented the offensive line, pointing out that by "blocking their butts off" all season they had set the stage for runners Johnson and Copeland to become only the second set of teammates in county history to each rush for more than 1,000 yards. Johnson, in just two years of varsity play, gained 4,044 yards, breaking the county career rushing record that had taken Broadneck's Martel Threadgill four years to set. It is mind numbing to think what numbers Johnson could have accumulated if he hadn't spent the fourth quarter on the bench in so many lopsided victories. Fittingly, for the second straight year he received the Touchdown Club's Rhodes award, and the 1999 Panthers joined Brown's 1989, 1992 and 1997 teams as winners of the Jerry Mears trophy given annually to the county's top prep football team.

The 2000 *Fighting Panthers*

Despite all the accolades, the way the 1999 season ended weighed heavily on everyone. To be undefeated for nine weeks and then lose the last two games by a total of two points seemed too cruel. As they cleared out their lockers for the last time, the team's senior leaders and all-county players – Johnson, Copeland, Charles, Phaneuf and Williams – challenged their younger teammates to set their sights the next year on what they had failed to accomplish: victory in a playoff game.

Coach Brown and his veteran staff were cautiously optimistic about the prospects for 2000. Despite losing so many of the previous year's starters to graduation, the squad had several quality underclassmen and an unusually large senior class, many with extensive game experience. Four 1999 all-county selections – all linemen – were back: James Forester, Nick Good-Malloy, Brandon Gulley and Kion Mackell. Good-Malloy kept a journal that chronicles the 2000 team's response to the challenge from last year's seniors. His first entry is on Monday, August 14th: *"At the end of last season, many people doubted that Annapolis High would get to the state play-offs in 2000 for the fourth straight year. Most of our talent was graduating. I was one of 18 juniors who would be returning for one more season. Many of us had played together since rec league days, and nine of us would be on the varsity for the third year straight. Vowing to make our last year together one to remember, we arranged to go to a Wing-T camp at Salisbury University in early August. Our confidence got a boost when we won the team competition on the camp's last day. Our hopes are high as we begin preseason camp tomorrow."*

It only took one morning practice session for Brown to sense unwarranted cockiness among some of the seniors. He pulled them aside to remind them, *"No one player is bigger than the team. No one on this team is a star – the stars are all gone. We lost the county's best* running back, linebacker and tight end. Our best quarterback is gone, too. What's left is the tradition of the Annapolis High Fighting Panthers and that's what will still be here when you're long gone." Most of the players seemed to take the coach's words to heart. They looked good in preseason scrimmages against Loyola and Frederick Douglass of Prince George's County. Seniors Andre Toney (guard, 6'0", 175), Camaro Henson (end, 6'4", 200) and Brian Powell (end, 6'2", 220) joined returning starters Baker and Good-Malloy (tackles), Gulley (guard) and Mackell (center) to become, in coach Bill Phebus' opinion, the "best overall offensive line in Annapolis High history." (33) Five stayed on the field for defense: linebackers Toney and Gulley, defensive end Henson and down linemen Mackell and Good-Malloy. "Big James" Forrester (nose guard, 6'2", 285) used his strength and size to clog the middle. Charlie Dammeyer (6'3", 200) moved to starting quarterback after two years' experience as a backup. Mike Melton (5'10", 170) was expected to play a key role blocking from the flanker position, while Brown thought he had several two-way backs with good speed, led by senior Kevan Simms (5'8", 180) and sophomore track stars Davon Watkins (5'7", 160) and Demario Harris (5'7", 155), the state triple jump champion. Simms talked his cousin Eric Venerable (6'0", 180) into coming out for the varsity. Back in the fall of 1997 Venerable had shown considerable promise as a freshman running back on the junior varsity before personal problems led him to quit. Although he hadn't played since, his size, athleticism and power landed him starting positions at running back and defensive back, and he also became the team's place kicker.

Everything seemed set for the opening game that was played on an extremely warm, humid night on Old Mill's field. Good-Malloy's entry on Monday, September 11th reveals what happened: *"We went into our first game with all the confidence in the world. We just knew we couldn't be stopped. We were wrong. Old Mill's veteran team beat us soundly. It hurt. Coach Brown kept all the seniors after practice today to tell us we had shown no leadership and even less heart. Our play, he said, had embarrassed the coaches. His words stung. Some guys got mad, others thought Coach Brown was unfair. But deep down we all know that we aren't yet the leaders – or the players – we thought we were. We are going to have to change. There hasn't been much said, but we know what we have to do: work harder, complain less, compliment teammates on their efforts and forget about our own individual glory."*

The soul searching, increased commitment and some roster juggling turned the squad around. By homecoming in early November the team had come a long way. The victory in a shootout with North County, 39-26, ran the Panthers' winning streak to eight games, none of which had been close. Venerable and Simms were on pace to break the previous year's rushing records. Both gave credit the offensive line. Venerable told a *Washington Post* reporter on November 10th, *"With the offensive line I have, it's pretty easy to get all those yards and touchdowns. Almost every time I get the ball I look up and there is a huge hole for me to run through."* Senior Phil Boyd, who transferred from Severna Park before the start of the season, and Camaro Henson were sure-handed hauling in Charlie Dammeyer's passes, filling the void left when Marvin Charles graduated.

The entire season now was riding on the outcome of the final game against Broadneck, but this year the tables were turned. The 2000 Bruins were unbeaten and seeking a top seed in the 4A playoffs, while a loss would most likely send the Panthers packing with no postseason berth. The game would be played on Al Laramore Field where none of the seniors had ever lost a regular season game (34). Good-Malloy captures the emotions of the night: *"Before the game I looked at my uniform and thought how much it has meant for me to wear it for four years. I thought about all the tradition that has been here before me, and how, as a senior, I was not ready to give up wearing it. Gulley put it well when he told a reporter that 'none of the 20 seniors are ready to go home yet.' And because of what happened on the field tonight, we're not. The game was a classic. It came down to their last possession when our defense stuffed them to preserve the do-or-die victory, 26-19. We're all emotionally drained but really happy to be able to put our uniforms on at least one more time."*

The victory vaulted the Fighting Panthers to their fourth consecutive regional title and a share of the league's best record with Broadneck (35). Annapolis now would host a state quarterfinal game for the fourth straight year. Their opponent would be the Panthers from Paint Branch High, who would be bringing their 9-1 record, a 12th place ranking in *The Washington Post* and a group of highly recruited players to Ensor Stadium. Camaro Henson recalled the pre-game building: *"Annapolis High had advanced [to the quarterfinals] for the past three years only to lose. We saw the game as our chance to restore our school's reputation, as well as that of Anne Arundel County football. Nick and I saw the game as personal. We wanted to*

The 2000 Panthers' 20 seniors pause for a photograph after practice the week of the state semifinal game against Douglass that would be their last time to play on Al Laramore Field. Kneeling in front is the offensive line (l to r): Brian Powell, Nick Good-Malloy, Andre Toney, Kion Mackell, Brandon Gulley, Bobby Baker and Camaro Henson. Behind them are Tyrico Morgan, Mike Melton, Neanders Nixon, Brandon Johnson, Erron Silva, Charlie Dammeyer, Delray Johnson, Kevin Jones, Phil Boyd, James Forrester, Delano Watkins, B.J. Zadera and Kevan Simms.

Two months later many of the seniors attended the 47th annual Annapolis Touchdown Clubs banquet to collect the Mears trophy as the top high school team in Anne Arundel County for the third time in four years. Joining them were all five coaches who took them to the state finals: Larry Brogden (far left), Ken Dunn (center), Dave Summey, Bill Phebus and head coach Roy Brown (on the right).

beat Paint Branch after the hurt their basketball team put on us last year at Cole Field House." The game was better than anyone could have imagined. Mike Melton tells the tale of what took place on Friday night, November 17th. *"Ensor Stadium was packed for the game. We only managed to score two touchdowns, but our defense held them and all their D-I players to just 9 points. We'd proved our doubters wrong again and met the challenge from last year's seniors. We won a playoff game."*

After the game ended some Booster Club parents were closing up the concession stand, celebrating the thrilling victory and beginning to store away equipment that wouldn't be needed again until spring lacrosse season. Everyone expected that third-seeded Annapolis would have to go on the road for the semi-final game against second-seeded Damascus. Talk was about avenging last season's overtime playoff loss. Two scouts from Damascus stopped by the stand to get some coffee before driving home when they got a cell phone call with the surprising news that the seventh-seeded Eagles from Frederick Douglass had upset the Hornets 22-21! So instead of avenging last season's overtime loss at Damascus, Annapolis would be hosting Douglass at Ensor Stadium in the state semi-final game the following Friday night, with the winner earning a trip to the state finals at Byrd Stadium.

Schools are closed in Anne Arundel County during Thanksgiving week for teachers' conferences and the holiday, but the players willingly gave up vacation to practice Monday through Wednesday afternoons and again early on Thanksgiving to prepare for the Eagles. Memories of the preseason scrimmage in which Annapolis had outplayed Douglass gave the Panthers confidence they could win, but the senior leaders made sure nobody the Eagles wouldn't be taken lightly. After all, Douglass was coming off a great upset win over previously undefeated Damascus, something Annapolis had failed to accomplish the previous. After practice boys scattered to share turkey dinners with their families. Nine Panthers especially enjoyed their meals after they found their names among those listed in the local papers' traditional Thanksgiving Day announcements of all-county football teams: seniors Forester (DL), Good-Malloy (OL), Gulley (LB), Mackell (C), Simms (RB), Toney (OL) and Kevin Jones (DL), along with junior Venerable (RB) and sophomore Harris (DB). Fittingly, Roy Brown was also named Anne Arundel Coach of the Year in *The Capital, Washington Post* and the Baltimore *Sun.*

Byrd Stadium State 3A Title game:

Captains meet at midfield for coin toss then race back towards the team and Coach Brown.

The offensive line carries out Wing-T blocking scheme to perfection: 62 Good-Malloy, 83 Henson, 56 Toney, 54 Gulley, 67 Mackell, 52 Baker and 19 Boyd.

QB Dammeyer (7) prepares to hand the ball to Venerable (35), who broke Rayvon Johnson's single season county rushing record with 2,346 yards and scoring record with 32 touchdowns.

Late the next afternoon the seniors trickled into the locker room to dress for a final time. Win or lose, they'd not be playing again at home. Good-Malloy's journal records what happened. "*We were united tonight in our determination to go off Al Laramore Field for the last time as winners. We were jittery at kickoff, but when play started we settled down. Midway through the first quarter the lights on the post in the western corner of the end zone went out, giving the cold, frosty field an eerie feeling. After a scoreless first quarter, we both scored two touchdowns, but our missed extra points gave them a 14-12 lead at halftime. The third quarter belonged to us. We scored twice, and a two-point conversion gave us a 12-point cushion. Then our defense took over. As the final seconds ticked off the clock, the scoreboard told the story: AHS 26, Douglass 14. We erupted into our last Panther Drill on Laramore Field, then stayed to celebrate with our fans as the band played on. Not until we got into the locker room did it really sink in. For the first time in 16 years, Annapolis would be playing for the state football title.*"

Back in school after Thanksgiving vacation, hallway chatter seemed to be about little else than the football team. Championship week was a whirlwind of activities and emotions: long practices that finished after dark, team meetings and dinners, newspaper interviews and photos. Thursday night was the Booster Club's awards banquet for all the fall sports teams that had been scheduled back in August with no thought that the football team might still be playing come December. Coach Brown called the names of all 20 seniors one by one to line up in front of the auditorium. He spoke with emotion about how proud the coaches were of them, a special, close-knit group who had pulled for each other both on and off the field to lead the team to a season they should treasure. Mike Melton remembers how surprised they were when Coach Brown "*did something he'd never done before: he gave each of us a replica helmet with our own number on the side, a tangible memento of how far we'd come since that embarrassing season-opening loss at Old Mill.*"

Two MPSSAA championship contests were to be played on Friday night and two on Saturday afternoon. Brown hoped the 3A title game that pitted Annapolis against Calvert (County) High would be slated for Friday night when his team was accustomed to playing, but instead the Panthers drew the last game late on Saturday afternoon. The Sports Boosters learned that the coaches were concerned about keeping the players busy and well fed, so the club agreed to host a spaghetti dinner for the team on Friday after practice, and then returned on Saturday morning to provide a healthy brunch before they boarded the bus to College Park at noon. Hopes were high that they would return after dark with the state championship trophy.

Good-Malloy succinctly relates the events that unfolded inside Byrd Stadium in the bitter December cold. "*Walking to the center of the field with the other co-captains (Mackell, Gulley and Toney) for the coin toss was the beginning of a surreal afternoon. Our opponent was a strong Calvert High team. At halftime the game was tied at 14, but then disaster struck. They ran back a punt for a score. Our offense broke down. Suddenly we were losing, 34-14. This couldn't be happening, but it was. Late in the fourth quarter we scored to narrow their lead to 12 points. We recovered an onside kick and again drove down the field. Nobody had ever stopped our offense when we got inside the five- yard line, and if we could score again we still had an outside chance of pulling out a miracle victory. But this time we couldn't punch it in. Calvert took over the ball and ran out the clock. Our comeback fell short. We had lost.*"

The players were subdued after the game. Some cried, but most realized they'd done their best and had just come up short. Brown told them he was proud of those who had refused to quit, and reminded them that their 11-2 overall record was the best in 20 years and they were one of only three Annapolis High teams to win more than 10 games in a season. Several months later, many of the seniors attended the Touchdown Club banquet to accept the Jerry Mears trophy awarded to the top team in Anne Arundel County, the third time in four years that Annapolis High had earned the distinction. Individual honors piled up for several players. Brandon Gulley won the Touchdown Club's Al Laramore award as Anne Arundel County's top lineman. Kion Mackell and Eric Venerable joined Gulley as first team all-state players, while Nick Good-Malloy, Kevan Simms and Andre Toney were named to the honorable mention all-state list. In March Roy Brown was inducted into the Arundel High School athletic hall of fame – an honor that was based on his lifetime accomplishments as player and coach.

* * * * * * * * *

The state championship was Annapolis High's last football game of the 20th century. The senior football players were part of the first graduating class of the 21st century. Most had plans to continue their education, and five would be playing on college football fields the next fall. They left Annapolis High looking forward to opportunities ahead, carrying with them the sense of good fortune they'd had to play on a team that had come within 24 minutes of winning the state championship.

Good-Malloy's chronicle of the season ends with a description of the final minute of the state title game. Although the story he tells centers on only two players, it undoubtedly represents how every one of the seniors felt about their experience playing football at Annapolis High. *"A knee injury forced me to watch helplessly from the sideline as Calvert ran out the clock. Next to me was one of several seniors who'd given four years to Annapolis High football without ever getting much playing time. I glanced over at him and saw there were tears in his eyes. Here was a guy who rarely started, whose name seldom made the papers, yet he cared so much about losing. We hugged each other, both of us crying now as we felt the exact same emotion. We knew we'd never be wearing the maroon and white Annapolis High football uniforms again. He spent most of his career on the sidelines, while I started both ways for two years. But it didn't matter. We felt the same emotions. Annapolis High lost that championship game, but the journey of getting there took us beyond just being a team. Now we were a family. I know each of us will always treasure our years on the Fighting Panthers football team, and we'll especially remember the 2000 season. And as for me, I'll never forget that tearful hug."*

EPILOGUE:
CHANGES AND CHALLENGES,
2001 – 2003

The real strength of Annapolis High School as it continues into the 21st century is found in its racial and economic diversity.

"I've been coaching at Annapolis for 24 years and I never missed a practice. Emotionally, I have a lot invested in this program. [We] tried to build on the legacy Big Al established and to continue the traditions he put in place. I'd like to see some of those traditions live on, but whoever comes in should coach the way they're comfortable."

Head Coach Roy Brown
The Capital, 23 July 2003

Changes and Challenges, 2001 - 2003

This book was intended to end with the 2000 state championship football game and the graduation of the Class of 2001, but so many major changes have occurred since then that a brief epilogue became necessary. While the freshly graduated seniors were enjoying the traditional beach week following their commencement ceremony, Anne Arundel County learned that the 21st century was going to usher in major changes – at least in its school system – much more quickly than anticipated. On June 5, 2001, popular school superintendent Carol Parham announced she was resigning her post effective in December to accept the senior teaching position at the University of Maryland's College of Education. (1). The first African American and the first woman to head the county public schools, Parham was leaving after eight fruitful years during which confidence was restored in the local education system. Her stature was such that at her farewell party the school board announced that the central office building on Riva Road would be named in her honor (2).

Although Parham's decision to depart was met with genuine regret, all was not completely rosy in the 78,000-student school system she was leaving behind. Test scores had stagnated since 1995, high school drop-out rates had increased slightly and – most importantly – one-third of all high school students had grade point average below 2.00, a "C" average. Particularly of concern was the gap in standardized test scores between various ethnic groups (3). The school board's search for a new superintendent focused on these academic issues as well as on the need to find an experienced manager who could fashion creative ways to live within the constantly constricting school budget. Appointed interim superintendent was Ken Lawson, a Severna Park graduate who had worked in a wide variety of administrative capacities during his 40-year career in the school system. Lawson, who had solid support among a group of school board members, announced in early April that he was throwing his hat in the ring for the permanent position (4). Despite his advocates' best efforts, however, the board's majority was looking to land a bigger fish for their pond, preferably somebody with a national reputation. By the end of April the board announced they had lured in their man, Dr. Eric J. Smith, with a salary package valued at $300,000, almost double what Mrs. Parham had been paid (5). An outcry was raised from those who had favored Lawson's candidacy,

The end of senior year is filled with special moments, including the traditional prom. No expense is spared as seniors Albert Johnson and Alex Malloy rent a limo to transport them to the dinner dance at the BWI Marriott. Graduation itself has moved out of the county to the Showplace Arena in Upper Marlboro since the Naval Academy no longer is able to offer its facilities and there is no other arena in the city large enough to house the event.

but the impressive credentials Smith compiled as superintendent of the 109,000-student Charlotte-Mecklenburg, North Carolina, school system soon quieted the controversy over his salary. The 2000 Urban Educator of the Year's major claim to fame was his success narrowing the test gap between majority and minority students, a goal the school board also hoped he'd be able to replicate here.

Smith hit Anne Arundel County running and has hardly slowed down since. The 400-person staff at the central offices quickly learned that he expected them to stay at their desks every day until he left the building, which was often long after traditional quitting time. One of the first issues he tackled was switching middle and high schools to a four-period-per-day schedule instead of the traditional six-periods in use throughout most of the county. Various teacher, parent and student groups voiced opposition based on their belief that 85-minute classes meeting on alternate A days and B days would negatively impact learning, but Smith revealed late in October his intention to implement the controversial schedule in all 31 county middle and high schools. Although he could point to the success of the four-period schedule at Chesapeake, Meade and Northeast during the past several years, the uproar of protest proceeded unabated until Smith made it clear that the decision rested with him, not the school board. He pointed out that he had been given a mandate to raise scores and improve the academic environment in the schools, and that after detailed study he had determined the four-period day would do just that. Prior to winter break in December 2002, Smith announced the schedule would go into effect on the first day of school in the 2003-2004 academic year (6).

Annapolis High was specifically in the superintendent's sites for an idea central to his vision for improving the county's high schools. Smith was concerned about the number of wealthy parents who routinely send their children to one of the 65 private schools in the area rather than to the county's public schools, especially at the middle and high school level. Smith decided to introduce a countywide International Baccalaureate program at two magnet high schools in hopes of convincing traditional private school families to reconsider a public school option. As its name implies, the I.B. program sets international curricular standards for particularly rigorous college preparatory courses. Generally college admissions officers regard I.B. as a step above advanced placement classes. Annapolis High administrators and teachers were excited to learn that Smith intended to use the county's oldest and most diverse school as the I.B. magnet for south county students. The program began at Annapolis High in the fall of 2003 with slots for 100 top students (7).

Overseeing these changes at Annapolis High would be a new principal. In the May 2003 *Annapolis High Newsletter* veteran principal Joyce Smith informed the school community that health concerns had led her to "accept an opportunity to work in a non-school based position." The loss of the popular principal was more painful because several key counselors and teachers were also retiring or transferring, including chair of the guidance department Tony Anzalone, science teacher John Rentch, math instructor Chris

Deterding and physical education's Donzella Parker-Bert. Speculation was that an administrator with experience within the Anne Arundel system would be rotated to Annapolis High, but on June 19, 2003, *The Capital* reported that the superintendent had selected Deborah Williams, an educator from Prince George's County, to head the school. Only the second African American to hold the position, Williams continues the run of female leaders at the school. Joining her from Prince George's County is assistant principal Jose Taboada, a Spanish-speaker tasked to "break down barriers" between the school and the growing Annapolis Latino population. Retiring guidance counselor Tony Anzalone applauded this move. In just this past year the size of the ESOL program had grown from 65 to 112 students. He believes the influx of non-English speakers will be the biggest challenges in the coming decade (8).

Then a month before the beginning of the new school year came news that rocked the entire Annapolis athletic community. Football coach Roy Brown publicly announced his resignation. His longtime assistants Ken Dunn and Bill Phebus also tendered their resignations, as did Dave Summey, who had joined the Panthers staff in 2000 after Larry Brogden's retirement (9). The news was startling because it came just 21 days before the start of preseason football camp. The reasons behind the decision of the entire football staff to quit center on problems that had developed after Brown retired in May 2002 as a physical education teacher but stayed on as head football coach. Brown intended to keep coaching several years and had not planned to retire until a successor was in place who was prepared to continue Annapolis traditions. He envisioned a replacement who would be on the Annapolis High faculty just as he had been when he took over following Al Laramore's death.

Although all three of Brown's assistants taught physical education, none were assigned to the Annapolis High faculty. Brown assumed a physical education teacher interested in coaching football would be hired to replace him, but this did not turn out to be the case. Thus during the 2002 football season Brown found it necessary to spend long hours at the school doing things he had hoped to turn over to an assistant in the building. He was confident, however, that a physical education teacher with a football background would be selected for one of several additional billets that were projected to be opening for the fall semester of 2003, but in late June he learned that no teachers with football interest had been hired. Brown summarized

Epilogue

Football coach Roy Brown (left) retired with a 103-48 record, good for the second best winning percentage in county history. Dale Castro brought a winning record from a decade at the helm of High Point High in Prince George's County, but after a season of frustrations trying to coach while commuting, he resigned in December 2003, leaving a vacancy yet to be filled.

his feelings to *The Capital*'s Bill Wagner, who broke the news of the resignation in a July 23, 2003, story: *"It's very difficult not having anyone in the building anymore. When I first came to Annapolis, all the football coaches were on the staff. Now we have none. You really need some help in the building, someone who can monitor the players and other things that are going on with the program."*

The decision of Brown and his staff to step down was particularly hard because the football team they had built was poised to continue its unprecedented success in the county. In 2002 Brown broke the century mark in victories as a head coach, and he topped all active county coaches with the most victories and the best winning percentage (103-48, .682), a record that leaves him just hundredths of a point behind his mentor Al Laramore. Brown had expected a good crop of players to report in August 2003 from last year's county and regional championship team that set a local record when it was the sixth in a row from Annapolis High to make it to the playoffs. Indeed, making the postseason will be easier in 2003 than ever because after much debate, the MPSSAA voted to expand the format from 16 to 32 teams, a move that virtually guarantees the Panthers will be there for an seventh straight year. The format features games to crown regional champions, rather than simply giving the title to the team in the region with the top number of points.

Named as Annapolis High's 14th head football coach on August 13, 2003, was Dale Castro, a Southern High multi-sport star who was a 1979 all-American place kicker for the University of Maryland and played briefly for Tom Landry's Dallas Cowboys. On paper Castro seemed an excellent selection. As head coach at High Point High School in Prince George's County, Castro compiled a 72-54 record (.571) and took the team to the playoffs four times before resigning to concentrate on his guidance counselor duties.

Castro brought with him an entire staff from Prince George's County, thus effectively ending the direct connection at Annapolis High to the Laramore era. Severna Park's retired coach Andy Borland, Laramore's longtime rival and friend, summed up the feeling of those who saw Brown as the link to those bygone days when he noted "Annapolis football won't be the same anymore."(10) Indeed, they weren't, as the Panthers suffered its first losing season in a decade. Despite his dedication to the job, Castro realized the impossibility of trying to run a football program without a fulltime coach in the school. Thus, In December 2003 Castro resigned essentially for the same reason that had driven Roy Brown away. Whoever is hired as the next head coach hopefully will not face this same problem.

The arrival of a new principal and the vacancy in the head football coaching position make a convenient stopping point for this history of Annapolis High. The challenges ahead as the first decade in the 21st century unfolds are obvious for their successors. Leading the list are the new four-period schedule, the implementation of the International Baccalaureate program and the increasing diversity as Latino and other ethnic minority groups move into the school. Those now in charge might turn the pages of this book to draw strength as they face these challenges. Over the past century Annapolis High has grown from a cluster of rooms on the third floor of the downtown grammar school with three teachers and a score of all white, mostly female students to a modern facility on the outskirts of the city with a student body that represents the ethnic and economic diversity of Maryland's capital city. Indeed, when asked what they most valued about their Annapolis High education, virtually every graduate responded in a manner similar to sisters Liz and Cindy Davis, valedictorians respectively in 1982 and 1984, who agreed that diversity is the bedrock of the school's strength, something that children sheltered in private schools will never experience. Annapolis High is the real world, with its share of problems, but also with a long history of success. The Class of 2003 is typical: 82 percent of its graduates are in college supported by over 2.2 million dollars in scholarships (11).

Certainly the 17 principals, 14 football coaches and over 500 other teachers should be praised for the roles they played in educating the more than 25,000 students who have filled the hallways, sat in the classrooms, worn the maroon, blue and white uniforms and earned Annapolis High diplomas over the course of 107 years, 1896 to 2003.

APPENDICES,
CITATIONS,
BIBLIOGRAPHY &
INDEX

The season is over. It is not the wins and losses that really count. The all-important numbers fade from the scoreboard, the empty stadium is swept, and the lights, one by one, go out. Yet it is what still remains: the echo of the band, the fallen confetti, the cleat marks in the mud, reminding us that you were "here at 7:30 and ready to play football." The Annapolis tradition is one of excellence, of sportsmanship, of determination and of spirit. And while that may not have been enough to take us to the very top, while it cannot change the papers, the rankings or the statistics, it does mean something to us, your fans, who would just like to say to all of you:

Fighting Panthers – you will always be our heroes.

1982 Annapolis High School *Wake* Yearbook

APPENDIX A: Annapolis High Football Season Results, 1899-2003
(Includes team captains and all-county selections, when available)

1899 (2 – 1 – 0) Coach: Walter L. Brady
Captain: John Strohm
AHS 0 St. John's Preparatory School 11
AHS 11 Laurel 0
AHS 29 Laurel 0 (Thanksgiving)

1900 (1 – 0 – 0) Coach Walter L. Brady
Captain: Arthur Ward
AHS 6 Polytechnic Institute 0

1904 (0 – 0 – 1) Coach Walter L. Brady
Tie game with Laurel

1905 (3 – 0 – 0) Coach Walter L. Brady
AHS 12 St. John's Prep 0
AHS 5 Colonial Outing Club 0
AHS defeated Baltimore Polytechnic Institute

1906 (0 – 0 – 1) Coach Walter L. Brady
Captain: Ben Blumberg
AHS 0 St. John's Prep 0

1908 (7 – 0 – 1) Coach Garey Lambert
Captain: Howard Thompson
AHS 6 Chesapeake Athletic Club 0
AHS 2 Mt Washington 0 (forfeit)
AHS 10 Wilmer's Naval Prep 5
AHS 36 Hagerstown High 0
AHS 21 Polytechnic Institute (Reserves) 2
AHS 0 Werntz Naval Prep 0
AHS 15 City College (Reserves) 0
AHS 40 Charlotte Hall 0

1909 (6 – 0 – 0) Coach Garey Lambert
Captain: Philip Clayton
AHS 26 Baltimore Latin 0
AHS 11 City College 5
AHS 35 Werntz Naval Prep 5
AHS 2 Hagerstown 0 (forfeit)
AHS 18 St. John's Scrubs 0
AHS 2 Charlotte Hall 0

1910 (0 – 1 – 1) Coach Ivan T. Morton
AHS 5 Werntz's Naval Prep 5
AHS 0 Wilmer's Naval Prep 5

1911 (1 – 1 – 3) Coach Ivan T. Morton
Captain: Warren Feldmeyer
AHS 6 Wilmer's Naval Prep 0
AHS 0 Werntz Naval Prep 0
AHS 10 Wilmer's Naval Prep 10
AHS 5 Maryland All-Stars 5
AHS 0 St. John's Prep 6

1912 (3 – 3 – 0) Coach Ivan.T. Morton
   Captain: Willis Martin
   AHS 19 St. John's College Freshmen 0
   AHS 0 Bobbie's Prep School 12
   AHS 0 City College 22
   AHS 7 Wicomico 6 (at Salisbury)
   AHS 7 Wicomico 0 (at Annapolis)
   AHS lost to Lancaster High School

1913 (1 – 2 – 0) Coach Ivan T. Morton
   AHS 0 Werntz Naval Prep 21
   AHS 6 Gilman Country Day 19
   AHS defeated Boys' Latin

1914 (3 – 0 – 0) Coach Ivan .T. Morton
   Captain: Edgar Clark
   AHS 13 Marsten School 0
   AHS 47 Baltimore Latin 0
   AHS 14 Friends School 0

* * * *(Break 1915 – 1919) * * * *

1920 (3 – 0 – 1) Coach A.Z. Holley
   Captain: Frank De Santis
   AHS 42 Werntz Naval Prep 0
   AHS 13 Donaldson 13
   AHS 21 Calvert Hall 0
   AHS 36 Werntz Naval Prep 0

1921 (2 – 3 – 0) Coach A.Z. Holley
   Captain: Frank De Santis
   AHS 6 Mt. St. Joseph 0
   AHS 0 Severn 21 at Boone
   AHS 6 Donaldson 0 at Ilchester
   AHS 6 Mt. St. Mary College freshmen 20
   AHS 0 Leonard Hall 16

1922 (3 – 2 – 1) Coach A.Z. Holley
   Captain: Robert Elliott
   AHS 12 Company M 0
   AHS 7 Severn 13 at Boone
   AHS 0 Mt. St. Joseph 26 at Irvington
   AHS 7 Rock Hall 7 at St. John's Field
   AHS 7 University School 0 at St. John's Field
   AHS 25 Army-Navy Prep 0 at St. John's Field

1923 (0 – 4 – 2) Coach: Byron Leitch
   Captain: Robert Elliott
   AHS 0 Mt. St. Joseph 27 at Irvington
   AHS 0 Loyola 14 at St. John's Field
   AHS 9 Calvert Hall 20 at St. John's Field
   AHS 0 Severn 13 at Boone
   AHS 7 Charlotte Hall 7 at St. John's Field
   AHS 6 Alexandria 6 at St. John's Field

1924 (4 – 2 – 2) Coach Willis "Bill" White
    AHS 0   Mt St. Joseph 0
    AHS 24 Donaldson 0
    AHS 0   Severn 7
    AHS 0   Devitt Prep 20
    AHS 6   Loyola 0
    AHS 58 Dunham 0
    AHS 0   Alexandria 0

1925 (2 – 4 – 0) Coach Willis "Bill" White
Captain: Norman Boettcher
    AHS 0   Mt. St. Joseph 47
    AHS 7   Severn 12
    AHS 46 Charolotte Hall 7
    AHS 13 Devitt Prep 34
    AHS 0   Loyola 33
    AHS 34 Alexandria 0

1926 (4 – 2 – 0) Coach Willis "Bill" White   *Maryland Public School State Champions*
    AHS 0   Mt. St. Joseph 7 at Irvington
    AHS 47 Charlotte Hall 0
    AHS 0   Loyola 7
    AHS 6   McDonough 0
    AHS 41 Severn 0
    AHS 13 Hagerstown 6 (Thanksgiving)

1927 (3 – 1 – 3) Coach Willis "Bill" White
Captain: William "Cy" Kimball
    AHS 7   Mt. St. Joseph 6
    AHS 20 Loyola 30
    AHS 6   MacDonough 6
    AHS 47 Army-Navy Prep 6
    AHS 0   City College 0
    AHS 0   Forest Park 0
    AHS 20 Severn 0

1928 (1 – 5 – 0) Coach Willis "Bill "White
    AHS 0   Mt. St. Joseph 6
    AHS 12 City College 13
    AHS 0   Loyola 12
    AHS 0   Severn 6
    AHS 12 Forest Park 0
    AHS 21 Hagerstown 27 (Thanksgiving)

1929 (2 – 6 – 0) Coach James W. McCauley
    AHS 0   Mt St. Joseph 12
    AHS 6   Polytechnic Institute 26
    AHS 12 Calvert Hall 6
    AHS 2   City College 7
    AHS 0   Forest Park 7
    AHS 6   Severn 20
    AHS 7   St. John's College "scrubs" 0
    AHS 6   Hagerstown 18 (Thanksgiving)

        * * * * (Break – no games from 1930 – 1947) * * * *

1947 Coach Bruce Rentschler — football revived; team played one exhibition game against an alumni team

1948 (2 – 2 – 1) Coach Bruce Rentschler
AHS 6 Cambridge 6
AHS 0 Dover 7
AHS 19 Harve de Grace 6
AHS 6 Westminster 32
AHS 19 Elkton 14 on Thanksgiving

1949 (2 – 6 – 1) Coach Norwood "Woody" Wetherhold
Captain: Robert Purdy
AHS 0 Frederick 7
AHS 0 Dover 20
AHS 6 Sherwood 6
AHS 0 Bethesda 26
AHS 27 Elkton 6
AHS 7 Westminster 34
AHS 24 Harve de Grace 2
AHS 0 Cambridge 20
AHS 6 Wicomico 12

1950 (7 – 2) Coach Norwood "Woody" Wetherhold
Co-captains: Dan Olson and Robert Purdy
AHS 7 Greenbelt 6
AHS 7 Frederick 13
AHS 31 Dover 7
AHS 56 Sherwood 0
AHS 12 Bethesda 0
AHS 21 Elkton 6
AHS 6 Maryland Park 7
AHS 27 Cambridge 20
AHS 6 Wicomico 0

1951 (7 – 2) Coach Norwood "Woody" Wetherhold
Co-captains: Bill Kennerly, Bill Kerchner, Roger Moyer & John Simmons
AHS 21 Frederick 6
AHS 19 Dover 20
AHS 21 Suitland 14
AHS 13 Bethesda 7
AHS 27 Elkton 6
AHS 12 Northwestern 6
AHS 33 Cambridge 19
AHS 20 Woodward Prep 21
AHS 39 Southern 0

postseason honors:
Roger "Pip" Moyer
Bill Kerchner

1952 (1 – 5 – 1) Coach Norwood "Woody" Wetherhold
Co-captains: Ralph Beavers and William Brown
AHS 7 Cambridge 7
AHS 7 Southern 6
AHS 0 Frederick 21
AHS 0 Suitland 6
AHS 0 Bethesda 20
AHS 0 Elkton 26
AHS 0 Northwestern 33

Appendices

1953 (2 – 6) Coach Norwood "Woody" Wetherhold
Co-captains: W. Fred Carlson and Gordon Catterton
AHS 20 Frederick 12
AHS 21 Cambridge 7
AHS 0 Suitland 33
AHS 6 Elkton 39
AHS 14 Northwestern 28
AHS 6 Westminster 27
AHS 0 St. Mary's 6
AHS 2 Southern 6

1954 (6 – 3 – 1) Coach Norwood "Woody" Wetherhold
AHS 8 Frederick 12
AHS 26 Cambridge 0
AHS 7 Suitland 13
AHS 28 Laurel 12
AHS 31 Elkton 0
AHS 0 Northwestern 19
AHS 7 Bethesda 7
AHS 13 Westminster 7
AHS 33 Southern 6
AHS 46 St. Mary's 0

1955 (1 – 7 – 1) Coach Norwood "Woody" Wetherhold
Captain: Charles Horton
AHS 6 Frederick 0
AHS 0 Cambridge 0
AHS 0 Sherwood 13
AHS 0 Laurel (DE) 6
AHS 6 Elkton 7
AHS 6 Southern 13
AHS 18 BelAir 31
AHS 12 Westminster 20
AHS 6 Wicomico 18

1956 (6 – 3) Coach Norwood "Woody" Wetherhold
Co-Captains: Bud Beardmore and Robert Gaither
AHS 32 Cambridge 0
AHS 20 Frederick 0
AHS 6 Richard Montgomery 0
AHS 12 Laurel (DE) 0
AHS 13 Elkton 31
AHS 25 Southern 0
AHS 7 Bel Air 38
AHS 0 Wicomico 20
AHS 13 Howard 0

Postseason honors:
Michael Byrne

1957 (5 – 2 – 1) Coach Bill Best
Captain: Harry Dobson
AHS 6 St. Mary's 7
AHS 16 Cambridge 0
AHS 14 Frederick 7
AHS 25 Richard Montgomery 7
AHS 49 Southern 0
AHS 0 BelAir 21

Postseason honors:
Harry Dobson
Dave Dulin
Buster Rankin
Skip Brown

AHS 40 Wicomico 7
AHS 13 Howard 13

1958 (4 – 4) Coach Bill Best
Co-captains: Buster Rankin, Jim Scible & Ed Roberts
AHS 19 Cambridge 0
AHS 0 Frederick 7
AHS 0 Seaford, De. 19
AHS 27 GlenElg 0
AHS 26 Edgewood 0
AHS 19 Southern 0
AHS 0 BelAir 7
AHS 6 Wicomico 35

1959 (6 – 1 – 2) Coach Neville Leonard
Co-captains: Charles Lewnes, Lloyd Wheeler, Wayne Kramer & Buster Rankin
AHS 15 Cambridge 0
AHS 13 Frederick 6
AHS 0 Seaford 12
AHS 0 Laurel (DE) 0
AHS 26 Edgewood 6
AHS 40 Southern 0
AHS 6 Bel Air 33
AHS 0 Wicomico 0
AHS 27 St. Mary's 7

1960 (5 – 3 – 1) Coach Neville Leonard
Co-captains: Joe Nicewarner & George Samaras
AHS 26 Howard 0
AHS 25 Brooklyn Park 6
AHS 0 Severna Park 0
AHS 32 Southern 6
AHS 6 BelAir 32
AHS 13 Wicomico 27
AHS 7 Cambridge 39
AHS 21 Forest Park 7
AHS 51 St. Mary's 0

1961 (2 – 7) Coach Neville Leonard
Co-captains: Jim Canary, John Clapp, John Neill.
George Samaras, Charles Russell & Dave Copenhaver
AHS 6 Oxon Hill 18
AHS 0 Howard 6
AHS 7 Brooklyn Park 0
AHS 6 Severna Park 12
AHS 13 BelAir 28
AHS 14 Wicomico 20
AHS 7 Cambridge 26
AHS 6 Forest Park 19
AHS 7 St. Mary's 0

1962 (10 – 0) Coach Neville Leonard *Perfect 10-0 season*
Co-captains: Alan Pastrana and Harold Grau
AHS 20 Oxon Hill 0
AHS 33 Howard 0

AHS 27 Brooklyn Park 7
AHS 29 Southern 0
AHS 13 Severna Park 0
AHS 13 Bel Air 0
AHS 12 Wicomico 7
AHS 13 Cambridge 12
AHS 14 Forest Park 0
AHS 48 St. Mary's 0

1963 (6–4) Coach Neville Leonard *Anne Arundel County Champion*
Captain: John Russell
AHS 26 Oxon Hill 0
AHS 6 Howard 7
AHS 17 Brooklyn Park 7
AHS 33 Southern 0
AHS 7 Andover 25
AHS 7 Bel Air 26
AHS 6 Wicomico 25
AHS 19 Cambridge 14
AHS 21 Allegheny 19
AHS 23 Severna Park 0

1964 (4–5–1) Coach Neville Leonard
AHS 0 Oxon Hills 38
AHS 6 Howard 14
AHS 14 Arundel 7
AHS 23 Brooklyn Park 7
AHS 0 Bates 19
AHS 13 Bel Air 26
AHS 12 Wicomico 6
AHS 14 Andover 14
AHS 21 Glen Burnie 7
AHS 7 Severna Park 44

1965 (5–5) Coach Al Laramore
Co-Captains: Dick Larrimore and Charlie Schuette

Postseason honors:
Mike Corbett
Charlie Schuette
Jerry Wilson
Joe Alton

AHS 19 Oxon Hill 7
AHS 26 Northeast 0
AHS 10 Arundel 18
AHS 13 Brooklyn Park 0
AHS 26 Bates 0
AHS 6 Bel Air 14
AHS 19 Wicomico 7
AHS 13 Andover 20
AHS 14 Glen Burnie 26
AHS 6 Severna Park 12

1966 (8–0–1) Coach Al Laramore *Anne Arundel County Champion*
Captain: Lee Corbett

Postseason honors:
Jeff Cheplowitz
Lee Corbett
Hank Kechington
Archie Pearman
Don Luongo   Dave Hart
Lou Thomas   Jim Chase

AHS 33 Glen Burnie 0
AHS 33 Wicomico 0
AHS 33 Brooklyn Park 14
AHS 27 Andover 0
AHS 18 Bel Air 0
AHS 33 Arundel 0

AHS 31 Southern 0
AHS 26 Northeast 0
AHS 12 Severna Park 12

Richard Gaar Gerry Wilson
Alan Harris   Bob Mason
Mike Chase   Lee Corbet

1967 (8 – 2) Coach Al Laramore
Captain: Gerry Hough
AHS 13 Northeast 6
AHS 25 Cambridge 7
AHS 38 Brooklyn Park 14
AHS 36 Southern 7
AHS 14 BelAir 12
AHS 46 Wicomico 20
AHS 39 Andover 0
AHS 0 Glen Burnie 7
AHS 0 Arundel 6
AHS 14 Severna Park 7

Postseason honors:
Murry Todd
Jim Coates
Archie Pearman
Murry Todd
Bill Kirby
Don Smith
Gerry Hough
Jack Reed
Spunky Perkins
Chilly Orme
Steve Bell

1968 (7 – 3) Coach Al Laramaore
Captain: Bill Kirby
AHS 18 Caesar Rodney 12
AHS 20 Northeast 6
AHS 25 Brooklyn Park 6
AHS 34 Southern 0
AHS 0 Bel Air 14
AHS 7 Good Counsel 12
AHS 34 Andover 0
AHS 12 Glen Burnie 6
AHS 41 Arundel 6
AHS 20 Severna Park 21

Anne Arundel County Champion
Postseason honors:
Don Smith
Archie Pearman
Bill Kirby
William Flood
Scott Williams
Mitch Kappesser
Joe Weresuk

1969 (7 – 2 – 1) Coach Al Laramore
Captain: Scott Williams
AHS 28 Caesar Rodney 12
AHS 44 Northeast 6
AHS 28 Arundel 20
AHS 38 Brooklyn Park 16
AHS 20 Southern 12
AHS 14 Bel Air 30
AHS 6 Good Counsel 52
AHS 39 Andover 6
AHS 22 Glen Burnie 6
AHS 6 Severna Park 6

Anne Arundel County Co-Champion
Postseason honors:
Chris Carter
Mike Patton
Scott Williams
Norman Davis
Dean Neal

1970 (7 – 3) Coach Al Laramore
Captain: Norm Davis
AHS 14 Oxon Hill 7
AHS 6 City College 7
AHS 6 Arundel 0
AHS 34 Brooklyn Park 0
AHS 20 Southern 0
AHS 8 Bel Air 77
AHS 27 Northeast 0
AHS 47 Andover 0
AHS 25 Glen Burnie 0
AHS 14 Severna Park 26

Anne Arundel County Champion
Postseason honors:
Scott Crandall
Norm Davis
Wendell Holland
Joe Lowman
Ridgely McGowan
Michael Queen
Ravon Downs
Angelo Wells
Mike Patton

Appendices

1971 (5 – 5) Coach Al Laramore
Captain: Pat Turner
AHS 0 Archbishop Carroll 20
AHS 14 City College 8
AHS 0 Arundel 27
AHS 0 Bel Air 35
AHS 8 Southern 14
AHS 0 Cedar Cliff 23
AHS 24 Northeast 6
AHS 25 Andover 0
AHS 20 Glen Burnie 6
AHS 26 Severna Park 12

Postseason honors:
Pat Turner
Pete Barrow
Angelo Wells
Ravon Downs
Bert Olson

1972 (5 – 5) Coach Lou Thomas
Co-captains: Dick Duden and Wayne Belt
AHS 6 Archbishop Carroll 38
AHS 26 City College 6
AHS 29 Arundel 22
AHS 15 Bel Air 21
AHS 28 Southern 0
AHS 8 Good Counsel 14
AHS 26 Northeast 6
AHS 28 Andover 8
AHS 8 Glen Burnie 16
AHS 0 Severna Park 20

1973 (9 – 2) Coach Al Laramore   *Anne Arundel County and District V Champions*
Co-captains: Terry Orr and Steve Simms
AHS 0 Archbishop Carroll 9
AHS 24 City College 14
AHS 14 Arundel 0
AHS 13 Bel Air 7
AHS 46 Southern 0
AHS 53 Parkville 0
AHS 39 Northeast 7
AHS 28 Andover 6
AHS 7 Glen Burnie 8
AHS 15 Severna Park 6
AHS 21 Arundel 20 *(District V championship)*

postseason honors:
Henry Downs
Kevin Slade
Steve Simms
Donald Downs
Kim Jones
Jeff Brooks
Jeff Donaldson
Bunk Stansbury
Howard Johnson

1974 (5 – 5) Coach Al Laramore   *Anne Arundel County Co-Champion*
Captain: Melvin Colbert
AHS 0 Archbishop Carroll 20
AHS 0 City College 6 (OT)
AHS 7 Arundel 6
AHS 0 Bel Air 14
AHS 38 Southern 14
AHS 2 Dunbar 8
AHS 21 Northeast 6
AHS 28 Andover 14
AHS 7 Glen Burnie 25
AHS 6 Severna Park 0

postseason honors:
Howard Johnson
Russ Kakaley
Carter Boston
Donald Downs
Bryan Brouse
Melvin Colbert

1975 (6 – 3) Coach Al Laramore
  Captain: Carter Boston
  AHS 7 Parkdale 23
  AHS 7 Archbishop Carroll 16
  AHS 12 Arundel 14
  AHS 30 Bel Air 21
  AHS 12 Southern 0
  AHS 6 Northeast 0
  AHS 21 Andover 0
  AHS 35 Glen Burnie 22
  AHS 14 Severna Park 7 (OT)

1976 (7 – 3) Coach Al Laramore *Anne Arundel County Champion*
  Co-Captains: Tom Coates and Jeff Styron   Postseason honors:
  AHS 34 Parkdale 6   Brian Varden
  AHS 0 Archbishop Carroll 22   Tom Coates
  AHS 20 Arundel 14 (OT)   Lodie Makell
  AHS 20 Bel Air 28   Jeff Styron
  AHS 46 Southern 24   Ron Downs
  AHS 6 Old Mill 7   Tom Coates
  AHS 20 Northeast 6   Carlos Sembly
  AHS 26 Andover 12   Randy Pittman
  AHS 12 Glen Burnie 7
  AHS 60 Severna Park 13

1977 (4 – 6) Coach Bruce Villwock *(temporary coach)*   Postseason honors :
  AHS 0 Archbishop Carroll 9   Virgil Wells
  AHS 6 Polytechnic Institute 21
  AHS 6 Arundel 14
  AHS 13 Bel Air 7 (2 OT)
  AHS 13 Southern 0
  AHS 0 Old Mill 7
  AHS 13 Meade 14
  AHS 6 Andover 7
  AHS 26 Glen Burnie 7
  AHS 2 Severna Park 0

1978 (12 – 0) Coach Al Laramore *Anne Arundel Count, District V & AA State Champions*
  Co-captains: Randy Pittman & Tom Parker   Postseason honors:
  AHS 45 Kenwood 0   Daryl Brown
  AHS 19 Westminster 12   Crandall Chambers
  AHS 22 South Carroll 7   Gary Dukes
  AHS 12 Bel Air 7   Jeff Jacobson
  AHS 27 Chesapeake 0   Dan Loman
  AHS 40 Old Mill 0   Philip Pearman
  AHS 48 Meade 13   Randy Pittman
  AHS 47 Andover 0   Kevin Thompson
  AHS 34 Glen Burnie 6   Daryl Parker Tom Parker
  AHS 19 Severna Park 13   Larry Riek Jim Quarles
  AHS 34 Crossland 10 (*State AA semi-finals*)
  AHS 28 Walt Whitman 14 (*State AA championship*)

1979 (5 – 5) Coach Al Laramore
  Co-Captains: John Rodkey and Jeff Smith   postseason honors:
  AHS 28 Kenwood 6   Tucker Pearman

AHS 12 Westminster 14
AHS 0 South Carroll 3 (OT)
AHS 14 Bel Air 26
AHS 46 Chesapeake 0
AHS 7 Old Mill 0
AHS 35 Andover 14
AHS 6 Meade 20
AHS 9 Glen Burnie 6
AHS 10 Severna Park 35

Jim Quarles

1980 (5 – 5) Coach Al Laramore
Co-Captains: Kost Kapchonick & Tucker Pearlman
AHS 26 Kenwood 6
AHS 21 Westminster 28
AHS 26 Salesianum 21
AHS 7 Bel Air 9
AHS 18 Chesapeake 7
AHS 22 Old Mill 28
AHS 12 Andover 6
AHS 7 Meade 25
AHS 17 Glen Burnie 14
AHS 25 Severna Park 29

postseason honors:
Donald Brown
John Dobyns
Delwin Brown
Jack Hall
Jack Guare

1981 (8 – 2) Coach Al Laramore
Co-Captains: Craig Wilson & Karl Rocher
AHS 27 Kenwood 0
AHS 15 Salesianum 25
AHS 40 Franklin 0
AHS 35 Arundel 34 (OT)
AHS 28 Glen Burnie 14
AHS 47 Westminster 22
AHS 20 Meade 19 (OT)
AHS 26 Chesapeake 0
AHS 7 Old Mill 14
AHS 30 Severna Park 24

Anne Arundel County Champion
postseason honors:
Craig Wilson
Woody Dove
Richard Johnson
Karl Rocher

1982 (4 – 6) Coach Al Laramore
Co-Captains: Greg Pinkney and Bruce Cotterman
AHS 54 Kenwood 0
AHS 16 Calvert Hall 38
AHS 39 Northeast 7
AHS 6 Arundel 28
AHS 3 Glen Burnie 6
AHS 30 Westminster 26
AHS 12 Meade 21
AHS 6 Chesapeake 19
AHS 0 Old Mill 7
AHS 21 Severna Park 18

postseason honors:
Greg Pinkney
Pete Alvanos

1983 (4 – 6) Coach Al Laramore
Captain: Leander Phelps
AHS 6 Ballou 0 (forfeit)
AHS 13 Woodlawn 20
AHS 0 McNamara 35
AHS 6 Arundel 25

postseason honors:
Bryant Hall

AHS 7 Glen Burnie 13
AHS 27 Westminster 21
AHS 25 Meade 14
AHS 39 Chesapeake 0
AHS 0 Old Mill 7
AHS 16 Severna Park 20

1984 (11 – 1) Coach Al Laramore *Anne Arundel County and AA District Champions*
Captain: Rico Stewart *Maryland AA State Finalist*
AHS 7 Northern 6 **postseason honors:**
AHS 21 Woodlawn 0 Rico Stewart
AHS 40 Southwestern 6 Randy Elliot
AHS 13 Arundel 6 Vince Johnson
AHS 33 Glen Burnie 7 Jay Johnson
AHS 37 Westminster 0 Mark Morgan
AHS 18 Meade 0 Craig Ross   Marcus Hayes
AHS 40 Chesapeake 7 Tom Herzog   Shawn Simms
AHS 46 Old Mill 14 Dan Laramore Stan Conley
AHS 52 Severna Park 12
AHS 32 Winston Churchill 15 (*state AA semi-finals*)
AHS 6 Randallstown 14 (*state AA championship*)

1985 (9 – 2) Coach Al Laramore ***AA District Champion***
AHS 48 Northern 0 **postseason honors:**
AHS 7 Arundel 17 Craig Ross
AHS 13 Meade 6 Marcus Hayes
AHS 52 Old Mill 0 Randy Elliott
AHS 39 Woodlawn 21 Kevin Blonder
AHS 21 Dulaney 0 Orlando Johnson
AHS 13 Westminster 10
AHS 37 Randallstown 0
AHS 14 Glen Burnie 6
AHS 21 Severna Park 0
AHS 0 Winston Churchill 3 (*State AA playoff game*)

1986 (8 – 2) Coach Al Laramore ***AA District Champion***
AHS 20 Arundel 12 **postseason honors:**
AHS 13 Meade 17 Robert Fischer
AHS 24 Old Mill 0 Chris Alexander
AHS 27 Woodlawn 12 Mike Hicks
AHS 34 Dulaney 7 Howard Alexander
AHS 13 Westminster 7 Carlus Watkins
AHS 27 Randallstown 20
AHS 35 Glen Burnie 7
AHS 24 Severna Park 6
AHS 20 Meade 35 (*State AA playoff game*)

1987 (8 – 3) Coach Al Laramore
Co-captains: Chris Alexander and Mike Hicks **postseason honors:**
AHS 16 Friendly 8 Keith Lomax
AHS 26 Arundel 13 Chris Alexander
AHS 7 Polytechnic Institute 0 Derek Chiari
AHS 15 Broadneck 9 Mike Hicks
AHS 7 Caesar Rodney 0 Mike Powell
AHS 7 Meade 17

AHS 28 Chesapeake 0
AHS 28 Old Mill 7
AHS 41 Glen Burnie 20
AHS 7 Severna Park 9
AHS 7 Severna Park 16 (*State 4A quarter-finals*)

1988 (8 – 3) Coach Al Laramore

AHS 14 Friendly 21
AHS 27 Arundel 12
AHS 31 Coolidge 12
AHS 14 Broadneck 7
AHS 33 Dunbar 0
AHS 15 Meade 7
AHS 3 Chesapeake 0
AHS 21 Old Mill 7
AHS 13 Glen Burnie 7
AHS 7 Severna Park 10
AHS 14 Churchill 31 (*State 4A Quarter-finals*)

postseason honors:
Nat Cook
Gary Williams
Dexter Turner
Bart Williams
Jamie Cook
Jon Holtzman
Jeff Diggs
Keith Lomax
Gene Slocum
Ray Conner
Chris Bellotte   Jim Westin

1989 (7 – 4) Coach Roy Brown   *Anne Arundel County and 4A East Region Champions*
Co-captains: Jamie Cook and Nat Cook

AHS 20 Friendly 26
AHS 13 Randallstown 14
AHS 26 Arundel 6
AHS 8 Old Mill 7
AHS 14 Broadneck 0
AHS 35 South River 22
AHS 41 Chesapeake 13
AHS 0 Glen Burnie 11
AHS 14 Meade 0
AHS 23 Severna Park 14
AHS 6 Gaithersburg 20 (*State 4A Quarter-finals*)

postseason honors:
Ahmed Middleton
Nat Cook
Harry Stepney
Jamie Cook
Archie Brown
Tim Riggins
Mike Linynsky
Jerold Parker

1990 (5 – 5) Coach Roy Brown
Co-Captains: Mike Linynsky & Titus Jeffries

AHS 0 Friendly 21
AHS 6 Randallstown 14
AHS 7 Arundel 3
AHS 0 Old Mill 28
AHS 14 Broadneck 6
AHS 13 South River 21
AHS 42 Chesapeake 0
AHS 26 Glen Burnie 0
AHS 14 Meade 10
AHS 20 Severna Park 34

postseason honors:
Mike Linynsky
Darrell Foote
Titus Jeffries
Carlos Evans
Eric Tooles

1991 (6 – 4) Coach Roy Brown
Captain: Ty Selby

AHS 17 Randallstown 18
AHS 15 Meade 8
AHS 33 North County 7
AHS 12 Broadneck 0
AHS 13 Arundel 15
AHS 7 Glen Burnie 3

postseason honors:
Andrew Yiannolou
Demond Galloway
Ty Selby
Jeff Golas
Brendon Tinker
Ray Henson

AHS 40 Queen Anne 6
AHS 14 Old Mill 22
AHS 20 Chesapeake 0
AHS 14 Severna Park 16

1992 (10 – 2) Coach Roy Brown   *Anne Arundel County and 4A East Region Champions*

AHS 16 Randallstown 18   **postseason honors:**
AHS 28 Meade 0   Shawn Taylor
AHS 20 North County 19   Brandon Tinker
AHS 35 Broadneck 20   Beau Watkins
AHS 51 Arundel 6   Matt Criscimagna
AHS 28 Glen Burnie 6   Jeff Ogle
AHS 14 Queen Anne 6   Brendan Bellotte
AHS 30 Old Mill 22   Tom Ford
AHS 40 Chesapeake 7   Chris Johnson
AHS 21 Severna Park 0
AHS 21 Friendly 6 (*State 4A State Quarter-finals*)
AHS 7 Gaithersburg 35 (*State 4A Semi-finals*)

1993 (7 – 3) Coach Roy Brown
Co-Captains: Matt Smear and Kevin Belt   **postseason honors:**
AHS 20 Largo 26 (OT)   Kenny Boyd
AHS 34 Westminster 6   Jeff Ogle
AHS 6 Mt. St. Joseph 0   Lamont Henson
AHS 35 Old Mill 7   Darnell Ravenell
AHS 34 Glen Burnie 8   Beau Watkins
AHS 35 Meade 13   Bernard Turner
AHS 14 Chesapeake 6   Chip Monger
AHS 6 North County 40   Chris Johnson
AHS 36 Arundel 0
AHS 0 Severna Park 6

1994 (5 – 5) Coach Roy Brown
Co-Captains: Victor Watkins and Orlando Downs   **postseason honors:**
AHS 20 Largo 19   Beau Watkins
AHS 21 Westminster 9   Orlando Downs
AHS 6 Mt. St. Joseph 26   Bernard Turner
AHS 6 Old Mill 3   Danny Edwards
AHS 7 Glen Burnie 32
AHS 13 Meade 0
AHS 26 Chesapeake 21
AHS 0 North County 7
AHS 12 Arundel 13
AHS 13 Severna Park 33

1995 (4 – 6) Coach Roy Brown
AHS 0 Mt. St. Joe's 32
AHS 28 Carver 6   **postseason honors:**
AHS 46 Southern-Balt 0   Carey Stone
AHS 12 Old Mill 9   Marty Sellers
AHS 0 Glen Burnie 18   Brandt Hager
AHS 14 Meade 20
AHS 31 Chesapeake 7
AHS 18 North County 32
AHS 6 Arundel 36   AHS 14 Severna Park 29

Appendices

1996 (5 – 5) Coach Roy Brown
Co-Captains: Danny Curran & Greg Gulley

AHS 28 Mt. St. Joseph 32
AHS 7 Bladensburg 6
AHS 40 Fairmont Heights 6
AHS 6 Old Mill 10
AHS 32 Glen Burnie 8
AHS 13 Meade 33
AHS 32 Chesapeake 20
AHS 6 North County 0 (forfeit)
AHS 6 Arundel 21
AHS 7 Severna Park 32

postseason honors:
Donnell Foote
Danny Curran
Greg Gulley

1997 (9 – 2) Coach Roy Brown   *Anne Arundel County and 4A East Region Champions*
Co-Captains: Mike Donlin and Derek Johnson

AHS 28 Largo 7
AHS 12 Paint Branch 9
AHS 41 Frederick 18
AHS 24 Chesapeake 0
AHS 28 Arundel 8
AHS 49 North County 6
AHS 25 Meade 21
AHS 40 Glen Burnie 6
AHS 40 Old Mill 13
AHS 14 Severna Park 21
AHS 14 High Point 33 *(State 4A Quarter-finals)*

Postseason honors:
Albert Creek
Mike Donlin
Donnell Foote
Derek Johnson
Curtis Jones
Pete Ludlum
Joe Plattner
S.J. Womack
John Paul Williams

1998 (8 – 3) Coach Roy Brown   *Anne Arundel County and 4A East Region Champions*
Co- Captains: DeWayne Hunt and Kyron Belt

AHS 20 Largo 29
AHS 6 Paint Branch 13 (OT)
AHS 60 Frederick 0
AHS 42 Chesapeake 0
AHS 35 Arundel 34
AHS 21 North County 0
AHS 35 Meade 0
AHS 49 Glen Burnie 0
AHS 35 Old Mill 7
AHS 47 Severna Park 7
AHS 7 Sherwood 17 (State 4A Quarter-finals)

postseason honors:
Kyron Belt
Jack Brooks
Charles Carter
Henry Downs
DeWayne Hunt
Eric Toney
Rashad Wills
Marvin Charles
Rayvon Johnson
Dan Harich

1999 (9 – 2) Coach Roy Brown   *Anne Arundel County and 3A East Region Champions*
Co-Captains: Aaron Copeland and Rayvon Johnson

AHS 41 Old Mill 34
AHS 37 Chesapeake 6
AHS 46 South River 7
AHS 47 Meade 0
AHS 42 Arundel 14
AHS 21 Severna Park 17
AHS 55 Southern 12
AHS 42 Glen Burnie 0
AHS 41 North County 24
AHS 21 Broadneck 22
AHS 27 Damascus 28 (OT – *State 3A Quarter-finals)*

postseason honors:
Marvin Charles
Aaron Copeland
Rayvon Johnson
Mike Phaneuf
Trevon Williams
James Forrester
Nick Good-Malloy
Brandon Gulley
Kion Mackell

2000 (11 – 2) Coach Roy Brown *3A East Region Champions and Maryland State Finalist*
Co-captains: Nick Good-Malloy, Brandon Gulley, Kion Mackell & Andre Toney

AHS 28	Old Mill 38	
AHS 32	Chesapeake 15	**postseason honors:**
AHS 52	South River 0	Nick Good-Malloy
AHS 35	Meade 15	Brandon Gulley
AHS 49	Arundel 8	Kion Mackell
AHS 38	Severna Park 14	Andre Toney
AHS 40	Southern 20	Kevin Jones
AHS 46	Glen Burnie 6	James Forrester
AHS 39	North County 26	Kevan Simms
AHS 26	Broadneck 19	Eric Venerable
AHS 12	Paint Branch 9 *(State 3A Quarter-finals)*	Demario Harris
AHS 26	Douglass 12 *(State 3A Semi-finals)*	
AHS 22	Calvert 34 *(State 3A championship)*	

2001 (8 – 3) Coach Roy Brown

AHS 28	Meade 6	**Postseason honors:**
AHS 0	Broadneck 6	Darren Johnson
AHS 34	Glen Burnie 21	Kareem Reed
AHS 34	Chesapeake 14	Eric Venerable
AHS 48	Arundel 0	Mike Womack
AHS 48	North County 0	Sung Yang
AHS 46	Northeast 6	Demario Harris
AHS 46	South River 6	Darius Johnson
AHS 14	Old Mill 20	
AHS 40	Severna Park 0	
AHS 19	Patuxent 27 *(State 3A Quarter-finals)*	

2002 (9 – 2) Coach Roy Brown *Anne Arundel County and 3A East Region Champions*
Co-Captains: Demario Harris and Davon Watkins

AHS 42	Meade 0	**Postseason honors:**
AHS 21	Broadneck 7	P.C. Cerone
AHS 35	Glen Burnie 13	Demario Green
AHS 28	Chesapeake 20	Demario Harris
AHS 26	Arundel 7	Darius Johnson
AHS 49	North County 7	Davon Watkins
AHS 27	Northeast 3	Cory Holland
AHS 49	South River 13	
AHS 14	Old Mill 20 (OT)	
AHS 27	Severna Park 7	
AHS 13	Seneca Valley 35 *(State 3A Quarter-finals)*	

2003 (3 – 7) Coach Dale Castro

AHS 26	Delmar (Del) 6	**Postseason honors:**
AHS 43	North County 0	Andrew Thomas
AHS 0	Severna Park 21	Steve Jones
AHS 0	Arundel 17	Larry Beavers
AHS 0	Broadneck 20	
AHS 14	Glen Burnie 16	
AHS 17	Northeast 13	
AHS 0	South River 27	
AHS 21	Chesapeake 27	
AHS 0	Southern 27	

APPENDIX B: Annapolis High Football Opponents, 1899 – 2003
(Other Anne Arundel County teams are in CAPITAL LETTERS)

Alexandria, Virginia (1 – 0 – 2) 1923, 1924, 1925
Allegheny (1 – 0) 1963
ANDOVER (14 – 3 – 1) every year from 1963 – 1980
Archbishop Carroll (0 – 7) 1971 – 1977
Army-Navy Prep (2 – 0) 1922, 1927
ARUNDEL (25 – 12) 1965 – 1977 and 1981 – 2003 (twice in 1973)
Ballou (1 – 0) 1983 (forfeit)
BATES (1 – 1) 1964, 1965
Bel Air (7 – 19) 1955 – 1980
Bethesda (2 – 2 – 1) 1949, 1950, 1951, 1952, 1954
Bladensburg (1 – 0) 1996
Bobbie's Naval Prep (0 – 1) 1912
Boys' Latin (Baltimore) (3 – 0) 1909, 1913, 1914
BROADNECK (8 – 3) 1987 – 1992, 1999 - 2003
BROOKLYN PARK (11 – 0) 1960 – 1970
Caesar Rodney (3 – 0) 1968, 1969, 1987
Calvert (0 – 1) 2000 (state championship)
Calvert Hall (2 – 2) 1920, 1923, 1929, 1982
Cambridge (11 – 3 – 3) 1948 – 1963, 1967
Carver (1 – 0) 1995
Cedar Cliff (0 – 1) 1971
Charlotte Hall (4 – 0 – 1) 1908, 1909, 1923, 1925, 1926
CHESAPEAKE (22 – 2) 1978 – 1984, 1987 – 2003
Chesapeake Athletic Club (1 – 0) 1908
Churchill (see Winston Churchill)
City College (5 – 5 – 1) 1908 (reserves), 1909, 1912, 1927, 1928, 1929, 1970 – 74
Colonial Outing Association (1 – 0) 905
Coolidge (1 – 0) 1988
Company M of Maryland National Guard (1 – 0) 1922
Crossland (1 – 0) 1978 (state semi-finals)
Damascus (0 – 1) 1999 (state quarter-finals)
Delmar, DE (1-0) 2003
Devitt Prep (0 – 2) 1924, 1925
Donaldson (2 – 0 – 1) 1920, 1921, 1924
Douglass – P.G. County (1 – 0) 2000 (state semi-finals)
Dover, Delaware (1 – 3) 1948 – 1951
Dulaney (2 – 0) 1985, 1986
Dunbar (1 – 1) 1974, 1988
Dunham Naval Prep (1 – 0) 1924
Edgewood (2 – 0) 1958, 1959
Elkton (5 – 4) 1948 – 56
Fairmont Heights (1 – 0) 1996
Forest Park (3 – 2 – 1) 1927, 1928, 1929, 1960, 1961, 1962
Franklin (1 – 0) 1981
Frederick (7 – 5) 1949 – 54, 1956 – 59, 1997, 1998
Friendly (2 – 3) 1987 – 90, 1992 (state quarter-finals)

Friends School (1 – 0) 1914
Gaithersburg (0 – 2) 1989 (state quarter-finals), 1992 (state semi-finals)
Gilman Country Day (0 – 1) 1913
Glenelg (1 – 0) 1958
GLEN BURNIE (29 – 11) every year since 1964
Good Counsel (0 – 3) 1968, 1969, 1972
Greenbelt (1 – 0) 1950
Hagerstown (3 – 2) on Thanksgiving Day in 1908, 1909, 1926, 1928, 1929
Havre de Grace (2 – 0) 1948, 1949
High Point (0 – 1) 1997 (state quarter-finals)
Howard County (3 – 3 – 1) 1956, 1957, 1960 – 1964
John Carroll (0 – 1) 1977
Kenwood (5 – 0) 1978 – 1982
Lancaster, PA (0 – 1) 1912
Largo (2 – 2) 1993, 1994, 1997, 1998
Laurel, Delaware (2 – 1 – 1) 1954, 1955, 1956, 1959
Laurel, Maryland (2 – 0 – 1) 1899 (twice), 1904
Leonard Hall (0 – 1) 1922
Loyola (1 – 5) 1923 – 1928
McDonogh (1 – 0 – 1) 1926, 1927
Marsten School for Boys (1 – 0) 1914
Maryland All-Stars (0 – 0 – 1) 1911
Maryland Park (0 – 1) 1950
McNamara (0 – 1) 1983
MEADE (18 – 9) 1977 – 2002 including 2 games in 1986 (state quarterfinal)
Mount St. Joseph (3 – 9 – 1) 1921 – 1929, 1993- 1996
Mount St. Mary College freshmen (0 – 1) 1921
Mount Washington (1 – 0) 1908
NORTH COUNTY (10 – 3) 1991 – 2003
NORTHEAST (16 - 0) 1965 – 76, 1982, 2001-3
Northern (2 – 0) 1984, 1985
Northwestern (1 – 3) 1951 – 54
OLD MILL (15 – 12) every year since 1976
Oxon Hill (4 – 2) 1961 – 65, 1970
Paint Branch (2 – 1) 1997, 1998, 2000 (state quarterfinals)
Parkdale (1 – 1) 1975, 1976
Parkville (1 – 0) 1973
Patuxent (0 – 1) 2001(state quarterfinals)
Polytechnic Institute of Baltimore (4 – 2) 1900, 1905, 1908, 1929, 1977, 1987
Queen Anne County (2 – 0) 1991, 1992
Randallstown (2 – 5) 1984 (state championship), 1985, 1986, 1989, 1990, 1991, 1992
Richard Montgomery (2 – 0) 1956, 1957
Rock Hall (0 – 0 – 1) 1922
St. John's College Reserves/Freshmen (3 – 1) 909, 1912, 1929
St. John's College Prep School (1 – 1 – 2) 1899, 1905, 1906, 1911
St. Mary's/Annapolis (5 – 2) 1953, 1954, 1957, 1959 – 62
Salisianum, Delaware (1 – 1) 1980, 1981
Seaford, Delaware (0 – 2) 1958, 1959

Seneca Valley (0 – 1) 2002
Severn School (2 – 7) 1921 – 1929
SEVERNA PARK (22 – 20 – 3) 1960-2003 (2 games in 1987)
Sherwood (1 – 2 – 1) 1949, 1950, 1955, 1998 (state quarterfinals)
South Carroll (1 – 1) 1978, 1979
SOUTH RIVER (5 – 2) 1989, 1990, 1999, 2000-2003
SOUTHERN – AA County (23 –43) 1951 – 1963, 1966 – 1977, 1999, 2000 , 2003
Southern – Baltimore county (1 – 0) 1995
Southwestern (1 – 0) 1984
Suitland (1 – 3) 1951 – 54
University School (1 – 0) 1922
Walt Whitman (1 – 0) 1978 (state championship)
Werntz Naval Prep (3 – 1 – 3) 1908, 1909, 1910, 1911, 1913, 1920 (twice)
Westminster (10 – 6) 1948, 1949, 1953, 1954, 1955, 1978 – 86, 1993, 1994
Wicomico (9 – 7 – 1) 1912 (twice), 1949, 1950, 1955 – 67
Wiley H. Bates (see Bates)
Wilmer's Naval Prep (2 – 1 – 1) 1908, 1910, 1911 twice)
Winston Churchill (1 – 2) 1984 (state semifinals), 1985, 1985 (state quarterfinals)
Woodlawn (3 –10) 1983 – 86
Woodward Prep (0 – 1) 1951

APPENDIX C: Annapolis High Football Coaches (1899-2002)

Years Coached	Name (record)	Winning percentage
1899-1906	Walter L. Brady (6–1–2)	.667
1907-1909	A.G. "Garey" Lambert (13– 0–1)	.929
1910-1914	Ivan T. Morton (8– 7–4)	.421
1920-1922	Andreas Holley (8–5–1)	.571
1923	Byron Leitch (0– 4–2)	.000
1924-1928	Willis "Bill" White (14–14–5)	.424
1929	J.W. McCauley (2– 6–0)	.250
1947	Bruce Rentschler (2– 2–1)	.400
1948-1956	Woody Wetherhold (32–34–1)	.464
1957-1958	Bill Best (9– 6–1)	.563
1959-1965	Neville Leonard (33–20–4)	.579
1965-1988	Al Laramore (156–68–2)	.690
1972	Lou Thomas, interim (5– 5)	.500
1977	Bruce Villwock , interim (4– 6)	.400
1989-2002	Roy Brown (103–48)	.682
2002-2003	Dale Castro (3-7)	.300
TOTAL	398 – 233 – 24	.611

APPENDIX D: Annapolis High Football Honors & Records

Touchdown Club of Annapolis
Jim Rhodes Memorial Trophy
given annually to top high school
player in Anne Arundel County

1959	Bill Glotzbach
1960	Bill Glotzbach
1961	Charles Russell
1966	Lee Corbett
1968	Archie Pearman
1973	Steve Simms
1978	Tom Parker
1981	Craig Wilson
1984	Douglass Johnson
1998	Rayvon Johnson
1999	Rayvon Johnson
2002	Demario Harris

Touchdown Club of Annapolis
Jerry Mears Memorial Trophy
given annually to best high school
team in Anne Arundel County

Six Annapolis High teams were named county best since award began in 1989: 1989, 1992, 1997, 1999, 2000, 2002

Top AHS Team Records

1978 (12-0) Maryland State Champs
1962 (10-0)
1909 (6-0)
1966 (8-0-1)
1908 (7-0-1)
1984 (11-1) Maryland state finalist
2000 (11-2) Maryland state finalist
1992 (10-2) Maryland state semifinalist

County Records (Individual)

Rushing (season): Eric Venerable
2,346 yards (2000)

Rushing (career): Rayvon Johnson
4,044 yards (1998-99)

Touchdowns (season): Eric Venerable
32 (2000)

Touchdowns (career): Eric Venerable 53

Associated Press Ranked Teams
(state of Maryland, end of season)
1992 – 9th
1997 – 15th
1999 – 15th
2000 – 10th
2002 – 21st

County Records (Team)

Rushing (season): 4,291 (2000)

Points scored (season): 445 (2000)

Number state playoff appearances: 14

1978	1992
1984	1997
1985	1998
1986	1999
1987	2000
1988	2001
1989	2002

Scoring average/season: 38.2 (1999)

APPENDIX E: Anne Arundel County Football Champions

1962		No official county league. Annapolis and Bates High both recorded perfect 10-0 season records.
1963	Annapolis	League consists of 6 teams (Andover, Annapolis, Bates, Brooklyn Park, Severna Park and Southern).
1964	Severna Park	League adds Arundel and Glen Burnie (8 teams)
1965	Arundel	Severna Park has identical 6-1 league record, but lost to Arundel 13-7. League adds Northeast but loses Bates.
1966	Annapolis	Annapolis undefeated for season (8-0-1)
1967	Glen Burnie	Glen Burnie undefeated for season (9-0)
1968	Annapolis	Arundel has identical 6-1 league record, but lost to Annapolis 41-6.
1969	Annapolis	
1970	Annapolis	Arundel has identical 6-1 league record, but lost to Annapolis 6-0.
1971	Arundel	Brooklyn Park leaves county league (7 teams).
1972	Glen Burnie	Severna Park has identical 5-1 league record, but lost to Glen Burnie 21-0. State begins district playoffs.
1973	Annapolis	
1974	Annapolis	MPSSAA state championship tournament begins.
1975	Arundel	Arundel wins Maryland AA State title (9-2).
1976	Annapolis	Old Mill's 1st season. County League grows to 8 teams.
1977	Andover (AA) Arundel (A)	Meade's 1st season. County League divides into 2 divisions to enhance chances to make playoffs. "AA" League (Glen Burnie, Annapolis, Old Mill & Severna Park) and "AB" League (Andover, Arundel, Meade, Northeast, Southern).
1978	Annapolis (AA) Arundel (AB)	Annapolis wins AA State Championship (12-0). Chesapeake and South River join AB League. Arundel records perfect regular season (10-0).
1979	Meade (AA) Arundel (A/B)	Arundel records 2nd straight perfect regular season (10-0).
1980	Severna Park (AA) Andover (A/B)	
1981	Annapolis (AA) South River (ABC)	County AA league grows to 7 teams (Annapolis, Arundel, Chesapeake, Glen Burnie., Meade, Old Mill & Severna Park.). Westminster joins them to form the "Big 8" Conference (comprising region IV of class AA). Four remaining county teams form "ABC" league with Brooklyn Park, South River, Northeast and Southern.

1982	Meade (AA) South River (ABC)	Broadneck joins ABC league.
1983	Old Mill (AA) South River (ABC)	Arundel also finished 5-1 but lost to Old Mill 34-14.
1984	Annapolis (AA) South River (ABC)	Annapolis records perfect regular season; advances to state final (11-1 final record).
1985	Arundel (AA) South River (ABC)	
1986	Meade (AA) Northeast (ABC)	South River also finished 4-1 but lost to Northeast 16-6.
1987	Severna Park (AA) 3-way tie (ABC)	Broadneck moves to AA classification. Northeast, South River and Southern all 2-1. Brooklyn Park leaves the county league in 4-team ABC League.
1988	Severna Park & Annapolis (4A)	State classification system changes. County 4A League has 8 teams (Annapolis, Arundel, Broadneck, Chesapeake, Glen Burnie, Meade, Old Mill & Severna Park). 3A/2A League has Andover, Northeast, South River & Southern.
1989	Annapolis (4A)	
1990	Severna Park (4A)	Andover and Brooklyn Park are closed; North County opens as county's ninth 4A school, leaving 3 3A/2A teams
1991	Old Mill (4A)	
1992	Annapolis (4A)	
1993	North County (4A)	Southern advances to 2A state finals, finishes season 11-2. Broadneck reclassified 3A.
1994	North County (4A)	North County wins 4A Maryland State Championship.
1995	Arundel (4A)	Arundel finishes perfect 10-0 regular season, but loses to Meade in quarterfinals of 4A playoffs.
1996	Meade (4A)	
1997	Annapolis (4A)	
1998	Annapolis (4A)	3A Broadneck has 10-0 regular season.
1999	Annapolis	Single league for all 12 county high schools is formed.
2000	Old Mill	Annapolis (9-1) and Broadneck (9-1) have best county records. Annapolis won the season-ending "county championship" game, but the MPSSAA point system adopted by athletic directors gives 8-1 Old Mill the title.
200	Broadneck	Athletic directors adopt winning percentage against other county teams as way to determine county champion.
2002	Annapolis	

APPENDIX F: Annapolis High Chronology
(Principals & Buildings)

Sept. 1896	**William E. Smith**	*first principal;* **Stockett House** on Green Street is used to house new high school department.
Sept. 1897		New **Annapolis Schoolhouse** on Green St. opens; high school department on top floor in assembly room until Stockett House is renovated
Sept. 1900	**Charles E. Dryden**	*second principal;* High school returns to **Stockett House** (8th through 11th grades).
Sept. 1902	**Irving L. Twilley**	*third principal*
Sept. 1903	**Henry R. Wallis**	*fourth principal*
Nov. 1905	**W.S. Crouse**	*fifth principal*
Sept. 1906	**Andrew J. English**	*sixth principal;* High school department returns to **Annapolis Schoolhouse** while Stockett House is torn down and new high school is built
Sept. 1907		New $20,000 **Annapolis High School** opens on **Green Street**
Sept. 1908	**George B. Pfeifer**	*seventh principal*
Sept. 1910	**Louise W. Linthicum**	*eighth principal*
mid-1920's		Classroom wing added to high school building
Sept. 1928	**Henry A. Kinhart**	*ninth principal*
Feb. 12, 1930		Fire destroys much of 3rd floor of high school
Sept. 1932		New **Annapolis High School** opens on the outskirts of the city (Spa View Heights)
Sept 1949	**Albert W. Fowble**	*10th principal* **Annapolis Jr. High** (7th and 8th grades) opens in old high school on Green St.
Sept. 1950	**Ernest H. Herklotz**	*serves as acting principal until Fowble returned from the Korean War in the fall of 1952*
Sept. 1953		New **Annapolis Jr. High** ($7^{th} - 9^{th}$ grades) opens on Chase St. next to Annapolis High building
1955-56		"Chesapeake" Hall to house band and shop rooms built behind high school
Sept. 1963		New **Annapolis Jr. High** opens on Forest Dr. Annapolis High becomes 3-building complex: main building (Maryland Hall), Science/shop/ band building (Chesapeake Hall) and former junior high building (Severn Hall).

June 1966	Bates High graduates its last class
Sept 1966	Annapolis High integrates completely; Former Bates building (renamed Annapolis Middle High School) houses 9th and half of city's 10th graders
April 1970 **Joeseph A. Mirenzi**	11th *principal*
Sept. 1973 **Richard G. Ensor**	12th *principal*
Jan. 1979	New **Annapolis High School** opens on Riva Road. Renovation of Severn Hall; reopens as **Bates Jr. High School** in 1980 (former Bates building on Smithville Rd. closes)
May 1984 **Kenneth W. Catlin**	13th *principal*
July 1986 **Kenneth Nichols**	14th *principal*
July 1990 **Laura Webb**	15th *principal*
July 1994 **Joyce Smith**	16th *principal*
July 2003 **Deborah Williams**	17th *principal*

APPENDIX G: Superintendents of Anne Arundel County Schools, 1865 - Present

1865-66	R.R.. Anspach, President of School Commissioners
1866-69	William H. Thompson, President of School Commissioners
1870-76	William H. Perveil, Examiner
1876-88	William Harwood, Examiner
1888-94	John C. Bannon, Examiner
1894-1905	Eugene Wathen, Examiner
1905-09	Henry R. Wallis, Examiner
1909-16	Samuel Garner, Examiner
1916-46	George Fox, Superintendent
1946-72	David S. Jenkins, Superintendent
1972-84	Edward J. Anderson
1984-88	Robert C. Rice
1988-92	Larry L. Lorton
1992-93	C. Berry Carter
1993-2002	Carol S. Parham
2002 -	Eric J. Smith

Citations

Chapter 1: The Tigers on Green Street, 1896-1900

1. R.C. Hammet, *St. Mary's County Maryland* (no publisher, 1977), 123.
2. Katherine Kibler, "Public Education," *Anne Arundel County Maryland, A Bicentennial History, 1649-1971* (Annapolis, Bicentennial Commission, 1973), 117.
3. *Ibid.* Jane Wilson McWilliams also generously shared information about the early history of Annapolis schools that she has gathered for her forthcoming book on the history of the city.
4. *Ibid.*, 119.
5. *Ibid.*, 117.
6. The various terms used in this manuscript in reference to African Americans reflect common usage during the period being discussed. Thus labels considered pejorative today – such as "colored" and "Negro" – are found frequently in the first six chapters (1896 – 1955), but are replaced by "black," "Afro-American" and "African American" in later chapters. I used as a guide the standard works about segregated education in Annapolis, Philip L. Brown, *A Century of 'Separate But Equal' Education in Anne Arundel County* (New York: Vantage Press, 1988) and Philip L. Brown, *The Stanton School* (Annapolis: Philip Brown, 2001). Quotation marks indicate direct citation.
7. *Evening Capital*, 7 September 1896.
8. Evangeline Kaiser White, *The Years Between; A Chronicle of Annapolis Maryland, 1800-1900* (New York: Exposition Press, 1957),106-110.
9. *Evening Capital*, 9 August 1896.
10. *Evening Capital*, 15 April 1897, 16 July 1897 and 26 July 1897.
11. *Evening Capital*, 7 September 1897 and 10 September 1897.
12. Information about the first commencement can be found in the *Evening Capital*, June 15, 1899. A photograph labeled "AHS's first graduating class" was published in Elihu Riley, *A History of Anne Arundel County* (Annapolis, G.T. Feldmeyer, 1905) is actually the second graduating class. Unfortunately this photo has been widely reproduced with the mistaken label attached.
13. The standard work that discusses the various rule changes in football in the first decades of the game is Allison Danzig, *The History of American Football* (Englewood Cliffs, N.J.: Prentice-Hall, 1956).
14. The quotation from the Princeton quarterback comes from Allison Danzig, *The History of American Football* (Englewood Cliffs, N.J.: Prentice-Hall, 1956), 219. The description of Michigan high school football can be found in John Armstrong, *The Way We Played the Game* (Napierville, IL.: Sourcebooks, Inc.), 104.
15. Allison Danzig, *Oh, How They Played the Game* (New York: MacMillan, n.d.), 149.
16. Mame and Marion Warren, *The Train's Done Been and Gone; An Annapolis Portrait, 1859-1910* (Annapolis, MD: Mame Warren, 1976), 47.
17. M. Howell Griswold, *Baltimore Polytechnic Institute; the first Century* (Baltimore, NPS, Inc., 1984), 92-3. By 1903 in Michigan anyone playing on a

team sanctioned by the state's Athletic committee had to be less than 22 years old and enrolled in school by October 1st. See John Armstrong, *The Way We Played the Game* (Napierville, IL), 286-87.
18. *Evening Capital*, May 26, 1900.
19. *Lucky Bag*, 1905.
20. *Evening Capital*, October 16, 1914, has a front-page story on the upcoming game between the Annapolis "colored" team and Howard University.
21. Information about the role managers played is found in John Armstrong, *The Way We Played the Game* (Napierville, ILL: Sourcebooks, Inc.).
22. *Evening Capital*, May 29, 1899.
23. Evangeline Kaiser White, *The Years Between; A Chronicle of Annapolis Maryland, 1800-1900* (New York: Exposition Press, 1957), 104-6.
24. *Evening Capital*, October 20, 1899.
25. *Evening Capital*, October 24, 1899.
26. *Evening Capital*, November 22, 1899.
27. *Evening Capital*, December 18, 1899.
28. Logan Cresap's life ended tragically on July 16, 1950, he and his wife were found dead in their Scarsdale, NY apartment from apparent suicide. The apartment's gas jets had been left on. Shortly before this Cresap had sent some old USNA papers to the alumni office, writing that he wished to be rid of "the volume of records I have saddled myself with over the years." His son, Logan Jr., graduated from USNA in 1936 and Harvard Law School in 1941.
29. The information on the subsequent lives of these players came from their obituaries, variously published in the *Evening Capital, Capital, Washington Post* and *New York Times*.

Chapter 2: Honoring their Home Town, 1900 - 1910

1. *Evening Capital*, 17 October 1900.
2. *Evening Capital*, 5 June 1901
3. *Evening Capital*, 8 August 1903.
4. *Evening Capital*, 15 November 1962, reported that the original school bell had been taken down following one of the school's fires and put in storage, where it was long forgotten when a school maintenance worker stumbled across it. Although it could not be remounted for use at the school, a wooden holder was constructed so that it could be put on display in the school's lobby.
5. *Evening Capital*, 14 June 1904.
6. *The Red and the Blue* (Vol. I, No 1), 2. Marjorie Layng Roxburgh ('55) generously shared complete copies of *The Red and Blue*, volumes 1 (1910-11) and 2 (1911-12) that she discovered among her uncle Russell Evans Smith's belongings. Smith had been in the Class of 1914, but left Annapolis High to prepare for entry with St. John's Class of 1918. The publication provides interesting detail about some school activities, but its format is more like a literary magazine with short stories and humorous anecdotes.
7. *Evening Capital*, 4 September 1905.
8. *Evening Capital*, 11 November 1905. Wallis remained in the examiner's post for five years before departing for the west.

9. *Burton Star Papers*, Maryland State Archives
10. *Board of School Supervisors Minutes*, June 12, 1906 and July 10, 1906.
11. *Evening Capital*, 10 September 1908; Jackson, p. 184.
12. Wallis returned to Annapolis in 1909 to marry Mary Feldmeyer, a 1901 Annapolis High graduate. They moved from Miles City to Boise, Idaho, where he became superintendent of schools. Robert McIntire, *Annapolis Maryland Families* (Baltimore: Gateway Press, 1980 and 1990), volume 2.- Wallis entry.
13. *Evening Capital*, 10 September 1908.
14. *Evening Capital*, 16 June 1910.
15. *Evening Capital*, 17 June 1910.
16. *Ibid.*, 10 July 1906.
17. *Ibid.*, 15 August 1906.
18. *Ibid.*, 15 October 1908.
19. *Ibid.*, 22 September 1908.
20. The Catholic Church supported St. Mary's parochial school for white children and St. Augustine's for "colored" children.
21. The early history of the Stanton School can be found in Joseph L. Browne, "An Earnest Interest in the Schools: The Struggle for Educational Opportunity in Anne Arundel County, 1869-1896." *Anne Arundel County History Notes*, Part I (Jan 1994); Part II (April 1994). For information about the meeting at which demands were made for a new school see *Evening Capital*, 11 May 1897. A school with almost the same layout as the Stanton School – eight rooms on two floors with attic and sloping basement - was built on N Street, NW in Washington, DC in 1890. This Wendell Phillips Colored School cost $26,156 to build. *Washington Post*, 6 April 2002, H1.
22. P. L. Brown, *The Stanton School* (Annapolis: Philip L. Brown, 2001), 3.
23. In 1905 the population of Annapolis was about 8,500. The education tax that year was 25 cents per $100 of income. See Elihu Riley, *History of Anne Arundel County* (Annapolis: Feldmeyer, 1905), 117-121.
24. *Ibid.*, 108.
25. P.L. Brown, *The Stanton School* (Annapolis: Philip L .Brown, 2001), 6-7.
26. *Evening Capital*, 10 September 1904. Few sports facilities were available to black athletes although the November 24, 1906 *Evening Capital* had a front page story about a "colored football team" (identified apparently erroneously as a "high school team") winning its "annual football game" against Howard University in Washington, DC. The lineup for Annapolis was: W. Addison (le), W. Brice (lt), L. Green (lg), Ducab (c), and C. Walker (rg), R. Steward (rt), E. Queen and V.G. Brice (re), W. Adams and J. Brown (qb), J. Brown and W. Pointer (lhb), Garber (fb), P. Tudell(rhb), J. Queen and V. Brown (substitutes).
27. *Evening Capital*, 1 October 1904.
28. Allison Danzig, *Oh, How They Played the Game* (NY: Macmillan) 149.
29. Allison Danzig, *History of American Football* (Englewood Cliffs, NJ: Prentice-Hall, 1956), 29.
30. *Ibid.*, 30-1
31. Mame Warren, *Then Again, Annapolis* (Annapolis: Time Exposures, 1990), 64.
32. *Evening Capital*, 5 November 1909.
33. *Evening Capital*, 7 October 1908.

34. *Evening Capital*, 12 October 1908.
35. *Evening Capital*, 5 November 1910.
36. *Evening Capital*, 10 November 1908. The only copy of the *Evening Capital* is on microfilm at Nimitz Library (U.S. Naval Academy). The 1908-09 gap is just one of many, all the result of a fire that destroyed the only original newspapers.
37. Childs, the next to last of 12 children born to a Conduit Street grocer, studied electrical engineering, stayed in Baltimore after graduating from Poly, married a teacher, fathered six children, and lived to age 95 before his death in 1988.
38. See discussion of eligibility for non-matriculated students in M.H. Griswold, *The Baltimore Polytechnic Institute: The First Century* (Baltimore: NPS, Inc., 1984), 92-3.This same agreement declared post-graduates ineligible, and also limited students to 4 seasons of participation. An age limit – under 21 years of age – was also set Other significant points of agreement were that all athletes had to be amateurs with good attendance and disciplinary records and enrolled in the school prior to October 12th.
39. *Evening Capital*, May 10, 1910.
40. *Evening Capital*, 21 October 1909.
41. *Evening Capital*, 29 October 1909.
42. *Evening Capital*, 6 November 1909.
43. *Evening Capital*, 9 November 1909.
44. *Evening Capital*, 16 May 1910 and 20 May 1910.
45. The achievements of the Annapolis High boys who went on to St. John's are documented in the college's yearbook, *Rat Tat*, from those years. The yearbooks are located in the special collection in the college library.

Chapter 3: Annapolis High's Warriors, 1910 – 1920

1. *Evening Capital*, 29 November 1916.
2. *Evening Capital*, 10 September 1910, 9 October 1912, 14 October 1913
3. Additional information about Annapolis High enrollment during this period can be found in Katherine Kibler, "Public Education," *Anne Arundel County Maryland, A Bicentennial History, 1649-1971* (Annapolis, Bicentennial Commission, 1973), 117-18 and Elmer Jackson, *Annapolis; Three Centuries of Glamour* (Annapolis: Capital- Gazette Press, 1937), 184. Student activities are reported in *Evening Capital*, 14 November 1911, December 4, 1911June 12, 1912, 29 November 1916, and 6 June 1917.
4. Armstrong, John, *How We Played the Game* (Napierville, IL: Sourcebooks, Inc., 2002) stresses that many high school team supporters were gamblers interested in betting on the games, a situation ripe for abuse. Fortunately this doesn't seem to have been the case in Annapolis.
5. *The Red and Blue* brims with stories about organizing class intramural teams for boys and girls. Particularly interesting is the obvious enthusiasm the girls had for playing basketball. The results of these games were often reported in the local newspaper. See *Evening Capital*, 20 November 1911, 9 October 1912 and 29 November 1916.
6. The names of the 73 boys who played football come from player rosters published in *The Evening Capital* and *The Red and Blue* as well as from team

photos with players' names identified. Probably several more may have played, but their identities and participation cannot be confirmed.
7. The game reports in *The Red and Blue* appear in December 1910 and November 1911. The 1910 story states that the loss to Werntz's Naval Prep was the first in three years, which reconfirms that the 1908 and 1909 teams were undefeated.
8. The quotation comes from John Armstrong, *How We Played the Game* (Napierville, IL: Sourcebooks, Inc., 2002), 10. The rule changes discussed are taken from Armstrong and Allison Danzig, *History of American Football* (Englewood Cliffs: Prentice-Hall, 1956), 29.
9. AHS game stories can be found in the *Evening Capital* on 10 November 1910, 28 October 1911, 1 November 1911, 21 November 1911, 15 December 1911, 5 October 1912, 9 October 1912, 2 November 1912, 9 November 1912, 23 November 1912, 29 November 1912, 11 October 1913, 30 October 1913, 1 November 1913, 29 October 1914.
10. *Evening Capital,* 14 October 1913 has both the West Point and Surgeon General reports.
11. Greg Downey, "Parks, Plans and Playgrounds: The Battle Over Baltimore's Leakin Park." Unpublished manuscript submitted to *Maryland Historical Magazine,* August 1999. The description of how field ball was played came from Anita Allio McIntire.
12. *Evening Capital,* 20 May 1916. Chapter Four will include additional information about PAL's annual Olympiads.
13. *Evening Capital,* 29 November 1916.
14. Information about Annapolis soldiers and sailors is from *Maryland in World War One; Military and Naval Service Records* (Baltimore: 20th Century, 1933).
15. *Dictionary of American Naval Fighting Ships* (1981), Vol. 7: 214. After dying in action on 23 May 1942 in the Philippines, the Navy commissioned the TISDALE (dE-278), an Evarts class destroyer, in his honor.
16. *Evening Capital,* 13 November 1918
17. *Evening Capital,* 31 May 1919
18. *Evening Capital,* 11 February 1919.
19. *Evening Capital,* 30 May 1919.
20. *Evening Capital* covered the return of Annapolis' warriors with front page stories beginning in February 1919, when rumor first circulated that the 29th would soon be shipping out of France, to 31 May 1919 when the parade was covered in detail.
21. See pages 51-52, for more information on Parlett.
22. News about the James and Revell Carr was reported on the *Evening Capital* on February 12, 1919 and February 22, 1919.
23. *Evening Capital,* 7 June 1917. Altogether 1403 county residents served in the Army and another 768 in the Navy. Forty percent in the Army (538) and 25 percent in the Navy (204) were African Americans. Besides the 351st Field Artillery, most of Maryland's African Americans were assigned to special "Colored" units: 372nd Infantry and 808th Pioneer Infantry. Information about these units and the overall experience of black troops in World War One can be found in Byron Farwell, *Over There* (New York: Norton, 1999), *148*-160. The

Annapolis men in Battery E were: Sgt. William Washington, Sgt. William Brice, Sgt. Charles McPherson, Corp. Hinton Coates, Corp. Frank Dorsey, Corp. Vanzy Hayes, Bugler Clarence Goghens, Cook Greenberry Thomas, Wagoner Arthur fisher, Blacksmith Moses Smith, Cook Ernest Zedricks, Pvt. Charles E. Stokes, Pvt. William Wright, Pvt. Augustus Darnell, Pvt. John Ayers and Pvt. Thomas Brown.

24. Gary Mead, *The Doughboys; America and the First World War* (New York: The Overlook Press, 2002), 69-70.
25. *Ibid.*, 71-2, cites the number of medical rejects as 182,325 (49.8%) of the 366,143 enlistees. Statistics back up Harbord's assessment; an average soldier's height was 5 feet 9 inches and weight was 142 pounds. See Byron Farwell, *Over There; The United States in the Great War, 1917-1918* (New York: Norton, 1999), 51, for a fuller description of the physical proportions of the soldiers. On page 450 Mead lists the other causes for rejection, including being too young, not being an American citizen, and illiteracy.
26. *Evening Capital*, 15 June 1916.

Chapter 4: Red Jackets in the Roaring Twenties, 1920 - 1929

1. 1922 *Crablines*, 5.
2. Among those who advertised in *Crablines* during the 1920's still around today are Annapolis Banking & Trust, Farmers National Bank, Annapolis Garden Theater, Capital-Gazette Press, Circle Playhouse, Coca Cola Bottling Company, McNasby Oyster Company, Johnson Lumber Company and Strayer Business College, etc.
3. Philip Brown, *The Stanton School* (Annapolis: Philip Brown, 2001), 12 and *A Century of Separate But Equal Education* (New York: Vantage Press, 1988), 21-24. Free bus transportation for African-American students did not begin until 1937, about a decade after it was provided for the county's white students.
4. Trench F. Tilghman, *Early History of St. John's College*, 172-175. Other major changes took place in 1923 after the retirement of Dr. Thomas Fell at the end of his 37-year tenure as the college's president. The curriculum was revamped and compulsory military training was abolished.
5. Severn School's history is discussed briefly on its web site, www.Severn.edu.
6. Katharine Kibler, "Public Education," *Anne Arundel County Maryland, A Bicentennial History, 1649-1971* (Annapolis, 1973), 118-119.
7. Banny Eppes mentioned the addition being built shortly before his freshman year of 1926-27. Since he went to Germantown School, he was not next-door in Annapolis Elementary when the addition was constructed and therefore cannot exactly place the date.
8. The displaced domestic science department was moved to the grammar school basement. See 1923 *Crablines*, 105 and 113 for discussion of the split-sessions.
9. Bernard P. Walters, longtime teacher, coach and athletic director at Arundel High, provided information about the school's early history, including a packet of unpublished materials. Especially useful is Kenneth Caitlin, *The History of Arundel High School* (unpublished manuscript, 2003). Also see *Evening Capital* 22 March 1910 and 2 February 1917; Katharine Kibler, *The First*

Hundred Years of Anne Arundel County School Superintendents (Annapolis, Board of Education, 1965), 118-119.
10. Katharine Kibler, *The First Hundred Years of Anne Arundel County School Superintendents* (Annapolis, Board of Education, 1965), 118-119; *Evening Capital,* 1 October 1926.
11. *Evening Capital,* 1 November 1928; *1928 Crablines,* 87.
12. Every *Crablines* from the 1920's has a small section devoted to the history of each class. Quotations are taken from these sections. Gessner's recollection about paddling comes from the *Evening Capital,* 13 May 1992. Anita Ailio McIntire also mentioned the paddles in interviews during December 2002.
13. Information about Linthicum's life and educational views come from *Evening Capital,* 14 June 1910, 14 June 1928 and 28 May 1931; *Crablines* from 1922, 1923, 1926, 1927 and 1928, and in an interview with Anitia McIntire. Philip Brown, *A Century of Separate But Equal Education in Anne Arundel County* (New York, Vantage Press, 1988) discusses how African American teachers commuted to New York City on weekends and during the summer to earn a graduate degree in teaching – they could not get a master's degree in Maryland because the only graduate program at University of Maryland was strictly segregated. Linthicum undoubtedly followed a similar course while earning her degrees at Hopkins and Columbia.
14. The commercial curriculum is first described in *The Evening Capital,* 8 September 1908.
15. The Class of 1926 commencement program comes from the personal papers of James Revell Moss (AHS, 1926); his sister Marjorie Moss Dowsett (AHS, 1929) and niece Ann Dowsett Jensen (AHS, 1958) gathered the papers and generously provided me with copies.
16. 1927 *Crablines,* 107.
17. Each addition of *Crablines* details that year's Literary Society activities.
18. Reports about the various orchestras come from the 1923, 1927 and 1928 *Crablines.*
19. See John Armstrong *How We Played the Game* (Napierville, IL: Sourcebooks, Inc., 2002) for a full description of the problems that resulted when local businessmen with ties to gambling had control of the local high school.
20. Descriptions of the Athletic Association activities can be found in 1922 *Crablines,* 73; Evening *Capital* 29 October 1921, 1 October 1924, 25 September 1925, 12 October 1926 and 13 October 1927.
21. This summary of AHS athletics in the 1920's comes from *Crablines* as well as numerous stories throughout the period in the *Evening Capital.*
22. The platoon system is described in Allison Danzig, *The History of American Football* (Englewood Cliffs, NJ: Prentice-Hall, 1956).
23. 1923 *Crablines,* 89.
24. Philip Brown, *A Century of Separate but Equal Education in Anne Arundel County (*New York: Vantage Press, 1988)*,* 24. Bowie Normal School was actually an outgrown of the Baltimore Normal School, which in 1908 had begun training teachers for the city's "colored" schools.
25. *Evening Capital,* 2 November 1925.
26. *Evening Capital,* 1 December 1925.

27. *Evening Capital*, 1 October 1926.
28. *Evening Capital*, 4 October 1926.
29. *Evening Capital*, 11 October 1926.
30. *Evening Capital*, 18 October 1926.
31. *Evening Capital*, 25 October 1926.
32. *Evening Capital*, 6 November 1926; 1927 *Crablines*, 129.
33. *Evening Capital*, 19 and 24 November 1926.
34. *Evening Capital*, 26 November 1926, Hagerstown *Morning Herald*, 26 November 1926.
35. *Evening Capital*, 3 December 1926 and 3 June 1927.
36. 1928 Crablines.
37. Mary Felter. "Daffy Russell, Legendary Lacrosse Coach, Dies at 91." *The Capital*, 31 August 2001.

Chapter 5: Depression and Wartime, 1929 - 1945

1. *Evening Capital*, 14 June 1928.
2. *Evening Capital*, 7 and 10 September 1928.
3. Kinhart's article is in the *Evening Capital*, 21 January 1932. Other aspects of curriculum were discussed in the *Evening Capital*, 7 September 1928.
4. *Evening Capital*, 29 June 1932.
5. Sheldon Shearer provided information about the CVL.
6. White discusses his plans for lacrosse in the *Evening Capital*, 2 June 1928. The report of the school's first lacrosse game comes from the *Evening Capital*, 23 May 1929. See the end of chapter four for more discussion of Daffy Russell's long career as a lacrosse and football coach.
7. The black list was so strict that even failing a 1/4 credit drawing or a 1/2 credit typing class made a player ineligible. This rule was relaxed in October 1931 when a faculty committee was appointed to supervise students having academic difficulty. See *Evening Capital*, 1 October 1931.
8. *Evening Capital*, 5 June 1929 mentions the Rotary baseball team on the sports page. In the summer of 1929 the team captured the city's American Legion title and went on to play in the state tournament at Hyattesville in July.
9. *Evening Capital*, 18 September 1929. A story about Bill White driving in a Labor Day race at Altoona, PA appeared 23 Aug 1929 in the *Evening Capital*. See the paper on 12 Oct 1953 for mention of White working for state.
10. *Evening Capital*, 26 February 1929.
11. The *Evening Capital* in November 1931, 1932 and 1934 has many stories about the Coca-Colas, who played against other semi-pro teams in the region. The *Evening Capital* stories about the 118-pound team's victories over Severn appeared 11 November 1931 and mid-November 1932.
12. *Evening Capital*, 15, 16, 29 and 31 January 1930.
13. The *Evening Capital* throughout January, February and March in the 1930's had good coverage of boys' and girls' basketball.
14. The fire was covered in the *Evening Capital* and the Baltimore *Sun* on 11-12 February 1930. Subsequent stories appeared almost daily for the next week.
15. *Evening Capital*, 15 February 1930.

16. *Evening Capital*, 20 June 1930.
17. *Evening Capital*, 16 February 1929.
18. *Evening* Capita, 25 April 1929.
19. *Manual of Information for the Visiting Committee of the Middle States Association of Colleges and Secondary Schools* (Annapolis: Annapolis Sr. High School, 1969), 18. For funding of Wiley H. Bates High see Philip Brown, *A Century of Separate But Equal Education in Anne Arundel County* (New York: Vantage Press, 1988),32-3.
20. The *Evening Capital* had front page stories about the possible locations of the new Annapolis High School virtually every day from 6 January 1931 – 23 March 1931.
21. *Evening Capital*, 6 January 1931.
22. *Specifications for the Annapolis High School* (Baltimore: Buckler & Fenhagen Architects, 1931).
23. *Evening Capital*, 21 January 1932.
24. *Evening Capital*, 7 September 1932.
25. *Evening Capital*, 14 September 1932.
26. *Evening Capital*, 15 September 1932.
27. This brief paragraph hardly does justice to the founding of Bates High School, but the interested reader should turn to Philip Brown, *A Century of Separate But Equal Education in Anne Arundel County* (New York: Vantage Press, 1988), 32-39.
28. *Evening Capital*, 11 September 1929.
29. *Evening Capital*, 25 April 1929. Elementary school graduates earned $1,400 per year; high school graduates earned $2,100 per year, and college graduates had annual salaries of $3,500.
30. *Evening Capital*, 16 June 1937 contains the employment statistics. The average number of male graduates per class comes from commencement stories that appeared each June in the local newspaper.
31. Information on the CSS/MSA can be found on its website, www.css-msa.org.
32. Teachers' salaries are discussed in length in Phillip Brown, *A Century of Separate But Equal Education in Anne Arundel County* (New York: Vantage Press, 1988), 69-85. See also *Evening Capital*, 18 June 1932.
33. *Evening Capital*, 17 June 1933.
34. The earliest Annapolis High School accreditation report is from 1969.
35. 1943 *Wake*, 37.
36. 1942 *Wake*, 2.
37. On May 1, 2003, 5 World War II and Korean War veterans who had left Annapolis High to enlist prior to graduation and never finished were given their diplomas in a small ceremony at the school. In 2000 the Maryland General Assembly passed a bill that allowed such World War II veterans to be honored with high school diplomas; in 2002 the bill was amended to include Korean veterans. *Capital,* 2 May 2003, 1.
38. Information about Annapolis High graduates and World War II came from *Maryland in World War II* (Baltimore: War Records Division of the Maryland Historical Society, 1958) and Robert McIntire, *Annapolis Maryland Families* (Baltimore: Gateway Press, 1980).

Chapter 6: Panther Pride Promotes School Spirit, 1945 – 1958

1. Population figures come from the United States Census records.
2. I am indebted to Jane McWilliams, who is writing a book on the history of Annapolis, for the bulk of the information about the city and Anne Arundel County in the post-World War Two era.
3. In the 1920's Anne Arundel was one of several counties in Maryland to reduce its school system to 11 grades. During World War II the Maryland board of education indicated that equalization funds would no longer be used to support 11-grade systems. Connie Neale, "School Chronology" (unpublished manuscript, 19 April 2002).
4. Information about the school bonds comes from Connie Neale, "School Chronology" (unpublished manuscript, 19 April 2002), 11. Neale quotes a board of education report entitled "The $7,000,000 Bond Issue and the Need for Additional Funds (1949), 12.
5. Marjorie Roxburgh and Jane McWilliams shared their recollections about junior high in the old Green Street school building.
6. Information about Fowble comes from his *Capital* obituary of 19 July 1996.
7. *Evening Capital*, 6 November 1951.
8. The biographies of Davis and Hicks are from the 1965 *Wake*. Presumably they retired in 1965 because they had reached mandatory retirement age of 65. they are also mentioned regularly in the 1916-1917 *Evening Capital* editions of the high school's newspaper, generally published the last week of each month.
9. The teacher shortage led the Anne Arundel County's board of education to hire 12 seniors from Salisbury State Teachers College in January 1943. An instructor accompanied the dozen to supervise them in their initial classroom experience. *Evening Capital*, 4 June 1943. None of these teachers, however, seem to have been assigned to Annapolis High School.
10. *The Sun*, 7 August 1947.
11. *Evening Capital*, 11 and 12 October 1953 and 14 October 1954. Unfortunately none of the letters are preserved among the school's memorabilia.
12. Katharine Cox and Norwood Wetherhold, *History of Annapolis Senior High School* (unpublished manuscript, revised 1974), 3-4.
13. *Evening Capital*, May 11 – June 15, 1946 has many stories about the founding of the AAA; see editorial on Sept 16, 1954, for summary of activities 1946-54.
14. *Tally-Ho*, 11 December 1946 and 30 January 1947.
15. Information on the founding of the MPSSAA is available on its website www.mpssaa.org/sports/records.html. Baltimore city's 16 public high schools continued in the Maryland Scholastic Association MSA) until 1992, when under mandate from the city school superintendent they joined the MPSSAA so they could participate in statewide championships in baseball, girls and boys basketball, girls and boys cross country, field hockey, football, golf, boys and girls lacrosse, boys and girls soccer, softball, tennis, boys and girls indoor track, boys and girls outdoor track, volleyball and wrestling (individual and dual). The remaining 25 private and parochial schools voted to disband the MSA, which was later reborn as the Maryland Independent Schools

16. *Evening Capital*, 27 October 1947.
17. *Evening Capital*, 7 December 1947; *The Tally-Ho*, 19 December 1947.
18. Information from the 1947-51 seasons comes from a series of phone interviews with Woody Wetherhold along with stories from *Tally-Ho* and *Wake* published during this period.
19. The 1950 loss to Annapolis was the only blemish on Dover High's otherwise perfect season. According to Jane McWilliams, the Annapolis Country Club was what today is the Annapolis Roads golf club. In the 1950's the country club was "quite the place" – with a large main building that offered lavish food service and had a ballroom for fancy dances (including the Annapolis High senior prom). The club also had a swimming pool and golf course. A fire in the 1960's destroyed the main building, and the entire club declined. Today all that remains is the 9-hole course and a small clubhouse.
20. Dover *Index,* October 1951.
21. *Evening Capital,* 14 – 18 September 1954.

Chapter 7: Same Neighborhood, Different Worlds, 1959 – 1970

1. Myra Bryan, a fifth-grader at the Stanton School, wrote "Moving An Eight Room School" for her school's contribution to the Anne Arundel Board of Education's 1953 School History Project She reports on her mother and grandmother's recollections of the abandoned Germantown School being moved in 1939 about 500 yards from West Street to the Bates site: "The building had to be carried across Smithville Street which has a bank on both sides of the street. My grandmother said it took three weeks to complete the job, which included the laying of the foundation, and moving the school. In moving the building it had to be sawed into three sections, jacked up high, then engineers built up under the building with huge pieces of timber. The pieces the building had to slide on were greased with heavy grease. The skids were built up so that they would extend several feet beyond the building. It was pulled by a truck. Before carrying it across the street, they had to build up what looked like a bridge in the street. It took a day to carry the building across the street."
2. Most Information about Bates in this chapter comes from interviews with Larry Brogden, Rhonda Pindell Charles and Butch Middleton. See also Philip Brown, *A Century of 'Separate But Equal' Education in Anne Arundel County* (New York: Vantage Press, 1988) and Connie Neale, "School Chronology for Annapolis," unpublished report dated 18 April 2002.
3. Philip Brown, *A Century of 'Separate But Equal' Education in Anne Arundel County* (New York: Vantage Press, 1988), 41. *Ibid.,* 41. The *Evening Capital*'s coverage of Bates' sports improved dramatically from the mid-1940's onward. By 1950 it appears all their game results were printed.
4. *Evening Capital,* 20 February 1952.
5. *Evening Capital,* 18 May 1956.
6. The fullest treatment of this period is Philip Brown, *A Century of 'Separate But Equal' Education in Anne Arundel County* (NY: Vantage Press, 1988), 99-157.
7. Useful in looking at the early period is Jay F. Wigley, "Guns, Laid and Ready: Resistance to Integration in Anne Arundel County, Maryland, 1954-1957,"

unpublished honors thesis, U.S. Naval Academy, 1989. Integration was more openly opposed in the southern half of the county, where the population was approximately 30 percent African American than in the north with its 93 percent white population. Petition committees and court cases challenging integration characterized the years 1955-1956, but Gov. T.R. McKeldin held staunchly to his insistence that Maryland "obey the law."

8. The preseason profile of the Panthers appeared in the *Evening Capital*, 14 September 1962.
9. *Evening Capital*, 24 September 1962.
10. *Evening Capital*, 29 September 1962.
11. Stories about the games against the other Anne Arundel county teams can be found in *Evening Capital*, 6, 13, 20 October 1962.
12. *Evening Capital*, 29 October 1962.
13. *Evening Capital*, 3 November 1962.
14. *Evening Capital*, 12 November 1962.
15. *Evening Capital*, 19 November 1962..
16. *Evening Capital*, 25 November 1962.
17. 1963 *Wake*, 100-104.
18. *Evening Capital*, 14 September 1962.
19. Stories about these seven games, as well as extended pre-game analysis, can be found in the *Evening Capital* from 14 September through 11 November 1962.
20. *Evening Capital*, 19 November 1962.
21. Joe Gross, "Pastrana Turns off the Light," *Capital*, 26 June 2002, D1.
22. Information about the career of Charles Kirby comes from Larry Brogden.
23. *Evening Capital*, 15 October 1962.
24. *The Capital*, 7 November 1999, discusses the Bates' bus trips.
25. Information on James Webb's life came from the *Capital*, 21 and 31 March 1996, as well as from the interview with Larry Brogden..
26. Philip Brown, *A Century of 'Separate But Equal' Education in Anne Arundel County* (New York: Vantage Press, 1988), 109.
27. *Ibid.*, pp. 104-9.
28. Connie Neale, "School Chronology," unpublished report, 18 April 2002, 12.
29. Philip Brown, *A Century of 'Separate But Equal' Education in Anne Arundel County* (New York: Vantage Press, 1988), 129-132.
30. *Ibid.*, 86-89. Since 1938 the Stanton School had been forced to utilize various building annexes to house all of its students, including 4 rooms in the Bates Annex (the former Germantown School that had been carted to Smithville Road in 1939). Adams Park allowed kindergarten through sixth grade to again be located in one school, but despite the fact that it was new and had the best of facilities, no white children "chose" to attend.
31. The opening of Severna Park High School in the late 1950's greatly reduced the potential student pool at Annapolis High. One reason Arundel may have led the way among county high schools in desegregating is that the junior high on the grounds of Ft. Meade was one of its feeder schools. In 1959 the post commander at Ft. Meade informed the county school board that it could not use a barracks that had been converted into classroom space "if colored students in the area are denied the right to attend." This led the board on April 1, 1959, to

issue an exclusion for the desegregation program in the Arundel High feeder area so that in the fall of 1959 – a year ahead of schedule – seventh and eighth grade pupils would be given the choice of schools. See Anne Arundel Board of Education Minutes, April 1, 1959, as mentioned in Connie Neale, "School Chronology for Annapolis," unpublished report dated 18 April 2002,

32. An early example of resistance in the south county occurred in August 1954 when parents from Owensville Elementary and Southern High presented the "West River Proclamation " to the school board. They argued for local autonomy within the county to decide what was best for their children, which in their case meant the continuation of a dual school system for whites and blacks. They objected to children being compelled to have "instructors not of their own race." See Philip Brown, *A Century of 'Separate But Equal' Education in Anne Arundel County* (New York: Vantage Press, 1988), 106-7.

33. The Board of Education minutes 1955-1965 contain details about finances. Over $32 million dollars was spent from 1956 through 1967 on new schools. Connie Neale, "School Chronology," unpublished report, 18 April 2002, 14-32.

34. For discussion about Annapolis Jr. High see Anne Arundel Board of Education minutes for 1961 and 1962, specifically 6 Sept 1961, 6 December 1961, 7 March 1962, 21 March 1962 and 5 Sept 1962. All are listed in Connie Neale, "School Chronology for Annapolis," unpublished report dated 18 April 2002, 23-24. In 1964 Annapolis High students named the three buildings Maryland Hall, Chesapeake Hall (science and band building) and Severn Hall (jr. high).

35. Anne Arundel County Board of Education minutes, 6 September 1964.

36. The HEW report is part of the Anne Arundel County Board of Education Desegregation Files, as noted in Connie Neale, "School Chronology for Annapolis," unpublished report dated 18 April 2002, 32.

37. Philip Brown, *A Century of 'Separate But Equal' Education in Anne Arundel County* (New York: Vantage Press, 1988), 135. A June 1966 brochure was prepared for distribution to anyone associated with the various schools now in the Annapolis Junior/Senior High complex. Connie Neale, "School Chronology," unpublished report dated 18 April 2002,

38. Philip Brown, *A Century of 'Separate But Equal' Education in Anne Arundel County* (New York: Vantage Press, 1988), 136-37. Fortunately two years later the name "Wiley H. Bates" was reattached to the site where it originated, and in 1981 when the building was closed the name was transferred to the newly-refurbished junior high/middle school on Chase Avenue (the 1953 school originally constructed as the first Annapolis Junior High).

39. *Ibid.*, 138.

40. *Ibid.*, 64, 137-38.

41. A number of *Evening Capital* stories in the early 1970's refer to the PTA's disappearance without explanation. The school's chapter may have been caught up in a larger struggle in the county, where there had been separate white and "colored" PTA's. Perhaps the adults – black and white – at Annapolis High were unable to overcome their own bigotry and distrust of each other.

42. *Manual of Information for the Visiting Committee of the Middle States Association of Colleges and Secondary Schools* (Annapolis, MD: Annapolis High School, 1969), 22.

43. *Evening Capital*, 12 February 1970 through 28 February 1970 had daily front-page stories about the situation at Annapolis High. The information about the disturbance and its aftermath comes from these stories.
44. *Evening Capital*, 9 April 1970. Fowble was reassigned to the central office as supervisor of testing.

Chapter 8: Big Al and the Boys, 1970 – 1989

1. The names of those killed in Vietnam from Annapolis and Edgewater can be found at the National Archives website, www.archives.gov. The four names listed are the only ones that matched exactly with names in Annapolis High School yearbooks.
2. The quotations in this paragraph come from Middle States Association of Colleges and Schools Commission on Secondary Schools, *The Report of the Visiting Committee to Annapolis Senior High School*, March 26-27, 1980.
3. *Evening Capital*, 28 October 1968. Butch Middleton was one of the witnesses interviewed. He recalls how fortunate it was that a policeman saw him running to help stop the assault because the barely conscious victim initially identified Middleton as the person who had assaulted him.
4. *Evening Capital*, 30 and 31 October 1968 contains the quotations from Moyer used in this chapter..
5. *The Capital*, 15 May 1984. Stories about the accident and Ensor's death appeared in *The Capital*, 29 April 13 May and 14 May 1984.
6. Annapolis Senior High, *Further Report on Progress, 1986-1987*, pp 3-4. Information about Catlin comes from *Wake* yearbooks of the 1980's and interviews with Anthony Anzalone and Fred Stauffer.
7. These Belichick quotations came from Ron Borges, "What Makes Belichick Tick?" *Boston Globe Magazine*, 10 September 2000.
8. *Evening Capital*, 20 October 1916.
9. *Evening Capital*, 28 December 1916.
10. The girls' interscholastic teams, 1920 – 1955 are discussed in chapters four (pages 91-2), five (pages 115-16) and six (pages 143-144). See also *The Capital*, 11 January 1989, p. 1.
11. *Evening Capital*, 6 September 1966, reports on the enrollment increase.
12. *Evening Capital*, 17 September 1965, discusses the dedication of this new stadium. The 1966 *Wake* has a lengthy description of the process involved to build the new Panther stadium. Al Laramore organized an adult Booster Club in the fall of 1964, a year prior to his promotion to head football coach and athletic director. According to Fred Stauffer, a math teacher at the school, Laramore was energetic in pressing for a facility larger than Weems-Whelan for night football games. The organization of a local professional football team, the Sailors, seemed auspicious. They, too, wanted a stadium facility. The Booster Club raised about $5,000 by the spring of 1965. According to the *Wake*, "Parents ran concession stands at the football and basketball games; they printed football and basketball yearbooks; and they made an arrangement to receive a percentage of the profit from the sale of tickets to Sailors' football games. The student Booster Club also contributed to the stadium fund by selling candy, pennants and stickers and by maintaining that glorious A.H.S.

tradition – Penny Day." Over the summer, parents and students under the leadership of John Hammond laid the sod and watered it. Although $40,000 was eventually raised, the school was left with over a $30,000 debt when the Sailors folded.
13. 1967 *Wake,* p. 147. The debt for the field was finally paid off by the school board in the 1970's after Al Laramore had given up the athletic director's position as a result of a 1972 county policy that for the first time paid teachers a stipend for no more than two specified activities. At the time Laramore held three positions that warranted stipends, so he was required to give one up. He chose to remain head football and basketball coach, but turned over the athletic director's job to Fred Stauffer, who held the job 28.
14. Department of Education, "Title IX: 25 Years of Progress," U.S. Department of Education report, Jun 1997.
15. *Evening Capital,* 16 November 1978.
16. *Evening Capital,* 25 November 1978.
17. *Evening Capital,* 20 November 1978.
18. *Evening Capital,* 27 November 1978
19. *Evening Capital,* 25 November 1978 has Simendinger's assessment. Laramore's quotation is in the paper two days later.
20. *Capital,* 17 November 1984 and 28 January 1992.
21. *Evening Capital,* 20 November 1978
22. *Evening Capital,* 11 January 1989, p. 1.
23. Bob Mosier, "A Winning, Caring Coach," *The Capital,* 11 January 1989, C1.
24. Borland's recollections of Laramore come from *The Capital,* 23 October 1992.
25. Bob Grening, "Heart Attack Claims Life of AHS Coach, " *The Capital,* 11 January 1989, A1.
26. *The Capital,* 3 March 1991, reports on the controversy about how best to memorialize Laramore at the school. The school's PTSO and Booster Club had spurred the decision to name the stadium in honor of former principal Ensor. They feared adding Laramore to the facility would diminish the honor they had given to Ensor. They eventually agreed to Ensor's name going on the outer entrance wall to the stadium and Laramore's name on the scoreboard. Identical plaques for both men were mounted under the press box inside the stadium, as reported in *The Capital* on 5 September 1991.
27. Belichick discussed his experience at Annapolis High on numerous other public occasions, including at the local Touchdown Club's annual football banquet, as reported in *The Capital,* 6 February 1991and in a speech at Annapolis High in *The Capital,* 25 February 1993. The Patriots' official website, www.patriots.org refers to the Belichick's scholarship at Annapolis High.
28. Nick Good-Malloy, *Journal from 2001 Football Season.* Good-Malloy papers (Annapolis, MD).
29. Phebus' recollections are found in *The Capital,* 7 October 1992 in a story about Laramore's posthumous induction into the county's Athletic Hall of Fame.
30. Brown is quoted in David Grening and Bob Mosier, "Annapolis Loses Coach, Friend," *The Capital,* 11 January 1989, C1.

Chapter 9: Into the 21st Century, 1989 – 2001

1. Information on Mirenzi's work on middle schools can be found in the *Evening Capital*, 6 March 1970. Twenty years later the concept was still being debated, for example in the *Anne Arundel County Sun*, 15 May 1990, pp. 8-9.
2. The down side of the change to middle schools meant the discontinuation of junior high interscholastic teams, which in the long run has hurt younger athletes in several ways. Athletic coaching and competition for pre-high school athletes was left to local recreation leagues. Children whose families didn't have resources to pay for participation and were without transportation were out of luck. Without the athletic teams it was also more difficult to develop spirit and pride in middle schools.
3. *Anne Arundel County Sun*, 15 May 1990, p. 4.
4. *Report of the Visiting Committee to Annapolis Senior High School* (Annapolis, Commission on Secondary Schools of the Middle States Association of Colleges and Secondary Schools, November 1989), pp. 7-10.
5. Nichols is quoted in Dianne Williams Hayes, "Discipline at School Criticized," *Anne Arundel County Sun*, 15 May 1990.
6. *The Capital*, 13 May 1994, includes biographical information on Webb in a tribute to her written when she retired.
7. Smith's quotes in this paragraph come from *The Capital*, 13 May 1994.
8. Annapolis High School, *Progress Report to Middle States*, 1991.
9. *The Capital*, 1 June 1991.
10. *The Capital*, 13 September 1993.
11. *The Capital*, 27 August 1993.
12. *The Capital*, 22 May 1992.
13. *The Capital*, 10 and 11 March 1993.
14. *The Capital*, 31 March and 1 April 1993.
15. *The Capital*, 24 September 1995 and 17 September 1997.
16. Stories about the Wall of Fame can be found in *The Capital*, 18 March 1996, 5 April 1996, 4 April 1997, 20 March 1998, 10 October 1998 and 29 October 1998. One of Smith's inspirational ideas was to include graduates from Bates High School on the Wall, a move that has contributed to creating a sense of the shared history of Bates and Annapolis High.
17. Information from the 1999-2000 accreditation is contained in the various reports listed in the bibliography.
18. *The Capital* featured the centennial homecoming weekend in stories on 29 August, 10, 29 and 30 October 1998.
19. Among the Division I boys' basketball players John Brady coached are: Brian Barber (Towson), Lenny Barber (UMBC), Keith Colbert (Virginia Tech), Ted Cottrell (Massachusetts), Boo Diggs (Florida A&T), Steve Foley (Loyola), Dwight Forrester (Temple), Terry Jackson (Howard), Marcus Johnson (College of Charleston), Marcus Neal (Nebraska), Londell Owens (Kent State), Dan Rowland (James Madison), Rob Wooster (St. Francis). C'vette Henson, a 2003 Annapolis High graduate, became Brady's first female basketball player to go to a Division I school when she signed to play for the University of Maryland. Information on John Brady's long career is summarized in stories that appeared

20. MPSSAA only began a statewide lacrosse tournament in 1990, so they do not list the championships Annapolis won in the 1980's when playoffs involved only teams in the eastern part of the state.
21. For discussion of Brown's career see the front page of the sports section in *The Capital*, 27 November 1997 and 23 July 2003.
22. *The Capital 1989 Football Guide*, 6 September 1989, p. 2.
23. According to Sheldon Shearer, prior to the first state championship football games in 1974, schools were organized in 9 districts corresponding to the political alignment for administrative and legislative purposes. Anne Arundel County was part of District V. MPSSAA held several district championships to test the weighted point system that determined 4 champions (one per school classification) in each district, then staged games between the AA and A champs, and between the B and C champs for district titles. "AA" Annapolis played "A" Arundel for the District V football crown in 1973.
24. Shearer explains that until the early 1990's the four regions were designated I, II, III and IV, but beginning in the early 1990's, this was changed to North, South, East and West, probably because the Maryland Scholastic Association broke up in 1994 so 15 Baltimore area public high schools joined the MPSSAA playoffs for the first time. The geographic designators made some sense originally. For example, in the 4A classification the Baltimore area was designated North, Montgomery County was West, P.G. County was South and Anne Arundel County was East. These designations have blurred since then as school enrollments have shifted.
25. See Appendix D for a listing of county football champions, 1963-2002.
26. Broadneck's classification down from 4A to 3A caused some controversy. Severn River Junior High ninth graders were allowed to play on the Broadneck teams but it is unclear whether they were counted in the school's enrollment.
27. *The Capital 1989 Football Preview*, 6 September 1989, p. 2.
28. *Ibid.*, p. 6.
29. *Ibid.*, p. 2.
30. North County's 1996 season ended in embarrassment when they had to forfeit all nine of their victories after it was discovered for using an ineligible player.
31. *The Capital*, 27 November 1997.
32. From 1993 through 1998, Broadneck took the somewhat unusual position of playing three weaker out-of-county teams rather than traditional opponents Annapolis, Chesapeake, Meade and Severna Park. In 1997 a new wing was completed that allowed the ninth graders to enroll and made Broadneck one of the largest schools in the county, but because of the timing of MPSSAA reclassification they did not rejoin 4A – and resume playing all the 4A schools in the county – until 1999.
33. Bill Wagner, "Rush to Success," *The Capital*, 2 November 2000.
34. The last regular season game the Panthers lost was the season finale in 1997 to Severna Park that ended the team's nine-game winning streak. The 2000 seniors were only freshman on the junior varsity when that game was played.
35. Annapolis and Broadneck shared 9-1 records at the top of the county league. Their season-ending contest was billed as the county championship game. In victory, Annapolis was called the county champions until Old Mill, with only

an 8-1 record against county schools, was found to be champion based on MPSSAA points. Because of the controversy, the athletic directors agreed the next year to base the championship on winning percentage in county games, with co-champions declared in case of ties (regardless of head-to-head results).

Epilogue: Changes and Challenges, 2001-2003

1. *The Capital*, 5 June 2001.
2. *The Capital*, 20 November 2001.
3. *The Capital*, 23 December 2001.
4. *The Capital*, 6 April 2002.
5. *The Capital*, 25 April 2002.
6. *The Capital*, 31 October 2002, 4, 5, 13 and 19 December 2002, Several court cases were threatened against the schedule,. Particularly upset were middle school parents who thought that electives like music and art might suffer, but eventually even the state school board backed the plan. See *The Capital*, 24 July 2003.
7. *The Capital*, 7 September 2002, 2 and 30 January 2003, 30, 6 February 2003.
8. *The Capital*, 19 June 2003.
9. *The Capital*, 23 July 2003, page C1; *The Sun*, 23 July 2003, 5C and *The Washington Post*, 25 June 2003.
10. *The Capital*, 14 August 2003.
11. *The Capital*, 17 August 2003.

BIBLIOGRAPHY

A. Archival Materials

ANNAPOLIS HIGH SCHOOL (unsorted photos and papers), 1899-2003, Annapolis High School Media Center Archive, Annapolis, MD.
ANNE ARUNDEL COUNTY BOARD OF EDUCATION (Annual Reports), 1916-1975, MSA T3202, Maryland State Archives.
ANNE ARUNDEL COUNTY BOARD OF EDUCATION (Desegregation File), 1954-1967, MSA T2407, Maryland State Archives.
ANNE ARUNDEL COUNTY BOARD OF EDUCATION (Minutes), 1916-1955, MSA T2622, Maryland State Archives, Annapolis MD.
ANNE ARUNDEL COUNTY BOARD OF EDUCATION (School histories), 1952-53, MSA T3204, Maryland State Archives, Annapolis MD.
ANNE ARUNDEL COUNTY BOARD OF SCHOOL SUPERVISORS (Minutes), 1888-1916, MSA T3203, Maryland State Archives.
BANNEKER-DOUGLASS MUSEUM (exhibit), "Nothing But Pure Love for the Teachers; African-American Schools during a Century of Segregation in Anne Arundel County, Annapolis MD.
GRAY, EDWARD E. PAPERS, including 1993 letters and photo of 1929 football team, Annapolis High School Archive.
MARYLAND HIGH SCHOOL YEARBOOK COLLECTION, Enoch Pratt Library, Baltimore, MD
STARR, BURTON PAPERS, Maryland State Archives, Annapolis MD. Diary and memorabilia from Burton Starr, AHS 1906.
STATE OF MARYLAND, DEPARTMENT OF EDUCATION (Annual Reports), Maryland State Archives, Annapolis MD.
UNITED STATES CENSUS RECORDS (Anne Arundel County, MD), 1900-2000, Maryland State Archives, Annapolis MD.

B. Interviews

Anzalone, Anthony (AHS guidance counselor)
Booth, Barry (AHS, '79)
Brady, John (current AHS boys' and girls' basketball coach)
Brogden, Larry (Bates, '62 and former AHS coach and teacher)
Brown, Roy (AHS football coach, 1989-2002)
Campbell, Bill (AHS, '58, father Ralph in '26)
Charles, Rhonda Pindell (AHS, '72, mother of Marvin '00 and Rishelle '02)
Collins, Pamela Knox (historian, Salisbury University)
Crosby, Al (AHS, '54)
Cross, Huntley (former AHS teacher and coach, 1965-72)
Davis, Edward Smith (AHS, '32)
Davis, Fred and Kathy (parents of Cynthia '82 and Liz '84)
Daywalt, Irma Dunbar (AHS, '31)
Downes, Vachel Jr. (grandson, A.Z. Holley, AHS '10)
Dowsett, Marjorie Moss (AHS, '29)
Dunn, Ken (AHS assistant football coach, 1990-2002)

Eppes, James Bancroft "Banny" (AHS, '30)
Eppes, Elizabeth Fuller (AHS, '36)
Finkle, Leslie (AHS, '75)
Fuller, Betty Brown (Bates, '53)
Gardener, James "Buck" (AHS, '63)
Gehrdes, Dave (current AHS athletic director and girls' lacrosse coach)
Good-Malloy, Nick (AHS, '01)
Hall, Howard (retired Asst. Supt of Anne Arundel County Public Schools)
Hanna, Della (AHS math teacher)
Henson, Camaro (AHS, '01)
Hersman, Sue (AHS English teacher)
Hopkins, Al (AHS, '43; retired sports editor of *Capital*, mayor of Annapolis)
Hopkins, Libby (AHS, '58, President AHS Alumni Association)
Jensen, Ann Dowsett (AHS, '58)
Malloy, Alex (AHS, '97)
Mason, Carol (mother of Cary '97, Joe '00 and Chet '02 Feldmann)
Matthews Keith (AHS, '75)
McIntire, Anita Allio (AHS, '32)
McWilliams, Jane Longfellow Wilson (AHS, '56)
Melton, Mike (AHS, '01)
Middleton, Butch (AHS, '70)
Phebus, Bill (AHS assistant football coach, 1980-2002)
Purdy, Dick (AHS, '58)
Purdy, Doris Jarosik (AHS, '31)
Reed, Jack (AHS, '69)
Reimer, Susan (mother of Joe '01 and Jessie '04)
Roxburgh, Marjorie Layng (AHS, '55)
Sachs, Helene Snyder (AHS, '58)
Shearer, Sheldon (Editor, *Maryland/Virginia Varsity Football*)
Smith, Joyce (AHS Principal, 1994-2003)
Stauffer, Fred (retired AHS athletic director, coach and math teacher)
Strickland, Barbara (archivist, Baltimore Polytechnic Institute)
Taylor, Blanch (AHS, '38)
Walters, Bernard J., Jr. (Arundel High teacher, athletic director and coach)
Wilson, Marty (archivist, Baltimore City College High School)
Wooster, Rob (AHS, '92)
Zartman, Eugene (Dover High School, '52)

C. Newspapers and Periodicals

Anne Arundel County Sun, 1989.
Crablines, Annapolis High School Yearbooks, 1922-28.
The Evening Capital and *The Capital* (Annapolis, MD), 1865-2003.
The Evening Sun and *the Sun* (Baltimore, MD), 1900-2003.
Green Bag. City College High School (Baltimore) Yearbooks, 1908-20.
The Index (Dover, DE), 1950-53.
Lucky Bag. United States Naval Academy Yearbooks, 1900-1910.
Herald (Hagerstown, MD), 1925-29.
Rat-Tat. St. John's University Yearbooks, 1900-1950.

Bibliography 301

Tally-Ho. Annapolis High School newspaper, 1946-48.
The Red and the Blue. Annapolis High School newspaper, 1910-11.
Wake. Annapolis High School Yearbooks, 1942-2003.
Washington Post (Washington, DC), 1900-present.

D. Private Collections

Good-Malloy papers. Annapolis, MD. Clippings, scrapbooks, photographs and other memorabilia from Alex Malloy ('97) and Nick Good-Malloy ('01).
Holley papers. Centerville, MD. Photos and service records of A.Z. Holley ('10) in the possession of his grandson Vachel Downes, Jr.
Moss papers. Annapolis, MD. Photos, memorabilia and clippings belonging to Revel Moss ('26) in possession of his sister Marjorie Moss Dowsett ('29) and Ann Dowsett Jensen ('58)
Smith papers. Cambridge, MD. Yearbooks, manuscripts and school newspapers belonging to Russell Smith (attended AHS for several years before entering St. John's College (graduated 1918) and Marjorie Evans Smith ('22). Collection in possession of Marjorie Layng Roxburgh ('55)

E. Reports and Memoirs

Annapolis Senior High School. *Reports to Middle States Association, Commission on Secondary Schools* (1969, 1984, 1986-7, 1991, 1996, 2002).
Anne Arundel County Board of Education. *Desegregation of Public Schools in Anne Arundel County: Ten Years of Progress* (15 September 1965).
Joint Civil rights and Citizens' Committee on Education. *Discrimination in Public Schools in Anne Arundel County* (15 January 1966).
Flexner, Abraham and Frank P. Bachman. *Public Education in Maryland: A Report to the Maryland Educational Survey Commission.* New York, 1916.
Maryland in World War One: Military and Naval Service Records (Baltimore: Twentieth Century Press, 1933).
Middle States Association of Colleges and Secondary Schools, *Reports of Visiting Committees to Annapolis Senior High School* (1980, 1989 1999)
Specifications for Annapolis High School. Baltimore: Buckler & Fenhagen, 1931.

White, Evangeline Kaiser and Clarence Marbury White, Sr. *The Years Between; A Chronicle of Annapolis, Maryland, 1800-1900.* New York: Exposition Press, 1957.

F. Secondary Works

Armstrong, John. *How We Played the Game.* Napierville, IL: Sourcebooks, Inc., 2002.
Brown, P. L. *A Century of 'Separate But Equal' Education in Anne Arundel County.* New York: Vantage Press, 1988.
_____. *The Stanton School.* Annapolis, MD: Philip L. Brown, 2001.

Browne, Joseph L. "An Earnest Interest in the Schools: The Struggle for Educational Opportunity in Anne Arundel County, 1869-1896." *Anne Arundel County History Notes.* Part I (Jan 1994); Part II (April 1994).
Browne, Margaret and Patricia Vanorny. "Foundations of a Modern Educational System." *The Archivist's Bulldog* XII (11 May 1998).

Browne, Margaret. *Piety, Chastity and Love of Country: Education in Maryland to 1916.* Annapolis, MD: Maryland State Archives, n.d.

Brugger, Robert J. *Maryland: A Middle Temperament, 1634-1980.* Baltimore: Johns Hopkins University Press, 1988.

Cox, Katherine and Norwood S. Wetherhold. "History of Annapolis Senior High School." Unpublished typescript in Maryland Law Library, Drawer GRD#54, 1974.

Dictionary of American Fighting Ships (1981).

Danzig, Allison. *the History of American Football.* Englewood, NJ: Prentice-Hall, 1956.

_____. *Oh, How They Played the Game.* New York: MacMillan, n.d.

Downey, Greg. "Parks, Plans and Playgrounds: The Battle Over Baltimore's Leakin Park. Unpublished manuscript submitted to *Maryland Historical Magazine,* August 1999.

Eisenhower, John. *Yanks: The Epic Story of the American Army in World War I.* New York: The Free Press, 2001.

Farwell, Byron. *Over There; The United States in the Great War, 1917-18.* New York: Norton, 1999..

Flexner, Abraham and Frank Bachman. *Public Education in Maryland.* New York: General Education Board, 1916.

Griswold, M. Howell. *Baltimore Polytechnic Institute: the First Century.* Baltimore: NPS, Inc., 1984.

Hammet, R.C. *St. Mary's County Maryland.* No Publisher, 1988.

Jackson, Elmer M. *Annapolis: three Centuries of Glamour.* Annapolis: Capital-Gazette Press, 1937.

Jenkins, David S. *A History of Colored Education in Anne Arundel County.* M.A. Thesis, University of Maryland, 1942.

Kibler, Katherine. *The First 100 Years of Anne Arundel County School Superintendents.* Annapolis: Board of Education, 1965.

_____. "Public Education." *Anne Arundel county Maryland, A Bicentennial History 1649-1971.* J. Bradford (ed). Annapolis: Bicentennial Committee, 1973.

Leonhart, James. *One Hundred Years of the Baltimore City College High.* Baltimore: Roebuck and Sons, 1939.

Marudas, Kyriakos P. *the City-Poly Game: Baltimore's Oldest Football Rivalry.* Baltimore: Gateway Press, 1988.

McIntire, Robert H. *Annapolis Maryland Families.* 2 volumes. Baltimore: Gateway Press, 1980 and 1990.

Mead, Gary. *the Doughboys: America and the First World War.* New York: Overlook Press, 2002.

Melville, Pat. "Grand Jury Inspections of County Government." *The Archivist's Bulldog* XII (n. 17: 28 September 1998).

Neale, Connie. "School Chronology for Annapolis." Unpublished report dated 18 April 2002.

Nasaw, David. *Schooled to Order; A Social History of Public Schooling in the U.S.* New York: Oxford University Press, 1976.

Nolley, Ralph F. *Boys of Annapolis and Anne Arundel County Fighting for Uncle Sam.* Baltimore: R.F. Nolley, 1918.

Riley, Elihu. *History of Anne Arundel County*. Annapolis: Feldmeyer, 1905.

Tilghman, Tench F. *The Early History of St. John's College in Annapolis*. Annapolis: St. John's College Press, 1984.

"School Records for Anne Arundel County, 1865-1916." *the Archivist's Bulldog* XIV (No 5: March 2000).

Warren, Mame and Marion. *The Train's Done Been and Gone; An Annapolis Portrait, 1859-1910*. Annapolis: M.E. Warren, 1976.

Warren, Mame. *Then Again, Annapolis 1900-1905*. Annapolis: Time Exposures, 1990.

Watterson, John. *College Football; History, Spectacle, Controversy*. Baltimore: Johns Hopkins University Press, 2000.

Wigley, Jay F. "Guns, Laid and Ready: Resistance to Integration in Anne Arundel County, Maryland, 1954-57." Unpublished honors thesis, U.S. Naval Academy, 1989.

Worden, Amy. *Education in Anne Arundel County, 1671-1937*. Crownsville, MD: Maryland Historic Trust, n.d.

PHOTO CREDITS

Annapolis High Photograph Collection: 1, 8, 30, 112, 122, 124, 142, 186 and 198

Annapolis High *Crablines:* 58, 71, 80, 86, 94, 100, 104, and 112

Annapolis High *Wake:* 131, 136, 152, 155, 174, 181, 186, 194, 198, 204, 208, 218, 226 and 233

Bates High 1962 *Beacon:* 160 and 174

Campbell, Bill: 86

Capital and *Evening Capital* microfilm collection: 30 and 252

Good, Jane E.: 8, 64, 240, 242, 247, 262 and 254

Good-Malloy, Nick: 213, 226 and 233

Grey, Edward: 105

Holley, A.Z. (Sandy and Cathy Downes): 23, 53, 58, and 64

Jensen, Ann Dowsett: 86

Malloy, Alex: 252

Nolly, Ralph: 64

Riley, Elihu: 30

Zartman, Eugene: 150

Index

Accreditation – See Middle States
Annapolis Athletic Association (AAA) – 41-2, 146-8, 153
Annapolis High School
   Athletic Association (AHSAA) – 21, 36, 40, 45, 57, 89, 102, 109, 115
   Baseball teams – 21, 61, 90, 91, 92, 115,116, 145, 207
   Basketball teams (boys) – 62, 115, 116, 145, 173, 193, 207
   Basketball teams (girls) – 90, 91, 115-17, 145, 173, 197-201
   Blue Ribbon School – 222
   Booster Club – 241, 243, 294, 295
   Buildings
      Green St. – 30, 34-6, 75, 107, 121, 135, 172
      Constitution Ave – 119-25, 187-91
      Riva Rd. – 186-92,
      Stockett House – 4, 7, 9, 10, 35
   "Celebrate Annapolis" – 232
   Committed Black Females – 220
   Concerned Black Males – 220
   Cross-country teams – 174, 200,
   Curriculum – 35-7, 45, 55-7, 73, 81-2, 108-9, 139-41, 158-59, 185-87
   ESOL – 251
   Field hockey teams – 173, 199, 200
   Fieldball teams – 61, 90-2, 115-17
   Fires – 77, 107, 117-19
   Football – see separate Football heading
   Football players – see under football heading
   Four-period-per-day schedule – 250
   Freshman Day – 220
   Green School – 222
   Hangouts
      Droll's – 76, 78, 87
      Dutch Mill – 157
      Chris' Pool Room – 145
      Jim's Corner – 145
   Homecoming – 168
   International Baccalaureate – 250-1
   Founding – 5-10
   Lacrosse team (boys) – 104, 154, 166, 188, 207, 227
   Lacrosse team (girls) – 200, 201
   Maryland's Tomorrow – 216, 230
   Musical activities – 55-7, 125, 129, 143, 159, 190, 225
   National Honor Society – 143
   National School Lunch Program – 144
   Navy JROTC – 219
   Newspapers
      Annapolitan – 26-7
      Red and Blue – 56, 197, 282, 284
      Tally Ho – 125, 143
   PRIDE organization – 192
   Principals – listed in order of service
      Smith, William E. (1896-1900) – 6, 8, 10, 15, 18, 19, 21, 26, 29, 33

Annapolis High School (cont'd)
   Principals (cont'd)
      Dryden, Charles (1900-1902) – 26-7, 29, 44
      Twilley, Irving L. (1902-1903) – 27-9
      Wallis, Henry R. (1903-1905) – 28-9, 31-3
      Crouse, William S. (1905-1906) – 29-31
      English, Andrew J. (1906-1908) – 30-33
      Pfeifer, George B. (1908-1910) – 30, 33, 43
      Linthicum, Louise W. (1910-1928) –10, 28, 34, 56-8, 70, 77-81, 89, 95, 113, 119
      Kinhart, Howard A. (1928-1949) – 79, 107-10, 112, 115, 117, 119, 121, 123, 125-30, 135-7, 139, 146-8
      Fowble, Albert W. (1949-1970) – 136-9, 178-9, 183
      Herklotz, Ernest H. (1950-1952) – 136-9, 148
      Mirenzi, Joseph A. (1970-1973) – 180, 183, 186, 193, 215
      Ensor, Richard G. (1973-1984) – 184, 186, 188, 193, 212
      Catlin, Kenneth W. (1984-1986) – 186, 192
      Nichols, Kenneth (1986-1990) – 186, 192, 216-19
      Webb, Laura P. (1990-1994) – 167, 192, 217-21
      Smith, Joyce (1994-2003) – 192, 217, 219-21, 251, 253
      Williams, Deborah (2003-) – 251
   PTA – 29
   Quill and Scroll – 143
   Reader's Digest Honor School – 143
   Red Cross – 57, 129
   Soccer teams – 61, 62, 91-2, 115, 116, 145, 200
   Softball – 173, 197, 199, 200
   Students (see also football players listing)
      Banks, Caroline – 135
      Barber, Brian – 296
      _____, Lenny – 296
      Bloom, Samuel - 78
      Cannelli, Erin – 206
      Charles, Rhonda Pindell – 174-179, 199
      Colbert, Keith – 296
      Cotrell, Ted – 296
      Diggs, Boo – 296
      Eppes, Carolin – 82
      Eppes, Elizabeth Fuller – 78, 110, 125
      Feldmann, Chet – 206
      _____, Joe – 226
      Feldmeyer, Mary – 283
      Finkle, Leslie – 183, 185, 200
      Foley, Stve – 296
      Forrester, Dwight – 296
      Fuller, John – 78

Annapolis High School (cont'd)
  Students (cont'd)
    Gibson, Hank – 227
    Good-Malloy, Alex – see Malloy
    Hatfield, Orville – 117
    Hawkins, Thomas – 226
    Henson, C'vette – 296
    Jackson, Terry – 296
    Johnson, Albert – 250
    _____, Phil – 194
    _____, Marcus – 226, 296
    Kaiser, Evangeline – 7
    Linthicum, Georgiana – 10-11
    _____, J. Francis – 10-11
    _____, John – 10, 11
    _____, Mathida, 10-11
    Malloy, Alex – 220, 250
    McIntire, Anita Allio – 77, 82
    McNew, Brian – 206
    McWilliams, Jane Wilson – 133, 135, 144, 157, 158, 281, 289, 290, 291
    Middleton, Butch – 174, 176-8, 183, 194, 196, 211, 294
    Moss, James Revell – 287
    Neal, Marcus – 226, 296
    Neall, Robert – 190
    Noble, Lillian – 86-7
    Owens, Londell – 296
    Owings, Frances – 78
    Pasqualucci, Emidio – 185
    Phillips, Will– 206
    Purdy, Dick – 140, 144, 154, 157
    _____, Doris Jarosik – 108
    Rice, Robert – 130
    Riley, Donald – 21
    Robinson, Scott – 226
    Rowland, Dan – 296
    Roxburgh, Marjorie Layng – 83, 135, 159, 282, 291
    Simms, Leo – 159
    _____, Rodrick – 226
    Smalley, Dan – 227
    Smith, Margaret – 116
    Smith, Russell – 282
    Snowden, Carl – 178
    Snyder, Frank – 227
    Starr, Burton – 29
    Stanton, Les – 144
    Talley, Lillian – 86-7
    Taylor, Blanche – 108, 135
    Thomas, Helen – 86-7
    Tucker, William E. – 185
    Waxman, Teddy – 185
    Wells, Frances – 10-1
    West, Dallas – 185
    Wiggins, Mark – 227
    Winegrad, David – 206
    Wooster, Rob – 206, 296
    Young, Devin – 227
  Swim Team – 92

Annapolis High School (cont'd)
  Teachers, Counselors & Staff
    Anzalone, Anthony – 172, 178, 180, 185, 190, 218, 219, 224, 251
    Ballard, Mike - 225
    Brady, John – 189, 191, 207, 216, 224, 226-7
    Brogden, Larry – 157, 160, 164, 166-7, 169, 176, 210, 224, 226, 230
    Carroll, Elizabeth – 91
    Carter, Robert – 224
    Clarke, Norma – 224
    Covington, Rod - 193
    Cox, Katharine – 136, 138
    Cross, Huntley – 178, 224
    Cundruff, Catherine – 224
    Davis, Elizabeth – 80, 82, 136-8, 290
    Deterding, Chris – 224, 225, 251
    Eskuchen, Joy – 227
    Flanagan, Mike – 225
    Ford, Mary – 224
    Gehrdes, Dave – 201, 226-7
    Gershon, Leslie – 224
    Greenfield, Phil – 216, 224
    Hack, Laura – 224
    Hanna, Dela – 224
    Harrison, John – 224
    Harshbarger, Linda – 224
    Hart, Dan – 224, 227
    Hersman, Sue – 225
    Hewlett, Andrew – 45
    Hicks, Mary Louise – 80, 82, 136-8, 290
    Hockenberry, Sherry – 224
    Kibler, Katharine – 136, 138
    King, Richard – 216, 224, 225
    Kinhart, Mildred – 136, 138
    Kolarik, Lynn – 224
    Marking, Lorene – 80, 82, 136-7
    Neighbors, Mary Frances – 82
    Neiles, Tom – 216, 224, 225
    Norris, George – 138
    Nouri, Jean – 224
    Parker-Bert, Donzella – 216, 224, 251
    Pauli, Robert – 200
    Peckham, Diana – 225
    Pogonowski, Dan – 224
    Ramey, Marlene – 225
    Rannels, Morris – 138
    Ray, John – 7
    Rentch, John – 224, 251
    Riordan, Elizabeth – 34, 80
    Rogers, Barbara – 224
    _____, Calvin – 138
    Rossiter, George - 224
    Ruddle, Joe – 224
    Russell, Neill – 225
    Salamy, Sam – 224
    Sheller, Helen Mary – 82
    Smallwood, Marietta – 224
    Smith, Pat – 225

Index

Annapolis High School (cont'd)
   Teachers (cont'd)
      Smithers, Lydia – 224
      Stafford, Ron – 224, 225
      Suriano, Pat – 224
      Svec, Judy – 200, 218-224-5
      ____. Mike –
      Stauffer, Fred – 137, 139, 174, 177, 179, 18, 184, 189, 191, 201, 210, 224
      Tate, Mary – 57
      Turner, Helen – 216, 224
      Verillo, Paul – 200
      Vain, Calvin – 201
      Wingate, Evelyn – 79-80
   T.E.A.M. Days – 222
   Tennis teams – 92, 200
   Track teams – 49, 51, 92, 173
   Traffic squad – 143, 180
   Trustees
      Melvin, George – 32, 35, 43
      Munroe, Frank – 78, 121
   Volleyball teams – 115, 145, 199-200
   Wall of Honor – 222
   Wrestling – 166, 226
   Yearbooks
      Crablines – 73, 108, 287
      Wake – 129, 143

Annapolis Schoolhouse – See listing for Annapolis Elementary under Elementary School heading

Annapolis Touchdown Club – 207
   Mears Trophy – 237, 244
   Rhodes Trophy – 166 , 237

Anne Arundel County Athletic Hall of Fame – 207

Anne Arundel County Board of Education – 6, 25-35 (*passim*). 39, 169-180 (*passim*)
   Florestano, Thomas – 249

Anne Arundel County School Superintendents
   Harwood, William (1876-88) – 4
   Wathen, Eugene (1894-1905) – 29
   Wallis, Henry (1905-9) – see listing AHS Principals
   Garner, Samuel (1909-16) – 33
   Fox, George (1916-46) – 75, 78-80, 108, 118, 119, 121, 126, 135
   Jenkins, David (1946-72) – 135, 147, 161, 170-1
   Anderson, Edward (1972-84) – 188-90
   Rice, Robert (1984-88) – 192
   Lorton, Larry (1988-92) – 219
   Carter, C. Berry (1992) – 176, 209
   Parnham, Carol S. (1993-2002) – 249
   Lawson, Ken (2002, interim) – 249
   Smith, Eric (2003 -) – 249-50

Bates High School – 73, 120, 123-5, 157-61, 164-9, 171-2, 179, 193-6, 293, 296
   Coaches
      Early, James – 158
      Webb, James – 160, 164-8

Bates High School (cont'd)
   Principals, Teachers, Staff
      Brown, Philip – 175-6
      Chase, J. W. – 37
      Hilliard, Herbert – 175
      King, Douglas – 159 –61
      Pindell, Gwendolyn – 174, 176
      Randall, Charles – 158
   Students
      Baden, Bill – 158
      Brogden, Larry – see AHS teachers
      Fuller, Betty Brown – 159
      Randall, Charles – 158

Bellamy Award – 140-3
Belichick, Bill – see listing under football players
Bladen Street Armory - 87
Brown v Board of Education – 37, 161, 169, 170, 173, 177
Cain, James – 11
Camp Meade – 66
Caroline County Schools – 29
CBS News – 178
Colleges and Universities
   Air Force – 206
   Alabama - 140
   American University – 82
   Anne Arundel Community College
   Arkansas – 221
   Army – 14, 60-1
   Bennett – 21
   Berkeley – 80
   Blue Ridge - 79
   Bowie State – 158
   Brigham Young (BYU) – 140
   California State – 140
   California Tech – 140
   Case Tech – 140
   Chesapeake Community College – 206
   Cincinnati – 83
   Colorado – 82
   Columbia University – 81, 82, 108, 138
   Coppin State – 158
   Cornell – 65, 137
   Dartmouth – 206
   Dickinson – 28, 31, 140
   Drake – 140
   Duke – 206
   East Carolina University - 140
   East Stroudsburg – 148
   Emory – 140
   Fairfield – 82
   Florida – 140
   Florida Southern – 140
   Frostburg – 139, 192
   George Washington University – 140
   Goucher – 82, 83, 137
   Hampton Institute – 158
   Hampden-Sydney – 208
   Harvard – 127
   Hood College – 82

Colleges & Universities (cont'd)
   Howard – 159
   Iowa – 140
   James Madison – 206
   Johns Hopkins – 14, 33, 81, 82, 83, 137
   Kentucky – 82
   Lebanon Valley – 82
   Lincoln University – 159
   Loyola – 8, 184, 206
   Mary Washington – 140
   Maryland Institute of Art – 83
   Maryland, U of (College Park) – 75, 84, 139, 166, 205, 206, 253 287
      Byrd, H.C. – 146
      Byrd Stadium – 231, 241, 242, 244
   Maryland State (see UMES)
   MIT – 140
   Minnesota – 82
   Morgan State – 158
   Mt. St. Mary's – 184
   Muskingum – 82
   New England College – 140
   New York University – 140
   North Carolina – 140
   Notre Dame of MD – 83, 84
   Nursing Schools – 83, 84
   Ohio State – 140
   Peabody – 84
   Penn – 206
   Penn State – 148
   Pittsburgh – 140
   Portland – 140
   Princeton – 78
   Rhode Island School of Design – 140
   St. John's (Annapolis) – 3, 13, 14, 26, 39, 46, 65, 67, 81, 82, 83, 95, 107, 113, 140
   St. Mary's of MD – 94
   Salisbury (State) – 206
   Shepherd – 206, 208
   South Carolina Military College - 33
   Strayer Business College – 83, 84, 116
   U.S. Naval Academy – see separate listing
   Virginia, U of – 82 , 206, 221
   Washington College – 4, 27, 138, 154, 206
   Wesley – 193
   West Virginia – 140
   West Virginia Wesleyan – 193
   Western Maryland – 4, 82-3, 139, 228
   Western Pennsylvania – 57, 83
Company M of Maryland National Guard – 52, 66-7, 69, 92, 94
Cronkite, Walter – 178
Desegregation of Anne Arundel County Schools – 169-177
Disney, Walt – 141
Education laws (Maryland)
   of 1865 - 3,
   of 1869 - 5
   of 1916 – 26, 75

Eisenhower, Dwight D. – 141
Elementary Schools
   Adams Park – 38, 171-2
   Annapolis – 7-9, 27, 32, 34, 56, 76-7, 80, 81, 108, 111, 134, 172
   Eastport – 172
   Germantown – 111, 144, 157, 196, 200
   Parole – 172, 179
      Wilber Mills – 179
   Stanton School – see separate listing
Football (at Annapolis High)
   Eligibility rules – 40, 48, 113, 281, 284, 288
   Assistant Coaches
      Dunn, Ken – 230, 251
      Phebus, Bill – 201-2, 205, 209, 210, 212 230, 234, 251
      Summey, Dave – 251
      Villwock, Bruce – 201-209
   Head Coaches – in order of service
      Brady, Walter (1899-1906) – 18
      Lambert, Gary (1907-9) – 39, 45-50 (*passim*)
      Morton, Ivan T. (1909-14) – 55-58
      A.Z. Holley (1920-22)
      Leitch, Byron – 82, 95
      White, Willis (1924-28) – 95-104, 107-13, 141
      McCauley, J.W. (1929) – 112-16
      Rentschler, Bruce (1947-48) – 147-49
      Wetherhold, Woody (1948-56) - 136, 148-54, 163
      Best, Bill – 62
      Leonard, Neville (1959-64) – 160, 162-4 167
      Laramore, Al – 167, 169, 180, 181, 193-7, 199, 201-12., 294, 295
      Thomas, Lou (1972) – 201
      Villwock, Bruce (1977) – 209
      Brown, Roy (1989 – 2002) – 172, 207, 209-12, 229-45, 251-3
      Castro, Dale (2003 -) – 252
   Panther Drill – 208, 210
   Players (see also names in Appendix A)
      Acker, Kyle – 226, 233-4
      Arth, Joe – 19, 21, 22
      Baker, Bobby – 234, 238
      Belt, Kyron – 234
      Bartlett, Owen – 16, 22
      Baskett, Rick – 162-4
      Belichick, Bill – 181,194, 196-7, 208-10
      Bernstein, John – 90, 98
      Boettcher, Henry – 60
      _____, Norman – 96-7, 104-8.
      Booth, Barry – 196, 211
      Boyd, Phil – 239
      Brooks, Jack - 234
      Brown, Daryl – 202-4
      _____, Donald "Turkey" – 205, 208
      Buckingham, Keith – 206, 227
      Burtis, Solomon – 17, 21

Index

Football (at Annapolis High, cont'd)
  Players (cont'd)
    Carr, Benjamin Skinner – 64, 67
    Carter, Chris – 176, 194, 209
    _____, Charles – 234
    Charles, Marvin – 226, 233-7, 239
    Chew, Alex – 204
    Childs, Walton – 48
    Clark, Albert – 46, 47, 49-52
    _____, Edgar – 58, 60, 63-4
    _____, Ray – 50-1
    Claude, Howard – 43, 46
    _____, Laurens – 63-4
    Clayton, Philip – 43, 47, 49, 51-2, 63
    Colbert, Arthur – 165
    _____, Mike – 202
    Conor, Frank M. – 63
    Cook, Jamie – 231
    _____, Nathaniel – 206, 231
    Cooper, Teshawn – 206
    Copeland, Aaron – 226, 232-7
    Creek, Albert – 232, 233
    Cresap, Logan – 16, 21-2, 282
    Criscimanga, Robert – 206
    Dammeyer, Charlie – 238, 239-40
    DeMeter, Ed – 204
    Dobyns, John – 202
    Donlin, Michael – 206
    Downs, Henry – 234
    Duckett, Bowie – 92
    Dukes, Gary – 202
    Dulin, Wilber – 97, 98-104
    Elliott, Richard – 52
    Ennis, Robert - 52
    Eppes, James B. "Banny" – 76-8, 82, 87, 92, 114, 117-18
    Feldmeyer, Harry – 97, 103
    _____, Warren – 60
    Fenwick, Aaron – 237
    Foote, Donelle – 232, 233
    Forester, James – 235, 237, 238, 241
    Frazier, John – 67
    Frieman, Arnie – 162, 164
    Gardner, Buck – 162-3
    Good-Malloy, Nick – 206, 210, 226, 234, 237-45
    Grau, Hal – 162,164
    Gray, Ed – 114
    Gulley, Brandon – 234, 237-41, 243-4
    Hall, David – 234
    Hanna, John – 164
    Hantske, Leo – 97, 98, 147
    Harris, Demario – 206, 238, 241
    Hendrick, Dick – 164
    Henson, Camaro – 210, 226, 238-42
    Hoban, Charles – 102
    Hoff, Louis – 60
    Holley, A.Z. – 43, 46-52 (*passim*), 59, 64, 66, 92-94
    Hortopan, Charlie – 144

Football (at Annapolis High, cont'd)
  Players (cont'd)
    Hunt, Dewayne – 234
    Hyatt, Melvin – 149
    Hyde, Fred – 60, 63
    Jacobson, Jeff –
    Jennings, Jack "Mule" – 149, 150, 152-4
    Jewell, Harry – 17, 21
    Johnson, Derek – 231, 233
    _____, Rayvon – 232-7
    Jones, Charlie – 48
    _____, Clifford – 97, 102
    Jones, Curtis – 232-3
    _____, Kim – 204
    _____, Kevin – 241
    Jordan, Ronald – 154
    Kaiser, John – 43, 49, 50-1, 64-5
    Kennerly, Bill – 150-1, 154
    Kerchner, Bill – 150-1
    Kimball, Cy – 86, 90, 96-8, 104
    _____, Jamie – 86, 88, 104
    Laramore, Dan – 181, 208
    _____, David – 181, 208
    League, James – 17
    Loman, Dan – 202-4
    Ludlum, Pete – 233
    Macey, Doug – 162, 164
    Machin, Isaac – 17, 20-1
    Mackell, Kion – 234, 236-8, 240-41, 243-4
    Martin, Willis – 60
    Mathews, Keith – 211
    Medford, Leslie – 52
    Melton, Mike – 210, 238, 241, 243
    Moreland, Stiff – 116
    Mosier, Bob – 207-8, 230
    Moss, James Revell -
    Moyer, Roger "Pip" – 150, 188
    Nyland, Tom – 164
    Olson, Dan – 149
    Parker, Tom – 202-5
    Parlett, George – 17, 21
    _____, Guy – 43, 52, 64, 67
    _____, Tom – 164
    Pastrana, Alan – 162-6
    Pearman, Archie – 194-5
    _____, Philip – 204
    Pennell, George – 21
    Phaneuf, Mike – 233-7
    Pittman, Randy – 202
    Plattner, Joe – 232
    Pope, Patrick – 206
    Powell, Brian – 238
    Prosperi, Augustus – 15, 22
    Purdy, Bob – 149
    Quarles, James – 204
    Rankin, Mark – 164
    Revell, James – 67
    Riek, Lenny – 201
    Reed, Jack – 194-5, 211

Football (at Annapolis High, cont'd)
   Players (cont'd)
      Rodkey, John – 202-4
      Russell, Charles "Daffy" – 104, 113
      _____, John – 164
      Schultz, Walter – 48
      Simmons, John – 150-1
      Simms, Kevan – 236, 238, 239, 241, 244
      Snowden, Donald – 206
      Springfield, George – 149
      Stevens, Frank – 48-52, 59
      _____, Gerald – 97
      Strange, Kenton – 60
      Strohm, John – 15, 19-21, 141
      Strohmeyer, William – 52, 122
      Stone, Arthur – 45-47
      _____, Raymond – 63
      _____, Richard – 17, 21-2, 45
      Sullivan, Richard – 149
      Taylor, Buck – 162-4
      _____, Burt – 164
      Thomas, Roland – 48-9
      Thompson, Howard Frank – 43, 46, 51-2
      _____, Kevin – 202-4
      Tisdale, George – 63
      _____, James – 65-6
      _____, Ryland "Dillard" – 57, 60, 63-4
      Tomanio, Ernie – 90, 97-104
      Toney, Andre – 238, 240, 241, 243, 244
      _____, Eric – 234
      Trader, Allison – 97-8
      Vanous, Will - 97-8
      Venerable, Eric – 234, 238, 244
      Ward, Arthur – 17, 21
      Watkins, Davon – 238
      Wemple, Bruce – 202-4
      White, Frank – 17, 19, 20-1
      Williams, Albert – 17, 20, 21
      _____, John Paul – 232-3
      _____, Trevon – 233-7
      Womak, S.J. – 232-3
      Wills, Rashad – 234
      Wilson, Maurice – 102
      Woodward, Nicholas - 60
   Schools played – see Appendix B
   Stadiums
      Panther – 153, 187, 195, 200
      Richard E. Ensor – 191-2, 209
      Weems-Whelan – 153, 162, 165
         Weems, George F. – 153
         Whalen, Joseph F. – 153
   Team captains – see Appendix A
   Teams –
      1899 – 1, 15-22, 45
      1900 – 21
      1908 – 44-48, 57
      1909 – 48-52, 57
      1910 –15, 57-61
      1920 – 92
      1921 – 94-5

Football (at Annapolis High, cont'd)
   Teams (cont'd)
      1922 – 95
      1925 – 96-7
      19 26 – 71, 97-104
      1927 – 103
      1928 – 111
      1929 – 106, 113-14
      1947 – 147-8
      1948 – 148
      1949 – 149
      1950 – 121, 149-5, 153
      1951 – 151-2, 153
      1952 – 153
      1962 – 155, 161-4
      1966 – 195
      1978 – 181, 201-7
      1984 – 205
      1989 – 231
      1992 – 231
      1997 – 232-3
      1998 – 233-5
      1999 – 235-7
      2000 – 237-45
   Season & Team Records – see Appendix A
Football (in Annapolis) – 13-14
   College teams – see separate listings for
      St. John's and U.S. Naval Academy
      under heading for colleges & universities
   Neighborhood teams
      Chesapeakes – 45
      Down-Town Boys - 14
      Murray Hill Gang – 14, 43-44, 47
      Young Tigers – 44, 45
   Professional teams (in Annapolis)
      Annapolis Sailors – 199-201
   Recreation teams – 146-8
   Semi-pro teams
      Coca-Colas – 116
Football - general
   Brutality of – 40-1, 59-60, 93
   NCAA – 42
   Origins of game – 12-13
   Rules – 12-13, 42-43, 59-61, 93-4
Football – high school in Maryland
   Coaches
      Borland, Andy – 202, 209, 229
      Mears, Jerry – 211, 228-30
      Papetti, Joe – 229
   Conferences in Maryland
      Anne Arundel County leagues – 229-30
      Big Eight – 228
      Cumberland Valley League – 97, 111
      Maryland Scholastic Association – 96-7,
         111, 115, 116
Football (NFL) – 205
   Chicago Bears – 228
   Cleveland Browns – 209
   Dallas Cowboys – 253
   Denver Broncos – 166

Index

Football, (NFL, cont'd)
  Miami Dolphins – 205
  New England Patriots – 196
  New York Giants – 205
  San Diego Chargers –205
G.I. Bill – 144
Gross, Bailey – 146
Grammar Schools – see Elementary Schools
High Schools (Private)
  Anne Arundel Academy – 3, 28, 75-6
  Army-Navy Prep – 74, 94, 103
  Bobbie's Prep – 4, 58
  Boys' Latin – 49, 58
  Calvert Hall – 92, 96
  Charlotte Hall Academy -3, 48, 50, 96, 98
  Devitt Prep – 96
  Donaldson Academy – 92, 94
  Friends' School (Balt) – 58
  Gilman – 58
  Good Counsel – 165, 188
  Leonard Hall –94
  Loyola of Baltimore – 94, 96-8, 103, 111
  Marsten School for Boys – 58
  McDonogh – 100, 103
  Mt. St. Joseph – 96, 97, 98, 103, 111
  Patapsco Academy - 3,
  Rock Hall – 94
  St. John's Prep – 4, 19, 20, 21, 50, 58, 74
  St. Mary's – 104, 152-3, 163, 188, 195
  Severn School – 4, 74, 95, 101, 103, 111
  St. John's College Prep - 3, 19, 50
  Tome Academy – 49
  Washington College - 3, 47, 49-50
  Werntz Naval Prep – 4, 47, 50, 58, 74, 92
  West River Institute – 3
  Wilmer's Navy Prep – 4, 19, 46, 58
  Woodward Prep – 152
High Schools (Public)
  Alexandria (Va) – 96-7
  Andover – 135, 167, 172
  Arundel – 34, 75-6, 79, 80, 95, 172
    Walters, Bernie – 286
  Bates, Wiley H. – see separate listing
  BCC – 3, 18, 47-49, 58, 96, 103, 111, 115, 165
  Bel Air – 202
  Bethesda-Chevy Chase – 149
  Broadneck – 209, 297
  Brooklyn Park – 135, 162, 165, 167, 172
  Calvert – 243-4
  Cambridge – 6, 58, 148, 163
  Centreville – 6
  Chesapeake – 169, 190, 202
  City College High (Baltimore) –see BCC
  Crossland – 203
  Damascus – 235-6, 241
  Denton – 4, 29
  Dover (DE) – 148-152
  DuVal – 200, 211
  Easton –3, 29, 58

High Schools (Public, cont'd)
  Forest Park – 103, 111
  Fort Hill – 111
  Frederick – 6, 19, 149
  Frederick Douglass – 238, 241-2
  Friendly – 231
  Frostburg – 27
  Gaithersburg – 231
  Glen Burnie – 74, 95, 120, 123, 127, 184, 202
  Hagerstown – 6, 47, 50, 97, 101-2, 111, 114
  Havre de Grace – 148
  High Point – 232, 253
  Hyattsville – 116
  Howard – 162, 165
  Kenwood – 201
  Largo – 232, 234
  Laurel - 6, 19-21
  Mace's Landing – 165
  Meade – 169, 202-5, 231-2
  Middletown – 6
  New Town – 3
  North County – 231-2, 239, 297
  Northeast – 135, 169, 172
  Old Mill – 169, 190, 202
  Oxen Hill – 162
  Paint Branch – 227, 232, 234, 240-1
  Pocomoke – 79, 108
  Polytechnic Institute of Balt – 15, 28, 47
  Pomonkey – 165
  Randallstown – 205
  Rockville – 6
  St. Augustine's – 283
  St. Mary's – 283
  St. Michael's – 29,
  Severna Park – 135, 162, 166-7, 172, 183, 195, 202, 205
  Sherwood – 149
  South Carroll – 202
  South River – 190
  Southern – 74, 91, 95, 120, 123, 152, 162, 173, 188, 253
  Sparks – 137
  Towson – 79
  Tracy's Landing – see Southern
  Walt Whitman – 203
  Westminster – 148, 202
  Wicomoco - 3, 58, 149, 151, 163
  William Jason – 165
  Winston Churchill – 205
Isaac Benesch & Sons – 39
Jackson, E.M. – 105, 113-16
Junior High Schools
  Annapolis – 134-5, 172, 183
  Corkran – 139, 184
  Glen Burnie – 183
  Severn River – 230
  Severna Park – 183
King, Martin Luther, Jr. – 196
Korean War – 137, 289
  Deaths of Annapolis High grads – 144

McKeldin, Theodore – 141
Middle Schools – 215
Middle States Association/Commission on Secondary Education – 126-7, 140, 159, 177, 185-6, 191,216-20, 222-3
Moss, Robert - 27
MPSSAA – 146-7, 203, 229, 243-4, 253, 290, 296-7
National Brotherhood Week – 159-61
Plessy v Ferguson – 169
Public Athletic League (PAL) – 61-2, 91, 92, 109, 115, 146, 197
    Burdick, William H. – 62-3, 110
    Garrett, Robert – 61
Pullen, Thomas – 120
Roosevelt, Theodore
    views on football – 13, 42, 53, 147
Stanton School – 4, 8, 25, 36-8, 40, 73, 95, 123, 171, 283, 286, 291, 292
Title VI – 1964 Civil Rights Act – 173
Title IX – 1972 Education Act – 197-201
United States Naval Academy – 13, 14, 61, 66, 74, 83, 84, 104, 119, 139-40, 153, 194, 227
    Coaches & administrators
        Belichick, Steve – 196
        Ingrahm, Bill – 99
        Miller, Rip – 147
    Naval Academy Athletic Association – 88-9, 95, 99
Vietnam War – 178, 185, 293
Villa, Pancho – 52, 69, 92
World War I – 62-7, 75
    African Americans from Annapolis in war – 128
    Annapolis grads who died in war – 64, 67
    Medical rejects – 286
    Pershing, Black Jack – 69
World War II – 103-4, 127-30
    Annapolis High deaths in, 128
    Diplomas for Veterans – 289
    Effect on local population growth – 133-4
Zartman, Eugene – 150-52

Jane E. Good serves as Director of Academic Counseling at the United States Naval Academy, where she has been teaching Russian and European history for 25 years. A *magna cum laude* graduate of Wittenberg University, she served as a Peace Corps volunteer in Morocco before completing her education, earning a MAT at Brown University and a PhD at American University. Good came to love football as a girl watching Ohio State and the Cleveland Browns with her father and older brother. An all-around athlete, she was inducted in the Wittenberg Hall of Fame to honor her career as a collegiate basketball and tennis player. Good lives in Annapolis, Maryland, where she enjoys golf, jogging, book club discussions, seeing independent films with her son Alex and cheering for her son Nick's football and basketball teams.